MW00386822

A NATION DIVIDED:
NEW STUDIES IN CIVIL WAR HISTORY

James I. Robertson Jr., Editor

CIVIL WAR PETERSBURG

Confederate City
in the Crucible of War

A. WILSON GREENE

University of Virginia Press

CHARLOTTESVILLE AND LONDON

University of Virginia Press
© 2006 by the Rector and Visitors of the University of Virginia
All rights reserved
Printed in the United States of America on acid-free paper
First published 2006

1 3 5 7 9 8 6 4 2

Library of Congress Cataloging-in-Publication Data
Greene, A. Wilson
  Civil War Petersburg : Confederate city in the crucible of war / A. Wilson Greene.
    p.   cm. — (A nation divided)
  Includes bibliographical references and index.
  ISBN-13: 978-0-8139-2570-7 (cloth : alk. paper)
  1. Petersburg (Va.)—History, Military—19th century. 2. Petersburg (Va.)—Social
conditions—19th century. 3. Virginia—History—Civil War, 1861–1865—Social aspects.
4. United States—History—Civil War, 1861–1865—Social aspects. I. Title. II. Series.
F234.P4G738 2006
975.5'03—dc22

                                                                      2006013148

CONTENTS

ILLUSTRATIONS

MAPS

PREFACE

Civil War scholarship during the past decade has moved beyond the battle-field to explore the impact of the war on noncombatants. Profiles of cities rank among the most popular vehicles for helping us understand the total-ity of America's most costly conflict. Recent books on the opposing capitals join numerous titles exploring lesser Confederate and Union towns. Among the most important of the South's second-tier cities, Petersburg, Virginia, provides a rare opportunity to examine a demographically unique commu-nity imbued with economic, geographic, logistic, and strategic significance matched by few small cities in either section.

Petersburg's experience during the Civil War captured my attention for several reasons. Living in the shadow of its historic spires provided me with a natural curiosity to learn more. Students of the war have long examined the extended campaign around Petersburg in 1864 and 1865, but less is un-derstood about the city's place in strategic thinking during the three years before Robert E. Lee and Ulysses S. Grant placed Petersburg in the head-lines. Petersburg played a supporting role in my earlier study of the last week of that campaign (*Breaking the Backbone of the Rebellion: The Final Battles of the Petersburg Campaign*, Mason City, Ia., 2000) and suggested to me that a great deal of source material remained untapped.

The city possessed a number of unusual attributes that made it an at-tractive subject. A river port, major rail junction, regional economic capital for two states, and a manufacturing center exceeded only by Richmond — its larger neighbor twenty-three miles to the north — Petersburg boasted one of the largest free African American populations in the South. Staunchly conservative in its politics, Petersburg would contribute enormously to the Confederate war effort in treasure and troops. Most of all, no American city endured a longer, more unrelenting military campaign than Petersburg. These ingredients promised a fascinating stew when blended under the in-tense heat of war.

Finally, I was blessed with the opportunity to follow the deep furrows plowed by the dean of Petersburg's historians, William D. Henderson, whose *Petersburg in the Civil War: War at the Door* (Lynchburg, Va., 1998) formed the foundation for my work. No one knows more about nineteenth-century Petersburg than Bill Henderson. While on the faculty of Richard Bland College of the College of William and Mary, Professor Henderson wrote articles on Petersburg's antebellum economy, produced regimental histories of the city's principal Civil War military units, and contributed a highly useful summary of Petersburg during Reconstruction, all in addition to his pioneering work on Petersburg's wartime experience. Bill served as a mentor during the development of this book, reading each chapter in draft and offering invaluable suggestions for new lines of inquiry. One could not ask for a more generous scholar and competent teacher than Bill Henderson.

The other master of Petersburg's Civil War history, Christopher M. Calkins, also read my manuscript and corrected factual errors that would have escaped practically anyone else. No one knows more about the campaign for Petersburg than Chris Calkins, who has served as historian at Petersburg National Battlefield for a generation. His command of the subject matter strengthened this book immeasurably.

Two colleagues employed their broad knowledge of the Civil War and remarkable editorial skills to improve my work. George C. Rable of the University of Alabama meticulously dissected what I thought was a finished product. His historical insights and tactful references to clunkers in my writing deserve my most profound thanks. Similarly, William Marvel of South Conway, New Hampshire, wore out several red pens in his gallant attempt to raise my writing to acceptable standards. Bill also employed his eye for the improbable to challenge questionable conclusions, causing me to rethink many of my initial arguments. Every writer should be so fortunate as to have friends like George Rable and Bill Marvel.

A number of colleagues, aware of my interest in wartime Petersburg, steered me toward source material that proved important in telling the story. Brian Wills at the University of Virginia at Wise; Robert E. L. Krick, historian at Richmond National Battlefield Park; Art Bergeron of the United States Army Military History Institute; Tom Powers of the University of South Carolina at Sumter; and Peter Carmichael of the University of North Carolina at Greensboro all provided valuable information and research leads. I also wish to thank Thomas DiGiuseppe of West Newbury, Massachusetts, for material on Milligan's Signal Corps; Duncan van Reijswould of Sydney, Australia, for insights regarding Andrew Dunn; Mrs. Charles Cuthbert of Petersburg for information about the Collier and Wallace families; and Julie B. Grossman for sharing her Petersburg letters.

The dedicated archivists who staff the repositories where the raw material of history resides always deserve special mention. I was fortunate to encounter several such people who helped me above and beyond the call of duty. Graham Dozier and the fine people at the Virginia Historical Society; Tom Crew and the staff of the Library of Virginia (both the archives and the interlibrary loan); John Coski of the Museum of the Confederacy; Susan Riggs at the Swem Library of the College of William and Mary; and Erica Jenkins, former clerk of city council in Petersburg all facilitated my research with uncommon courtesy and competence. The museum and curatorial folks of the Petersburg city museums, Chris Meekins at the North Carolina State Archives, and Mike Musick at the National Archives also earned my sincere thanks. The outstanding professionals in the manuscript departments of the Southern Historical Collection at the University of North Carolina, the Alderman Library at the University of Virginia, and the William R. Perkins Library at Duke University are allies to any student of history.

I am especially grateful to Richard Holway at the University of Virginia Press for extending my deadline with gracious understanding and to James I. Robertson Jr. of Virginia Tech, a dear friend of many years, who recommended this work as a part of the series he edits.

As is true of all public historians and historic site administrators, I conducted the research and writing for this book before sunrise, after supper, on weekends, and during authorized vacation time so as not to infringe on obligations to my employer. My obligations as a husband and helpmate, sadly, often went unmet. Thus I dedicate this book with profound gratitude to my wife, Margaret, who has endured the mistress of history in her home without complaint for twenty years. Believe me MSB, I could not do it without you.

CIVIL WAR
PETERSBURG

Petersburg, Virginia, as viewed looking south across the Appomattox River. Petersburg ranked second only to Richmond among Virginia cities in both population and strategic significance. (Courtesy of Valentine Richmond History Center)

⌐ 1 ⌐

"Helping to Inaugurate Revolution"

JOHN TROWBRIDGE traveled to Petersburg in the summer of 1865 during an ambitious tour of Southern places made famous by the Civil War. Not surprisingly, his itinerary included Virginia's second largest city— a place that had dominated the headlines for most of the war's final year. Trowbridge interviewed various residents ranging from former slaves to deposed Confederate officers, but the city's visual scars left the deepest impression on the New Englander. "Its well-built, pleasant streets, rising upon the south bank of the Appomattox River, were dirty and dilapidated," thought Trowbridge. "All the lower part of the town showed the ruinous effect of the shelling it had received." Although some buildings displayed evidence of recent repair, "uninhabitable houses, with broken walls, roofless, or with roofs smashed and torn by missiles, [bore] silent witness to the havoc of war."[1]

A Union army survey conducted in the spring had quantified the devastation that so appalled Trowbridge. Some 625 of Petersburg's structures had been pummeled by shells between June 1864 and April 1865. Few Confederate cities had endured worse devastation, and no event in Petersburg's long history rivaled the impact of the conflict on the city's political, economic, and social fabric. John Trowbridge could not know that summer that the Civil War would define Petersburg for generations, leaving a legacy that echoed into the twenty-first century.[2]

Petersburg was an ancient community by American standards. It began in 1645 as Fort Henry, a frontier trading post and military strong point on the Appomattox River where Tidewater Virginia met the Piedmont at the head of navigation. The possibility of commerce at this advantageous location attracted one Peter Jones, who would lend his Christian name to the town that blossomed near the site of his rustic commercial venture. Subsequently two other villages, Blandford and Pocahontas, arose nearby. The three settlements became the unified Town of Petersburg in 1784. In 1850 the state legislature elevated Petersburg to the status of a city, only the third such municipality in Virginia at the time. Residents proudly referred to their home as "The Cockade City," from a compliment that President James Madison paid to Petersburg's War of 1812 volunteers.[3]

A fire that consumed close to two-thirds of the town's wooden buildings in 1815 led to the erection of more durable and fire-resistant brick structures in a building boom that continued through midcentury. "You would be struck with the changes of this place," wrote a Petersburg woman in 1841. "New churches with their white steeples, large additions to public and private buildings, a strong love of the town and [other] outward embellishments would scarcely suffer your recognition of the old place." Petersburg earned a reputation for hospitality and enterprise in the decades before the Civil War, prompting one writer in 1854 to credit the growing community with "vastly more life, according to its size, than Richmond." Two years later a Richmond newspaper begrudgingly admitted that "there is no place in Virginia where there is more true refinement, more genial, social warmth, and less of the stiff and starched pretension which sometimes follows prosperity and wealth, and is always the mark of weak & vulgar minds, than in the City of Petersburg."[4]

Petersburg's prosperity, growth, and social distinction had by 1860 elevated it to Virginia's second—and the slave states' eleventh—largest city. Petersburg owed much of its economic success to its role as a transportation nexus. Its fall line location made Petersburg an international port of some importance during the early decades of the nineteenth century. Once the shallow, often silted channel of the Appomattox began to restrict access to larger ships, Petersburg developed a vital rail link to deep water. Completed in 1838, the City Point Railroad connected Petersburg with the hamlet of this name eight miles downstream at the confluence of the James River, restoring the Cockade City's all-weather connection to the sea.[5]

By this time two other railroads connected Petersburg with its markets and hinterlands north and south. The Petersburg Railroad, begun in 1830, linked the Cockade City with Weldon, North Carolina, sixty-five miles to the south. The line opened in the summer of 1833 with its northern terminus at a station, which local residents frequently called the Southern depot, on Petersburg's primary east-west thoroughfare, Washington Street. Tobacco grown in Southside Virginia and the northern tier of counties in the Tarheel State found its way to Petersburg via the Petersburg Railroad. Like most Virginia railroads, this new line carried far more freight than passengers.[6]

The Richmond & Petersburg Railroad received its charter on March 14, 1835, and replaced the Manchester Turnpike, the old wagon road to Richmond, as the busiest route between Virginia's two largest cities. By 1838 this railroad linked Pocahontas, a Petersburg neighborhood on the left bank of the Appomattox River, with Richmond, twenty-three miles to the north. Passengers and freight used the old turnpike bridge to cross the Appomattox, relying on wagons and omnibuses to make the short journey from the Pocahontas depot to the city's business district. Neither the Petersburg nor the Richmond & Petersburg Railroads embraced the vision of an integrated transportation system. In fact, business interests in town—including the hotels, restaurants, draymen, and warehouse operators—vigorously opposed any suggestion that the lines connect. Gaps in the tracks ensured that all through-travelers and commodities moving from North Carolina to Richmond would rely on Petersburg businesses for local transportation and other services.[7]

Petersburg's other two antebellum railroads began operation in the 1850s, although the South Side Railroad received its charter in 1846. This line ran 124 miles west to Lynchburg and superseded wagon roads and the Upper Appomattox Canal, a system of locks that bypassed the river's unnavigable sections as far west as Farmville. In 1847, the city of Petersburg purchased the City Point Railroad and renamed it the Appomattox Railroad. Seven years later, the city sold it to the South Side Railroad, allowing the two lines to merge.

The last of Petersburg's railroads ran southeast to Norfolk, but the city's business interests opposed construction of this line. Business owners feared that connecting Norfolk with Virginia's interior would render Petersburg's port economically irrelevant. After years of fall line obstructionism, Tidewater prevailed, and the Norfolk & Petersburg Railroad commenced operation in 1858, quickly demonstrating that Petersburg's commercial fears had merit. The Civil War, however, would compromise Petersburg's waterborne economy before the great port of Hampton Roads could do so.[8]

In addition to its railroads and river, a number of prominent highways complemented the city's transportation network. The Richmond & Petersburg Turnpike (successor to the Manchester Turnpike) ran north to the capital; Cox Road paralleled the South Side Railroad as a western extension of Washington Street; Halifax Road provided a southbound alternative to the Petersburg Railroad; and a wagon road heading southeast toward Suffolk hugged the Norfolk line. Two toll roads lacked railroad competition. Jerusalem Plank Road left the Blandford section of the city heading south and southeast toward its namesake village. Boydton Plank Road meandered southwest through a rich tobacco region. A Petersburg newspaper characterized Boydton Plank Road as "an abominable burlesque . . . that even the natural intelligence of the quadruped, be his ears ever so long, may be perfectly conscious of."[9]

If success as a transportation hub placed Petersburg on the economic map, manufacturing vaulted it into the top echelon of Southern cities. Petersburg's business community understood full well that while shipping raw materials could be profitable, adding value through processing these materials for distribution to a world market would make the city even more prosperous. By 1860 Petersburg ranked forty-ninth among all American cities in industrial investment—an anomaly for the agricultural South, although it had not enjoyed the same meteoric commercial growth that other towns experienced during the 1850s.[10]

Tobacco reigned supreme in Petersburg, as it did in Richmond, the two largest tobacco towns in the world. Petersburg sold 23 percent of the state's tobacco in 1861 (compared to Richmond's 61 percent) and supported twenty factories (Richmond had fifty) that processed raw tobacco. The tobacco factories relied primarily on African American labor, slaves and free blacks toiling side by side, with male workers outnumbering women about two to one. Only in the last years of the antebellum period did the Petersburg tobacco factories experiment with white workers. The companies owned some of their slave labor and leased the rest, while they paid free black men approximately $152 per year and free women barely half as much. By contrast, it required more than $1,000 to purchase a healthy slave man and as much as $220 to hire him for one year. As the price of slaves increased during the antebellum period, the companies frequently preferred to employ free workers.

These factories required no water power and thus could be located away from the river near the center of town around Washington and Sycamore Streets. They were imposing brick structures rising two or three stories and resembled tidy apartment buildings. Inside, the workers enjoyed running water, central heat, and gas lighting, although no one could argue that the intense handwork of processing tobacco was an easy way to earn a living. Petersburg also boasted four tobacco warehouses, which stored the raw product prior to auction. Local tobacco inspectors examined 17,530 hogsheads in 1860 alone.[11]

Three other industries shared the balance of the local manufacturing output. Because of its surprisingly mild climate, Petersburg held the distinction of being the northernmost American city both growing and processing cotton. Beginning in the 1830s, Petersburg's cotton industry relied on water power from the Appomattox. The river dropped one hundred feet in the five miles above the fall line, aided by dams and canals that channeled its energy to the factories.

On the eve of the Civil War the Petersburg area supported four cotton mills, three of which were run by the local businessmen Benjamin Lynch and David Callender. Their Ettrick and Matoaca mills stood three miles apart on the north bank of the Appomattox just west of the city, while their Battersea Mill sat across the river. Small industrial villages emerged around these factories that employed white men and white women in roughly equal numbers. Wages exceeded those paid in the tobacco factories, averaging about $192 annually for men and $122 for women, but still providing a meager living. The Merchant's Manufacturing Company, independent of Callender and Lynch, straddled the river near Campbell's Bridge, Petersburg's upriver crossing point to Ettrick near the fall line. Approximately one-third of Virginia's cotton industry called Petersburg home.[12]

Water power also sustained three flour mills in Petersburg. James M. Venable, John Kevan and Andrew Kevan, and Sylvanius Johnson ran profitable businesses along the river, employing among them thirty-eight men in 1860. These operatives averaged wages of about three hundred dollars per year, half again what the cotton workers earned but not quite as much as laborers in Petersburg's five iron foundries. Uriah Wells owned the Petersburg Iron, Bell and Brass Foundry on Old Street near the river, the best known of Petersburg's foundries. It pounded out items ranging from steam engines to ploughs in addition to ornamental ironwork. Approximately one-third of Virginia's iron production came from Petersburg, which trailed only Richmond in its volume of both iron and flour.[13]

Although industrial production accounted for much of Petersburg's antebellum wealth, commission merchants—the middlemen between farmers and consumers—led the city economically. Thirty-nine Petersburg firms pursued this profession in 1860. They bought and sold wheat, corn, and cotton, and many acted as retail or wholesale purveyors of agricultural supplies to planters and farmers. Thomas Branch and Sons on Old Street operated one of the largest commission houses in Petersburg, but there were many others, such as the successful ones run by Dinwiddie Grigg, Archibald G. McIlwaine, and John M. Rowlett. Along with the commission merchants, nearly two hundred retailers helped sustain three banks and encouraged the formation of a fourth in late 1860. Four savings and loan institutions specializing in real estate financing rounded out Petersburg's thriving antebellum financial community.[14]

Neighboring Dinwiddie County illustrated Petersburg's status as the urban hub for a huge rural area to its south and west. Dinwiddie produced nearly 4,000,000 pounds of tobacco in 1860, 355,000 bushels of corn, 134,000 bushels of wheat, and large quantities of sweet and Irish potatoes, oats, and peas. Beeswax, honey, slaughtered livestock, wool, and butter poured into Petersburg from Dinwiddie farms. Petersburg's manufacturing, transportation, wholesale, and retail capabilities made trips to Richmond unnecessary for Virginians living in a wide stretch of the state called Southside, as well as the central North Carolina counties bordering the Old Dominion. Petersburg had become a regional economic capital, and its sophistication and wealth made it a cultural center as well.[15]

Although Petersburg's white population enjoyed the vast majority of this

sophistication and the prosperity that spawned it, the city's African American residents provided Petersburg's demographic distinction. Only 34 percent of Virginia's 1860 population was black, but Petersburg had been a
majority African American city until that year. The enumerators counted
18,266 souls during their 1860 canvass, of whom 5,680 were slaves, 3,244
were free blacks, and 9,342 were whites. Nearly 26 percent of free persons
in Petersburg were black—the highest proportion in any Southern city.
More than 36 percent of African Americans in Petersburg were free.[16]

Petersburg's free black community survived despite efforts by whites to
limit its numbers. Legislation made it increasingly difficult for persons of
color to relocate to Petersburg, and voluntary manumission became nearly
impossible. Nevertheless, the number of free blacks increased 24 percent
between 1850 and 1860, although this rate of growth failed to keep pace with
Petersburg's total free population. Such a large community naturally developed its own identity and culture.[17]

Free black women in Petersburg outnumbered their male counterparts;
they owned nearly half the property controlled by their race and held half
the jobs. Free African American women worked as stemmers in tobacco
factories or as washerwomen, seamstresses, or laborers, while some earned
a living as prostitutes or concubines. Free black men worked as tobacco
twisters and in the iron foundries. There were free black Appomattox River
boatmen, draymen, and cab drivers conveying freight and passengers between the depots. Skilled craftsmen such as brick masons, wheelwrights,
coopers, and blacksmiths plied their trades. Most of the city's barbers were
free black men.[18]

As might have been expected, the city's property owners were dispropor-
tionately white. Less than 20 percent of the total property owners came from
the free black class, and only one-tenth of all free blacks owned any real
estate at all. Still, 246 free African Americans—about one out of three families—owned town lots, and some achieved surprising wealth for the time.
The restaurant owner Jack McRae amassed a healthy sum, including two
houses and lots. Thomas Scott developed a successful contracting business,
and even some tobacco factory employees clawed their way out of poverty.
The Jarratt family made a comfortable living as boat operators on the Appomattox and James Rivers. The carpenter James Carter, the draymen
Leander Slaughter and Eleazar White, and the livery owner Robert Clark
all hired slaves to assist in their businesses. Even some of the more affluent
free black women who served white men as prostitutes or concubines could
afford to buy slaves of their own.[19]

Of course, the overwhelming majority of Petersburg's slaves belonged
to either white families or white-owned businesses. Tobacco factories and
railroad corporations owned substantial numbers. As the cost of this labor

increased due to the sale of Virginia slaves to the cotton South, entrepreneurs found themselves investing more capital in their workforce than on industrial development. The first of every year Petersburg's streets teemed with slaves whom their owners brought from nearby plantations to offer for hire. There were 843 slaveholding households in Petersburg, but only 309, less than 37 percent, kept more than two adult slaves. More than 40 percent of Petersburg's slaveholders owned just one servant. Petersburg conformed to industrial and urban slavery patterns typical of the upper South.[20]

Despite their large numbers and relative comfort, Petersburg's African Americans existed under the same rigid restrictions imposed in all Southern communities. Free blacks clustered in the poorest sections of town, which the whites derisively named Niggertown or Little Africa. Proscriptions against education and denial of fundamental civil rights defined black life in Petersburg as surely as in any Southern city.

Nevertheless, the free black community developed cultural institutions that flourished amid the repressive atmosphere of antebellum Virginia. Free blacks enjoyed greater access to literature, professional services, and the company of other African Americans than agricultural workers. The black congregation of Gillfield Baptist Church obtained title to its land as early as 1818 and erected a seven-thousand-dollar brick structure in 1859. Remarkably, the members paid for the church in advance through mandatory contributions and fund-raising events presented for the benefit of enthusiastic white audiences. The Petersburg African Baptist Church owned its own sanctuary, as well. The Beneficial Society of Free Men of Color added another layer of culture to the free black community. This organization acquired a burying ground for the use of its members and supported people in sickness and emergency. Aside from the cursory supervision of white ministers required by law, blacks ran these organizations independently.[21]

Petersburg's pervasive class stratification left many whites with bleak prospects, beyond their racial pride. Although whites owned 95 percent of the city's real estate, nearly nine out of ten Petersburg whites owned no property. Thus a tiny fraction of wealthy families controlled an overwhelming portion of the city's private assets.

Petersburg offered little ethnic diversity beyond race. Nearly all whites claimed Anglo-Saxon heritage from England and Scotland and followed Protestant faiths. A small Jewish community established its own synagogue on Sycamore Street in 1858. A Catholic church operated on Washington Street, but these congregations paled in comparison to the Episcopal and Presbyterian adherents who dominated the city—along with, to a lesser degree, the Methodists and Baptists.[22]

Churches were the most important but not the only cultural institutions in antebellum Petersburg. The city sustained about two dozen schools,

Charles Campbell (1808–76).
A newspaper editor, historian,
and the headmaster of Anderson Seminary, Campbell kept
a diary that is the single best
source on wartime Petersburg.
This image was taken in the
1850s. (Courtesy of Valentine
Richmond History Center)

including the Anderson Seminary on Washington Street. This facility, phil-
anthropically founded in 1821 to educate white children of all economic
classes, operated on the eve of the Civil War under the supervision of the
well-known historian and scholar Charles Campbell. The Petersburg Classical Institute on Union Street offered classes to as many as one hundred and
fifty students and ranked as the city's leading private school. Petersburg
offered no advanced education for men but did boast a variety of "female
colleges" during the 1850s.[23]

The city's intellectual life revolved around Library Hall, dedicated in
1859 and operated by the Petersburg Library Association. There, in addition
to enjoying a fine lending library, citizens gathered to hear distinguished
lecturers. Petersburgers interested in less erudite diversions could patronize
the horse races at Newmarket, east of the city—a venerable track once
described as the most popular in Virginia—or attend a performance at
Phoenix Hall, a seven-hundred-seat venue built in the 1850s and sufficiently
commodious to host the 1858 Democratic gubernatorial convention. Visitors to town had their choice of numerous hotels. The Bollingbrook catered
to passengers using the Norfolk & Petersburg Railroad, and Jarratt's appealed to patrons of the Petersburg Railroad. Guests and residents alike
could peruse several daily, weekly, or semiweekly newspapers reflecting a
variety of political perspectives. The most popular papers were the *Daily*
and *Weekly Express,* the *Daily Bulletin,* and the *Daily Intelligencer.*[24]

The homes, businesses, churches, schools, and cultural institutions of the Cockade City occupied a compact area of roughly one-and-a-half square miles. Streetcars had not yet appeared in Petersburg, so by necessity it was a walking city. The main thoroughfares, Sycamore and Washington Streets, traversed the length and breadth of town, running north–south and east–west, respectively. Sycamore Street from the Appomattox River south to Washington included a commercial district with retail shops on the ground floor and apartments in the second and third stories that were often leased to young, unmarried men just starting their business careers. The Petersburg Courthouse stood on the east side of North Sycamore Street next to the municipal jail. South of Washington Street, Sycamore became one of the town's most prestigious residential addresses, particularly around the fashionable Poplar Lawn, which was ringed by a number of elegant new homes. On high ground at the city's southern limits, the tobacco manufacturer William Cameron built his luxurious dwelling, Mount Erin, in a developing neighborhood dubbed Delectable Heights for its exquisite views across the valley of Lieutenant Run, a tributary of the Appomattox River.

Washington Street boasted its share of fine homes, as well, particularly west of Sycamore, but it also provided space for many of the city's tobacco factories and churches. East of Sycamore, Washington Street descended into the ravine cut by Lieutenant Run and then climbed into the Blandford sector of the city. Businesses, industries, and homes for the middle and working classes nestled along Old Street, a block south of the river. Some of the city's oldest mansions competed for space on Bollingbrook Street, a block south of Old and running east of Sycamore, with the Bollingbrook Hotel, Phoenix Hall, and a number of commercial and professional offices. The city possessed a modern, substantial appearance by the standards of the time. The finer homes featured gas lighting, running water, kitchen sinks, and bathtubs. Coastal ships from New England filled the iceboxes of Petersburg's elite.[25]

Militia units in antebellum Virginia did more for municipal social life than national defense. State law required that all white males aged eighteen to forty-five enroll in the unorganized militia, although men in certain occupations, such as the clergy, and those with physical disabilities received exemptions. These outfits existed mostly on paper. Muster rolls listed the men assigned to each unit, and these holiday soldiers gathered on July 4 to elect officers and strut about to the delight of their neighbors. In Petersburg a militia muster, often held at Poplar Lawn, usually included a reading of the Declaration of Independence by some prominent (if duly humbled) citizen, followed by much toasting.[26]

A second category of militia pursued a more serious military course. The organized militia or volunteer corps consisted of men willing to devote more time to their martial pursuits. Officers and men in the volunteer corps

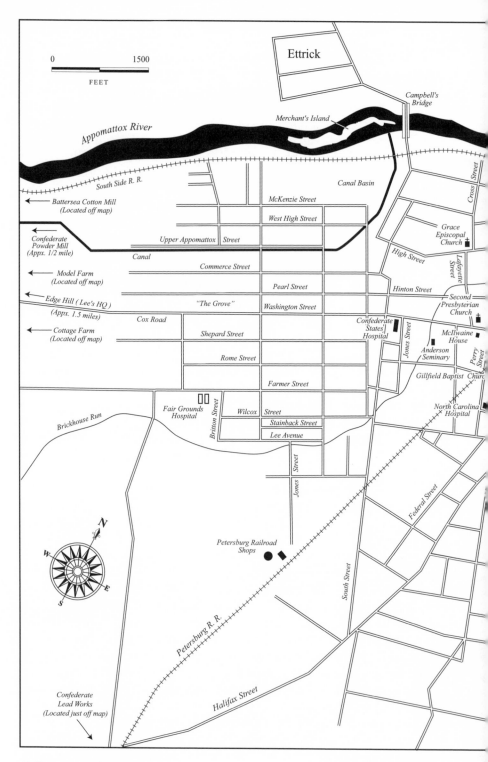

Civil War Petersburg, Virginia

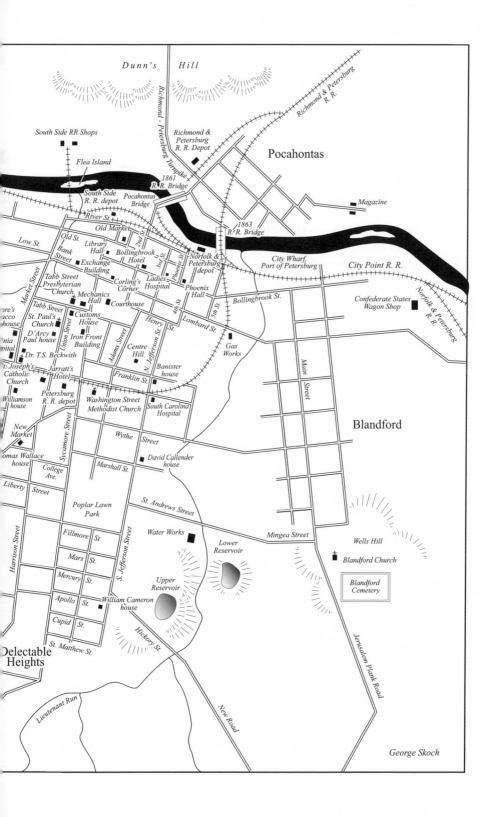

Dunn's Hill

South Side RR Shops

Richmond & Petersburg R. R.

Richmond - Petersburg Turnpike

Richmond & Petersburg R. R. Depot

Pocahontas

Flea Island

1861 R. R. Bridge

South Side R. R. depot

Pocahontas Bridge

Magazine

River St.

Old Market

1863 R. R. Bridge

Low St.

Old St.

Library Hall

2nd St.

3rd St.

Phoenix St.

Norfolk & Petersburg depot

City Wharf, Port of Petersburg

City Point R. R.

Bank Street

Bollingbrook Hotel

Exchange Building

Corling's Corner

Ladies' Hospital

Phoenix Hall

Confederate States Wagon Shop

Norfolk & Petersburg R. R.

Market Street

Tabb Street Presbyterian Church

Mechanics Hall

4th St.

5th St.

Bollingbrook St.

Tabb Street

St. Paul's Church

Customs House

Courthouse

Lombard St.

ore's bacco house

D'Arcy Paul house

Union Street

Iron Front Building

Adams Street

Henry St.

N. Jefferson Street

Centre Hill

Gas Works

Main Street

Blandford

nia ital

Dr. T.S. Beckwith

Jarratt's Hotel

Banister house

Franklin St.

t. Joseph's Catholic Church

Williamson house

Petersburg R. R. depot

Washington Street Methodist Church

South Carolina Hospital

New Market

omas Wallace house

Sycamore Street

Wythe Street

David Callender house

College Ave.

Marshall St.

Liberty Street

Harrison Street

Poplar Lawn Park

St. Andrews Street

S. Jefferson Street

Water Works

Lower Reservoir

Mingea Street

Wells Hill

Blandford Church

Fillmore St.

Mars St.

Upper Reservoir

Blandford Cemetery

Mercury St.

Apollo St.

William Cameron house

Cupid St.

St. Matthew St.

Hickory St.

Delectable Heights

Lieutenant Run

New Road

Jerusalem Plank Road

George Skoch

furnished their own uniforms and arms. Administratively the volunteer companies belonged to the same state militia regiments as the unorganized troops, but the organized militia participated in more frequent drills and musters, and they often maintained their own armories. Three Petersburg companies served in the organized militia prior to 1859: the Petersburg Artillery, the Petersburg Light Infantry Grays, and the Petersburg City Guard. These companies combined with the unorganized militia of the city to form the Thirty-ninth Regiment of Virginia State Militia commanded by the Petersburg commission merchant David Addison Weisiger, a native of Chesterfield County and a respected Mexican War veteran.[27]

Both the Petersburg Grays and the Petersburg City Guard journeyed to Charles Town, Virginia, in the autumn of 1859 to provide security in the tense atmosphere surrounding the hanging of John Brown, convicted traitor and instigator of servile rebellion. Brown's raid on Harpers Ferry that October electrified the white South and spurred an interest in the militia not seen since the Mexican War. Four new companies of organized militia began to drill in Petersburg by the year's end: the Petersburg Grays, called the New Grays, under the popular Thomas H. Bond; the thirty-five-year-old William H. Jarvis's Lafayette Guard; the Petersburg Riflemen under the bank president Daniel Dodson; and the Petersburg Light Dragoons—also called the Petersburg Cavalry—commanded by Robert Emmet Robinson, a physician well past fifty.

The sudden rush of enlistments across the state prompted an officers' convention in Richmond in early January 1860 to discuss ways to improve the state's volunteer force. The General Assembly quickly adopted the Militia Act, authorizing the establishment of militia battalions and instituting measures for improved training. Under the provisions of this statute, four of the seven companies of organized Petersburg militia joined forces to become the Fourth Battalion of Virginia State Militia under the command of Weisiger; the unorganized companies, the Petersburg Cavalry, and the two companies of Petersburg Grays remained in the Thirty-ninth Regiment.[28]

Politics, like military affairs, played an important role in the lives of some antebellum Virginians. Office holding in Petersburg remained almost the exclusive province of the city's elite, as conservative as the leadership in most Virginia cities. A twenty-four-member common council presided over municipal matters, and the elected mayor exercised influence in every aspect of city administration, including presiding over the Mayor's Court, which heard criminal cases. William Waverly Townes served as Petersburg's mayor from 1854 through 1866. Just thirty-five years old when first elected, Townes had studied law at the University of Virginia and established a successful practice in his hometown by the 1840s. Voters also elected a number of petty officials, ranging from the commissioner of the revenue to the keeper of the hay scales. The city collected numerous taxes and benefited from dividends earned through ownership of substantial shares of railroad stock.[29]

The 1860 presidential election was the most important antebellum political event in Petersburg, as it would be across the nation. Following the rupture of the Democratic convention in Charleston, South Carolina, the Northern wing of the party nominated Senator Stephen A. Douglas of Illinois while Southern Democrats tapped Vice President John C. Breckinridge of Kentucky. Breckinridge appealed to voters most interested in protecting slavery in the national territories, although he never endorsed disunion. Douglas energized Northern Democrats and maintained a substantial following in the border slave states, including Virginia. In fact, on August 28 he made a campaign appearance in Petersburg. The third hopeful, John Bell of Tennessee, ran on the Constitutional Union ticket, a contrived political movement invoking many of the conservative Whig principles so popular in cities such as Petersburg. The Republican standard bearer, Abraham Lincoln, did not appear on the ballot in Petersburg.[30]

Douglas attracted the support of Governor John Letcher and wore the mantle of the legitimate Democratic nominee in many parts of Virginia. Numerous party loyalists viewed Breckinridge as a stalking horse for Deep South secessionists and thus gravitated toward the Little Giant of Illinois. Prominent local Douglas men included Charles Fenton Collier, an attorney, and Thomas Branch, a commission merchant and former mayor. Collier and Branch typified Petersburg's Douglas voter because both linked economic prosperity with preservation of the Union.[31]

Breckinridge inspired the few true fire-eaters in Virginia, but the Kentuckian also retained a substantial minority of more orthodox Democrats who shrank from endorsing secession. These men viewed Breckinridge as the only candidate capable of beating Lincoln, and they cast their ballots more against the Republican rail-splitter than for the vice president. The *Petersburg Bulletin* endorsed Breckinridge, arguing that he could best protect the racial and sectional interests of white Southerners. Henry Clay Pate, a former Missouri border ruffian and antagonist of John Brown on the Kansas frontier, made his pro-Breckinridge stance widely known in Petersburg.[32]

Bell's candidacy resonated with former Virginia Whigs, a conservative and pro-business faction that retained considerable vitality even after the death of the national party. The *Petersburg Intelligencer* endorsed Bell. As election day approached, one nearby resident observed that "political feeling is now running higher than I have ever seen it, absorbing the thoughts of almost every patriot that the dark cloud that rests over the prosperity of our country may pass away and we may live in Union." Evidently, the majority of Petersburg voters felt the same. Bell collected a clear majority of Petersburg's ballots, outpolling Breckinridge and Douglas combined. The results

Charles Fenton Collier
(1827–99). The son of a prominent Petersburg attorney, Collier served on the Petersburg
Common Council and later in
the Confederate Congress
despite being a unionist early
in the secession crisis. This
image captures Collier in his
later years. (Courtesy of the
Petersburg Museums)

were similar in neighboring Dinwiddie and Prince George Counties, although in the rural areas Breckinridge outpaced Douglas. Clearly, the citizens of the Petersburg region hoped to avert secession, a national catastrophe that appeared increasingly likely after Lincoln carried the national
election with less than 40 percent of the popular vote.[33]

Lincoln's victory would indeed send the country spiraling toward disunion and war, but in Petersburg these calamities seemed avoidable in the
days following the election. Although a correspondent from the *New York
Herald* reported that "every man [in Petersburg] feels that something
terrible is impending," the Republican triumph unleashed nothing in Virginia like the secessionist passions that engulfed the lower South. These
calls for immediate secession faintly echoed in Petersburg when the pro-
Breckinridge *Bulletin* asserted that the triumph of a "Black Republican"
candidate signaled the practical end of the Union. But on December 23,
when a small group of disaffected citizens erected a "secession pole" in front
of the Bollingbrook Hotel displaying the "Bonnie Blue Flag," a symbol of
Southern independence, a mob of one hundred people tore down the offensive banner and replaced it with a national ensign.[34]

Rather than providing the South with a motive to seek independence,
Lincoln's election would instead "put a stop to the slavery agitation more
effectively than the election of . . . the other candidates," wrote the editor of
the *Petersburg Intelligencer*. Few voters east of the Blue Ridge shared this

naively conservative opinion. Petersburgers, like most Virginians, instead found comfort between the two extremes. They firmly rejected the notion that Lincoln's election provided adequate justification for rending the Union while recognizing that a looming national crisis demanded attention to uniquely Southern concerns shared by the Old Dominion.[35]

South Carolina, the first state to secede, declared itself independent from the United States on December 20, 1860. Governor Letcher responded by expressing the prevailing Virginia viewpoint, shared by the majority of Petersburg voters. The Lexington Democrat condemned South Carolina for its revolutionary action, promoted a national convention of reconciliation, and predicted a gloomy future if disunionism prevailed elsewhere in the South. At the same time, the governor articulated a six-point plan to protect slavery, including free entrance for slaveholders to the territories, protection of slavery in the District of Columbia, and the abolition of the personal liberty laws in the North that had hampered the recovery of fugitive slaves.[36]

The former governor Henry A. Wise and the Prince George County agriculturalist and editor Edmund Ruffin provided the most outspoken Virginia opposition to Letcher's moderate course. Congressman Roger Atkinson Pryor of Petersburg lagged only a few paces behind. A native of Dinwiddie County and barely in his thirties, the brilliant and colorful Pryor had used his editorship of the *Petersburg South-Side Democrat* and a keen sense of political destiny to gain election to Congress in 1859 as a states' rights Democrat. He and Letcher had been political allies in earlier days, but the secession crisis drove them apart. In late December Pryor publicly despaired over the future of a nation controlled by "Black Republicans," who showed little inclination to provide the South with the guarantees required to keep it in the Union. Although he wrote Letcher on December 30 that "no difference of opinion on the policy of the state & the South, which may be developed between us, will detract from [the] confidence & regard" in which Pryor held the governor, it became obvious that in the new year the question of disunion would test Virginia and its political leaders as had no other issue.[37]

Members of the Petersburg Common Council who took their seats on New Year's Day 1861 embraced the same qualified unionism that characterized most of the eastern half of the state. The *Petersburg Daily Express* cleverly articulated this feeling in a January 8 article satirizing the departure for Norfolk of three artless if enthusiastic Petersburg Southern nationalists. Virginia's premier port city shared Petersburg's unionist sentiments, but its strategic location suggested to many that if war came to the Old Dominion, it would call first at Hampton Roads. The *Daily Express* ridiculed the trio of Southern patriots by noting sarcastically that they were "armed with navy revolvers and regulation overcoats, the former for close quarters, the latter to make them look formidable in the distance—Glory is their only object—

Roger Atkinson Pryor (1828–1919). Pryor edited a newspaper in Petersburg before the war and, unlike most residents, earned a reputation as a states' rights advocate. Pryor resigned from the United States Congress during the secession crisis, served one term in the Confederate Congress, and became a brigadier general. His wife's memoirs provide colorful insights into wartime Petersburg. (Courtesy of Valentine Richmond History Center)

board and lodging included. We hope our Norfolk friends will be able to accommodate them."[38]

Four days later the *Daily Express* reported on the activities of the Petersburg native Richard Kidder Meade Jr., an army lieutenant on duty in Charleston Harbor. Meade was the handsome and intelligent twenty-five-year-old son of Richard Kidder Meade Sr., a former states' rights congressman, United States minister to Brazil under President James Buchanan, and a leading member of Petersburg's social and political elite. Lieutenant Meade arrived at Fort Moultrie near Charleston in mid-December, and along with the rest of the garrison, removed to Fort Sumter, provoking quite a stir. Meade played a prominent role during these politically charged days, defending the integrity of the United States Army during a confrontation with the South Carolina governor. The *Daily Express* walked a fine line in its account of Meade's exploits. It praised the honorable behavior of the native son, voiced no opinion as to the nature of the controversy, and declined to either condemn or condone South Carolina's defiance of government authority. Later in the month, however, the paper spoke out against the course of the Palmetto State, suggesting that South Carolina be left "to the grandeur of that amazing destiny which her ravished vision sees looming up in the future."[39]

The unfolding crisis of the Union did not go unnoticed in Petersburg's free black community. Many African Americans from the upper South with both the legal standing and financial means to leave the slave states were doing so. Demand for passage to the northwest had increased sufficiently that one railroad established special fares for use by blacks interested in fleeing the South before secession potentially threatened their status as free men. For $11.30 an African American could purchase a ticket from Petersburg to Parkersburg, Virginia, on the Ohio River, and for another $12.00 passage could be obtained to St. Louis, Missouri. Both of these river towns bordered free states. The first leg of a trip from Petersburg to the west entailed a ride to Richmond, and any African American booking a seat was required to show the agent of the Richmond & Petersburg Railroad "a genuine certificate of his freedom" or risk arrest on suspicion of being a runaway slave.[40]

Meanwhile, some in Petersburg called for armed preparation to meet any contingency caused by the North's intransigence. The young attorney Giles Buckner Cooke, a graduate of the Virginia Military Institute and a future Confederate staff officer, wrote the school's superintendent from Petersburg on January 21 recruiting VMI graduates for a Zouave company he was forming in Norfolk. The common council received several petitions, including appeals from the tobacco inspector and future councilman Thomas M. Rowlett and the wealthy attorney Thomas Wallace, who requested that the council appropriate fifteen hundred dollars to arm the unorganized militia. The lawmakers referred these requests to the Committee on Public Property, which reported on February 1 that it considered such an appropriation "inexpedient" at this time. Clearly, Petersburgers were not yet ready to cast their lot with the new Confederacy or even arm themselves in anticipation of conflict.[41]

Petersburg voters demonstrated their continued unionism during the brief campaign for a representative to a state convention authorized on January 14 by the General Assembly to consider Virginia's relation to the new Confederate states. Conservative members of the legislature supported submitting the question of holding such a convention to the vote of the people, but the measure failed. The conservatives did manage to enact a provision asking the voters to decide whether any ordinances that the convention adopted should be "referred" back to the electorate for ratification. This requirement plainly intended to retard the hasty removal of Virginia from the Union in the overheated atmosphere of a Richmond hall. The election would be held on February 4, and the convention would assemble on February 13.[42]

Petersburgers chose between Thomas Branch and Thomas Wallace to represent them in the convention. The fifty-eight-year-old Branch, one of the city's most successful businessmen, ran on a pro-union platform. The forty-eight-year-old Thomas Wallace advocated that Virginia join the new Confederacy. An "overwhelming" anti-secession majority sent Branch to Richmond on February 4 and voted almost four to one to refer the convention's verdict on secession back to the electorate for ratification, evidence of the Cockade City's pronounced conservatism.[43]

The state convention gathered in the capital as scheduled with 152 delegates representing every corner of the commonwealth. Like Branch, the largest number were moderates or conditional unionists who accepted the constitutionality of secession, acknowledged Southern grievances with Northern policy, and believed that Virginia had just cause for alarm from the upcoming Lincoln administration. They determined, however, that nothing had yet occurred that justified shattering the Union, and they hoped that by working with like-minded men in the North and the border slave states, they could prevent further secession and eventually lure the Deep South back into the nation.

The remaining delegates occupied one of the extreme ends of the political spectrum. A substantial number of outright unionists, almost exclusively from the far western and northern portions of the state, opposed secession under almost any circumstance. The convention's smallest faction favored immediate secession and sought to marry Virginia's destiny with that of the Gulf States, Georgia, and South Carolina. Clearly, moderates such as Branch held the key to Virginia's political future.[44]

Branch plainly articulated the moderate position on February 20 when he introduced seven resolutions for consideration by the convention. Describing himself as "a slow coach" and someone who would "save the Union," Branch also explained that "if the exigency arises and events transpire . . . which require action, I shall be one of the readiest voters." Branch's resolutions defined the fine line that conditional unionists walked. He stated that Virginia would not tolerate military action by the Lincoln administration against the Confederacy, but Branch agreed that the North should be given reasonable time to offer guarantees for the South's future safety, such as those recently introduced by Senator John Crittenden of Kentucky. Branch further proposed deferring Virginia's "inherent right of declaring herself an independent sovereignty" until the forces of compromise and reconciliation had been provided a chance to succeed. Finally, Petersburg's delegate declared that Virginia's "natural ties, her clear rights and sacred honor . . . dictate a firm and prompt adhesion . . . to the common cause of the Southern States, and the blending of their interests and destiny with her own."[45]

When John R. Chambliss, pro-secession delegate from Greensville County, arose to congratulate Branch on his resolutions and suggested that they reflected a position favorable to secession, Branch quickly corrected him. "I do not concur . . . that the interests of this new confederacy and the interests of the Southern States in the Union are to be perfectly analogous," he scolded Chambliss. "I have no sympathy with the action of the Southern Confederacy; for, through their action . . . Virginia . . . is placed in a [very] delicate relation to the West, the North and the South. . . . I was elected on a moderate platform. I am now a moderate man, and whilst I go against coercion . . . still I feel it to be the duty of Virginia to cling to the Union as long as she can."[46]

This Petersburg brand of national loyalty manifested itself in a different way on February 25 when Robert Ruffin Collier, a fifty-six-year-old attorney and the father of unionist Charles F. Collier, sent an unsigned petition to the capital that Delegate Chambliss read on the convention floor. Building on the principles that Branch articulated and those embodied in Crittenden's proposal, Collier recommended that Virginia leave the Union on March 4, 1861—the day of Lincoln's inauguration—but with one important qualification: that secession would be automatically repealed on October 19, 1861, if the Northern states had by then ratified a series of constitutional amendments vital to Virginia's interests. These amendments would guarantee the existence of slavery in present and future territories south of latitude 36°30′ (the old Missouri Compromise line) and the perpetuity of slavery where it existed; reaffirm the right to traffic domestically in slaves; continue to outlaw the African slave trade; provide federal compensation for all fugitive slaves not returned from the North; and prohibit persons "in whole or in part of the African race" from holding federal or territorial office or enjoying the right to vote in elections for such offices. An effort to table this petition met decisive defeat, and it was referred to committee for consideration.[47]

The hope for a negotiated resolution of the sectional crisis championed by Branch and his moderate colleagues in the state convention received encouragement from the Peace Convention meeting in Washington. This informal gathering at Willard's Hotel had been organized by the Virginia General Assembly on January 19 to find a peaceful adjustment to the nation's travails. Delegates from twenty-one states convened on February 4— the same day that the new Confederate government had its first meeting in Montgomery, Alabama, and Virginians elected their delegates to the state convention.

From the beginning the Peace Convention was a creature of the Old Dominion. John Tyler chaired the proceedings, lending the prestige of a former president to the assemblage. One hundred and thirty-two men representing most of the Northern states and all of the border slave states debated Senator Crittenden's proposals that Branch and other moderates favored as the blueprint for restoring union. Encouragement came from influential elements of the Republican Party, including William H. Seward of New York, who many assumed to be the most powerful voice in Lincoln's new administration. Even Congress suspended its hapless efforts to hammer out a compromise pending the secret deliberations of the Peace Conference.[48]

The delegates wrangled throughout the crucial days of February, finally presenting Congress with a seven-point plan on the twenty-seventh. The program comprised a diluted version of Crittenden's ideas and failed to generate enough support to be brought to a vote, the Republicans rejecting any measure that guaranteed expansion of slavery into the territories. Virginia moderates lamented the failed Peace Convention while a new round of secession agitation and increased sympathy for disunion engulfed the state.[49]

This backlash included the Petersburg area. Delegate James Boisseau of Dinwiddie County maintained close ties to the Cockade City. In the wake of the failed Peace Convention, Boisseau introduced an explicit resolution calling for Virginia's secession. The *Daily Express* supported his position, blaming radical Republicans for thwarting Virginia's sincere efforts to restore the Union through compromise. The editor admitted that he was "so much disgusted and sickened with Black Republican impertinences, insolence and meanesses [*sic*] . . . that we have arrived at the state of feeling in which we are utterly indifferent about any further political connection with such a graceless, miserable set of scamps" who had "pretty essentially and effectually cured us of *unionism.*"[50]

This transformation in sentiment gathered momentum from Lincoln's inaugural address on March 4. The president elect had been careful to avoid making inflammatory statements prior to his arrival in Washington. Lincoln based a great deal of hope for resolving the sectional crisis on the evident unionism of the upper South. His speech combined a conciliatory appeal to "the mystic chords of memory" that bound the nation together, with a firm resolve to sustain the union of states and hold federal property in the South. For many conditional unionists in Virginia such as Branch, Lincoln's address failed to abjure coercion—an absolute condition of their continued loyalty. The *Daily Express* took advantage of this disappointment to publish an unflattering description of the inauguration provided by two Petersburg citizens who attended the event. When asked if "the Illinois sucker" was good looking, these witnesses reported that "he is as ugly as they ever make them in Illinois, and that state is famous above all others for ugly men." In a less personal analysis, both the *Daily Express* and the *Petersburg Intelligencer* deemed Lincoln's speech an endorsement of coercion and roundly condemned it.[51]

The failure of the Peace Convention, the rejection of Crittenden's compromise, and Lincoln's controversial inaugural address combined to unleash a flurry of pro-secession rhetoric in the state convention. On March 5 the Goochland County delegate Walter D. Leake introduced a proposal for immediate secession endorsed by Lewis E. Harvie of Amelia County, one of the state's leading disunionists. Thomas Branch rose in response to these firebrands, stating that "I really cannot see any necessity for such hot haste as is manifested to-day in the presentations of such resolutions." Branch considered Lincoln's words "moderate" and saw nothing in them to warrant drastic action on the part of the convention. To the laughter of the delegates, Branch advised the younger Harvie, "don't be in such hot haste, my friend from Amelia. You have your whole life-time before you in which to attend to these matters."

Instead of embracing disunion, Branch counseled the convention to await the report of its influential Committee on Federal Relations before taking action, expecting this body to act in a matter of days. "When I went home to Petersburg on Saturday, I could not tell my constituents what we were doing or going to do, and hence I left town," Branch joked to the continued amusement of his colleagues. But Branch expressed his intention to press the committee for its report, recognizing that the moderation that had thus far controlled the convention was rapidly unraveling.[52]

Events in Petersburg also began to overtake the deliberate pace set by the moderates in the state convention. Mrs. Thomas G. Keen, wife of the pastor of the First Baptist Church, wrote her daughter that "the standing dish at every table is POLITICS." George S. Bernard, a young Petersburg attorney, agreed, describing the nature of the political discourse dominating Petersburg's street corners and supper tables: "The secession fever is almost universal—certainly among the more enlightened portion of the community." The common council felt the pressure for action. Robert A. Martin, a candidate for council in the upcoming elections, the wealthy industrialist Archibald Graham McIlwaine, and the successful tobacconist David Dunlop requested the council "to furnish the volunteers of Petersburg with arms," an unambiguous acknowledgment of the likelihood of war. The council appointed a committee to investigate the needs of the local militia, which verified that the volunteers lacked the necessary weapons for a military emergency. The council initially deferred action, but on March 15 it voted to supply Enfield rifles to two of the companies and Hall's rifles to another.[53]

By this time a critical event had abetted Petersburg's transformation into a secessionist city. The March 11 editions of the local newspapers carried an announcement requesting "All true lovers of CONSTITUTIONAL LIBERTY, and of the Union, as our fathers formed it" to attend a meeting that night at Phoenix Hall "to instruct our Delegate in the State Convention . . . to go for IMMEDIATE SECESSION." The *Daily Express* noted that although Branch had been elected on a unionist platform, "we believe that since the adjournment of Congress there have been changes enough in the city to reverse that majority, and as it has been here in Petersburg so it has been in every other conservative stronghold in the state." The *Daily Express* predicted that the March 11 meeting would "probably [be] the largest which has ever convened in Petersburg" and urged its readers to speak out against "the obstinate, perverse, and demented course of the Black Republicans."[54]

The meeting convened as scheduled and elected the forty-two-year-old attorney and railroad president William T. Joynes as chair, with the young *Daily Express* editor Andrew F. Crutchfield and the thirty-three-year-old attorney and militia captain John Lyon as secretaries. The former Douglas supporter and unionist Charles Collier offered four resolutions that reflected how much opinion had shifted since the presidential election and confirmed the centrality of slavery to the sectional crisis.

The first affirmed that "the point of substantial dispute, from which all minor disputes radiate as from a common centre, between the slaveholding and the non-slaveholding States, is *whether negroes are property.*" Collier called on the federal government to defend Southern property rights "in order to make that Union again illustrious with the beams of the old-time brotherhood." The second proposal cited the failure of Congress to accept the recommendations of the Peace Convention and called on Virginia to "resist the authority of the Union over us" and "declare this State absolved from any allegiance to that Union." This provision also pledged Virginia never to rejoin the Union "except on the basis that negroes held to service are property, as well as persons, and that the element of property in them must be created as property in the territories, and especially in the matter of delivery of fugitives from labor when escaped into any of those States or into any territory." Collier's third resolution called for these guarantees to be incorporated into an amendment to the Constitution. Last, the petitioner proposed that his resolutions be forwarded to Branch with instructions to support them.[55]

George W. Bolling, a wealthy fifty-two-year-old lawyer, offered an alternative to Collier's proposition: "That having full confidence in the intelligence, patriotism and firmness of our delegate in the Convention, for the protection of Southern rights and honor, it is inexpedient to instruct him on any question now pending before the Convention." This effort to quash an endorsement of secession received the support of Secretary Lyon. Roger Pryor, who had resigned his seat in Congress on the eve of Lincoln's inauguration, and Charles Collier's father, Robert Collier, spoke in favor of his son's resolutions.

Sensing an impasse or even a rejection of the secession proposal, Pryor moved that both Charles Collier's and Bolling's resolutions be tabled and the meeting adjourn. At this point the elder Collier advanced a proposal that would allow the electorate to place Petersburg either in the secessionist camp or continue the course of conditional unionism favored by Branch. Collier's motion stated "that the resolutions offered to this meeting by Charles F. Collier . . . and the substitute therefor offered by Col. George W. Bolling, be published in the newspapers of this city to-morrow (Tuesday), and the next day . . . and the next day . . . and that a poll be opened at the

Court House on each of those days, at which the legally qualified voters of the city may vote *aye* or *no* on the said resolutions."[56]

Between March 12 and 14, 1,641 voters cast ballots in what amounted to a plebiscite on Petersburg's endorsement of immediate secession. A slim majority, 53.6 percent, voted in favor of Collier's resolutions. This result hardly defined Petersburg as a hotbed of secession. It did, however, represent a major political shift since Branch's election to the state convention six weeks earlier and since the presidential contest in November, when seven out of eight voters supported either Bell or Douglas.

In Richmond on March 19, Branch sadly read his new instructions to the assembled convention. "The members of this Convention well know my position here," intoned Branch. "They know upon what platform I have stood, and stand now in my own individual opinion." But he felt obliged to obey what he considered the clear preference of Petersburg's voters. "I now bow with submission to the will of my constituents . . . that this Convention should pass an ordinance of secession." Invoking his flair for ironic humor to elicit sympathetic laughter from his fellow delegates, Branch concluded by admitting that "my people have changed very suddenly, and they have a right to change again so soon as the daylight breaks upon our hopes; and when they do, I shall be ready to carry out their views then."[57]

Although unionists claimed that local slave traders spent large sums of money to manipulate the March vote in Petersburg, similar manifestations of secessionist sentiment appeared in Fredericksburg, Portsmouth, and Norfolk at about the same time. Closer to home, a mass meeting at Dinwiddie Court House on March 18 declared that "we consider Lincoln's inaugural as an open declaration of war upon the South" and that "the old Union being irreparably dissolved, there is no option left us save to unite our destinies with our sister Southern States, or to remain a helpless appendage to the Northern Confederacy—the latter alternative being utterly repugnant to *all true Southern men*."[58]

"Secession, like Aaron's rod, absorbs everything and everybody," observed Mrs. Keen on March 14. "The party had a procession last night, and sent up quantities of fireworks, quite a *feu de joie*, and the cannon were fired. A rash expenditure of gunpowder for nothing I think. But then, I am no politician." The elected officials in Petersburg shared Eleanor Keen's skepticism of both secession and its likely military consequences. The common council took multiple votes at its March 16 meeting regarding the purchase of additional small arms for the militia. It eventually agreed to do so for both companies of Grays, but the council appended several safeguards to ensure that the guns would not fall into the wrong hands—those who were tempted to act outside constituted authority. President Joynes of the Petersburg Railroad sought military exemptions for his employees—hardly the impulse of a

Southern nationalist girding for war. Although the *Daily Express* lauded the ardor with which Petersburg's women encouraged displays of martial preparedness, even in late March Petersburgers evinced substantial ambivalence regarding Virginia's course of action. The city's move toward secession was evolutionary, not revolutionary, and still dependent on events beyond its control in Washington, Richmond, and Charleston, South Carolina.[59]

By mid-March the coalition of unconditional unionist and moderate delegates at the state convention realized they were losing control of the proceedings. Virginia's secession had become a real possibility. Should Lincoln decide to reinforce Fort Sumter, it would be difficult for the unionist-moderate coalition to maintain its supremacy. The coalition's strategy centered now on promoting a border states conference while endorsing their Committee on Federal Relations' majority report that called for federal guarantees on slavery, similar to those proposed in Crittenden's compromise. The coalition leadership hoped that such acknowledgment of Southern rights would stymie the disunionists long enough to allow the convention to adjourn without passing an ordinance of secession. Then, with more time, a solution to the crisis might yet emerge that would hold Virginia in the Union.[60]

Thomas Branch participated in implementing this strategy. The Petersburg delegate addressed the convention on March 28 , referring to his political situation as a "predicament in which but few men here are placed." He felt obligated to support secession as instructed by the voters of Petersburg, but he personally hoped to keep Virginia in the Union on honorable terms. Branch urged his colleagues to dispense with prolonged speech making and get on with the business at hand: determining Virginia's position on the great question of the day. "I came from home yesterday," Branch told the convention, "and the universal cry among my constituents was: what are you doing, and when are you going to act? We are a commercial city, and business languishes from your non-action."

Branch promised to introduce an ordinance of secession the following day, knowing that for the moment the disunionists did not have the votes to approve such a measure. Then, Branch and his political allies hoped, the convention would approve the federal relations committee's report and adjourn. "I give notice to gentlemen, then, that they must take their choice, whether they will stay in or go out. Let us act, and thereby put an end to so much unnecessary and unprofitable discussion." As it turned out, Branch did not introduce the secession motion, but Harvie from Amelia County did. On April 4, as the moderates hoped and expected, the convention voted 88 to 45 against disunion. For the time being, the secessionist engine had been derailed.[61]

Some minor incidents related to the political crisis occupied the Petersburg Common Council during early April. It authorized the purchase of sixty additional Enfield rifles, ensuring, however, that they were closely guarded. The council also endorsed the petition of the Petersburg tinker George C. Davis to take charge of the manufacture of tin items such as canteens and camp kettles at the Gosport Navy Yard in Portsmouth, anticipating a sudden increase in demand, despite the state's lack of jurisdiction at this federal facility. These halting steps toward martial preparation reflected the lingering devotion to peace and the Union in the Cockade City. As late as April 12, when news of the firing on Fort Sumter reached Petersburg, one observer noted that "I did not meet with so many *secessionists* as I expected to find. . . . The excitement here is not as great as one would suppose."[62]

Petersburg's fate depended, of course, on what the state decided to do, and events on the national stage began to steer Virginia toward disunion. The convention's anti-secession coalition of unionists and moderates had always been predicated on opposition to coercion of the Southern states by the federal government. Moderates such as Branch considered efforts by Washington to collect revenue, enforce the laws, or retain military installations in seceded states against the will of those states to constitute such coercion. As the sectional crisis escalated, a clash between the Lincoln administration and moderate Southerners grew more likely.

Virginia secessionists, such as Roger Pryor and Edmund Ruffin, recognized that by precipitating an incident in which the Lincoln government would be compelled to take overt action, the moderates' conditional unionism might become untenable. These firebrands also understood that Virginia preferred to act in concert with the rest of the border slave states and that the convention was disinclined to lead the upper South out of the Union. Thus Pryor and Ruffin journeyed to Charleston hoping to persuade the South Carolina authorities to attack Fort Sumter as a means of compelling Virginia to choose between abetting or resisting coercion.[63]

Lincoln's new secretary of state, William Seward, hoped that the United States would bow to Southern pressure and evacuate Fort Sumter, but this approach garnered little support in the White House. The president preferred to keep faith with the voters who elected him and made preparations in early April to resupply Sumter, while carefully denying any intention to precipitate a military conflict. Virginia moderates found little comfort in Lincoln's course. They instead pinned their hopes on two measures designed to defer another vote on secession and bring the state convention to an early adjournment, while seeking adequate redress of Virginia's concerns.

The convention sent three members to Washington to ascertain Lincoln's intentions toward the Southern states, hoping to gain some useful assurances. They also continued to promote a border slave states convention as a means of applying increased pressure on the administration for compromise, and as an alternative to unilateral Virginia action. Straddling the fence between secession and union grew increasingly uncomfortable for moderates such as Thomas Branch. These men still held the political balance of power, but their position had grown precarious.

The three delegates finally obtained an interview with Lincoln on April 13, the day after the Confederates opened their bombardment on Fort Sumter, including an early shot fired by Ruffin. The president, naturally, could offer the Virginians no hope of voluntarily abandoning the forts, particularly since hostilities had now erupted. When the delegates returned to Richmond on April 14, the die appeared cast in favor of disunion.

The convention met on April 15 amid an electric pro-secession sentiment throughout the capital. The last hope of the unionists and their dwindling moderate allies was to delay a vote on secession until Virginia could consult with the rest of the border states and act in unison, perhaps finding a way to avoid disunion and war in the interim. Lincoln's call that day for seventy-five thousand volunteers to put down the rebellion in South Carolina, including a quota from Virginia, destroyed this slim possibility. Branch fired off a telegram to Pryor and Ruffin in Charleston predicting that "an ordinance of secession will pass . . . in sixty hours."[64]

In Petersburg affairs followed suit, albeit more slowly and cautiously. Several Petersburgers made their way toward Charleston on the evening of April 12, fired with the ardor of Southern patriotism, but this instinct represented a trickle and not a torrent. Charles Collier was in the South Carolina metropolis, where events in Richmond garnered great attention. "Cheers for Virginia & her governor have been given today," Collier telegraphed Letcher from his Mills House chambers. "War is imminent—I wish to be in it." The common council continued martial preparations so incremental as to seem ludicrous against the frenzy of the next four years. The city solons approved the purchase of gunpowder, predictably specifying that it be closely guarded, and approved requests from the local militia to acquire "sixty-five knapsacks & six swords or sabers & 4 Navy or Army pistols" and to build a carriage for the brass cannon owned by the city. George Bernard told his father that one of his cousins had joined the secessionists but "is by no means zealous in the cause having very little confidence in the permanency of the Southern Confederacy."[65]

By April 17 nothing could stay the rush to secession. Encouraged by the floor-side histrionics of the former governor Henry Wise and the impotence of the shrinking unionist-moderate coalition, the convention now overwhelmingly favored disunion. The official tally counted eighty-eight delegates in favor of secession and fifty-five opposed. Thomas Branch cast his vote with the majority. Although the convention's action would be submitted to the voters for ratification, there was no question that Virginia had left the Union.

That evening, amid the unprecedented excitement of the convention's decision, Branch addressed his colleagues. He did so, as he explained, "as the representative of that patriotic city, which is known to be such throughout the country, to take the responsibility of sustaining the honor of the State that is now no longer part of the Union." But Branch made no secret of his personal feelings as he cast his vote to withdraw Virginia from the United States: "I wept this day as I witnessed the severance of that tie which bound Virginia to this once glorious Confederacy. . . . Yes, sir, I could not resist the influence of the sad reality, of having to desert the flag which sustained and protected me and my forefathers, and which commanded respect in every clime and on every sea."[66]

Many in Petersburg no doubt shared his reluctance and remained deeply ambivalent about secession. Virginia left the Union as a last resort in opposition to the perceived coercion of the Southern states, in defense of its right to hold property in slaves, from a fear of social and political anarchy should racial controls be eased, and out of a deep distrust of Republican intentions. Sentiment in Petersburg mirrored these motivations.

Petersburg's rural neighbors to the south and east, Prince George and Surry Counties, had elected Timothy Rives to represent them in the state convention. A renowned orator and owner of a farm south of Petersburg that would witness one of the city's most famous wartime events, Rives had defeated Edmund Ruffin Jr. for a seat in the convention on a pro-union platform. He and Branch shared a similar orientation toward the great issue of the day.

Rives addressed the convention on April 17 and delivered a particularly poignant speech on this historic occasion. He reconfirmed his well-known conditional unionism and told the convention that some of his constituents had recently attempted to present him with a set of instructions similar to those delivered to Branch. Rives had faced down this challenge by promising to resign should he be prevented from voting his conscience and submit to another election that he believed would sustain his position on preserving the Union consistent with Virginia honor. His defiance worked, the petitioners retreated, and Rives had returned to Richmond with a worried eye focused on events in Washington and Charleston.

When word arrived of the failure to achieve guarantees from Lincoln, and the president's demand for volunteers circulated through the convention, Rives informed the citizens of Prince George and Surry that "I know when the point of honor is past . . . I know when to strike the blow." Rives, like most Virginia moderates, had now become a secessionist, but he did so with great foreboding. "When I sign that ordinance of secession," Rives explained to his colleagues, "I shall sign it as an act of revolution. I tell you that the passage of this ordinance is the inauguration of revolution; and I tell you that in less than thirty hours afterwards, there will be acts done in the Convention that no man would now regard as possible. I tell you I go into this fight, and look every man in the face, and say, I did what I deemed best for my country, meanwhile believing that in signing the ordinance, I was helping to inaugurate revolution." The next four years would prove, for Petersburg and the rest of the South, the painful prescience of his words.[67]

⌈ 2 ⌋

"War Had Come Indeed"

APRIL 18–JULY 1861

THE CITIZENS OF Petersburg understood the political arithmetic on April 18, 1861: the attack on Fort Sumter plus the secession of Virginia equaled war. "The popular mind [is] so absorbed in war news and preparations," wrote Mrs. Thomas G. Keen. "Awful war! Thou horrid monster!!!" Yet Eleanor Keen willingly played her part in the Cockade City's transformation into a Confederate community. She produced the first eight-star secession banner in Petersburg and proudly displayed it in front of her home on High Street. "It attracts considerable attention and has elicited some compliments," she noted with pride. Her flag proved to be merely one among many Confederate symbols appearing on residences and public buildings throughout town that springtime Thursday. A group of inspired patriots climbed to the top of the Customs House, located with unnoticed irony on Union Street, and hoisted a particularly striking set of Confederate colors. "An immense assemblage of persons, who, already wild with excitement, cheered and hurrahed till their throats were hoarse," reported a gleeful newspaper correspondent.[1]

And at last, tangible military preparations began. On April 18 Major David A. Weisiger, commander of the city's Fourth Battalion of Virginia State Militia, complained to Adjutant General William H. Richardson in Richmond that he had "only two thousand Enfield, one thousand musket cartridges and twenty-eight canister shot—send a supply." He also requested that forty muskets be shipped on the early morning train to supplement the equipment that suddenly assumed urgent importance to a community and its citizen soldiers confronting the likelihood of war.[2]

Weisiger bore initial responsibility for Petersburg's military response to the crisis. On April 19 six of the city's militia companies gathered at Poplar Lawn to be sworn into active state service for a term of one year. Distinctive in their tailored militia uniforms, with each company attired uniquely, about

The Petersburg Courthouse one block east of Sycamore Street in the heart of Petersburg's commercial district. This building symbolized the city and witnessed many momentous wartime events, including political rallies, lurid trials, and the flying of the first United States flag when Petersburg surrendered on April 3, 1865. (Courtesy of Library of Congress)

four hundred local volunteers attracted the attention of admiring citizens who watched the spectacle and grasped the import of the moment. "A thrill of horror ran over me & I felt that war had come indeed," remembered Margaret Stanly Beckwith, teenaged daughter of the physician Thomas Stanly Beckwith and granddaughter of the fire-eater Edmund Ruffin.[3]

This somber reality became even more apparent the following day, as the troops prepared to board a special train bound for Norfolk. During the morning the young lawyer-turned-soldier George S. Bernard found time to jot a quick note to his father: "We are not yet off but are in hourly expectation of being ordered off. We are all in readiness for immediate motion. The excitement here for the past twenty-four hours has been very great." Bernard then confessed to a sentiment typical of so many naive volunteers during the Civil War's inaugural spring: "It may be that I do not fully realize the horror of war but I feel the greatest anxiety to commence the conflict now that it is about to be on us and this anxiety I believe pervades our whole force. All seem eager to be off."[4]

Bernard would not have long to wait. Shortly after noon Petersburg's volunteers wended through throngs of friends, neighbors, and family from Poplar Lawn to the Norfolk & Petersburg depot. The members of the Petersburg Grays, Companies A and B, the Petersburg Riflemen, the Petersburg City Guard, the Petersburg Artillery, and the Lafayette Guard paused for a collective moment to participate in what one observer called "the most affecting scene I have ever beheld." Mothers, fathers, sisters, and wives gathered around their loved ones to wish them farewell. "That day . . . seemed the end of the world," recalled Margaret Beckwith. Tears flowed freely, and above the commotion rose an occasional shriek of feminine emotion. "What made the scene the more touching," wrote a correspondent for the *Richmond Daily Dispatch,* "is the fact that the troops are composed of the very flower of our youth, fully three-fourths being under twenty years of age," or so it seemed. "Pen cannot portray the terror of that day," admitted Miss Beckwith, but "the consciousness of being in the Right gave us courage & hope."[5]

About 2:00 PM the time arrived to begin the journey east. The Reverend William H. Platt, rector of St. Paul's Episcopal Church and veteran of the Mexican War, stepped forward to address the departing troops—and their friends and loved ones gathered about them. "Soldiers! Go forth upon your mission of defence," Platt intoned, "strong and sustained in the mighty convictions of right. . . . Drive back the invaders from our soil, and the most deep prayers of mothers, sisters and wives will hourly ascend to the God of battles for your safety and success." The volunteers boarded the cars, the engine unleashed a defiant whistle blast, and "vociferations and cheers from

Fletcher Harris Archer (1817–1902). Archer saw action as a volunteer officer in the Mexican War and practiced law in Petersburg. Despite being a political conservative, Archer organized a volunteer company in Petersburg in 1861 and later served as a militia officer during the Petersburg campaign. His wartime letters to his wife, written while he was just a few miles from their home, are illuminating. (Courtesy of the Petersburg Museums)

thousands of voices" filled the afternoon air as the cars rumbled away from Petersburg's familiar streets toward an uncertain future. "The parting at the depot was the most severe trial of my life," wrote the Petersburg soldier John A. Weddell.[6]

The attorney Thomas Wallace reported to the governor on April 20 that the Cockade City was "blazing with excitement & new companies are rapidly forming," but the least exhilarated Petersburgers at the moment were the members of the Petersburg Cavalry. They had been ordered to remain in the city while their comrades left for the seat of war, and many of the troopers objected. Such was the enthusiasm of Petersburg's young men to meet the enemy that Thomas Branch predicted dire consequences should the cavalry remain idle. He warned Governor John Letcher that if the Light Dragoons were not quickly ordered to the front, their members were likely to resign and join units already in the field.[7]

As the six infantry and artillery companies entrained for Norfolk and the Petersburg Cavalry chafed at being left behind, new units began forming in Petersburg. Fletcher Harris Archer, a forty-four-year-old attorney and Mexican War volunteer officer, began recruiting an infantry company to be called the Archer Rifles. Like so many of Petersburg's leading citizens, Archer had been a conditional unionist until the waning weeks of the secession crisis but now embraced the Confederate cause. Joseph V. Scott, a thirty-eight-year-old commission merchant, organized the Cockade Rifles, using his reputation as a prewar militia captain in the Petersburg Grays to attract volunteers. Both companies enlisted one hundred men within forty-eight hours. James S. Gilliam, a twenty-two-year-old native of Prince George County, formed the McRae Rifle Guards about the same time, although this unit drew fewer recruits in the days immediately following secession. Other units rallied to the cause in nearby Ettrick, just across the Appomattox River in Chesterfield County.

At fifty-nine Major General Walter Gwynn, a renowned railroad engineer temporarily residing in Petersburg, was well past his military prime. Nevertheless, Governor Letcher appointed Gwynn the militia officer in charge of the initial defense of Norfolk and thus the commander of the Petersburg troops assigned there. Gwynn left Petersburg for Hampton Roads on April 21, taking with him the Colliers, father and son, and the former Petersburg Cavalry commander Robert E. Robinson as members of his unofficial staff. It seemed as though every white man in Petersburg had contracted war fever.[8]

Petersburg's African Americans watched all this commotion with great interest. The mobilization of so many white men, many of them slave masters and employers, promised a disruption of the delicate social and legal equilibrium that allowed slaves, free blacks, and whites to coexist peacefully in Petersburg. The South's interracial society rested on a strict system of controls, regulated by whites. Now that many of the men charged with this control were gone, how would the remaining whites respond?

Petersburg's free blacks had the most to lose from any disruption to the system. Always an unsettling presence for Petersburg's white population, free African Americans faced the real possibility of losing their few privileges should they be viewed as a threat in the city's evolving new order. They attempted to allay such fears and defer any deterioration in their legal status by expressing an avid willingness to assist the Confederate cause, either as soldiers or as laborers. "One hundred free negroes the pick of the place good & true men will offer their services to the state & ask me to command them," wrote the thirty-two-year-old James Read Branch to his influential father, Thomas, on April 22. "I will do so if the Governor will give me a Captain's commission. See him at once." Letcher received similar correspondence on April 23 from a Petersburg citizen who reported that "there is a number of negroes in this place that offer their services to you for any purpose."[9]

Virginia authorities were unprepared to arm blacks, and Governor Letcher initially rejected offers to supply black labor. Soon, however, Letcher changed his mind and permitted recruiting African Americans to work on the fortifications around Norfolk. On April 22 he approved Gwynn's request to enlist six hundred African American laborers. Petersburg's free black community rallied to this call in impressive numbers, as more than three hundred men immediately volunteered.

On April 25 a large portion of these men gathered outside the courthouse prior to departing for Norfolk. The former mayor John Dodson, an attorney of considerable prestige, made a fine speech commending their patriotism, and Petersburg's white ladies presented them with a homemade ensign. If this seemed oddly reminiscent of the departure of Petersburg's white sons five days earlier, the public reply of Charles Tinsley, a twenty-nine-year-old bricklayer and spokesman for the black volunteers, cemented the incongruous analogy. "We are willing to aid Virginia's cause to the utmost extent of our ability," promised Tinsley. "We do not feel that it is right for us to remain idle here, when white gentlemen are engaged in the performance of work at Norfolk, that . . . is more suitable to our hands. . . . There is not an unwilling heart among us . . . and we promise unhesitating obedience to all orders that may be given us." As an exclamation point on his people's Confederate patriotism, Tinsley added that "I could feel no greater pride, no more genuine gratification than to be able to plant [the Confederate flag] upon the ramparts of Ft. Monroe." Some of Petersburg's free blacks contributed as much as two hundred dollars, an enormous sum in the African American community, to defray the costs of sending their neighbors to the front.[10]

It is difficult to accept at face value Tinsley's explanation for the alacrity of Petersburg's free blacks. There can be no doubt that the city's whites sought gainful employment for their black neighbors, both to maintain control over them and out of a sense of duty to them. Early proscriptions against trading with the North and the interruption of commercial shipping instituted by the Lincoln government immediately affected Petersburg's tobacco factories, depriving many free African Americans of their jobs. "It would be a mercy to give them some useful work to perform, if only for their bread and meat," wrote one sympathetic Petersburg observer.

But as a resident of nearby James City County explained, assigning African Americans to work on the fortifications "would be putting them out of harm's way, thereby lessening the chances of servile insurrection, which it is well to guard against as far as possible." Although some of the black volunteers may have felt a genuine loyalty to Virginia and found sincere motivation in serving their native state, it is difficult to believe that men like Charles Tinsley did not exaggerate their Confederate patriotism out of a sense of self-interest. Free blacks in Virginia had become experts at accommodation and survival, and their eagerness in volunteering for unarmed military service comported with this instinct. Calculations of self-protection undoubtedly tipped the scales in favor of cooperating with the rapidly mobilizing whites.[11]

The reaction of the Petersburg Common Council to the national crisis proved much less ambiguous. An informal group of more than two hundred citizens met at the courthouse on the morning of April 22 to express unanimous support for providing $20,000 to arm and equip local volunteer troops. Heeding these popular sentiments, the fiscally conservative council debated a motion later that day to appropriate $5,000 immediately for such purposes and to provide an additional $15,000 if necessary. A companion proposition suggested a $1,000 distribution to the families of those volunteers "who have left their homes in defense of the state that in their absence they may not suffer for the necessaries of life." The members initially tabled both of these measures but readily approved them the next day.

The common council also resolved to provide $150 "for the benefit of the families of such free Negroes who have volunteered to go into the service of the state." This represented a fraction of the per capita appropriation for white soldiers' families. It did demonstrate, however, that the city held some small paternalistic solicitude for African Americans who left Petersburg to do their part for the Confederate cause. The allocations also signaled a significant departure from the laissez-faire fiscal traditions of Petersburg's municipal government.[12]

The council turned first to North Carolina for help in providing arms to its citizen soldiers. Some of the Petersburg companies left town carrying obsolete .69 caliber smoothbore muskets, converted from flintlocks. An agent for the city journeyed south in late April to purchase a quantity of modern rifles seized by Tarheel agents. "North Carolina . . . will, of course, spare us a portion of them," predicted a newspaper correspondent.[13]

The women of Petersburg willingly contributed to the support of the city's volunteers as well. Sara Rice Pryor, Roger Atkinson Pryor's wife, remembered that once the soldiers left Petersburg "silence and anxiety fell upon the town like a pall." The ladies instituted a prayer meeting each afternoon at 4:00 PM to assuage their anxiety, rotating the venue among various residences.

Besides seeking the favor of the Almighty, Petersburg's well-to-do women dedicated themselves to providing for their soldiers' material needs through the production of clothing and camp items. Mrs. Pryor assumed a leadership role in this work. "To be idle was torture," she declared, and her sewing circle met daily, including Sundays, to churn out everything a volunteer in the field might need. "We embroidered cases for razors, for soap and sponge, and cute morocco affairs for needles, thread, and court-plaster, with a little pocket lined with a bank note," she boasted.[14]

The women prepared bandages and lint, baked biscuits and cakes, and boiled hams to be sent to the Petersburg boys in Norfolk. Haversacks, shirts, and other clothing items emerged from sewing machines humming in Petersburg homes and churches. The young Jennie Friend, daughter of the

wealthy businessman and planter Charles Friend, recalled going to the basement of the Tabb Street Presbyterian Church, where "for every child and
woman there was work, scraping old linen into lint, tearing bandages, making sheets, pillow cases and tents." Thus in April 1861 virtually the entire
population of Petersburg—men and women, blacks and whites—was engaged in the prosecution of what had been, up to this point, a bloodless and
thoroughly exhilarating war.[15]

Little evidence of Petersburg's former unionism remained, while the few
dissenters attracted attention and soon learned that failure to adhere to political orthodoxy exacted a price. Colonel Edgar L. Brockett, a forty-year-old
store owner and lieutenant colonel of Petersburg's unorganized militia, reported four such individuals to the governor on April 19. The following day
John A. Ford, a thirty-five-year-old painter and native Marylander, received
orders to leave town "on account of his approval of Northern men and
means." He had become notorious by speaking freely in support of the Lincoln administration and its policies. "He was advised to seek the society
of more congenial spirits, and warned that his presence was neither needed
nor desired" in Petersburg. On April 20 several others, identified only as
"abolitionists . . . guilty of some offensive language," received similar treatment.[16]

Thomas H. Campbell, president of the South Side Railroad, understood
that the threat that outspoken unionists posed to his business paled in comparison to the dangers of a shooting war. Less than one week after Virginia's
secession, Campbell urged the governor to give top priority to military dispatches involving the transportation of troops. Campbell's counterpart at
the Petersburg Railroad, William T. Joynes, took the security issue one step
further by requesting that the state provide one hundred muskets for use in
protecting his company's vulnerable bridges. Other citizens hoped that
some of the heavy ordnance passing through town bound for Norfolk would
remain in the Cockade City. "We now have [in Norfolk] more than we can
use," a Petersburg correspondent explained to Governor Letcher. "There is
not a single cannon here." The city did have a fully stocked powder magazine,
and the authorities ensured that it was well guarded at night.[17]

Virginia's secession and Petersburg's consequent metamorphosis into a
Confederate town trapped Northern shipping in transit on the Appomattox
River. On April 18 a group of citizens, supported by a portion of the Petersburg Riflemen, descended on City Point, at the confluence of the Appomattox and James Rivers, and seized a Northern ship, the *Jamestown*, directing
it and its cargo to Richmond. Over the course of the next few days, Petersburg authorities detained more than a half-dozen vessels bound for Northern ports. The captors unloaded coal, flour, corn, and even gunpowder,
either in Richmond or Petersburg. Armed citizens, described as " a posse

of men ... to act as a river police," established themselves at City Point under the command of Colonel Brockett to monitor shipping at this key location. Mayor W. W. Townes wrote the governor on April 23, inquiring if vessels loaded with tobacco and cotton products sold by Petersburg businesses before secession to customers in New York would be allowed to leave port. When Letcher denied permission, the Petersburg tobacco industry suffered a sudden and near mortal blow. The Southern and blockade-restricted European markets for Petersburg's tobacco products could never absorb the city's prewar production.[18]

The military geography in April 1861 compelled Petersburgers to focus on Hampton Roads, the port of Norfolk, and the James River as the points of greatest interest and potential danger. The city had dealt almost effortlessly with Yankee sympathizers and Northern shipowners, but the Federal military and naval presence in southeastern Virginia could not be cavalierly dismissed. It was Norfolk and vicinity, after all, that required the presence of Petersburg's volunteers. The Union army occupied Fort Monroe at Old Point Comfort on the tip of the peninsula separating the York and James Rivers. The United States Navy had virtually free reign in Hampton Roads, although they had hastily abandoned the Gosport Navy Yard at Portsmouth, scuttling several ships, including the renowned *Merrimack*. Governor Letcher occasionally heard from Petersburg citizens, who reported alleged Union plans to attack Norfolk or described Yankee deployments around Fort Monroe.[19]

On one occasion during these heady days, the fear of Union power gained moral supremacy over Petersburg's unsoiled defenders. Reports originating with General Gwynn in Norfolk reached Petersburg on Sunday, April 21, warning of the possible approach of the USS *Pawnee* along the James River. Union Secretary of the Navy Gideon Welles had dispatched this eight-gun steamer to Hampton Roads a few days earlier as part of Washington's effort to protect the Gosport Navy Yard. The *Pawnee* made a dramatic but fruitless appearance opposite Norfolk on April 20, returning to Fort Monroe the next morning. Somehow the inexperienced Gwynn concluded that the *Pawnee* intended to attack Richmond or Petersburg. The militia general notified Governor Letcher that he had ordered Colonel Brockett to take command of two guns sent to City Point and to arrest the progress of the *Pawnee* or any other vessel passing up the James from Hampton Roads.[20]

The ill-prepared soldiers at City Point, Petersburg's Thirty-ninth Virginia State Militia, leapt into action. A flurry of correspondence passed between City Point and Richmond as citizens and soldiers prepared to do battle. "We have just received intelligence that steamer *Pawnee* is on her way to City Point," Lieutenant Colonel John M. Davenport, a wealthy commis-

Southern Virginia and Eastern North Carolina

sion merchant in civilian life, informed Governor Letcher. "Will thank you to send us immediately by special train fifty eighteen pound balls." The situation assumed comic dimensions: Petersburg's amateur soldiers manned ammunition-less guns posted at a wide spot in the James River, all intent on stopping a phantom United States warship. Fortunately, the *Pawnee* was on its way to Washington, not Richmond or Petersburg, but rumors of its approach created a memorable day, referred to in both Virginia cities for many years as *Pawnee* Sunday.[21]

Richmonders heard the reports and either panicked or prepared to give the *Pawnee* a warm reception with brooms, spades, old axes, and other makeshift weapons. In Petersburg the courthouse bell sounded at midday, warn-

ing the citizens of the approaching danger. Some Prince George County residents along the James appeared in Petersburg, apoplectic about the presumed impending attack of a tribe of Indians that the Lincoln government
supposedly sent to ravage the countryside.

In the midst of the "crisis," Jennie Friend and her family arrived at White
Hill, their home east of town, from Sunday services at Grace Episcopal
Church in Petersburg. Anxious neighbors urged them to return to the city
because the *Pawnee* (or to their minds, the Pawnees) had landed at City
Point. The Friends, envisioning tomahawks and scalping knives, loaded a
few valuables in a carriage and made haste for Petersburg, where Charles
Friend, patriarch of the family, had remained to attend afternoon worship.

When the terrified Friends reached town they saw chaos in the streets as
citizens, some armed with ancient firelocks, roamed about in search of news
and on the lookout for savages. Friend spotted his family in a dither and inquired as to the meaning of all the ruckus. Nonplused by the excited explanation, Friend calmly instructed his carriage driver to "turn around and go
home." Mrs. Mary Friend protested the recklessness of such a course, but
Charles insisted, and the family resignedly headed back east, young Jennie
remembering that "if I had been going into the jaws of death, the gloom
could not have been deeper." By sunset, when neither the United States Navy
nor bloodthirsty Indians had appeared, the panic subsided and everyone returned home. "All this seems foolish now," wrote Bessie Meade Callender,
wife of a cotton mill manager, "but it was real trouble at the time."[22]

Pawnee Sunday did nothing to stem the tide of office seekers who were
more nettlesome to Governor Letcher than a Yankee gunboat, imagined or
real. The outbreak of hostilities created opportunities for some Petersburgers to exercise their patriotism, while others sought only personal advantage. Robert R. Collier embodied the ideals of self-sacrifice. Before leaving
for Norfolk with General Gwynn, Collier wrote Letcher seeking a military
post in the service of his state: "I am fifty six years old, but I am willing to engage in the defense of the South, a section which . . . is in the right in the
great matter at the bottom of our national troubles." On a somewhat less
elevated note, John Herbert Claiborne, a thirty-three-year-old Petersburg
physician, member of the state senate, and surgeon in the Fourth Battalion,
beseeched the governor on April 18 to provide basic medical supplies to the
Petersburg troops before they left for the seat of war. He also used the occasion to suggest himself for a higher medical post: "I presume it is the purpose of the Executive to organize the medical force at once," Claiborne wrote
Letcher. "If I can be of any service in Richmond . . . please let me hear."[23]

The governor received numerous requests for appointments in late April
from, or on behalf of, Petersburgers from all walks of life. William A. Dudley, a young Market Street physician, immodestly promoted himself as a

Dr. John Herbert Claiborne (1828–1905). Claiborne had been a physician in Petersburg for a decade when the war began. He sacrificed his statewide political career to lead the Confederate hospital administration in Petersburg for much of the war. This image was taken in 1871. (Courtesy of the Petersburg Museums)

candidate for surgeon general of the state, using the former border ruffian Henry Clay Pate as a reference. Thomas Branch advocated a youthful Virginia Military Institute graduate from a prominent Petersburg family, Washington F. Sydnor, for a commission. The thirty-two-year-old businessman Richard H. Baptist recommended himself as a staff officer with endorsements from Mayor Townes, Councilman Benjamin B. Vaughan, and Roger Atkinson Pryor, the former congressman. The city residents James Lafsey, Robert C. Donnan, Dr. Algerson J. Cousins, and B. G. Black all approached the governor with personal letters, or through surrogates, to gain state appointments or commissions. Few were as blatantly self-serving as William B. Michie, who sought a position as a tobacco inspector in the Center Warehouse on the grounds that an incumbent, Nat Blick, was almost (but not yet) dead. Acknowledging that his appeal might appear "heartless, unfeeling and so on," Michie wanted to be certain that Letcher considered his application in a timely manner when Mr. Blick went to his eternal reward.[24]

During the last twelve days of April, virtually all of the city's residents, especially the white males, scrambled to find their places in the new order that the war had occasioned. "The business of the city is entirely suspended," proclaimed a Richmond newspaper, and the cause could be largely found in the efforts of Petersburg's businessmen and their employees to obtain a position in the military or in some support role. "Truly a martial spirit pervades the whole city," wrote one observer. "Efforts are now making, and with eminent success, to form other companies. The response of the people to volunteer for the defense of their native state is generous and hearty."[25]

The new recruits of the Cockade Rifles and the Archer Rifles drilled diligently from their creation on April 20 through the end of the month. Archer's company conducted a public parade on May 2 and elicited praise as "fine, able-bodied men." Two days later these units entered state service, and shortly thereafter they departed for Fort Powhatan on the James under command of Major John P. Wilson, a twenty-seven-year-old Virginia Military Institute graduate assigned to the river post.[26]

Captain James Gilliam's McRae Rifle Guards enlisted on May 9, 1861, just a few days after the Cockade Rifles and the Archer Rifles departed for Fort Powhatan. Like most of the Petersburg volunteers before them, the McRae Rifle Guards reported to the Norfolk area, eventually serving in the Confederate defenses on Craney Island at the mouth of the Elizabeth River. James D. Maney, co-owner of a wood planing mill, organized the Ragland Guards. They entered state service on June 20 and reported to the Norfolk defenses. The Cockade Cadets also trained in Petersburg under the guidance of William Platt. These volunteers drilled twice daily in late May and early June as they attempted to fill up their ranks. Any able man with a height of at least 5 feet 5 inches was deemed worthy of enlistment. "Some are very anxious to get the co[mpany] commissioned so as to be ordered to the field," wrote one of the men.[27]

Some Petersburg men preferred service in the cavalry. The firebrand attorney Henry Clay Pate organized a mounted company referred to variously as Pate's Rangers, the Letcher Mounted Guards, or the Petersburg Rangers, and he equipped the unit from his own pocket. On April 29 Pate advertised in the *Petersburg Daily Express* for volunteers, enticing recruits with promises of free uniforms and horses. Pate journeyed to Norfolk and salvaged small arms that had been thrown into the Elizabeth River when the Federals abandoned the Gosport Navy Yard. The innovative Pate also designed a revolving cannon cast at a Petersburg foundry, which he made available to his unit. The Rangers lacked pistols and sabres, however, and in June sought help from the state in supplying them, a request that the commonwealth could not honor. The Rangers joined the Wise Legion, commanded by the former Virginia governor Henry A. Wise, on July 4, and reported to western Virginia to secure the Kanawha Valley.[28]

Petersburg's original cavalry company finally saw its opportunity to serve in the field on May 17. The Petersburg Cavalry enlisted in state service under the leadership of Christopher Fry Fisher, the forty-two-year-old cashier at Petersburg's Exchange Bank, who had replaced Dr. Robinson as captain. An "immense assembly" of well-wishers watched as fifty-five members of the Light Dragoons departed for Norfolk on the seventeenth, "one of the finest companies of Dragoons in the state."[29]

The Cockade City would contribute two more artillery batteries to the Confederate cause, although one company of gunners spent the war's first year serving as infantry. The thirty-two-year-old attorney Richard G. Pegram organized an infantry company called the Lee's Life Guard, which entered state service on May 11. They reported to Craney Island in Norfolk, where James Branch, a future commander of the unit, requested ninety rifles and ammunition for the company, which had arrived in Hampton Roads unarmed. In March 1862 Lee's Life Guard became Branch's Field Artillery. The tobacco manufacturer Gilbert V. Rambaut recruited a battery of heavy artillery that bore his name and entered state service on June 1. This unit would also be known as the Cockade Mounted Battery. Thus within three months of the state's secession, Petersburg contributed ten companies of infantry, two companies of cavalry, and three artillery batteries to the Confederacy. These approximately twelve hundred soldiers represented roughly 53 percent of the city's white men of military age.[30]

Some Petersburg men declined to volunteer for state duty away from the city. Whether limited by advanced age, family concerns, business obligations, or opting for simple self-preservation, many of these citizens joined home guard units. Organized throughout Virginia in the spring of 1861, these outfits provided local community protection and an honorable option for those men who would not or could not take the field. Captain John Pollard, an accountant at the Exchange Bank, and later Captain David G. Potts, a member of the common council, commanded such a unit in Petersburg numbering about two hundred volunteers.

By the last week of April the home guard could be seen parading daily through the city's streets, the men carrying firearms of every description and uniformed solely with a red ribbon in their lapels. Potts sought to maintain his men as an independent unit rather than enlisting them in the state's formal militia system, which he thought had sufficient numbers without his troops. "We want to keep our company as large as we can, believing that it will have a good moral effect in our community," Potts explained to the Virginia adjutant general.[31]

In late April, William Pannill, a venerable commission merchant and Petersburg's most popular auctioneer, organized the Home Guard Troop of Cavalry. The sixty-six-year-old Pannill, "an elegant gentlemen," clearly had no intention of leading his mounted troops much farther than the city limits. Another organization, the Home Artillery, under the leadership of the thirty-four-year-old grocer Robert A. Young, recruited fifty volunteers to man two cannon "for home use entirely, unless urgent necessity should require their services elsewhere." The Reverend William Platt organized a fourth home guard company, called The Young Men's Reserve Guard comprised entirely of underage boys.[32]

Within a matter of days following Virginia's secession, Petersburg's volunteers had to compete for attention with Confederate units from other states passing through the Cockade City on their way to Richmond, northern Virginia, or Hampton Roads. At first the arrival of out-of-state troops elicited great excitement. Over time the novelty diminished, and Petersburgers turned to meeting the practical needs of these armed strangers.

The first transient soldiers to arrive in Petersburg came, appropriately enough, from South Carolina, the birthplace of the Confederacy. The Second South Carolina Infantry, commanded by Joseph B. Kershaw, a future Confederate general, arrived at the Petersburg Railroad depot on Washington Street shortly before noon on April 24. They received a welcome that must have warmed their hearts and made them grateful that they had been sent to the Old Dominion. William Joynes presented an official greeting to the six hundred Carolinians, as a stern-faced home guard attempted to appear martial and a large contingent of ladies, boys, and old men looked on approvingly. Milledge L. Bonham, a newly minted Confederate brigadier general and one of the Palmetto State's Fort Sumter heroes, provided a "spirited response" to Joynes's welcome.

The South Carolinians were bound for Richmond, and like all travelers making the connection to the Richmond & Petersburg line from North Carolina, they had to traverse nearly one mile of city streets and the Pocahontas Bridge to reach the Richmond depot. While some of the bronzed veterans of Charleston Harbor dined at Jarratt's Hotel near the Petersburg Railroad depot, others marched ceremoniously to the Bollingbrook Hotel on the route to the Richmond station. "The greatest enthusiasm prevailed during their transit through the city," wrote a newspaper correspondent. "Flags innumerable were suspended across the streets and flying from the principal buildings, and ladies from the windows waved their kerchefs and lent their approving smiles."

Some women did more than that, providing cool drinks of water, cleansing bloody noses (presumably sustained during intramural scuffles), and thrilling to the duty of holding a regimental banner while its bearer satisfied his hunger in a local eatery. The Carolinians had their band strike up "Dixie" and "La Marseillaise" as they marched down Sycamore Street, while some companies enlivened the scene with banjo and fiddle music provided by slaves attached to Kershaw's regiment as body servants or camp attendants. Others softened their dusty and road-worn appearance with yellow jasmine flowers tucked in their caps. An opinion circulated through town that these fine men and their companions were out to capture Washington, and if appearances could forecast deeds, most observers believed they would do so.[33]

The South Carolinians continued to tramp through Petersburg for the better part of a week. On April 27 several companies reprised the experience that their comrades had enjoyed three days earlier. They encountered enthusiastic "waving of handkerchefs from fair hands" and a rousing cheer in honor of the Palmetto State flag displayed near the corner of Sycamore and Bank Streets as well as an "eloquent address" that the distinguished local jurist Thomas S. Gholson delivered at the Richmond depot and that the Carolina captain William H. Casson answered in a kindred spirit. More South Carolinians arrived on April 30, only to repeat what by then had assumed the cadence of a ritual. The Reverend Theodorick Bland Pryor, Roger's fifty-six-year-old father, and Captain John D. Kennedy (another future general) played the roles of effusive host and grateful guest. One reporter took note that some of the Carolinians had lost their hats while leaning out the windows of the train, but eager Petersburgers quickly remedied the deficiency with proffered headgear, to the delight of all. In April 1861 this was war.[34]

Over the course of the next few weeks countless companies and regiments from North Carolina, Alabama, Louisiana, and other Southern states poured through Petersburg daily. The Petersburg correspondent for the *Richmond Daily Dispatch* observed that "one might almost suppose that mother earth was in the act of giving birth to a martial offspring so many are the military companies that daily pass through our streets." The First North Carolina Regiment attracted considerable attention due both to its size and to Petersburg's long association with the Tarheel State. One soldier in the Third Alabama Infantry reported that "the enthusiasm [from Petersburg citizens] was even greater than at Lynchburg. The Depot was crowded to excess by the citizens & numbers of ladies, all of whom welcomed us with smiles & cheers & entered freely into conversation with the 'boys.'" This regiment proved so popular in Petersburg that townsfolk contributed money to buy its colonel a new horse.[35]

Volunteers from nearby Virginia counties also arrived in Petersburg, where they paused to receive assignments and muster into state service. City authorities decided to create an encampment at the Union Agricultural Society Fair Grounds on the western outskirts of town for these soldiers whose stay exceeded the few hours it took to change trains. Boasting "refreshing shade and a cool, sparkling fountain," the fairgrounds soon provided shelter for new recruits from Chesterfield, Dinwiddie, Prince George, Mecklenburg, and Nottoway Counties as well as the occasional out-of-state unit. One observer estimated that as many as three thousand men could be accommodated under canvas at the fairgrounds.[36]

The presence of so many Confederate soldiers bivouacking in or passing through Petersburg, combined with the city's volunteers mustering and departing for Norfolk or other military destinations, smothered Petersburg in a welter of martial sights and sounds. "War is all the talk and all the occupation with the great and small," wrote Eleanor Keen to her daughter. "The Northerners are determined to worry us in every imaginable way. . . . I have just heard the bell ringing for another train coming full of soldiers. Everything is in a stir." While en route to Norfolk on May 4, Governor Letcher paused in Petersburg and attempted to assuage citizen anxiety. The governor reassured a large crowd that there was no immediate threat of a military collision around Hampton Roads, where so many Petersburg units had gone. The executive urged the people to "be calm and firm, and not to be led away by any undue excitement."[37]

Petersburg's annual municipal election, held on Monday, May 6, attracted relatively little attention either from office seekers or voters who remained too focused on the war to care much about the local campaign. "The present incumbents, if they desire it, will be elected without opposition," reported one newspaper correspondent. The new Petersburg Common Council experienced little turnover, with Mayor Townes presiding again over the usual assemblage of wealthy, conservative, commercial men. Martial matters dominated municipal business in May: Townes sought more arms from the state for Petersburg units; the council required all white men aged sixteen to fifty to register for the home guard; and the city appropriated additional funds to both the families of soldiers and black volunteer laborers serving in Norfolk.[38]

Governor Letcher's mailbox continued to fill with solicitations from job-seeking Petersburg residents. Colonel Brockett of the militia pursued a position as a quartermaster officer in the volunteer service; Thomas Branch lobbied on behalf of his son, James, who desired a staff appointment at Fort Powhatan; Alexander Watson Weddle, son of the wealthy Petersburg merchant James Weddle, marshaled the recommendations of many of the city's leaders for a quartermaster's commission; and the railroad engineer William N. Bolling, the Petersburg physician Richard Boyd, D'Arcy Paul Jr., son of a Petersburg councilman, as well as other less prominent residents all beseeched the governor for special favors involving diminished combat dangers and increased opportunities for material gain.[39]

On a less mundane level, war bred unrealistic aspirations in the city's leaders—a group particularly vulnerable to flights of boosterism. Petersburg vied to replace Montgomery as the Confederate capital when it became obvious that the little Alabama town could no longer serve the military, political, or logistical needs of the national government. The *Petersburg Daily Express* gleefully reported: "It is a source of pride to hear that the suggestion has been made in influential quarters, that Petersburg should be the seat of government of the Confederate states. If there is one city more peculiarly entitled to the honor, than any other, it is certainly the Cockade. She is always foremost in every noble deed." Petersburg's promoters offered the Old Market House near the river, noted for its "graceful pillars and architectural proportion," as the national capitol building. A local editor declared it "far more eligible than the crumbling walls of the Capitol at Richmond." Of course, the Confederate Congress gave Petersburg little serious consideration and selected Richmond instead, but the city's proximity to the new capital still ensured it enhanced status in the neoteric Confederacy.[40]

Despite this reflected prestige, daily life in Petersburg grew increasingly difficult in May. Economic forces precipitated by the war began to take effect in the Cockade City two weeks after Virginia's secession. Abraham Lincoln's blockade of Southern ports, a labor force largely absent in military service, and a state embargo on trade with the North idled tobacco factories and trimmed retail inventories, undermining the prosperous commission merchants. Uncertainty in the credit system reduced the economy to a cash-only basis, creating a temporary currency shortage that was resolved by printing more bank notes, which fueled inflation. Prices rose immediately. "We may expect to experience much inconvenience," predicted a Petersburg newspaper correspondent on May 2 with unwitting understatement, "but it will be cheerfully borne."[41]

Common services routinely available to Petersburg citizens suddenly became problematic. Normal operations at the telegraph office suffered from a tremendous increase in military traffic, an inconvenience exacerbated by the departure of the office manager to Norfolk with his volunteer company. Unhappy and confused postal workers stopped receiving pay from the United States, plunging the domestic mail system into chaos until the new Confederate government could fill the void. Even then, Petersburg citizens wishing to maintain communication with Northern correspondents endured the costly expedient of sending letters through Louisville, Kentucky, by commercial express.[42]

Fire companies dwindled as their members left for the front, and a large late April blaze on Harrison Street near the New Market consumed buildings that one fortnight earlier would have been saved. Railroad travel grew more complicated as the lines attempted to cope with military priorities and a system of government passes that reduced their revenue. Anna Birdsall Campbell, wife of the headmaster of the Anderson Seminary on West Washington Street and a New Jersey native, lamented the lack of tolerance shown a neighbor who had once lived in the North. Various Petersburg women had cruelly targeted this poor soul as a scapegoat for the domestic woes already so keenly felt in Petersburg. "This is one of the terrible evils of the times," regretted Mrs. Campbell.[43]

A different kind of tragedy befell Petersburg in late May. Captain Christopher F. Fisher, popular commander of the Petersburg Cavalry, committed suicide a few days after arriving in camp near Suffolk. Reportedly overwhelmed by his new responsibilities, Fisher was the first Petersburg soldier to die in uniform. His body arrived at the Norfolk depot on May 23 and was transported to the Baptist church, where the Reverend Thomas Keen conducted a funeral service, an event starkly at odds with the glorious image of war that so many credulous citizens embraced.[44]

Trains carried other notables to Petersburg in May, under happier circumstances, including North Carolina's governor, John W. Ellis. Petersburg's most popular visitor, Confederate President Jefferson Davis, arrived on May 29 about 8:00 AM, en route from Montgomery to the new Confederate capital. Accompanied by his secretary of state, Robert Toombs of Georgia, the former Texas senator Louis T. Wigfall, and others, the president's journey to Richmond had become a grand celebration with adoring crowds at every stop demanding an appearance by the chief executive—an obligation an ailing Davis always accommodated. Governor Letcher, Mayor Joseph Mayo of Richmond, and other dignitaries from the capital joined local people in welcoming the famous Mississippian to Petersburg.

"The whole city was in a stir" as Davis's train pulled into the Southern depot. "He is a tall slim man very neat in his dress, and has a mild, benevolent countenance," reported one admiring onlooker. "I was never more favorably impressed by any one, and if looks indicate his character he must be the man for the times, and under whose guidance the South will be sure to prosper." Davis made a few almost inaudible remarks outside the depot, then boarded a hack and rode to the Richmond station in Pocahontas, where he and his entourage continued north.[45]

The following day two more Confederate luminaries arrived, Brigadier General Pierre Gustave Toutant Beauregard and Confederate Attorney General Judah P. Benjamin. Beauregard was at the moment the leading Confederate military hero, having directed the conquest of Fort Sumter. With uncharacteristic modesty he disembarked on Washington Street, ascended the porch of Jarratt's Hotel, and explained to an enthusiastic crowd that "he was not to be praised for the victory at Sumter, but God alone." All city business ground to a halt in anticipation of Beauregard's arrival, which drew "everybody except the sick folks" to the station. The general's appearance impressed one Petersburg witness more than his eloquence: "He was much confused and is nothing of a speaker, though as perfect a model of a soldier as I ever saw." The assembly showered the Louisiana Creole with bouquets that became so numerous Beauregard sought the assistance of the crowd in carrying the surplus. Less conspicuous but no less important, Benjamin, another Louisianian, tried his best to avoid the multitude at Jarratt's.

The cabinet officer "lit out" for the Richmond depot, but some citizens corralled him and demanded a speech, which he delivered with what Confederates would learn was his customary grace. Later that day Beauregard and Benjamin arrived in Richmond to assume their duties.[46]

Amid the excitement generated by these distinguished visitors, Petersburg continued to serve as a funnel for Confederate soldiers streaming north. "All is well" in Petersburg, reported one correspondent, "nothing except continual arrival of troops and trains." While Petersburgers always provided a warm welcome to these strangers during their brief transit through the city, by early June parades and speeches began to prove less of a priority than food, shelter, and more efficient transportation. "About 900 troops arrived here last night about 10½ o'clock from the south & were detained for want of transportation on the Richmond & Petersburg Road 'till this morning & without anything to eat," complained Thomas Branch to the governor. "There is a screw loose somewhere."[47]

The absence of rail connections between the city's two north-south lines explained much of the transportation bottleneck. Shortly after the influx of Confederate troops began, rumors circulated that the two lines would be joined. The common council affirmed these speculations on May 1 when it passed a resolution authorizing the state of Virginia to lay new tracks through the city for military use only, stipulating that they must be removed at the end of the war or as soon as the military situation no longer required them. It would take nearly three long months to accomplish this critical logistical improvement.[48]

The city of Petersburg, a major stockholder in the Petersburg Railroad, had a vested interest in sustaining its transportation economy and sought assurance that wartime necessity would not create postwar problems. The Virginia government, the Confederate government, and the railroads all had bureaucracies to navigate and special interests to protect. The result was administrative gridlock. "I consider it very important to the military operations within Virginia that proper and easy connections of the several railroads passing through or terminating in Richmond or Petersburg should be made as promptly as possible," General Robert E. Lee explained to the Virginia State Convention on June 18. "The want of these connections has seriously retarded the operations so far." The lawmakers introduced an ordinance to effect the connection of the Petersburg and the Richmond & Petersburg Roads the following day, and they approved the measure on June 24. The Petersburg Common Council added its blessing in mid-July, and the line was designed on July 15, at last clearing the way to begin construction.

President Joynes of the Petersburg Railroad explained to Confederate Secretary of War Leroy P. Walker his company's reluctance to undertake the expense of making the connection. Citing the "great repugnance" in Peters-

burg to unifying the roads, Joynes argued that once the war had concluded
there was little chance that the city would allow the linkage to remain. Thus
there would be no advantage to his railroad in paying for an improvement
that would likely be dismantled in a matter of perhaps a few months. Joynes
suggested that the Confederate government bear the cost. He did volunteer
to undertake the work in return for payment in Confederate bonds equal to
his expenses, supplemented by government contracts to transport passengers and mail. Although the tracks eventually would be laid and efficiency
improved, this episode illustrated Petersburg's willingness to sacrifice her
sons to the war effort more readily than relinquishing her business interests.[49]

While the authorities wrangled, Confederate troops and supplies continued to move slowly between the Washington Street and Pocahontas depots. According to the schoolmaster Charles Campbell, who maintained a
meticulous diary throughout the war years, North Carolina soldiers most
frequently passed through Petersburg, although Georgians and South Carolinians arrived in great numbers as well. Some units featured military
bands that entertained residents during their trek along Sycamore and
Bollingbrook Streets. Troops unable to make a seamless connection by rail
to Richmond frequently bivouacked near the New Market at Halifax and
Harrison Streets, making the best of a makeshift situation.[50]

The common council at last responded to the needs of these transient
soldiers at their July 17 meeting by appropriating $450 for the erection of
"a house on the Poplar Lawn." Charles Campbell approved of the location,
citing as its attributes its "fine spring, pleasant shade & no groggeries near."
Petersburg's five saloons had enjoyed a booming business from the visiting
soldiers, commerce not entirely appreciated by Campbell and like-minded
citizens who valued order and propriety.

Assisted by funds from the Confederate government, the city contracted
with local carpenters, who agreed to donate their labor for the soldiers' shelter. The building was to be 150 feet by 40 feet and large enough to house five
hundred men. Charles Campbell suggested that the city's ladies make mattresses filled with corn shucks provided by local farmers. He also urged the
city to install water hydrants at the New Market for the troops and to erect
gas lamps in front of Jarratt's to illuminate the area for soldiers arriving
at night. Campbell's most innovative suggestion, a stark reminder of racial
hierarchies in the city, entailed compelling a "corps of Negroes always ready
with buckets of water & dippers attached by a chain to give water to the soldiers when they get out of the cars."[51]

As Confederate armies prepared for battle in northern Virginia in July,
an average of fifteen hundred soldiers passed through Petersburg each day.
Campbell estimated that as many as twenty-five to thirty thousand men had

traversed the Cockade City in the eight weeks after the arrival of Kershaw's South Carolinians on April 24. This traffic would eventually seem insignificant, but early in the war such a military presence far eclipsed any experience in the city's history.[52]

Managing transient soldiers presented but one problem facing the common council, which struggled to administer a city at war. Reluctance to appropriate funds for Petersburg's volunteers had disappeared by the end of June. The council voted on June 1 to outfit any Petersburg members of Captain Pate's cavalry company entirely at city expense. Two weeks later Petersburg's leaders provided $9,000 to equip volunteers, pay for military supplies, and support the families of absent white soldiers and black laborers. Through the end of the month the city had expended $26,721.05 to equip troops, $1,588.15 to purchase gunpowder, and $489.84 to buy small arms. This represented approximately 20 percent of the entire municipal budget for the fiscal year ending June 30. The council added another $800 for family support on July 1, $700 of which went to white dependents of Petersburg soldiers, with the remainder earmarked for African Americans.[53]

These large expenditures required revenue that the council raised through a complex array of municipal levies instituted on July 1. Every white or free black male over the age of sixteen was liable for a two-dollar head tax. The council assessed slave owners three dollars for each bondsman over the age of twelve. The city taxed real property at the rate of seventy-five cents per one hundred dollars' valuation and imposed a personal property levy of 2 percent on pleasure or riding carriages, horses, mules, watches, clocks, pianos, harps, and gold and silver plate jewelry. All other personal property required an annual payment equal to 3 percent of its value.

The city taxed income at the rate of 0.5 percent on the first $1,500 and 1 percent on all additional earnings, although citizens earning less than $1,000 annually received an income tax exemption. Interest on bonds or stock dividends required a municipal payment of 5 percent. Owners of "negro jails or slave pens" were liable for a $50 annual fee. Even dog owners had to pay the city one dollar for their first canine and three dollars for each additional pet. The city attempted to meet its new obligations by cutting expenses as well, instituting a "system of rigid economy" that included reducing the pay of certain municipal employees. Selling portions of the city's supply of gunpowder to the Confederacy generated additional revenue.[54]

Petersburg's leaders also perceived internal threats to the safety of the city and took steps to address them. On June 12 the council created the Committee of Safety, which exercised the authority to bring "all persons suspected of disloyalty to the state of Virginia or the Confederate states" before the mayor or a justice of the peace. This committee, numbering "40 of the city's finest citizens," had the power to establish "its own police rules and regulations" and "keep a strict watch over persons of suspicious character." The committee received a $200 appropriation to sustain a "secret service fund" to pay informants and otherwise detect and prosecute disloyal persons, such as the two Northerners arrested under suspicion of spying after registering under false names at a local hotel. Three weeks later the Petersburg Common Council adopted an ordinance making it a felony to "tamper with slaves, inciting them to rebel or make insurrection, or to escape from their owners," or to aid the government of the United States in any invasion of the state. These security measures revealed that a fifth column of unionists and slaves loomed in the consciousness of Petersburg's leaders as alarmingly as the presence of Union armies on the lower Peninsula or in northern Virginia.[55]

By June most of Petersburg's office seekers had found a place in the new government or army, but Governor Letcher continued to entertain the occasional solicitation from the Cockade City. One of the more interesting appeals came from Anthony M. Keiley, a twenty-eight-year-old Petersburg attorney and former copublisher of the *Daily South-Side Democrat*. Keiley, like Letcher, had supported Douglas in the 1860 presidential election and had opposed secession in the winter of 1861. Seeking to establish his political bond with the governor, Keiley explained that "having fought . . . at your side against fanaticism . . . recognizing, as you did, that the Proclamation of Lincoln was the obituary of the Union, I obliged your summons, left my home, a subaltern . . . and came to this spot [Norfolk] . . . resolved to show the maligners of Douglas Democrats . . . that the spirit of the leading Douglas Democrat [and] 'submissionist' in the state [Letcher] was not wanting in his followers." Keiley had joined the Petersburg Riflemen as a sergeant on April 19, explaining to Letcher that he assumed, like so many other eager volunteers, that his unit would see action immediately, and he wished to partake in the earliest battles. "That suspicion proved unfounded," he wrote on June 16, "and I am sure that it will not be thought an inordinate ambition if I desire service in some more important field than the modest one I find myself in." Keiley despaired of his chances for promotion through normal military channels because "my politics differed so much [from his superiors'] in the late canvas[s] . . . that it became my duty to tread heavily on their party prejudices, and it may be that all is not forgotten." Letcher noted on the back of this letter that he would like to help but lacked the proper authority to offer Keiley a line officer's commission or other relief.[56]

Alexander Falconer of Petersburg submitted an equally unusual petition to Letcher on June 18. Falconer, a Scottish citizen, considered himself exempt from obligatory service in the Virginia military, a position in conflict with the local authorities. Falconer had paid fines to the state before the war for his failure to report for militia duty, and with the advent of formal hostilities the pressure for him to participate in militia musters had only increased. "All my interests and sympathies are . . . with the South, and I am ready to aid in her defence all I can, but I am unwilling to be compelled to muster or pay fines that I do not legally owe," Falconer asserted. Letcher's response is unknown, but the Committee of Safety likely took note of Falconer's behavior and attitude.[57]

The ladies of Petersburg revealed no such ambivalence in their devotion to the Confederacy, sustaining the enthusiasm they had demonstrated during the heady days following secession. Bessie Callender wrote her brother, serving with the Petersburg Riflemen in Norfolk, "how gladly I would change places with you were it possible. Never before did I regret being a woman, but now it grieves me to be unable to fight." A newspaper correspondent praised Petersburg's affluent white women as "so zealous in the public cause that their activity is exerted in every way in which it can be rendered available." These distaff patriots provided meals to the transient troops, manufactured bedding for the new soldiers' pavilion at Poplar Lawn, and sewed various articles of military clothing. Petersburg's churches provided the organizational structure for the women's labors, the ladies sometimes dividing large tasks among the denominational groups, using materials that the Confederate government supplied. "There never was a war sustained by such a spirit," gushed one local admirer.[58]

Petersburg's women shared the general certainty in the early summer of 1861 that no Union military threat menaced their city. Still, as armed conflict erupted in the Old Dominion, some expressed concern for Petersburg's safety. "Our victory at [Big] Bethel has elated us and we feel more confident of the superior excellence of our soldiers," wrote Bessie Callender, but "rumours of the evacuation of Harpers Ferry makes [sic] our community anxious." The *Daily Express* expanded on this theme in its June 18 edition. "There is an urgent and pressing need for laborers to build fortifications while the recruits drill," wrote the editor. "Frequent appeals have been made. Some have responded. Others are indifferent."[59]

The newspaper also questioned the blind faith in Petersburg's invulnerability. "Some economical clod-hoppers of this vicinity who have as much knowledge of military matters as a James River sturgeon has of . . . theology declare that . . . they know the enemy will never come here and they, in the plenitude of their wisdom, consider this post unnecessary, notwithstanding the opinion of General Lee and other accomplished officers to the contrary." One armchair strategist, more well-meaning than practical, suggested that Petersburg could enhance its defenses by stockpiling thousands of bales of cotton in barns between Hampton, Richmond, and Petersburg to use as mobile barricades. Charles Campbell proposed the erection of more traditional earthworks around the city, but it would be some time before the authorities believed that Petersburg required permanent fortifications.[60]

Various circumstances in the late spring and early summer distracted Petersburgers from the war. The Baptist Association held its meeting in early June, filling Petersburg's churches, including the new Second Presbyterian Church on West Washington Street, with visiting ministers. The citizens welcomed David Humphreys Todd, Mary Todd Lincoln's half-brother, who was on his way south to aid the Confederate war effort. The *Daily Express* sardonically complained about the inexplicable rise in the cost of fowl. "The very chickens themselves would no doubt flap their wings and cackle in astonishment" at the high prices, the editor quipped. Fire wardens fretted about inadequate staffs reduced by enlistments; railroad owners successfully lobbied to exempt their employees from militia musters; and the Surveyor of the Port of Petersburg offered to return his pay. Citing the port's blockade-induced inactivity, Samuel V. Watkins wished to donate his salary to help hospitalized Confederate soldiers. "If you think it best to put it into the treasury you can do so," Watkins told the governor, but "I . . . would prefer that it . . . be given [to] the ladies in my neighborhood . . . for the benefit of our sick soldiers." Letcher approved this selfless gesture.[61]

Throughout the early summer the city experienced few problems with slave tampering or disloyal persons. Mayor Townes gained approval from the governor to open a letter addressed to "a suspected person of this place" in early June but, due to security concerns, failed to receive permission to allow a New York resident working for a Petersburg mercantile house to travel to the North. The most infamous local enemy, Union General-in-Chief Winfield Scott of Dinwiddie County, remained out of reach of Petersburg authorities at his desk in Washington, but this did not prevent the *Daily Express* from lambasting the native turncoat. "The truth so plainly but unintentionally told, when Gen. Scott said his long career had been more remarkable for its length than its brilliancy will meet with the hearty concurrence of every man in the south," wrote the editor. "He is notoriously the vainest man on the face of the earth."[62]

Troubles with slaves in Petersburg were confined to petty crimes and runaways, unremarkable except for the increased difficulty in retrieving truant bondsmen due to the absence of their owners serving in the army. One Petersburg woman complained to her soldier son about a runaway named Atchison who was at large and frequently seen in Blandford. "I wish you could get up & go catch him—and have him well whipped. I see no other way of bringing him to his senses," she advised.[63]

During the third week in July, military events in distant corners of the Confederacy competed with local affairs for Petersburg's attention. One correspondent noted that "we heard yesterday at Church of our success in Missouri and hope it is as great as reported in Saturday's paper. . . . The situation of our armies every where now keeps us always on the *qui vive*." With the situation at Hampton Roads relatively static, the forces under Beauregard and

Brigadier General Joseph E. Johnston in northern Virginia dominated Petersburg's war news.[64]

On July 18 Beauregard's forces clashed with a Union army under Brigadier General Irvin McDowell along the banks of Bull Run. The antagonists met in the first large-scale battle of the war at nearby Manassas Junction three days later. Anticipation of what many hoped would be the climactic battle of the war animated large crowds that gathered around the *Daily Express* office during these several days, awaiting dispatches from northern Virginia that arrived at the neighboring American Telegraph Company headquarters on Sycamore Street. The excitement distracted Charles Campbell, who still managed to note the arrival of Confederate Vice President Alexander Stephens on July 20. The Georgian impressed Campbell with "his eye dark & piercing[,] expressive of genius, his figure decrepit." Four hundred Florida troops, the first from that state to visit Petersburg, appeared the next day. The Floridians escorted nineteen prisoners of war captured earlier in the month at Cedar Key, Florida. A few local citizens joined Campbell to gawk at the Northern captives, some jeering and taunting the unfortunate Federals—an act that Campbell regretted.[65]

The days immediately following the Confederate victory at Manassas marked a turning point in Petersburg's Civil War experience. Although no local soldiers fell victim to Yankee bullets along Bull Run, the sons of many other Southern families passed through Petersburg either dead or badly wounded. Northbound trains carried the relatives and friends of Manassas casualties rushing to the battlefield to search for their loved ones. These scenes exerted a profound effect on the citizens of Petersburg. "Services at St. Paul's were beautiful," reported one Petersburg lady, but "it wont [*sic*] much like rejoicing for many eyes were wet." A furloughed Petersburg soldier agreed: "Everyone down here is elated with the news of the great victory. But the corpses & the wounded that have been passing through this place during the last day [demonstrated that the victory] was not without blood." Little could the citizens of Petersburg know how familiar they would become with blood, death, and suffering in the coming months.[66]

⌐ 3 ⌐

"The World Is Turned Upside Down and Topsy Turvey"

LIFE IN PETERSBURG
JULY 1861–DECEMBER 1862

THE SEAT OF WAR appears to be hermetically sealed against authentic news," complained Charles Campbell shortly after the battle of First Manassas. "Fame with her thousand tongues multiplies rumors." Petersburgers, like Southerners everywhere, maintained an insatiable interest in the recent conflict. They quizzed witnesses from the battle lines, devoured newspapers, and gathered around a large bulletin board outside the *Petersburg Daily Express* office that posted the latest reports. But as the ebullience of the spring and early summer of 1861 succumbed to the myriad disruptions, inconveniences, hardships, and dangers inherent to wartime, the challenges of everyday life competed with distant battlefields for Petersburgers' attention. As Margaret Stanly Beckwith phrased it, "This year of 1861 was spent endeavoring to meet the daily anxiety."[1]

During the summer and fall this routine stress included coping with thousands of transient Confederate soldiers. Petersburg hospitality had early in the war earned an enviable reputation among units from the Carolinas, Georgia, Alabama, and Florida. Local citizens extended seemingly endless kindness and generosity to visiting Southern troops, maintaining their gracious accommodation long after the novelty of greeting soldiers from different states had evaporated. Campbell witnessed a sick soldier borne through Sycamore Street on a cart, a local citizen striding along beside using his umbrella to shield the unfortunate volunteer from the blazing sun. Margaret Beckwith remembered tired and hungry soldiers "lining the pavements" of town while the ladies in the neighborhood "could be seen up & down the street carrying biscuits . . . which they had made with their own hands."[2]

Campbell collected reading material for a soldiers' library at the Union Agricultural Society Fair Grounds, while Petersburg churchgoers from various denominations organized the Evangelical Tract Society. This charitable organization produced more than one hundred different religious tracts and, assisted in Petersburg by the local Bible Society, distributed "more than a million pages of these little messengers of truth" within one year. Grateful soldiers responded to these gestures by bestowing tiny handmade keepsakes on their benefactors. One South Carolina regiment published its thanks in a Richmond newspaper for the warm reception the men received in Petersburg.[3]

On July 25 the city's various tradesmen, under the direction of a prominent local business, commenced construction of the Soldiers' Pavilion at Poplar Lawn. "The entire mechanic force of the city, white and black, have promptly and willingly come forward and offered their services . . . for free," reported the *Daily Express*. Using lumber obtained at discounted prices, the work required less than one week. The finished product combined adequate size with "fine shade and excellent water." The Relief Committee thanked the pavilion's builders with a free dinner and then used their new facility to prepare a meal for eleven hundred soldiers on August 7, serving food provided by the Confederate government but cooked and delivered by local volunteers.[4]

The relationship between soldiers and citizens did not lack problems. Charles Campbell complained that if the officers failed to control their men, the soldiers would drink at any hour of the day and "fill their canteens with grog." Campbell condemned some Alabama cavalrymen for their disorderly behavior, terming them "lewd fellows of the baser sort." Still, during the war's first summer and fall most of the townsfolk and soldiers enjoyed a relationship of mutual trust and esteem.[5]

The volume of visiting soldiers diminished on August 14 when crews completed the long-anticipated connection between the Petersburg and the Richmond & Petersburg Railroads. In spite of political pressure from the capital, work had not commenced until July 26. The new line ran east on Washington Street from the Southern depot, veered north, passing just west of the gas works, twisted back west, and, finally, turned north again to connect with the Richmond depot via a new span across the Appomattox River, immediately east of the Pocahontas wagon bridge. The South Side and the Norfolk & Petersburg roads extended their tracks to effect a junction as well, overcoming differences in gauge by running a third lateral rail at the required calibration.

After prolonged foot dragging in authorizing the execution of this vital improvement, the government provided but a short time to complete the work, imposing fines of one hundred dollars per day for tardiness. As a result, designers and mechanics rushed to meet their deadlines. Their hasty labors led to poor engineering and shoddy construction, causing frequent derailments at overly tight curves. Charles Campbell considered the new route "tortuous." Nevertheless, regiments on the move through Petersburg at last could avoid the inefficient delay marching between depots—an improvement Campbell deemed long overdue.

Improvements to the Petersburg transportation network coincided with an increasing volume of southbound traffic. Trains carried the casualties from Manassas and victims of camp sickness in northern Virginia. Townspeople also took notice on July 27 when the corpses of the two greatest martyrs from the July 21 battle, Brigadier General Barnard E. Bee and Colonel Francis S. Bartow, passed through town en route to their Deep South graves.[6]

The local citizens prepared to receive the sick and wounded in a variety of ways. Andrew F. Crutchfield of the *Daily Express* urged his readers to supply blankets for three makeshift hospitals that were quickly organized throughout the city. The Petersburg Common Council authorized funds to transform the exhibition buildings at the fairgrounds into hospital wards, a process that took several months, and appointed a committee of five to oversee hospital administration throughout town. The wealthy businessman Robert B. Bolling donated his magnificent home, East Hill, for sufferers of contagious diseases. By the end of July at least sixteen soldiers found refuge in the house, tended by white and black assistants and Petersburg doctors, all compensated by the city for their services. A facility for measles patients opened on North Market Street, and work began to convert the Classical Institute on North Union Street for medical use.

Until workers could complete the alterations, patients boarded at the city's leading hotels, Jarratt's and the Bollingbrook, the common council paying the proprietors for the rooms. It soon became clear that although Petersburg's transportation system, proximity to Richmond, and building inventory suggested an ideal location for a major Confederate medical community, the city's financial resources could not meet the challenge. By the end of August the Confederate government assumed responsibility for hospital administration in Petersburg, paving the way for a rapid and dramatic enlargement of the city's medical infrastructure.[7]

Sick and wounded Confederates were not the only soldiers to arrive in Petersburg from the north. Beginning in early September large numbers of Federal prisoners, captured at First Manassas and subsequent skirmishes in northern Virginia, moved south to prisons in the Carolinas, Louisiana, and Alabama. This parade of captives never failed to arrest the attention of the local newspapers and curious citizens.

Substantial numbers of Northern prisoners first appeared about September 9. These men, captured at Manassas, were on their way to Castle Pinckney, an obsolete island fortress guarding Charleston's inner harbor. They apparently arrived at a time when the connection between the railroads was under repair, as these unfortunates had to march from the Richmond depot in Pocahontas to the Southern depot near Washington Street.

The novel appearance of the vanquished enemy "attracted an immense crowd of spectators," primarily women and children, whose behavior elicited differing interpretations. The *Daily Express* reported "no evidence of rudeness" from the onlookers, while the Michigan colonel Orlando B. Willcox, wounded and captured at Manassas, recorded that "the town turned out *en masse* to stare at us & evince various tokens of hate." The *Daily Express* took notice of the diverse nationalities represented in the Union army, including the native Northerners who "appeared to be in high spirits, looking as shrewd and impudent as ever, as if they were going on an expedition which was expected 'to pay.'" Their demeanor contrasted with the Irish prisoners who acted "downcast . . . as though their memories were reverting to the Green Isle of which they were natives." Thus the editor Crutchfield evoked pejorative stereotypes of the greedy Yankee and the deluded, benighted immigrant that soon became staples of Confederate propaganda.[8]

A couple weeks later as many as two hundred and fifty Union prisoners passed through town en route to New Orleans. Charles Campbell noticed two black assistants who accompanied the guards and distributed water to the captives. Again a large crowd assembled to view the bluecoats. This time Crutchfield admitted that "taunts were given and returned" but claimed that the exchanges were made "seemingly in a very good humor." Newspaper readers once more learned of the "impudent looks, sharp features and glassy eyes" of the Northerners who also displayed unspecified crude manners that "accorded perfectly with their appearance."[9]

The martial exodus continued throughout the fall, with one hundred and ninety Federal prisoners passing through Petersburg on Halloween, this time shielded from public scrutiny behind the locked gates of the South Side Railroad yard. When one hundred and fifty prisoners trekked through town a month later, a large crowd followed them, but by then the sport of baiting Union prisoners had begun to grow old. The newspaper reported no incidents of abuse or derision, although it could not resist commenting on the "impudent and . . . very mean appearance" of the captives.[10]

Local citizens who engaged the Yankees in conversation characterized them as good humored, an attitude the Federals reciprocated. Some ladies distributed food to the captives and expressed sympathy for the prisoners' suffering from the chilly November wind, while the less charitable called for the blue-clad soldiers to be "drowned in the Appomattox." Charles Campbell noticed the interest in these Northern soldiers exhibited by blacks who hovered on the outskirts of the crowd. Although the demeanor of some Petersburgers toward these unlucky and impotent enemies might have softened over time, Crutchfield continued to describe them with unrelenting vitriol. When one prisoner escaped from a transport train at Belfield, forty miles south of Petersburg, the editor reported that "we are unable to give any description of him, only that he is a Yankee, and that is enough to betray him." When one hundred and seventy Federals traversed through town in December on their way to a military prison in Salisbury, North Carolina, the *Daily Express* called them "Hessians," reprising a familiar epithet from the Revolutionary War.[11]

Union soldiers were not the only prisoners who attracted interest in Petersburg. On September 13 city officials arrested a Canadian citizen named Daniel Flood, charging him with using seditious language and confining him in the city jail for several months. Flood's situation came to the attention of the British consul in Richmond, Frederick J. Cridland, who traveled to Petersburg in early December to effect Flood's release. After meeting with Mayor W. W. Townes, Cridland returned to Richmond believing he had achieved his mission, only to discover in January that Flood remained incarcerated. Later that month Townes freed Flood, who was taken to Norfolk and then escorted under a flag of truce to Fort Monroe. The mayor hoped that the incident would not become "a 'cannon ball' between [Queen Victoria] and the Confederate States."[12]

The exodus of volunteers in the spring and early summer of 1861 left few local troops to compete for attention with Northern prisoners and transient Confederate regiments. The small home guard and militia units rambled about town with the casual irregularity characteristic of such organizations. The Reverend William H. Platt of St. Paul's Episcopal Church formed a new company called the Independent Guards and relinquished command of the Cockade Cadets to the Reverend John B. Laurens, a thirty-four-year-old Methodist minister described as resolute, quiet, and sensible. So many of Petersburg's men of military age had enlisted in other units that Laurens had to scour neighboring counties and entice volunteers as old as sixty and as young as thirteen to fill his ranks.

By late August the unit counted merely fifty-six members, barely half a full company's complement, although the common council assisted Laurens with funding for proper uniforms. Enough volunteers appeared by late September to allow the Cadets to take the field. They assembled at Washington Street Methodist Church on the twentieth to hear an inspiring discourse before departing for Sewell's Point near Norfolk.[13]

The departure of the Cockade Cadets just about exhausted the voluntary martial manpower in Petersburg. Although patriotic ladies continued to display their ardor by making and presenting flags to the boys protecting Hampton Roads, the city's remaining white men of military age sought ways to avoid active army duty. Some found refuge in Petersburg's Thirty-ninth

Regiment of Virginia State Militia, which met weekly for musters and drill. Such requirements disrupted Petersburg's dwindling industrial workforce, already drastically diminished by volunteering. On August 20 the Petersburg Railroad president William T. Joynes, along with the presidents and general superintendents of all of Virginia's major railroads, had expressed frustration at the "intolerable inconvenience" of mandatory militia drills. Joynes pleaded that without exemption from this obligation, Virginia's railroads would suffer.[14]

Other businesses sought similar relief for their employees. Lemuel Peebles, a member of the common council and owner of the Petersburg Locomotive Car and Agricultural Implement Manufacturing Company, petitioned the governor to exempt five of his mechanics. "The scarcity of such laborers is so very great that we have been unable to . . . work our power beyond half its capacity and . . . the loss of these men will be a serious interference with the production of the works," he explained. John E. Wills, ticket and freight agent for the Petersburg Railroad and captain of a new home guard unit styled the Petersburg Cadets, sent a similar request to the governor seeking exemption from militia service for his recruits as had been done for other home guard outfits in the city. "I can assure your Excellency that we are gaining more information than we would be under the Militia officers and are at all times ready to render any service . . . in the repelling of invasion or putting down any disorderly conduct in our midst."[15]

Prominent individuals also sought exemption from military service. None of this implies that Petersburgers had not answered the call of their fledgling nation with remarkable alacrity. It does suggest that by the autumn of 1861 their focus had changed from the creation of military units to the support of existing regiments in the field, the maintenance of industrial production, and coping with the vicissitudes of daily life.

Chief among these challenges were the twin scourges of inflation and shortages. Just before the battle of Manassas, Petersburg's one-man economic barometer, Charles Campbell, recorded his first complaint about skyrocketing prices: "I gave 10 cents for a glass of soda water—double price; I asked a boy the price of peaches[,] it was 5 cents a piece for small ones worth about 5 cents a dozen. . . . What is the world coming to?" Within the next two months Petersburgers grumbled about the scarcity and cost of butter, salt, bacon, lard, candles, soap, matches, coal, and flour. When the *Daily Express* took notice of the city markets' lack of fruit, it encouraged readers not to complain: "As long as we are able to eat the bread of freedom a crust will be sweeter than the luxuries in a state of bondage."[16]

The editor Crutchfield and others mixed such patriotic appeals with accusations against unnamed self-serving speculators. "Within a few days we have heard some severe comments on the tendency exhibited to concentrate in a few hands the monopoly of some articles of prime necessity with a view of receiving exorbitant profits," reported the *Daily Express* on August 29. "If this is persevered in, these articles will be placed beyond the reach of the poor, and suffering and destitution must be the consequences." Crutchfield called on Petersburgers to banish "all idea of greed" from their hearts to avoid "civil discontent" among the working poor in the city.[17]

Although prices moderated temporarily in September, the inflationary trend generally continued through the fall, along with the virtual disappearance of items such as school books that had been imported from the North before the war. Even the *Daily Express*, a stalwart advocate of the stiff upper lip and personal sacrifice, raised its subscription price 25 percent in order to offset a 50 percent increase in paper costs. Hostility toward shadowy speculators rose. A public meeting in Dinwiddie County labeled speculation "worse than Yankeeism and Lincolnism and in perfect keeping with that people and their government." Charles Campbell agreed, observing that a man speculating on the necessities of daily life "may do us more harm than 20 Yankees."[18]

Transportation problems and a flood of paper money also contributed to inflationary pressures. The supply of fuel offered a prime example. Before the war Petersburg relied on anthracite coal from the North and bituminous coal from mines in western Chesterfield County for home heating and to power the municipal gas works. The blockade excluded the former; availability of the latter was limited by competition from the military for transportation via the Clover Hill branch of the Richmond & Petersburg Railroad and the absence of miners serving in the army. The proliferation of local, state, and Confederate currency immediately deflated its value to the point that merchants and railroads began to stipulate which bills they would accept. Attempts to horde hard currency in turn created a severe shortage of gold and silver.[19]

The Christmas season of 1861 provided a benchmark for measuring the decline in Petersburg's standard of living. Although some of the churches decorated their sanctuaries with evergreens, many families in the city simply ignored their holiday traditions rather than indulge in diluted versions of treasured customs. One Petersburg girl remembered Christmas 1861 as "oh so changed, so flat!" The candy stores offered the usual sweets for sale, but the delicacies had risen 50 percent in price, beyond the reach of middle- and lower-class families. "The prospects are that Santa Claus will not be so generous at . . . Christmas eve as he has been in times past," warned the *Daily Express*. "The 'little folk' will receive fewer presents, and probably will eat less confections. Pop crackers and fireworks generally will be scarce." The editor Crutchfield lamented the paucity of turkeys, hot plum pudding, spiked eggnog, and other esteemed holiday treats, and he suggested that

Confederate generals orchestrate a great battle at Christmas "to terminate in a Bull Run stampede of the Yankees" to nourish the souls if not the stomachs of patriotic Petersburgers.[20]

Inflation and scarcities created inconveniences for every resident, but they threatened disaster for the city's poor. Petersburg responded in various ways to assist their least fortunate neighbors. The Petersburg Women's Relief Association, an organization formed in September and composed of the city's wealthier ladies, solicited used clothing for distribution to needy families and sought employment for poor women in making items for the army. Bessie Meade Callender, wife of a cotton mill manager and treasurer of the association, succeeded in obtaining a contract in October to make ten thousand pairs of drawers for the army using local female labor.

A meeting in early November at the Washington Street Methodist Church attracted large numbers of the city's elite. The Reverend Theodorick Bland Pryor, William Joynes, and the Reverend Churchill J. Gibson, rector of Grace Episcopal Church, gave speeches in the cause of aiding the poor. Everyone in attendance contributed, totaling $3,000 in donations accruing to the relief efforts. Citizens organized theatrical performances, *tableaux vivants* they called them, and a lecture series to benefit the destitute. The *Daily Express* extended an invitation to the "Amateur Histrionic Society" of the Twelfth Virginia Infantry to come to Petersburg and present a show for the indigent families of local soldiers. "The simple appearance of Petersburg boys before a Petersburg audience is a sufficient inducement to extend them a hearty invitation," proclaimed the editor Crutchfield. The common council did its part by appropriating fourteen hundred dollars for soldiers' families in November and negotiating with the railroads to provide firewood to the city's needy at discounted prices.[21]

Petersburgers opened their hearts and their pocketbooks for their kinfolk in the army as well. Ward committees formed to collect blankets for distribution to Petersburg soldiers. The *Daily Express* boasted that only one family declined to contribute, but Charles Campbell thought that donors found motivation as much from "fear of popular odium [and] the show of liberality" as from "patriotic beneficence & real sympathy." The common council supplemented War Department supplies by providing uniform and camp items to Petersburg units in the field.[22]

Beginning in early November, Phoenix Hall hosted a series of public entertainments presented for the relief of local and out-of-state soldiers. Performers appeared from Richmond, New Orleans, and other distant locations. Patrons doubtlessly suffered bravely through novelty acts such as "Capt. King's Infant Drum Corps" featuring "Masters Fred and Charlie, 8 and 6 years old." No shows proved more popular than the amateur productions offered by the girls of the Petersburg Female College, the city's best-known school for young ladies. On December 23 the students packed Phoenix Hall for an evening benefit. The girls delighted their audience with various musical numbers. In conclusion the entire company performed "a stirring rendition of Dixie . . . which . . . set every heart aglow with patriotism." The newspaper critic did suggest that future productions be shortened, "as four hours was too long to expect people to stand or children to resist 'the wooings of the drowsy god.'"[23]

Proceeds from such theatricals helped support the sick and wounded in local hospitals, succor Petersburg troops stationed around Norfolk, and aid out-of-state Confederate regiments. The free African American community also pitched in to support Petersburg soldiers, motivated by an undeterminable mix of habitual ingratiation, fear of white retaliation for failing to do so, and genuine regional loyalty. "The Negroes are to have a concert tomorrow for the benefit of any Petersburg company at Norfolk that the Mayor of Petersburg may name," noted Charles Campbell the day after Christmas. "They sing far better than the whites."[24]

Petersburgers also tended to the needs of nearby troops. When the Twenty-fourth North Carolina Infantry encamped west of the city at the Model Farm around Christmas, their tented bivouacs lacked straw. Local farmers quickly responded. The city also orchestrated an elaborate New Year's Day feast at Poplar Lawn for the Tarheels, complete with music. Townspeople rejoiced when a Confederate soldier, jailed for overstaying his furlough while courting a Petersburg girl, obtained his release and married his local love.[25]

The city always turned out in force to honor Confederate dignitaries. Petersburgers suspended business during the summer in memory of recently deceased Governor John Ellis of North Carolina, whose body arrived at the South Side depot en route to Raleigh. The appearance of General and Mrs. E. Kirby Smith in September provided a much less somber diversion. Smith's new bride, the former Cassie Selden, maintained a close friendship with Mrs. John Donnan, wife of a wealthy Petersburg wholesale grocer. When the newlyweds arrived in town, the Cockade Cadets and Independent Guards provided an honor guard outside the Donnan home at 26 Perry Street, where William Platt greeted the general with a brief address before an enthusiastic crowd.[26]

Such displays of public celebration, however, were rare in 1861 Petersburg. "Our town is very quiet," admitted Bessie Callender in October. "So many have dear ones absent that there is no heart for gaiety."[27]

No portion of the population had more reason to despair than the city's blacks. The free African Americans who in the spring had volunteered to construct fortifications around Norfolk had still not received their pay by the end of July. William Joynes wrote an impassioned letter to Governor John

Letcher on their behalf and in the interest of their suffering families. "They volunteered their services with great alacrity," argued Joynes, "and it seems a gross injustice that they cannot receive their stipulated wages."[28]

Throughout the fall hundreds of additional blacks, slave as well as free, passed through Petersburg on their way to Yorktown or Jamestown to build works. Two men caught gambling in October were sentenced to work on the defenses in lieu of whippings or jail time. African American women idled by a lack of employment in the tobacco factories accepted jobs as laundresses in the field, leaving their Petersburg homes as a matter of economic necessity, rather than patriotic choice.[29]

Significant numbers of African Americans ran afoul of a criminal justice system grown increasingly harsh due to continuing fear that, with so many white men absent in the army, free blacks might exploit the lack of supervision to incite the slaves. Typical violations included disorderly conduct and failure to display a pass. These offenses exacted various punishments, such as jail time, whippings, or assignment to the work crews building fortifications on the Peninsula. Blacks convicted of other petty crimes, including gambling, smoking in public on Sunday, or attending a gathering without permission, drew sentences of ten to fifteen lashes or remission to the chain gang. The appearance of blacks in municipal court became so commonplace that their absence from the docket for any length of time prompted a sarcastic remark in a local newspaper. "The Mayor's Tribunal has been treated with the utmost contempt by the darkies for the last two or three days[,] not one of that numerous class having vouchsafed to make his or her appearance there," jested the *Daily Express*.[30]

More serious violations committed against whites — theft, for instance — warranted a standard sentence of twenty to thirty-nine lashes, the same punishment applied to the slave Albert Parker for shooting Tom, another slave. When an overseer shot a black man attempting to steal corn from the field outside the city poorhouse, the local press applauded the act. One Petersburg slave owner expressed concern about a growing lack of slave discipline and an increase in runaways: she blamed the problems on masters who curried obedience by promising not to inflict punishment. "In another year you must take them all under your own supervision," she wrote her soldier son about the family's disorderly slaves. "I will not continue this. You must hire them out and make them know they have a master."[31]

African Americans were not the only lawbreakers in Petersburg. In early December one Mrs. Hymandinger "thrashed a man and concluded the performance by choking him and kicking him down the stairs," for reasons that remain obscure. A row on Christmas Day at Sweeney's Tavern resulted in the apprehension of a New Orleans man who subsequently assaulted the arresting officer. The city jail filled with the accused and the convicted. Due to rotten mortar and restive inmates, the building proved unequal to the job of confining its charges, and prisoners routinely escaped into the streets. Soldiers guilty of overimbibing at one of the city's five saloons or seven restaurants added to the workload of the police and the court, but in general, the mayor treated cases involving intoxicated troops leniently.[32]

In a city consumed by worries about the war and the resulting social tensions, Petersburg's business community performed remarkably well during the war's first year. The flour mills, cotton manufacturies, and iron foundries thrived for a time, thanks to government contracts. The ironmaster Uriah Wells manufactured gargantuan bowie knives, so popular early in the war, featuring blades ten to twenty inches in length. By December 1861, however, Wells found it increasingly difficult to obtain reasonably priced iron from his sources in North Carolina and western Virginia. One Petersburg carpenter prospered by making bedsteads for military hospitals in Richmond and Petersburg. Similarly, the railroads made money transporting troops and war materiel for the Confederate government. The shops of the Petersburg Railroad manufactured freight cars, employing blacks in unprecedented numbers to compensate for the absence of so many white men in the army. The company operating the Appomattox River canal system reported good financial results in 1861.[33]

Not every Petersburg firm benefited from the war. The Union blockade suffocated any business that relied on the North for transportation or markets. Petersburg's primary industry, tobacco manufacturing, suffered almost immediately. By early autumn some of the largest factories had closed all together. Their remaining inventory became disposable only at great risk, if potentially high profit, through the blockade. The *Daily Express* commented on the shortage of lime, previously supplied from the North, resulting in numbers of unfinished buildings scarring the municipal landscape. The harbor filled with sloops, their cargoes unable to reach Chesapeake Bay via the lower James River. With so many of its citizens absent in the military, Petersburg's rental housing market grew soft. Thrifty boarders commuted to jobs in Richmond to avoid higher leases in the capital.[34]

The Northern blockade proved a mixed blessing for Petersburg's commission merchants and retail business owners. Most sold their complete inventories at inflated prices, realizing enormous profits. What to do with these massive sums became a challenge. Investments in Confederate bonds attracted some money, but many entrepreneurs purchased stockpiled tobacco or cotton for shipment to England on blockade runners, with proceeds flowing into British bank accounts. In this manner the wealthy simultaneously shielded income from inflation and the possible collapse of the Confederacy.[35]

The war itself created new but often complex ways to make money. In

August 1861 the attorney Thomas Wallace, William T. Joynes, and the forty-year-old banker and businessman Reuben Ragland teamed with the steamship clerk John Garnett Guthrey to represent them in New York City. The Virginians ostensibly instructed Guthrey to buy stock in Southern companies—a legal option open to everyone during those days—and to raise money for the building fund at Grace Episcopal Church. It is probable that Guthrey also established New York accounts for the Virginians to handle investments in Northern businesses.[36]

Winter is a brief but sometimes harsh visitor to Southside Virginia. The wet season of 1861–62 interfered with the lecture series held at Library Hall featuring topics ranging from the Holy Land to Brazil. Snow and ice also occasionally inconvenienced those interested in the frequent *tableaux vivants* and musical programs presented at Phoenix Hall to aid Petersburg soldiers, particularly the Twelfth Virginia Infantry. A twelve-year-old autistic savant named Thomas "Blind Tom" Wiggins provided the highlight of the season in early March. This black youth, sightless from birth and "incapable of intelligent conversation on any subject," toured the South during the war years, amazing audiences with his proficiency at the piano. "He performs inimitably selections from the operas of 'Norma,' 'Lucrezia,' 'the Battle of Manassas,' his own composition, etc.," observed one admiring Petersburg patron. "He played at once 'Yankee Doodle' and the Fishers Hornpipe and sang at the same time 'Dixie.'" By early April the city's entertainment scene had faded, causing one resident to complain that "the dullness of Petersburg is now oppressive."[37]

At times during the winter, city life enlivened in an undesirable fashion. For a number of weeks the gas works refused to pay the high prices charged for coal, and as a result, the streetlights went dark. The nocturnal gloom increased vandalism in Petersburg. One February night unidentified pranksters overturned cotton bales and store displays on Sycamore Street, a brazen if essentially harmless act unlikely to have been attempted under the glow of the lights. Charles Campbell reported a more unsettling situation in the death of an elderly man named Cochrane who was discovered in his house almost entirely eaten by his dog, a victim of either crime or terminal illness. Some households reported extensive sickness that winter, but the ailing and healthy alike suffered on February 24 when a terrible nor'easter blew into town, toppling the steeple on the new Second Presbyterian Church and destroying roofs, fences, and trees.[38]

Large numbers of blacks returned to the city from the Peninsula that winter to collect pay they had earned building fortifications. Mayor Townes distributed as much as forty dollars to each of these men, at a rate of fifty cents per day, "a snug little sum," thought the *Daily Express.* "They seem to be well satisfied with their treatment while away," explained the reporter, "in fact none of them offer any complaint whatsoever. Good lodgings, plenty to eat, and not overworked, with good wages, they come home as smiling as 'a basket of chips.'" The perspective of the workers, though unrecorded, was undoubtedly less cheery. African American women, delighted with the return of their absent husbands and sons, still gathered around the depots by the dozens with containers of sweets to sell to the soldiers who continued to stream through town.[39]

Petersburg society decried the presence of drunken Confederates on the streets, staggering under the effect of five-dollar-per-gallon whiskey. Alcohol and armed men could equal trouble. An intoxicated soldier from the Fifty-ninth Virginia Infantry died from a pistol shot to the forehead at the hand of a captain who took offense at the soldier's abusive and threatening language. Another inebriated graycoat was cited for robbing the city's blacks at the point of a bowie knife.[40]

The most infamous stranger to roam the streets of Petersburg that winter was a Yankee. Colonel Michael Corcoran, a well-known Irish American leader in New York City, had been wounded and captured leading the Sixtyninth New York Infantry at Manassas. The authorities confined Corcoran in Charleston's Castle Pinckney and then transferred him to the city jail in Columbia, South Carolina, more as a hostage than a prisoner of war. They used Corcoran as leverage on behalf of Confederate privateers captured by the Federals whom the United States government treated as pirates and common criminals, denying them status as military prisoners. Corcoran's situation received ample coverage in newspapers on both sides of the Potomac.

While the Union colonel traveled from South Carolina to Richmond in late February, his escorts made a stop in Petersburg. Accompanied by a set of friendly guards, Corcoran and a few other privileged prisoners visited some of the city's drinking establishments. Corcoran even managed to slip away for a time. The Irishman's little furlough ended when citizens recognized him and compelled the guards to return him to the Richmond depot to await transport to the capital. When he came back through Petersburg in May en route to Salisbury, North Carolina, the *Daily Express* noted that he was not allowed the run of the city as he had been previously.[41]

By then Petersburg confronted its first real military threat. During the late winter of 1862, Confederate arms suffered a succession of setbacks, including an army-navy offensive at nearby Roanoke Island, North Carolina, that resulted in the defeat of Confederate forces led by the former Virginia governor Henry A. Wise. Everyone knew that with the advent of warmer weather and improved road conditions, military activity would recommence in the Old Dominion.

The Union army in northern Virginia caused particular concern. Many speculated (accurately, as it would turn out) that the Federal commander there, Major General George B. McClellan, would advance against Richmond via the Peninsula following an amphibious landing at Fort Monroe. Refugees from Norfolk began pouring into Petersburg in anticipation of such a campaign. Workers loaded tobacco onto cars at the South Side depot for transport to Farmville, where the valuable commodity would be safer from possible Union capture. About the first of March one million pounds of Southampton County bacon passed through Petersburg, its owners hoping to shield it from potential seizure in the event of a Federal invasion.[42]

Besotted soldiers wandering the streets, battalions of blacks operating outside their traditional constraints, strangers by the score arriving at the depots, and military threats within a few days' march of Petersburg all suggested to many citizens a crisis of remarkable dimensions demanding equally unprecedented remedies. On February 27 the Confederate Congress authorized President Jefferson Davis to suspend the writ of habeus corpus and declare martial law in "such cities, towns, and military districts as shall, in his judgment, be in . . . danger of attack by the enemy." Davis acted immediately to so declare in Norfolk and Portsmouth, and on March 1 he placed the Confederate capital under military control as well. Within forty-eight hours of this act, approximately three hundred Petersburgers signed a petition calling for Confederate authorities to assume the same powers in the Cockade City.[43]

On the evening of March 4 the distinguished Richard Kidder Meade Sr. chaired a large gathering at the courthouse to consider the matter of martial law. The Reverend Theodorick Pryor of the Second Presbyterian Church called the meeting to order. Several speakers offered opinions on the wisdom of subjecting Petersburg to military control, an infringement on local autonomy inconsistent with the fundamental principles of the Confederacy. The attorney H. L. Hopkins spoke out against such a Draconian measure, "fearing its impact on personal liberty guaranteed by the constitution and tradition." J. B. Hardwick, a thirty-two-year-old Baptist minister, endorsed martial law, citing "instances of drunken soldiers embracing innocent and virtuous women on the streets of Petersburg with impunity" as ample justification. Another speaker warned that disloyal people "as thick in our midst as the fingers on our hands" threatened the community's safety. When William Joynes attempted to find a middle ground, suggesting that the resolution be amended to ask Davis to suspend civil jurisdiction in Petersburg only when the president thought it necessary, dissenters objected that with such authority suspended in Norfolk, Portsmouth, and Richmond, "nefarious characters from those cities would flock to Petersburg making it the 'great whisky mart of the state.'"

Theodorick Pryor ultimately introduced two resolutions approved by the majority of those in attendance. The first explained why military justice seemed necessary: "The establishment of martial law in the city of Petersburg and the surrounding country, would conduce, in an eminent degree, to the safety and security of the city; quiet the apprehensions of our people, and guard against the machinations of disloyal and traitorous persons, if any such there be in our midst." The second resolution created a committee to lobby the president to declare martial law in the Cockade City "and the surrounding country to the distance of ten miles, on the same terms upon which it is established in Richmond." Meade served as chair of this delegation composed of Joynes, Dr. T. Stanly Beckwith, Councilman Robert A. Martin, Dr. Thomas Withers, and a Mr. B. Wells.

This group arrived in Richmond on March 6 and met with the president, who agreed to consider the matter and promptly make known his decision. Davis was as good as his word. War Department General Orders Number 11, issued on March 8, announced the immediate suspension of most civil jurisdiction in Petersburg and the surrounding counties within ten miles. Adjutant General Samuel Cooper named William Pannill provost marshal of the city and authorized him to recruit military police to enforce the law. Cooper also ordered the distilling and sale of all "spirituous liquors" to cease immediately under penalty of up to one month hard labor imposed by military court martial.[44]

Meade and Beckwith helped the elderly Pannill form his military police, initially using men from Company B of the Thirty-ninth Regiment of the Virginia State Militia, commanded by Captain John Butte. This force posted around the city and enforced an increasingly unpopular system of military passes required of all citizens to enter or leave Petersburg. Within one week complaints arose about the inconvenience of such travel restrictions, while the guards suffered from standing in the cold and rain for hours without adequate shelter, food, or relief.[45]

The looming military crisis precipitated another infringement on individual freedoms late that winter when on April 16, 1862, the Confederate Congress adopted a conscription act. During the two months prior to the implementation of a national draft, however, the citizens of Petersburg experienced the imposition of mandatory state military service. Governor Letcher had recognized the need to field more troops and organize reserve forces throughout Virginia. As a first step, he convinced the state legislature to enact a statute on February 8, 1862, requiring all white males between the ages of eighteen and forty-five not serving in active Confederate units to register with militia officers. This measure essentially echoed the antebellum policy of militia enrollment, but the new law also provided that "every man enrolled . . . hold himself in readiness for draft for active service." Letcher issued a stirring proclamation on February 13, appealing to his fellow Virginians to "repel the foul tyrant" by volunteering for active service in existing Virginia regiments, implying that those who chose to remain only on the compulsory militia rosters would likely be conscripted to take the field. March 10 would be the deadline for volunteers to join existing Confederate units of their choice.[46]

Petersburgers, like other Virginians, inquired about the criteria for exemptions from the militia enrollment and active duty. Some men sought to hire substitutes. The legislature amended the state code, carefully enumerating all occupations qualifying for exemption. The governor also established a board in each county and city to review exemption issues. These measures precipitated a flurry of activity in Petersburg, including a sarcastic offer published in the *Daily Express* by local ladies offering themselves as substitutes for "any of those gentlemen who lately visited Richmond to obtain such substitutes, and may have failed to do so."

By March 6 as many as 991 eligible Petersburg men had enrolled in the state militia. The local newspapers filled with advertisements from existing Petersburg companies soliciting volunteers. The March 3 edition of the *Daily Express* contained no fewer than seventeen such appeals. John Laurens of the Confederate Cadets traveled from Norfolk to entice volunteers to join his company. Edward A. Goodwyn, the thirty-eight-year-old general ticket and freight agent for the South Side Railroad and a future Petersburg mayor, helped recruit an entirely new company of mounted troops, the Cockade Cavalry, organized on March 5 and enlisted in Confederate service one week later. Local citizens contributed between eight and nine thousand dollars to provide this new unit with horses.[47]

On March 7 the state legislature significantly modified the provisions of its February 8 act. The new law declared that men aged eighteen to forty-five listed on the state rolls would be considered the First Class Militia. It then provided for the establishment of the Second Class Militia to be manned by boys aged sixteen and seventeen and men aged forty-six to fifty-five in and around several cities, including Petersburg.

The next day Confederate Secretary of War Judah P. Benjamin asked Governor Letcher for forty thousand Virginia troops, and the governor responded by activating the First Class Militia. "This war has attained a point which requires brave men and true patriots to leave their homes and grapple sternly with the foe," declared the governor. "We will not tamely submit to degradation or slavery. We will have Virginia independent and all our liberties maintained or perish in the attempt to secure them." Petersburg's militia units, along with those from twenty-seven counties, received orders to report to Major General Benjamin Huger in Norfolk. The pursuit of liberty had, ironically, suddenly subjected large numbers of Petersburgers to active compulsory military service while depriving the rest of their civil rights through the imposition of martial law.[48]

The impending mobilization of so many men caused great excitement and no little anxiety in Petersburg. "Crowds discussing the news . . . people in fine spirits," recorded an observer. On March 13 the activated militia, estimated to number from five hundred to eight hundred men, gathered at Poplar Lawn prior to reporting to the Model Farm the next morning. From there the recruits would march to the Norfolk depot and board trains for the seat of war.

By then sentiments in Petersburg began to turn against the governor. "Letcher's levy *en masse* is generally denounced," reported Charles Campbell. Campbell speculated that Letcher's intent was to stimulate volunteerism for the regular units, not deploy the militia on the front lines. Lieutenant Colonel John M. Davenport, commander of Petersburg's Thirty-ninth Regiment of Virginia State Militia, posed just this question to the governor on March 13: "The militia of this city are now under orders. Can any of them volunteer?" Letcher, in fact, had issued a supplemental proclamation two days earlier stating that "any person, enrolled in any militia company, who shall designate . . . the company now in service to which he is willing to be assigned . . . for the war, shall be allowed to do so." It is difficult to calculate how many men exercised this option.[49]

The Petersburg Common Council scrambled to exempt as many citizens as possible from the militia activation, an instinct that would persist throughout the war. They excused themselves, the mayor, chamberlain, auditor, superintendent, all officers of the municipal water works, superintendent and all employees of the gas works, the keeper of Blandford Cemetery, the coroner, constable, jailer, night watchmen, bailiff, members of the fire department, and one teacher, totaling sixty-one individuals. All but the teacher avoided service. Some of these men no doubt watched, perhaps with a mixture of relief and guilt, as Petersburg's First Class Militia marched into town and entrained for Norfolk.[50]

The departure of even more of Petersburg's men underscored how the war had grown to dominate everyday life in the late winter and early spring of 1862. Fear of imminent attack, concern for loved ones in the military, and worry about Confederate fortunes in distant theaters combined to unnerve and depress nearly everyone. "The *Express* describes the excitement and commotion here as a sort of panic," wrote Charles Campbell. "I do not see evidences of alarm among those I meet with, although there are anxiety and apprehension. Rumor with her thousand tongues is busy." The Confederate attorney general, Thomas Bragg, visited his family in Petersburg in late February and thought "the town seemed gloomy. . . . Great uneasiness is felt there, as there is in fact everywhere." A "union prayer meeting" held at the Washington Street Methodist Church on February 28 attracted a large crowd to worship under the guidance of five or six ministers.[51]

Naval affairs briefly diverted public attention from matters of internal security. Robert B. Pegram, a fifty-year-old member of a prominent Petersburg family and one of Virginia's most celebrated sailors, arrived in the Cockade City on March 1 fresh from adventures on the high seas. As commander of the commerce raider CSS *Nashville*, Pegram had navigated the Atlantic, eluded the federal blockade, and steered his ship into a North Carolina port. Pegram requested that Petersburg churches return thanks for his safe return, a gesture the congregations readily offered. About one week later the legendary contest in Hampton Roads between the CSS *Virginia* (formerly the USS *Merrimack*) and the USS *Monitor* reminded Petersburgers that the *Virginia* promised the best deterrent to a Federal naval expedition up the James and on to Petersburg.[52]

Meanwhile, the provost guard elected new officers and mustered seventy fresh men into its ranks, the Second Class Militia received orders to drill Mondays and Fridays from 3:00 PM to 6:00 PM, and the names of suspected disloyal persons appeared on the community's informal bulletin board at Corling's Corner, Petersburg's most popular gathering spot at the northeast intersection of Lombard and Sycamore Streets. "The world is turned upside down and topsy turvey," lamented Charles Campbell. "Frequent speculations are made as to the probabilities of Petersburg's shortly falling into the enemy's hands." The city's churches began to offer their bells to be cast into cannon to defend the South—a powerful sign of persistent patriotism but also of the Confederate supply situation.

Anxiety and fear increased in late March as Petersburgers learned that their earlier fears of Union invasion had come true. Tens of thousands of Federal troops under McClellan began landing at Fort Monroe in preparation for an advance up the Peninsula. Citizens and the press also noted the arrival of the arrested mayor of Washington, North Carolina. This man stood accused of aiding the Union army in his city, a treasonous act that no doubt prompted many in Petersburg to scrutinize the loyalty of their neighbors.[53]

The French ambassador to the United States, Henri Mercier, also passed through Petersburg in April en route to Richmond, wishing to discuss Confederate relations with France as well as to look after French-owned tobacco that the blockade had bottled up in the capital. Petersburg units continued to recruit, the common council appropriated more funds to equip the militia recently sent to Norfolk, and efforts continued to gain exemptions from military service. But the looming strategic crisis dominated many people's thoughts only one year after Virginia had optimistically declared its independence from the federal Union. Charles Campbell's April 2 observation that few people were on the streets save for "here and there a group gravely talking over the signs of the times" might have applied at any time during the month.[54]

May brought warm springtime temperatures and a heightened sense of vulnerability. Apropos for residents of a port city, Petersburgers looked to the water as the source of their greatest peril. The common council dispatched a delegation to Richmond to see about measures to prevent the Federal navy from ascending the James and Appomattox Rivers. Andrew Crutchfield called on readers to contribute funds for the construction of a gunboat to protect the Cockade City. "Our immense storehouses and their contents would offer some inducements to the Yankees to pay us a visit to say nothing of the great advantages they would gain and the tremendous injuries they would inflict by getting possession of our railroads," argued Crutchfield with unwitting prescience. "We believe a sufficient sum could be raised here and in the South Side counties to build a formidable gunboat. . . . Who will make the first deposit?"[55]

General McClellan's investment of the Confederate defenses near Yorktown prompted General Joseph E. Johnston to withdraw his outgunned Confederate forces on the evening of May 3. Johnston's retreat isolated General Huger in Norfolk, including the Petersburg troops stationed there, and forced the evacuation of the Virginia port. Deprived of a home base, the commander of the *Virginia* scuttled his ship, and the virtually defenseless lower James River beckoned to the Union navy as far upstream as Drewry's Bluff, seven river miles below Richmond and well above City Point.

As sick and wounded soldiers from Yorktown and Norfolk reached Petersburg, Thomas Bragg, no longer serving in Davis's cabinet and now living in the city, sullenly weighed his options:

> I cannot well move my family for I know not where to go or what to do with them. Means would soon fail me, and may fail me here, for our currency and Banks would be worthless. They would stand a better chance here. But what to do with myself is another matter. It is hard to abandon my family, though they would be among friends—but if I remain, I shall probably be arrested. . . . I have little hope that we can keep them back. Every chance is against us. I am in great trouble. Ruin seems almost inevitable.[56]

Bragg's prominence distinguished him from the average citizen, but the entire community shared his distress as McClellan's army advanced up the Peninsula. "There is great panic in Richmond [and] the panic is scarcely less here," wrote Bragg. "Everyone is casting about to save something." Investors scrambled to pay cash for real estate, seeking to obtain tangible assets in exchange for currency that promised to depreciate drastically. The tobacco and cotton still stored in Petersburg created a unique dilemma. With rail transportation monopolized by the military crisis, neither commodity owners nor the government could readily move an appreciable amount of these goods into the interior. The military authorities prepared to burn what could not be displaced, while city leaders took hurried measures to protect Petersburg from a general conflagration. "We would state that several of the [tobacco] warehouses are contiguous to the most crowded parts of the city & if burnt would possibly if not probably cause a destruction of other portions of the city," warned several of the governor's appointed tobacco inspectors.[57]

By the second week of May soldiers and civilians fleeing Norfolk had utterly transformed Petersburg. "All is excitement and confusion here," recorded Thomas Bragg. "The town is crowded with soldiers." An article in the May 14 edition of the *Daily Express* described the dramatic changes that had engulfed the city, with a flourish of bravado typical of this patriotic journal:

> Petersburg no longer reminds one of a . . . provincial town. . . . The quiet of the last twelve months has been broken, and our streets and stores, which but a little time back were so still, are now crowded. . . . Hundreds of refugees from other quarters have taken up their residence among us. Our streets re-echo with the tread of armed soldiers. From early morning till dark . . . a continuous stream of human beings pour up and down the thoroughfares. . . . We are an important city in our location; but no matter how big and important we are, will the Yankees ever take us? No, sir.[58]

Unconvinced by such wishful thinking, Bragg decried the apparent lack of order and organization among the arriving soldiers and despaired of the future. "I fear all will soon be over—God help us!" wrote the North Carolinian. Agnes Beckwith, Margaret's mother, reported on May 13 that their family was sheltering four Confederate soldiers "and expect to have as many or more as long as there are many in town to be attended to—they are dying fast in the hospitals." This brave woman admitted that her family had considered evacuating Petersburg, "but we came to the conclusion that it is best to remain. . . . We are all . . . expecting the Yankees unless our troops can keep them back." A dejected Bragg agreed, citing the lack of a competent commander or practical plan and the presence of deserters and shirkers from the Norfolk garrison. "We have only to submit or die . . . the former will be as bad as the latter," he confessed.[59]

On May 15 the Virginia legislature appropriated two hundred thousand dollars for the defense of Richmond and Petersburg. Of course, such action carried mere symbolic significance as McClellan's army inched toward Richmond and the Union navy moved up the James River. The May 15 defeat of the Federal flotilla below Richmond at Drewry's Bluff and the decision of General Johnston to at last contest McClellan's advance accomplished infinitely more to safeguard Petersburg than the politicians in the capital. Johnston's attack on May 31 at Seven Pines and the fighting the next day presented the city with its first significant hometown casualties. The Twelfth Virginia Infantry was in the thick of the action, its beautiful flag made by the ladies of Petersburg riddled with bullet holes. A large committee of citizens immediately left for Richmond to tend to the city's combat victims.[60]

General Johnston was among those wounded at Seven Pines, his place filled the next day by General Robert E. Lee. Lee gathered troops from the Shenandoah Valley and North Carolina to assemble an army large enough to defeat McClellan, whose forces remained east of the capital. He launched an offensive on June 26 that resulted by July 2 in McClellan's withdrawal from the outskirts of Richmond to an armed camp along the left bank of the James downstream from City Point.

Some of this fighting could be heard in Petersburg, and nighttime artillery fire flashed in the northeastern sky. News of Lee's victories buoyed spirits, including the chronically pessimistic Thomas Bragg. In the midst of rumors that McClellan would cross the James, capture Petersburg, and threaten Richmond from the south, residents turned their attention in early July to nursing wounded Confederates who filled both private homes and the government's military hospitals. "Two rooms were given up entirely to soldiers and our time was fully occupied," remembered Margaret Beckwith.[61]

Although Petersburgers focused intensely on military matters during the spring and early summer of 1862, some familiar rhythms of municipal life continued. Petersburg and eight predominately Southside counties comprised the Fourth Virginia Congressional District. Roger A. Pryor had represented the district since the formation of the Confederate government in Richmond, splitting time between his legislative responsibilities and those as colonel of the Third Virginia Infantry. When McClellan's army advanced on Yorktown in early April, Pryor resigned his seat to devote full time to soldiering, and he quickly received promotion to brigadier general. Four men competed as Pryor's replacement, including the future Confederate secretary of war James A. Seddon and two Petersburg luminaries, Richard Kidder Meade Sr. and Charles F. Collier. The *Daily Express* found all four candidates worthy, but when the April 24 ballots were counted, Collier emerged victorious. The thirty-four-year-old Harvard-educated lawyer already served on the Petersburg Common Council and brought outstanding credentials to his new office.[62]

Collier also won reelection on May 5 to his East Ward seat on the common council. Despite the looming military threats, competition for municipal offices proved surprisingly keen, stimulated, perhaps, by the opportunity to gain exemption from the draft. Dr. Samuel H. Procise, mayoral candidate and headmaster of a local school, wooed voters with a pledge to contribute five hundred dollars toward the gunboat fund should he be elected. Procise challenged the incumbent W. W. Townes to a debate on the steps of the courthouse, informing readers of the *Daily Express* that if the mayor failed to appear, he would betray his "leanness of mind and contempt of the people." The tactic failed. The voters returned Townes to office along with most other incumbents. Among the failed challengers was Andrew Crutch-field. Myriad lesser offices attracted multiple candidates, including nine hopefuls for the petty post of clerk of the Old Market.[63]

Nor did the scramble for patronage abate much during this season of war. Appeals to the governor had declined during the summer of 1861, but Letcher's desk still filled with requests from Petersburg for jobs such as notary, inspector of tobacco at one of Petersburg's four warehouses, or bank director in one of the city's several financial institutions. Solicitations written for or by Petersburgers sought to obtain promotions or initial army commissions for favored men. Mayor Townes and many members of the common council lobbied Letcher on behalf of Robert R. Collier, seeking a military appointment for the distinguished lawyer. Anthony M. Keiley received help from Thomas Wallace in his enduring quest to escape the vengeful discrimination of his former political enemies in the Twelfth Virginia Infantry.[64]

The new year brought little change to Petersburg's business community. Manufacturing stocks, such as those in cotton factories and iron foundries, rose steadily in value thanks to lucrative government contracts. Railroads remained profitable by hauling Confederate freight. Banks did well, and new telegraph facilities opened on Bollingbrook Street in February, "the most handsomely finished office of the kind in the South."[65]

Enormous profits, both real and inflationary, continued to push up consumer prices, and wartime shortages only grew worse. "The stores were becoming depleted of pretty things," remembered Jennie Friend, daughter of the businessman and planter Charles Friend, "and prices were rising rapidly." The staunch Southern patriot Edmund Ruffin thought in the midst of the April pandemonium engendered by the Peninsula campaign that "the continuation of the Yankee blockade threatens more danger to our cause, by the consequent scarcity & high prices of necessaries of life, than do the Yankee arms & armies & fleets." With everything from salt to leather to city gas either exorbitantly high or unavailable at any price, Charles Campbell believed that the spring of 1862 would "try men's souls."[66]

Campbell's prediction contained more than a grain of truth. In late April one Petersburg resident complained that for two days nothing had been available in the city markets, government purchasing agents having gobbled up all the available beef. The *Daily Express* advised its readers to plant vegetable gardens, cheerfully extolled the virtue of produce over meat, and facetiously recommended that readers eat dried apples and then drink hot water so that the fruit would expand and fill their stomachs. Bacon, butter, lard, coffee, salt, sugar, and molasses—staples in most Petersburg diets—sold at prices unthinkable even a few months earlier. The morose Thomas Bragg linked the scarcities to speculation and was convinced that "we shall be near starvation very speedily."[67]

With the price of everything on the rise, including the cost of a marriage license (subject neither to shortage nor speculation, economically speaking), Charles Campbell worried about the impact on wage earners. "It requires 2 dollars in paper to buy 1 dollar in gold," he observed. "Those living on salaries are great sufferers as while they receive nominally the same salary as before the war yet it buys them only ½ as much." The appearance of counterfeit notes from a nonexistent Petersburg bank added another dimension to the fiscal chaos of the times.[68]

Although the "enormous prices of the necessaries of life" were "the subject of continual remark & general indignation," the temptation to cash in on Petersburg's woes sometimes overwhelmed even stalwart patriots. In early July, Sergeant George W. Wills of the Forty-third North Carolina Infantry was in Petersburg recuperating from an illness. Noticing the outrageous prices of various commodities, particularly food, Wills advised his sister that "if you want to make a fortune, just git [*sic*] a lot of chickens, vegetables & c. and come down here to Petersburg. . . . Chickens that we call 6 cent size are bringing $1. . . . Pa's garden would bring him an independent fortune were he to have it all here and sell it all."[69]

During the summer and fall, food and consumer items reappeared in Petersburg markets in greater quantity but were no lower in price. Goods arrived from beyond Union lines or through the blockade. "Mother, you all ought to see the market every day," wrote the North Carolina soldier James King Wilkerson in the fall. "We can buy any thing for money enough."[70]

Those lacking adequate means learned to live without. Edmund Ruffin recorded that he no longer indulged in coffee or butter due to their high cost. "I can live on as little & as humble food as any one accustomed to plenty & to luxury," wrote Ruffin. Angry citizens, such as Superior Court Judge Thomas S. Gholson, recommended that any food or other necessities hoarded or used for speculation should be subject to government seizure, another instinct at odds with Confederate orthodoxy. Responding at last to runaway inflation, the common council authorized salary increases for city officials to help municipal workers keep pace with the rising cost of living.[71]

No commodity attracted more attention in 1862 than salt, a vital component in the preservation of meat. Its absence or exorbitant price elicited numerous comments from desperate householders, particularly during the autumn. "There is literally no salt as far as I can discover," Thomas Wallace told the governor in October. Letcher's secretary responded the next day, appointing Wallace agent for salt in the city of Petersburg and charging him with the responsibility of preventing the preservative from leaving Petersburg for destinations outside Virginia. North Carolinians immediately raised a howl, claiming that they had contracted for salt deliveries via Petersburg prior to the governor's embargo. Petersburg Railroad president Joynes warned the governor that certain people were using his railroad to carry salt "to some point near the state line," then shipping it by wagon into North Carolina. A statewide government distribution scheme predicated on population satisfied a portion of Petersburg's salt requirements in November, but problems with transportation limited distribution. The governor's office worked directly with the railroads to expedite shipment as some of the salt destined for Petersburg from Saltville, Virginia, languished on sidings.[72]

The plight of Petersburg's needy, including soldiers' families, grew worse as prices rose. The Association for the Improvement of the Condition of the Poor obtained funding from the common council and private contributions in almost equal amounts to address this problem. In addition to paying the salary of its administrator, the association purchased and distributed shoes, firewood, and foodstuffs to Petersburg's poor, including military dependents, organizing their charity according to the city's electoral wards.[73]

The Petersburg Common Council appropriated thousands of dollars every month for the relief of soldiers' wives and children. The city's monthly contribution rose from fifteen hundred dollars in January to twenty-five hundred by September. In the summer city officials convened a special meeting to consider the offer of Petersburg's millers to sell flour to the city at cost for resale "to the more needy inhabitants." This measure passed ten votes to five, although the council reduced its purchase from one thousand to five hundred barrels.[74]

Charles Campbell described the plight of one Petersburg victim of inflation and shortage. This woman, whose spouse served in the army, had already lost two children during the war. She could get no work, had not heard from her husband in three months, and despaired of feeding herself and her one surviving child. Campbell appealed to the association on this poor soul's behalf, but the response of the charity, whose resources stretched ever thinner with each passing week, can only be imagined.[75]

The city continued to aid its fighting men throughout 1862. Captain Goodwyn's new cavalry company received thirty dollars from the common council for every recruit who volunteered. The councilmen created a committee to supply the needs of Petersburg units beyond what they received from the Confederacy. In addition to lobbying the secretary of war on the behalf of the troops, the common council purchased cloth and negotiated with local cotton mills to manufacture shirts and drawers at reduced prices. They purchased shoes, socks, and blankets and also accepted donations of clothing and cash. A Committee of Distribution arranged for free transportation of these articles, ensuring that each item found its way into the tents of only Petersburg residents.

The council did expand its charitable instincts in December, following the devastation suffered during the Union occupation of Fredericksburg. Councilman (and Congressman) Collier offered a resolution at the December 23 meeting to provide ten thousand dollars "for the relief of the suffering people of Fredericksburg." Although some councilmen balked at committing such a large sum, efforts to delay the appropriation pending citizen comment or to reduce the amount to five thousand dollars failed.[76]

Surprisingly, little evidence suggests that shortages or inflation increased crime in Petersburg. Although the newspapers occasionally carried stories about the conviction and punishment of men such as the slave Erasmus, who suffered thirty-nine lashes for stealing bacon from the South Side depot, lawbreakers were more likely to be detained for fighting, disorderly conduct, arson, or even speeding—transgressions unrelated to hunger or want. Blacks continued to provide a disproportionate number of cases. Stringent proscriptions against assembly and travel without proof of free status subjected African Americans to elevated police scrutiny. Whites who allowed substantial numbers of blacks to gather on their property received substantial community scorn.[77]

Some Petersburg African Americans prospered and actually purchased property during the war. The continued absence of so many white men meant that demand for black labor—free and slave—intensified. In late 1861 the South Side Railroad employed 378 workers, more than 80 percent of whom were black. African American workers found employment cutting wood under contract to the railroads, repairing wharves at City Point, and building carpenter shops. Wear and tear on rail beds required the installation of ballast under the ties, providing extensive work for blacks. Most domestic slaves remained at home, executing the orders of their masters and sharing proportionate reductions in material welfare. "Our servants were all faithful helpers doing double or treble work cheerfully," remembered Margaret Beckwith after the war (with probable Lost Cause exaggeration).[78]

Some families, such as the Friends, took their loyal servants and evacuated their homes during the height of the spring military crisis. Accompanied by three slaves, the Friends refugeed in Lunenburg County. Some slave owners living along the James, weary of their laborers running away to the Yankees, brought them to Petersburg either for safekeeping or to sell.[79]

With McClellan's departure during the summer, most of the families who had fled the city returned. The social scene, however, paled by comparison to previous years. Petersburg had become a city of old men, women, and children. The young ladies in town who would have otherwise competed for the attention of admiring beaux, contented themselves with female companionship. "We are all going to be old maids together," confessed one young woman. "Well! it will be no disgrace to be an old maid," replied her friend. "We can always swear our going-to-be-husband was killed in the war."[80]

Visiting Confederate soldiers sometimes substituted for missing Petersburg boys. "There is some nice looking girls here in old Virginia," wrote Private Thomas W. Gaither of the Fourth North Carolina Infantry in November 1862, "but the most of them can not get a meal . . . they do not suit a North Carolina boy. I would not give a good North Carolina Girl for a half dozen of them."[81]

Corporal Joseph J. Cowand of the Thirty-second North Carolina Infantry found the Petersburg women more to his liking. "I have got fifteen little lassies here," he wrote his cousin Winifred. "I have got six engaged to me now and expect to have six more before the war ends." Cowand shamelessly confessed that his irresistible appeal lay in the liberal telling of "sweet lies and they believe it all for they love a North Carolinian." Cowand's favorite fib was to reveal to the Petersburg girls the depth of his fictitious wealth by casually mentioning the loss of numerous runaway slaves, pretending to own so many blacks that the disappearance of a dozen or so mattered little. "Then they would lean to me like a sore eyed kitten to a basin of milk. I am as bad a boy as ever was and as coning as a fox."[82]

The war's second Christmas proved to be even less festive than its predecessor. Gaither managed to enjoy a good holiday meal, but during his visit to town on Christmas Day he "saw nothing but a general stir among children and women. One fine thing the people could not get enough liquor to get drunk." Corporal Cowand, the Tarheel lothario, saw the restrictions on drinking in a different light: "I have spent one more crismas and the dul[l]est I ever saw in my life. I only taken three drinks and pade $1.50 for them."[83]

The Cockade City had experienced unprecedented turmoil since the summer of 1861. The exhilaration of independence and the euphoria of victory at Manassas had given way to the fear of invasion and the agonies of privation. Still, as one observer noted in late 1862, "children go to school . . . families visit each other; churches and Sunday-schools go on; and the whole machinery of social life moves as though 'the war' was on the other side of the globe. Except [for] the passing troops and [the] hospitals . . . the Petersburg of to-day is very much the Petersburg of two years ago."[84] The presence of Confederate soldiers and numerous government facilities, however, ensured that any midwar comparison of Petersburg to antebellum days, no matter how cheerful, could not stand the most superficial scrutiny. Beginning in the summer of 1861, Petersburg had become a military city, a status it would retain for the duration of the conflict.

⌐ 4 ⌐

"We Are Entirely Defenseless Here"

THE CONFEDERATE MILITARY IN PETERSBURG
JULY 1861–DECEMBER 1862

IT HAS LONG BEEN my opinion that the true base for the Yankees to attack Richmond [is] . . . by way of Petersburg," asserted Confederate Major General Daniel Harvey Hill in November 1862. Few military men early in the war shared the perspective of this former and future commander of Petersburg. The War Department in Richmond considered the Cockade City little more than a transit point for troops and supplies, albeit an important one, between North Carolina and the Confederate capital. Union strategists ignored Petersburg's proximity to Richmond in their quest to conquer the Confederate capital. Throughout 1861 and 1862 Petersburg's military significance gradually grew more apparent, although the town would remain a strategic afterthought during the first twenty months of the Civil War.[1]

The battle of First Manassas on July 21, 1861, settled little beyond demonstrating that more than one large engagement would be required to win the war. Both armies in northern Virginia concentrated on recruitment and drill, avoiding large-scale campaigning for the remainder of the year. As trains funneled new units from the South to the front lines, Petersburg continued to greet an intermittent stream of eager soldiers.

Troops from North Carolina, Georgia, Alabama, and elsewhere passed through town all summer. Some soldiers spent a night or two in the Cockade City, bivouacking on the bricks around the New Market or at the fairgrounds in the city's West End. Those making only a brief stop enjoyed the facilities at the soldiers' pavilion at Poplar Lawn.

Petersburg's citizens warmly welcomed units such as the Fourth North Carolina Infantry in late July 1861, "the ladies waving their handkerchiefs & gentlemen their hats" and the volunteers responding with cheers. The city prepared formal meals for some regiments. Cavalry units enlivened the city as they rode through the streets. The frequency of such arrivals diminished in the autumn as accretions to General Joseph E. Johnston's army at

Manassas slowed. Nevertheless, the appearance of a particularly large or distinctive regiment, such as Colonel Robert Ransom's First North Carolina Cavalry on October 17, continued to elicit notice. In the fall, Confederate units began to move south as well. In what would become the norm until the spring of 1864, military events in North Carolina and southeastern Virginia determined Petersburg's strategic role, rather than the fortunes of the larger and more famous armies to the north.[2]

The North Carolina coast features a series of sounds separated from the Atlantic Ocean by barrier islands. Union control of these waters would threaten Hampton Roads via a network of commercial canals. Federal dominance in eastern North Carolina would also provide a base from which Northern troops could menace the Wilmington & Weldon Railroad, a vital link in the transportation system connecting Richmond and Petersburg with the southern Atlantic seaboard. In late August 1861 a combined Union naval and army expedition overwhelmed the Confederate fortifications guarding Hatteras Island and Albemarle Sound beyond. Major General Benjamin F. Butler, a cockeyed Massachusetts politician turned general, strode ashore to take possession of Fort Hatteras, causing a strategic splash that rippled as far as the Cockade City.[3]

Robert R. Collier, the Petersburg attorney, fancied himself a military thinker and readily shared his insights with Governor John Letcher. Collier composed a long letter on August 31, arguing against the rumored activation of the state militia by denying that Butler's triumph threatened Virginia's immediate security. "The enemy can't go to Norfolk except through the canals from Hatteras through the sounds and his passage . . . might . . . easily be prevented," advised Collier. "Nothing so unsettles our society as calling out the militia." Letcher decided against mobilizing Virginia troops, but events in the Tarheel State did prompt the shuffling of several Confederate commands and caused more activity in Petersburg.[4]

In late September the Confederate War Department assigned Harvey Hill responsibility for the defense of northeastern North Carolina. Hill understood that Roanoke Island, a small slash of sand, pines, and thick scrub oak between Pamlico and Albemarle Sounds, held the key to Confederate fortunes in this theater. He immediately sought to reinforce the small garrison charged with the island's protection. Hill departed for an assignment in Virginia three weeks later, and the former Virginia governor Henry A. Wise, now a Confederate brigadier general, took over. The War Department placed Wise under Major General Benjamin Huger, commander in Norfolk, thus formally recognizing the strategic relationship between North Carolina and southeastern Virginia, including Petersburg.[5]

Huger, an aging, unimaginative officer described by one colleague as "a barnacle on the Confederacy," shared Collier's skeptical view of the threat that the Federals posed in the North Carolina sounds. He therefore all but ignored Wise's repeated calls for reinforcements. In December, however, elements of the Virginian's old command, the Wise Legion, began to pass through Petersburg from western Virginia to strengthen the tiny garrison on Roanoke Island, and the trickle continued into January.[6]

Not all of the troops coming out of western Virginia made it to Roanoke Island. On November 11, Special Orders 216 assigned the Twenty-fourth North Carolina Infantry under Colonel William J. Clarke to garrison duty in Petersburg, the first Confederate regiment deployed in the Cockade City. The lead elements appeared on November 26, resting at Poplar Lawn before moving to their permanent bivouac at the Model Farm. Although Clarke's troops endured the winter in tents and cooked their meals over open fires, "the boys had fun and a good time generally." On New Year's Day 1862 Petersburgers organized an elaborate dinner for their Tarheel defenders. The North Carolinians behaved themselves "in a most becoming and gentle-manly manner and give no cause of trouble or complaint." The comfortable relationship between soldier and townsfolk continued until events at Roanoke Island dramatically changed the situation in both Petersburg and Albemarle Sound.[7]

Major General Ambrose Burnside led an amphibious assault against Wise's forces on Roanoke Island on February 8, 1862, routing the Confeder-ates. Twenty-five hundred Southerners became prisoners and more than one hundred fell killed or wounded, including Wise's son. The Twenty-fourth North Carolina broke camp within seventy-two hours of the defeat, marching to the Petersburg Railroad depot bound for their native state. Charles Campbell noticed that some of the soldiers were carrying bottles and cursing loudly, while others gave the citizens a rousing cheer. Several days later, additional troops and quantities of ammunition headed south to deal with the crisis.[8]

By then the hospitals in Petersburg had improved significantly under the Confederate government's direction. The city's makeshift facilities at the fairgrounds underwent extensive expansion in September 1861: a combi-nation of new and converted buildings provided five wards, each accom-modating thirty to forty patients. Thirty-one-year-old John Blackwood Strachan, a Petersburg native trained in medicine at the Universities of Virginia and Pennsylvania, administered what became the Confederate General or Fair Grounds Hospital. Dr. Hugh Stockdell, another young Pe-tersburg physician, served as Strachan's assistant.[9]

Each ward had cots arranged in a circle around a central stove. The hos-pital featured separate kitchen and dining buildings along with storerooms, a medicine room, and a dead house. "Altogether, this will be one of the most complete, comfortable and convenient hospitals in the South," thought the

Benjamin Huger (1805–77).
General Huger abandoned
Norfolk in May 1862 and
moved his headquarters to
Petersburg, where he com-
manded the short-lived
Department of the Appo-
mattox, the first of many
Confederate military jurisdictions centered in Petersburg. (Courtesy of Library
of Congress)

Petersburg Daily Express. In late October the Fair Grounds Hospital had expanded to a capacity of three hundred beds. Charles Campbell delivered
bundles of magazines and newspapers that citizens contributed for the patients' use, hoping that wholesome reading would deter convalescents from
resorting to the city's grog shops. Patients approved of the facilities and the
treatment rendered by Strachan and his staff. "This is the nisest place for
sick that I every have come across since I have been in service," testified Private Thomas W. Gaither of the Fourth North Carolina Infantry, "but a horse
pittle is not for me."[10]

In late September 1861 the state of North Carolina began converting
the Cameron Tobacco Factory at the corner of Perry and Brown Streets into
a hospital for Tarheel troops; it started accepting patients in October.
Mrs. Kate De Rosset Kennedy of the Old North State volunteered there as
a nurse—the first woman to do so. This intrepid lady worked as many as
twelve hours a day to tend the sick, many suffering from typhoid fever. "They
have been the most quiet orderly men I ever saw for such a number of rough

soldiers," she reported. "I could not help telling them how it gratified me that no bad word from any of them had reached my ears & no unruly temper been exhibited." At a time when women were discouraged from exposure to coarse environments or keeping company with unknown men, Mrs. Kennedy flourished. "I find really more pleasure than toil in the duties to be performed," she wrote. "The consciousness of being in the way of duty & the gratification that flows from being useful to others, contribute not a little to my real enjoyment."[11]

More hospitals opened in Petersburg during the war's first winter. The Robert Leslie Tobacco Factory on West Washington Street became the Virginia Hospital. A few blocks east the Osborne and Chieves Factory at Washington and Jefferson Streets housed the South Carolina Hospital. New buildings appeared at Poplar Lawn to treat the sick. The Confederate States Hospital, a four-hundred-bed facility in the Dunn and Beasley Tobacco Factory at West Washington and Jones Streets, opened in early 1862 under the direction of Dr. John H. Claiborne, recently the surgeon of the Twelfth Virginia Infantry. Under the leadership of Miss Nora F. Davidson, the Ladies' Hospital at Second and Bollingbrook Streets operated by private subscription, supplemented by contributions from the Confederate government.[12]

All of these institutions periodically lacked supplies. Appeals appeared in local newspapers seeking cloth, straw for ticks, linen, or food for the hospitals. The Confederate government appointed the Reverend J. B. Hardwick, pastor of the Byrne Street Baptist Church, as minister to the Petersburg hospitals. The Petersburg Evangelical Tract Society collected religious reading material for the patients. The converted buildings suited their new missions, most having gas lighting, central heating, and plenty of windows for illumination and fresh air.[13]

The Confederate government established more than medical facilities in Petersburg. In October 1861 the Navy Department purchased land near the Appomattox River upstream from the city to accommodate a powder mill. Two months later the *Daily Express* reported that a large workforce had made significant progress erecting structures and installing machinery, most of which had been produced locally. "Small lots of powder have been manufactured by hand, merely for experiment, and found to answer every purpose," claimed the newspaper. The mill opened in late February under the direction of an experienced manager trained in Delaware's DuPont mills. The powder works employed seventeen whites and fifteen blacks, supervised by Chief Engineer Thomas A. Jackson; it operated until the summer of 1862, when production shifted to Columbia, South Carolina.[14]

Rumors of plans to locate a shot tower in Petersburg circulated as early as January 1862. These plans took shape during the summer thanks to Lieutenant Colonel Josiah Gorgas, miracle-working Confederate chief of ordnance. In a few short months Gorgas constructed a lead works in the southwest corner of the city on Halifax Road, near the Petersburg Railroad. The plant used lead mined in North Carolina and southwestern Virginia to produce pellets and bars that were sent to Richmond and elsewhere to be cast into bullets. By the winter of 1862 the Petersburg Lead Works could smelt one thousand pounds of raw material daily.[15]

Gorgas also established niter beds in Petersburg during the summer of 1862 to facilitate the production of gunpowder. By year's end more than two dozen slaves labored in the fetid niter beds, tending a noxious blend of decaying vegetable matter, dead animals, stagnant water, and urine to produce potassium nitrate. Gorgas's Petersburg Copper and Zinc Works helped manufacture percussion caps for rifles. During the war's second winter the navy created a ropewalk in Petersburg to furnish cordage for gunboats, railroads, and quartermasters—a plant that would remain operational almost through the end of the war.[16]

Expanding prominence and the establishment of martial law earned Petersburg its first official inclusion in a Confederate military department. On March 26, 1862, Special Orders 69 placed "the city of Petersburg and the adjoining and surrounding country to the distance of 10 miles" within the Department of Henrico commanded by Brigadier General John H. Winder, whose headquarters were in Richmond. Nothing much of military significance occurred in Winder's Petersburg jurisdiction until early May, when events on the Peninsula and in Hampton Roads sent Petersburgers into a panic.[17]

General Johnston had never been sanguine about containing Major General George B. "Little Mac" McClellan's huge Federal army on the lower Peninsula, although the Union commander had dithered away weeks preparing to bombard Johnston's defenses near Yorktown. Johnston understood that once McClellan's siege guns opened his lines were bound to crumble. By May 2 the Confederate commander had issued orders to evacuate the doomed entrenchments and retreat toward Richmond. He also directed General Huger to abandon Norfolk and fall back along the south side of the James River. Johnston left the Yorktown lines on the night of May 3–4. One week later Huger slipped out of Norfolk a few steps ahead of the Yankees. Deprived of their home port and unable to cross the shallow bar into the James, the crew of the *Virginia*, guardian of Hampton Roads, exploded their vessel on May 11. In a dizzying week of reversals Confederate strategists now faced threats to Richmond from both McClellan's army on the Peninsula and the Union navy along the James.[18]

William Pannill, aged auctioneer turned provost marshal, served as the ranking officer in Petersburg during this crisis. "We are entirely defenseless here," cried the overmatched Pannill in a May 5 dispatch to Adjutant General Samuel Cooper. Betraying his focus on property rather than positions (Pannill was part owner of Moore's Tobacco Warehouse and a commission merchant), the provost marshal frantically inquired about the disposition of vast quantities of tobacco, flour, and cotton that filled Petersburg warehouses.

Secretary of War George W. Randolph instructed Pannill to prepare the commodities for destruction "in case it is necessary to prevent [them] from falling into the hands of the enemy." Randolph admonished Pannill to use care in preventing fire from consuming the city and authorized him to dump the tobacco into the river. As an afterthought, Randolph attempted to reassure the panicky provost marshal: "I should be sorry for the people of Petersburg to think . . . that the Government has no intention of defending the town or that its capture is considered probable. On the contrary, we confidently expect to repel the invasion from the interior of the State, and are preparing for it by withdrawing troops from exposed points." Randolph also dispatched an engineer officer, Captain Charles H. Dimmock, to obstruct the Appomattox River below Petersburg, counting on Pannill to provide Dimmock with materials and conscripted slave labor.[19]

General Robert E. Lee served in Richmond at this time as military advisor to President Jefferson Davis and the de facto mastermind of Confederate strategy in Virginia. Lee explained to Huger and Major General Theophilus H. Holmes in North Carolina the War Department's intention to protect the Petersburg Railroad all the way to Weldon. Lee ordered Huger and Holmes to place troops at convenient points east of the railroad where they could meet specific Union threats. Randolph suggested that Captain James Read Branch deploy his Petersburg artillery battery (formerly Lee's Life Guard) along the Appomattox River to contest the approach of gunboats, while he ordered the government agent William Turnbull to work with authorities in Petersburg to fill private schooners with rocks and sink the hulks in the channel.[20]

None of these measures impressed the outspoken Robert Collier. "Am sure you will excuse my suggesting that Petersburg ought to be defended," Collier scolded Secretary Randolph on May 11. "Let a stand be made here, where an army can be collected whose resistance would spread over the world and go down to latest times." Collier made a case for the importance of Petersburg's cotton and flour mills, her transportation network, and the "large numbers of negroes in all the surrounding country. If it is not to be defended strenuously ought not the people know it?" The chronically pessimistic Thomas Bragg predicted on May 8 from his Petersburg residence that within one week McClellan would be in Richmond, adding that when that should happen, "all is lost."[21]

McClellan's offensive forced Confederate strategists to react. On May 13 Secretary Randolph and General Lee renamed Huger's former Norfolk-based military jurisdiction the Department of the Appomattox, with head-quarters in Petersburg, superseding the city's relationship with General Winder. Two days later Huger issued General Orders 31, instructing all commanders to keep their troops in camps on the outskirts of Petersburg and prevent them from straggling into town — a tempting destination, espe-cially for the men in local companies.[22]

By then the city's perimeter had filled with troops pouring in from Nor-folk. Elements of the Twelfth Virginia Infantry were among the first to ap-pear, arriving by train from Suffolk on the evening of May 8. The soldiers slept that night in vacant buildings or in tents and then established a bivouac on Dunn's Hill, across the Appomattox from Petersburg. This high and healthful ground soon swelled with thousands of Huger's men, who turned the plateau into a forest of canvas by May 16. "I like this camp better than any place I have been yet," wrote Private Robert C. Mabry of the Sixth Virginia Infantry. "The water is . . . good . . . and I think the most we have to fear [is] from sickness [from] the large number of troops . . . stationed here [who] will make the camp filthy unless they are forced to keep it clean." Confeder-ate units also occupied bivouacs at Poplar Lawn and the Model Farm.[23]

Some of the infantry regiments, including the Twelfth Virginia and the Third Alabama, eventually moved north to Drewry's Bluff, the strongpoint on the right bank of the James below Richmond. Here on May 15 a make-shift force of sailors and artillerists turned back a Union flotilla, including the *Monitor,* temporarily ending the waterborne threat to the Confederate capital. McClellan had squandered a chance for victory by failing to assist this naval expedition. Instead, the Union commander inched his way to the eastern outskirts of Richmond, where he fortified his lines straddling the Chickahominy River and pleaded with Washington for more troops. Huger's arrival and the defeat of the Union navy at Drewry's Bluff quelled immedi-ate anxiety in Petersburg, although McClellan's presence menaced nearby Richmond.[24]

Huger relocated his headquarters and most of his division closer to Rich-mond on May 26, ceding informal administrative control of Petersburg to General Holmes, who was still in North Carolina. Brigadier General Lewis A. Armistead's Brigade of Huger's command remained behind to garrison the city and territory to the east. Holmes would not arrive until May 30, but on the twenty-seventh the vanguard of his force, Brigadier General John G. Walker's Brigade, appeared in Petersburg. Additional soldiers followed Walker as General Lee scrambled to concentrate as many forces as possible near Richmond. The Thirtieth Virginia Infantry of Walker's Brigade ini-tially deployed at City Point to discourage a Union landing south of the James. Walker's men then shifted north to Drewry's Bluff.[25]

Captain James Fisher Milligan commanded one of the more unusual Confederate units to serve in Petersburg that spring. Milligan had worked in the United States Revenue Service prior to the war, resigning to accept a commission in the Confederate navy. The thirty-three-year-old Missourian, described by one acquaintance as "profane to an alarming extent," took command of the signal corps in the Department of Norfolk in April 1862. After Huger's evacuation Milligan relocated his headquarters to Petersburg. The signal officer dispersed 127 observers to a series of posts on the James River from Drewry's Bluff down to Gregory's farm and along the Appomattox from a building at the southwest corner of Sycamore and Tabb Streets in Petersburg to City Point. Dubbed the Independent Signal Corps and Scouts, Milligan's specialists perfected an efficient system of communication that could transmit messages from City Point to Petersburg in twenty minutes.

Milligan's expertise came in handy on May 27 when he notified his superiors that two Union steamers, the *Coeur de Lion* and the *Stepping Stones,* had ventured up the Appomattox River from City Point. Commander William Smith of the Union navy hoped to cut communications between Petersburg and the capital by destroying the new railroad bridge over the Appomattox. Smith ultimately concluded that the recently constructed fortifications guarding the river and the obstructions blocking the channel probably precluded an operation up the Appomattox, and Armistead's fire from the shore validated his caution. The Federal probe did lead Armistead and Captain Robert B. Pegram of the Confederate navy to suggest improvements to the river's defenses—including moving the obstructions downstream from the mouth of Swift Creek, to deter Union naval traffic on this important tributary.[26]

All eyes soon turned east of Richmond when General Johnston launched a complicated and poorly executed attack against the portion of McClellan's army south of the Chickahominy. The battle of Seven Pines on May 31 and June 1 (heard in Petersburg) brought intense personal sorrow to the Cockade City. Two local boys, Private Julian Beckwith and Sergeant Theophilus Meade of the Twelfth Virginia Infantry, fell dead in the battle, and Private Lemuel Peebles Jr. of the same regiment sustained a mortal wound—on his twenty-third birthday.[27]

Private John Walters of the Norfolk Light Artillery Blues—his unit encamped near the city—stayed in Petersburg during the battle, sifting through the rumors that swiftly circulated about town. He learned of the death of the commander of the Third Alabama Infantry, Colonel Tennent Lomax, who had made an impression among local citizens when his unit passed through Petersburg. The ladies of town had entertained the Alabamians, and in thanking them for their hospitality the gallant colonel promised his hosts that "if ever the enemy desecrated this beautiful city, it could only be done after his arm should have lost the power to wield a sword in its defense." Walters noted that although "his stalwart arm has lost that power, his manly voice is hushed in death . . . the remembrance of his worth will nerve his men to deeds of daring."[28]

The fighting around Seven Pines concluded with little change to the strategic situation, but it elevated Robert E. Lee to command of the army. Lee consolidated as many troops around Richmond as possible as he prepared to launch an offensive of his own. During the first three weeks of June, Confederate units continued to stream from North Carolina through Petersburg as a part of Lee's plan. Robert Ransom, now a brigadier general serving under Holmes, became the ranking local officer while Holmes returned to the Tarheel State to manage the transfer of the rest of his forces.

Elements of Ransom's Brigade launched raids against Federal forces near the Blackwater River, forty miles southeast of Petersburg. Other Confederates took position along the lower Appomattox. The Forty-eighth and Forty-ninth North Carolina Infantry regiments of Ransom's Brigade ventured downstream to the Eppes plantation, Appomattox, in mid-June to retrieve supplies of ice for the North Carolina Hospital. They returned the next day accompanied by Brem's (North Carolina) Battery, which lobbed a few shells at the Union navy anchored near the mouth of the river, occasionally striking their targets until superior Federal firepower drove them off.[29]

Ransom organized several grand reviews while the North Carolinians camped around Petersburg. "The ladies were out in full trim and fascination," wrote a Tarheel colonel, "and were numerous, well pleased and beautiful." Corporal Joseph J. Cowand had already discovered that Petersburg's women made pleasant companions: "I have been enjoying myself with the ladies for the last t[w]o weeks as good as I ever did in my life. I tuck a nice walk with a young lady . . . to church and also friday night to the theater and you may [k]no[w] I felt happy. I have got the purties Sweethart you ever saw in your life. You tell the ladies if they dont wright me I will bring me a wife from forginnia."[30]

A soldier in Ransom's Brigade confirmed that duty in Petersburg had its pleasant moments: "We hav had a prety time since we left home . . . the laides comes out from town every day to se us some times about too hundred of them . . . That makes a prety site here but they dont favor you as much with eating stuff [.] they don't look like the old NC ladies atoll[.]" The North Carolinians, who often had to obtain their own "eating stuff," experienced the same shocking inflation Petersburgers had endured for nearly one year. "I never saw things so high in all my life," complained one Tarheel volunteer.[31]

In addition to the Confederate troops moving north, and for the first time since the previous summer, Petersburgers saw Union prisoners of war traveling south. Major General Thomas J. "Stonewall" Jackson completed his brilliant Shenandoah Valley operations on June 9, and a few days later his captives passed through Petersburg en route to Salisbury, North Carolina. Henry D. Bird, president of the South Side Railroad, reported to Secretary Randolph that in addition to Union prisoners, his cars transported sick Confederates to hospitals in Petersburg and shuttled reinforcements northward to Lee. He pleaded with Randolph to issue all of the War Department's transportation orders through him, to avoid collisions and reduce confusion.[32]

Meanwhile, General Lee continued to plan his offensive. Lee wired Holmes at Goldsboro, North Carolina, on June 18 erroneously reporting that Union General Burnside's forces were advancing toward Drewry's Bluff from south of the James River. Lee instructed Holmes to oppose any such movement by concentrating all his available troops at Petersburg. Three days later Lee officially made Petersburg the headquarters of Holmes's Department of North Carolina. The fifty-seven-year-old Holmes, whose expanded authority now far exceeded his modest ability, bore responsibility for protecting the rail connection from Wilmington to Richmond, defending the south side of the James River, including Drewry's Bluff, and reinforcing Lee's Army of Northern Virginia east of Richmond.[33]

On June 23 Lee established the timetable for his attacks and ordered Holmes to forward Ransom's Brigade from Petersburg to Richmond. Twenty-five hundred of Ransom's men broke camp on Dunn's Hill to prepare for their advance. The Forty-eighth North Carolina Infantry boarded trains the next day and arrived on the grounds of the state capitol about dark. While combat units moved north, large numbers of patients from Richmond's hospitals arrived in Petersburg. "The clearing of the Hospitals and going forward of troops indicate an early battle at Richmond," surmised one observer. Indeed, in less than forty-eight hours, the war's greatest engagement to date, the Seven Days' battles, would commence, with the fate of Richmond and Petersburg hanging in the balance.[34]

While costly Confederate attacks on June 26 and 27 pushed McClellan's forces across the Chickahominy River, the Federal navy moved against Petersburg. President Abraham Lincoln remained distressed by the ease with which Lee had been able to draw troops by rail from North Carolina through Petersburg to Richmond. On June 19 he sent his trusted assistant secretary of the navy, Gustavus Vasa Fox, to City Point (under nominal Union control since May 13) to meet with the ranking naval officers and prepare to destroy the railroad bridges over the Appomattox River and Swift Creek. Commanders John Gillis and John Rodgers reminded Fox that the reconnaissance in May had confirmed the narrowness of the river channel and the strength of Confederate firepower along the banks. Fox replied that Lincoln considered the mission sufficiently important to authorize a reward of up to fifty thousand dollars for any civilian who might destroy the bridges, if the navy could not do so. When Gillis departed for Norfolk, Rodgers inherited responsibility for executing the president's order.

Rodgers considered employing the navy's first submarine, the *Alligator,* to ascend the Appomattox and take out the bridges. This novel vessel arrived at City Point on June 25, but Rodgers quickly (and sarcastically) rejected her for offensive operations: "In going up the Appomattox to Petersburgh the Machine will show above water, since on the bars there is not depth to submerge her. Regiments and field artillery will fire at her. Should she escape these, as the rebels are badly off for food, and fish with nets very diligently, which nets extend entirely across the drain called a channel, some poor negro fisherman will drag her to shore. She is . . . utterly powerless to help our cause."

Rodgers relied on more conventional ships to achieve his mission. On the evening of June 26 he boarded the *Port Royal,* which led a flotilla of nine other vessels, including the *Monitor,* up the Appomattox River. The warships exchanged fire with Confederate artillery and infantry on the riverbanks beginning about 9:30 PM. Thirty minutes later the *Port Royal* grounded as the tide ebbed. The lighter draft craft proceeded until the lead boat, a converted tug named the *Island Belle,* caught fast on Gilliam's Bar, one-fourth of the way to Petersburg. The Surry (Virginia) Light Artillery and Branch's Petersburg gunners pounded the helpless steamer from the shore, firing that was clearly audible in an excited Petersburg.

The next day Yankee sailors attempted to refloat both the *Port Royal* and the *Island Belle* while landing parties torched buildings at City Point. The *Port Royal* lifted free, but the *Island Belle* remained mired on the river bottom. By then Lee's attacks had prompted McClellan to relocate his supply base from the Pamunkey River to Harrison's Landing on the north bank of the James. As McClellan needed the navy to secure his new camp downstream from City Point, Rodgers abandoned the fruitless expedition up the Appomattox, leaving the railroad bridges intact. Rodgers ordered the *Island Belle* stripped and burned on June 28.[35]

The navy secured McClellan's refuge on the James before the Union army's withdrawal from Malvern Hill on the evening of July 1. This retreat marked the end of Lee's audacious offensive, which had relieved Richmond from the immediate threat of capture at an enormous cost. Petersburg's hospitals admitted more than 2,500 of Lee's 16,261 wounded. In addition to the Fair Grounds, North Carolina, Virginia, South Carolina, and Confederate States Hospitals, the Poplar Lawn facility—now called the Pavilion Hospital—expanded to accommodate the influx, as did the Ladies' Hospital on Bollingbrook Street. Dr. Peter Hines of the North Carolina Hospital became the post surgeon at Petersburg and assumed general authority over the city's medical establishment. Private homes, such as the Beckwiths' on Market Street, accepted the overflow.

Women and slaves rolled up their sleeves to help the doctors provide around-the-clock care for the suffering multitude. Typhoid fever and pneumonia competed with battle wounds for the physicians' attention. Ambulatory casualties wandered about the streets, seeking aid and shelter from distraught citizens.

Petersburg's soldiers bore their share of the casualties. Among the many, Captain Virginius L. Weddell, son of a leading dry goods merchant, died of wounds sustained at Malvern Hill. Lieutenant Colonel Joseph V. Scott of the Third Virginia Infantry fell in action on June 30 at Frayser's farm (Glendale) in one of the horrific charges against artillery common in the engagement. Major Richard Kidder Meade Jr., son of the prominent diplomat and Petersburg statesman (the same young soldier who began the war as a United States Army officer in Fort Sumter), died at home of disease contracted during Lee's offensive. "He was one of the best & most intimate friends I ever had," wrote Lieutenant Colonel Edward Porter Alexander, destined for fame as a Confederate artillerist, "being my very first roommate . . . at West Point." Anthony M. Keiley, the young attorney who had persistently sought promotion from Governor Letcher, received a debilitating wound at Malvern Hill, ending his active military career.[36]

Lee's victory during the Seven Days did not end the Peninsula campaign. McClellan rested at Harrison's Landing, protected by gunboats and the security of his numerically superior force. General Lee worried that Little Mac might renew his offensive by moving his divisions across the James and against Richmond from the south by way of Petersburg. Rumors to that effect circulated throughout town.[37]

To meet this potential threat, Lee sent Holmes back to Petersburg with the brigades of Walker, Ransom, and Colonel Junius Daniel, reinforced by three regiments of Brigadier General James Martin's Brigade from North Carolina. Some of these troops strengthened the fortifications downstream from Petersburg or patrolled the south shore of the James. Others bivouacked in their old camps on Dunn's Hill, while General Holmes established his headquarters at the Petersburg Customs House on his arrival on July 7. Artillery units unlimbered at Drewry's Bluff and between this strongpoint and Petersburg. When Martin's troops began to appear on July 10, Ransom's Brigade shifted a few miles east of Petersburg to a spot they called Camp Lee. Holmes eventually accumulated nearly fifteen thousand troops between Petersburg and Drewry's Bluff. When McClellan betrayed no discernible intention of crossing the James, soldiers and civilians in Petersburg breathed a collective sigh of relief.[38]

Idle troops now roamed the streets much as they had during the early spring. Except for an occasional incident fueled by too much liquor, the men generally behaved themselves. The Fifty-third North Carolina Infantry encamped once again on Dunn's Hill with pleasures other than alcohol on their minds. "We return to our factory girls again," said one member of the regiment. "All O.K., you bet." Another soldier praised the hospitality of the local women "for they have shown their appreciation by giving us several very substantial dinners."[39]

Holmes, too, could be seen about town. Charles Campbell considered him "a stout good-looking old man . . . white haired . . . said to be very deaf." Shortcomings coincident to the general's physical maladies had been mitigated by his friendship with Jefferson Davis, a relationship that dated from their days together at West Point, where Holmes graduated two rungs from the bottom of his class. The North Carolinian, like so many of Lee's generals during the Seven Days, failed to distinguish himself. He nevertheless retained the confidence of the president, who in mid-July promoted him to command of the Trans-Mississippi Department. Special Orders 165 dated July 17, 1862, named Major General Daniel Harvey Hill as Holmes's replacement in the Department of North Carolina, a move that promised (but would not necessarily deliver) a more efficient and aggressive defense of Petersburg.[40]

Hill was a native South Carolinian but more closely associated with his adopted North Carolina, where he had been superintendent of the state's military academy at the outbreak of the war. He graduated in the middle of a West Point class that would produce fifteen Civil War generals, and he served with distinction during the Mexican War. The forty-one-year-old Hill, a former professor and among the most erudite of all Civil War generals, earned accolades from the press and the public during the war's initial battles, and along with them the respect of his soldiers. He could, however, be abrasive and blunt to a fault when addressing fellow officers and government authorities. He brought both his prickly personality and military professionalism with him to Petersburg in July 1862, when, "with unfeigned pain and reluctance," he left his division in Lee's army and reported for duty.[41]

Hill was appalled to discover the city's apparent vulnerability. "Not a spadeful of earth had been thrown up about Petersburg, and it was in a wholly defenseless condition," he reported. Indeed, relatively little thought or effort had been invested in protecting Petersburg during the first year of the war.

In March 1862 the Petersburg Common Council had appointed a committee "to inquire as to the propriety of putting the city in a state of defence & report what, if anything, is necessary for that purpose." Little resulted from this initiative. The Confederate government told Councilman D'Arcy Paul two months later that the city and the Lower Appomattox Company were empowered to "obstruct the Appomattox River at such points as they may deem best," but that no significant assistance would be provided from Richmond. More than two hundred and fifty slaves from Mecklenburg,

Daniel Harvey Hill (1821–89). Hill became a familiar figure in wartime Petersburg. He commanded the Department of North Carolina, with headquarters in Petersburg, in July and August 1862 and again from January to July 1863. Hill returned to Petersburg in the spring of 1864, but as a result of his feud with President Jefferson Davis, he held no specific command and served as a volunteer aide. (Courtesy of Valentine Richmond History Center)

Brunswick, and Nottoway Counties toiling under the guidance of Captain Dimmock had placed the navigational impediments and fortified positions on the banks that had helped repulse the Union navy in May and June. Hill had good reason to worry, however, considering that substantial enemy naval and military forces remained just a few miles away.[42]

Almost immediately on assuming command, Hill detailed troops to build fortifications. Men of the Forty-eighth North Carolina Infantry reported to the Charles Friend farm east of the city on July 26 and started a line of entrenchments. On the twenty-eighth the Carolinians were joined by the Thirtieth Virginia Infantry, Second Georgia Battalion, and the Second, Twenty-seventh, and Forty-sixth North Carolina infantry regiments. Hill also impressed local slaves, "causing quite a stampede among the blacks and some dissatisfaction among the masters." Hill's initiative prompted General Lee to dispatch Lieutenant Colonel Walter H. Stevens to Petersburg on August 4. This distinguished engineer, who helped design the Richmond fortifications, would assist Hill to establish a similar line around the Cockade City. Colonel Jeremy F. Gilmer, chief engineer of Lee's army, also contributed his skills.[43]

Stevens and Gilmer gave Dimmock responsibility for completing the works they eventually planned. Dimmock used a combination of soldiers and slaves, many from North Carolina, for the backbreaking labor required to erect an elaborate system of fifty-five artillery batteries and connecting infantry berms that would eventually ring Petersburg for ten miles on the east, south, and west. Hill assigned the brigades of Walker, Ransom, and Daniel to work in rotation under the steaming August sun. The soldiers generally plied their shovels in the mornings and late afternoons, avoiding the hottest part of the day. One North Carolina officer recorded on August 14 that in a day and a half his regiment of five hundred men built 619 feet of rifle pits. A complement of 264 slaves from as far away as the Eastern Shore and about 1,000 more from North Carolina augmented the labor force. Hill also ordered the erection of a pontoon bridge to span the Appomattox east of the railroad bridge and the placement of planks on the railroad span to facilitate the river crossing. These defensive precautions assumed a special urgency following a sharp military action along the James on August 1.[44]

By late July the strategic situation in Virginia had changed. McClellan's Army of the Potomac still rested in its camps at Harrison's Landing and Westover Plantation twenty miles below Richmond. General Lee could not ignore this coiled serpent lying one day's march from the Confederate capital. But now Lee also worried about a new Union army forming in the northern Piedmont headed by Major General John Pope. This force (primarily the units defeated by Stonewall Jackson in his Shenandoah Valley campaign) threatened to move against Richmond from the northwest, destroying Lee's rail links to the Valley in the process. Lee sought to suppress Pope's army, and he detached nearly half of his infantry under Jackson to do so. But in order to avoid fighting simultaneously on two fronts, Lee needed to drive McClellan off the Peninsula entirely or at least paralyze him until Pope could be defeated by Lee's reunited army.

Lee decided to attack McClellan's waterborne supply line along the James as a means of compelling his retreat, and so he instructed General Hill to discomfit McClellan's fleet with a massive artillery bombardment launched from the river's right bank. Lee suggested using old Fort Powhatan in Prince George County, familiar to the Petersburg troops assigned there in 1861, as the best place from which to make the attack. Lee assigned his artillery chief, Brigadier General William Nelson Pendleton, to command the guns that would execute the task and recommended that Brigadier General Samuel Gibbs French accompany Pendleton with infantry. French, a Northerner, West Point graduate, and distinguished veteran of the Mexican War, was a new figure in Petersburg. General Holmes had summoned French from dis-

Samuel Gibbs French (1818–1910). General French
arrived in Petersburg during the summer of 1862
and by late August was in command of the Department of North Carolina, with headquarters in the
Cockade City. He remained in department or district command in Petersburg through May 1863.
(Courtesy of Valentine Richmond History Center)

trict command in Wilmington, North Carolina, prior to his departure for the
West. Lee sought to ensure secrecy for Hill's operation and proposed that the
War Department announce a movement against Suffolk or Norfolk as mis-
direction to the press and spies, or place "an enigmatic paragraph in the
[*Richmond Daily*] *Dispatch*."[45]

Lee instructed Pendleton to select "his best and longest-range light batteries" along with several larger cannon from the Reserve Artillery, a total of
thirty-six guns. Batteries from the battalions of Colonel J. Thompson Brown
(a native Petersburger), Lieutenant Colonel Allan S. Cutts, and Major William Nelson made the trip to Petersburg. The most powerful ordnance in
Pendleton's command had been captured from the Union army at Manassas. Nicknamed Long Tom, this oversized thirty-two pounder joined three
other siege guns to bolster Pendleton's firepower. All the artillery arrived in
the Cockade City, overland and by rail, by sunset on July 29.[46]

While Pendleton's guns rumbled south from Richmond, Hill conducted a
personal reconnaissance along the James. He decided to make his attack
from Coggin's Point and Maycox Landing, a few miles upstream from Fort
Powhatan. These positions lay immediately opposite the main Union camps,
a tempting target, but at 3,000 feet across, the river here was wider than at
Fort Powhatan. Hill reported his decision to Lee on July 29. "I am not certain that Coggins Point is as good for your purpose as Fort Powhatan or some
point in the neighborhood below," Lee warned Hill. The Confederate commander, however, deferred to his subordinate, and Hill ignored Lee's reservations.[47]

Lee had suggested French for the expedition because French had participated in similar operations along the Potomac River earlier in the war. On
July 29 Hill selected the brigades of Junius Daniel and John G. Walker (temporarily led by Colonel Van Manning of the Third Arkansas Infantry) from
French's command to accompany Pendleton's guns. They would shield the

cannoneers from potential Union counterattacks from either directly across the river or via an amphibious landing at City Point. Ransom's men would provide general support. Hill directed that the task force leave Petersburg on the morning of July 30, intending to make the attack that night under cover of darkness. Artillery from Hill's department joined the column, providing Pendleton a total of forty-three cannon.[48]

Hill's infantry and artillery, with a scattering of cavalry scouts, marched out of Petersburg about 7:00 AM on July 30. Orders circulated through the infantry camps earlier in the morning to prepare two days' rations, indicating a substantial operation. The men of the Second Georgia Battalion set out toward Coggin's Point near the head of Manning's brigade. "The route led us down a long straight hill and at the bottom, turning and looking back, for half a mile can be seen nothing but a mass of moving heads and shining gun barrels, forty feet wide and [a] half mile long," wrote Private Henry Graves of Company B. The soldiers jabbered with the animation typical of the opening hour of any comfortable march, reminding Graves of " a set of blackbirds or . . . noisy women trying to out talk each other." Soon the chatter died out as the column tramped about seven miles to Perkinson's sawmill where they halted for a brief rest. French rode up about 10:00 AM and encountered Hill and Pendleton. General Hill now explained his battle plan for the first time and quickly described the terrain at Coggin's Point.[49]

French and Pendleton rode forward to Beechwood, Edmund Ruffin's family plantation near Coggin's Point, to reconnoiter. Ruffin lent considerable assistance in suggesting prime locations for the guns, simultaneously remonstrating against placing artillery in Beechwood's front yard. French removed his uniform jacket, donned a straw hat, and raised an umbrella as he rode to the riverbank disguised as a farmer. The general, accompanied at times by Pendleton and Ruffin, surveyed the riverbank for nearly half a mile before returning to the rendezvous point. The fussy Pendleton found the reconnaissance "laborious and perplexing" and fretted about positioning his batteries in the dark. Ruffin also considered the intelligence-gathering slow and inefficient. While the generals plotted, the troops lounged in the woods, seeking relief from the heat. They knew little about their mission but suspected that their targets would be the boomerangs—soldier slang for the Union gunboats. At 4:00 PM they resumed their march toward the river.

The delay occasioned by the tedious reconnaissance disrupted Hill's timetable and discouraged the expedition's testy commander. Late that evening Pendleton, French, and Hill met at Merchant's Hope Church, a short distance due south of Coggin's Point, to review the situation. French advised that the attack be deferred because "the night was far advanced, the darkness intense, and . . . many of the officers who would command batteries had not examined the ground, the roads, nor the shipping they designed to fire on, and many pieces were far in the rear." Pendleton agreed. Hill grumbled that by waiting another day they would sacrifice the element of surprise and thus compromise the entire operation, but he deferred to his lieutenants' judgment. Disappointed and a little disgusted, Hill departed for Petersburg, leaving French in command. The soldiers and artillerists hunkered down amid rumbles of thunder and flashes of lightning that illuminated the evening sky but produced little rain.[50]

The next morning French issued orders for Pendleton and his battery commanders to reexamine the ground at Coggin's Point and the nearby bluffs and select specific locations for their guns. The artillery would remain concealed during the day and then proceed to its designated points after dark. A coordinated fire would commence on French's signal, with each battery concentrating on its target until return fire rendered its position untenable. Then, as the circumstances required, the guns would be withdrawn one by one. Pendleton anticipated that each cannon would fire between twenty and thirty rounds before being compelled to disengage. Daniel's Brigade would lead the artillery on its return march to Petersburg, with Manning's troops protecting their rear. The Second Georgia Battalion would deploy at Ruffin's plantation to watch this landing point. Ransom would remain closer to Petersburg. "All noise, all fires, and approach during the day when a soldier can be seen by the enemy is forbidden, the whole being a secret expedition," French explained.[51]

Pendleton and his subordinates spent July 31 busily selecting battery positions. The gray-bearded Pendleton, a fifty-two-year-old Episcopal cleric from Lexington, Virginia, assigned locations for forty-three pieces, including the four heavy siege guns, from Maycox Landing, along Coggin's Point, and upriver to near Beechwood. French had the gunners erect stakes to guide their fire at night, each battery selecting a specific floating target among the anchored Union fleet, which numbered about 150 vessels within cannon range of the shore. The Confederates kept within the wood lines to avoid being seen by McClellan's observation balloons, which hovered over the Federal bivouacs. The gunners and their infantry escorts remained in camp, although Private Graves, among others, could not resist slipping to the river to gaze at their enemy across the James: "There before me . . . lay the Yankee camp, the wharf and steamboats and transports without number lin[ing] the river near the opposite shore. The drums are beating merrily and everything seems lively. I can almost distinguish the different tunes." Graves and the battery commanders returned to their camps late in the afternoon as a fine rain began to fall.[52]

About 6:00 PM the teams lurched forward and the Confederate artillery rolled toward its assigned positions escorted by the Second Georgia Battalion. The carriage wheels quickly carved the muddy farm lanes into a series of deep ruts, and the night grew unusually dark from the clouds and drizzle that obscured the moon. Out of the blackness glimmered thousands of lights from the Union fleet and camps, although by the time the batteries had taken their places around midnight, all was quiet on the river. Edmund Ruffin had extracted a promise from General Pendleton to fire the first gun in a reprise of Ruffin's reputed exploits at Charleston Harbor in April 1861. The old fire-eater struggled through the pitchy night to a battery position near the landing at Coggin's Point, hampered by night blindness, only to discover that the signal gun was to be fired elsewhere. Pendleton had managed to emplace all but two of the guns in their assigned positions when at 12:30 AM on August 1, the south shore exploded with the roar of forty-one Confederate cannon. "A sound, whose grandeur and power words cannot describe and which cannot be imagined by anyone who has never heard the like, breaks out, shaking the very ground and rolling, echoing and reechoing through the woods and ravines on the riverbank," wrote one witness.

The Confederate barrage caught the Union navy and McClellan's slumbering soldiers completely by surprise. Shell bursts revealed astonished sailors dashing about their decks. Infantrymen at Harrison's Landing rushed from their tents, wondering what in the world had disturbed their repose.

The gunboat crews recovered from their confusion and shock and slowly began returning fire. "The shells come over now and then, but making up in precision what they lack in number and frequency," commented Graves. One of the first missiles found its target at Long Tom and exploded near the muzzle of the famous piece, killing a Confederate gunner and wounding two others. Most of the navy's rounds, however, sailed over the Confederates' heads. McClellan had posted no artillery to fire across the river, relying on the navy to handle any annoyances from the south shore, although he eventually directed some heavy guns to positions near the bank. Still, the counterfire was sufficiently hot to impress Corporal Cowand: "They throwed bums all around us and I tell you they struck the grown and I thought at that time I never should see you again," he told a correspondent.[53]

The most intense portion of Pendleton's bombardment ran its course in about thirty minutes. In accordance with their plans, French and Pendleton began removing the batteries as their ammunition dwindled or the gunboats zeroed in on them. All the firing ceased around 1:30 AM, and the Confederates rested far enough from the riverbank to avoid incoming fire. They commenced the sixteen-mile march back to Petersburg at dawn.

French estimated that his guns fired approximately one thousand rounds. Although admitting that he could not accurately determine the damage inflicted, he presumed that "it could not have been otherwise than destructive." In addition to the casualties sustained around Long Tom, the Confederates suffered three men wounded by the premature discharge of a gun, two injured when their piece overturned on the road, and three horses slightly hurt. In his after-action report General Pendleton repeated estimates obtained from witnesses that twenty Union ships sustained serious damage and thirty or forty Federals had been killed, along with fifty horses.

McClellan's report issued later that morning belied such optimistic estimates. "Enemy opened with light guns from Coggins Point about half an hour after midnight," wrote the Union commander. "fire very heavy for more than half an hour—lasted perhaps an hour. Did not do any injury, that I can learn as yet, except one man hit in the leg. Firing very wild." A Union diarist admitted that the Rebel fire had "scared the contrabands [runaway slaves] & sutlers, but did no great damage." When McClellan had a proper chance to assess the impact of French's attack, he determined that ten men had been killed by the barrage and twelve wounded. The fleet sustained no meaningful harm.[54]

Hill's troops arrived in their Petersburg camps late on the afternoon of August 1. He reported the results of the expedition to General Lee, who congratulated the Carolinian but urged him to continue harassing McClellan's shipping and sever the unionists' communications via the James. "This will require continuous and systematic effort and a well-digested plan," Lee advised. "Marse Robert" reiterated his preference for using Fort Powhatan as the point from which to execute the attacks, reflecting his muted disappointment with Hill's conduct.[55]

Ruffin used less tact in assessing the outcome of the Coggin's Point offensive: "It seems to me that it is as ridiculous as useless to have made this whole movement—of so large a force not only of artillery, but of supporting infantry, & then marching all back after merely throwing 800 balls & shells, in half an hour, which I do not suppose served to kill 20 men, or sunk, or seriously damaged a single vessel." McClellan ensured the futility of the expedition by ferrying a force to the south shore on August 1. The Union commander ordered the Maycox house burned and the woods along the riverbank destroyed to prevent a repeat of the night's surprise.[56]

This foray provided a hint of McClellan's preferred course of action. He had explained in late July to Major General Henry W. Halleck, Lincoln's new general-in-chief, that he wished to cross to the south side of the James, capture Petersburg—and with it all but one of the rail lines serving the Confederate capital from the south—and entrench there to await Lee's response. Deprived of his supplies, argued McClellan, his opponent must either attack at Petersburg or abandon the capital—McClellan's ultimate objective.

Halleck thought this plan too risky. He credited McClellan's exaggerated reports of Confederate strength and worried that the army's removal to Petersburg would allow Lee to crush Pope without fear of interference from the Army of the Potomac. Events in distant theaters also spared Petersburg from

Little Mac's stillborn strategy. When the Union campaign against Chattanooga, Tennessee, met delay, McClellan feared that Chattanooga's defenders might shuttle to Virginia by rail and threaten his army from south of Petersburg. Thus nothing came of McClellan's viable scheme to capture the Cockade City.[57]

McClellan's toehold on the south bank of the James and the potential for an offensive from this quarter spurred Hill's determination to complete Petersburg's defenses, eventually known as the Dimmock Line. Assuming this undertaking and organizing the Coggin's Point expedition proved to be the most significant achievements of Hill's brief tenure as Petersburg's commander. When the soldiers were not involved in fatigue work on the trenches, they passed their time in the expected ways. "These Virginia girls, as usual, are trotting after our battalion," wrote one Georgian. "They crowd out here from Petersburg every evening, and the boys in their shirt sleeves and dusty, and ragged, 'buck up' to them and play the gallant very extensively." The North Carolina lieutenant Julius S. Joyner observed that "we are having a fine time as we have very little to do. Watermelons and fruit plentiful."[58]

McClellan sent more troops to Prince George County on August 2 to pacify the south bank of the James. Although a few Federal cavalrymen ventured inland to explore the countryside, the Union initiative posed no real threat to Petersburg. Hill dispatched various units east of town to keep an eye on the enemy, while the rest of his men labored on the fortifications. One North Carolina officer patrolling near the county seat considered Prince George Court House "the poorest apology I ever saw for a country town in my life, 3 houses constitute the whole town, and they hard cases." The Yankee presence did persuade Edmund Ruffin to abandon his James River plantations and seek refuge in Petersburg. He leased " a very old & ordinary house" on High Street and encountered the lofty prices and material shortages so common in the city.[59]

A few days after the fighting at Coggin's Point, Halleck and Lincoln achieved what Harvey Hill and Robert E. Lee could not. Weary of McClellan's inactivity and endless whining for reinforcements, and concerned for the well-being of Pope's army, they ordered McClellan to abandon the Peninsula and transport his army to northern Virginia to support Pope. Lee soon learned of McClellan's withdrawal and prepared to strike Pope before the Federal forces could unite.

On August 19 a mass exodus of Confederate troops commenced at Petersburg. Infantry and artillery units broke camp and made their way toward Richmond and a rendezvous with the units already jousting with Pope. This shift allowed Lee to execute an administrative change at Petersburg.

The Confederate chief had entertained doubts about Hill's competence as a department commander since the disappointing expedition to Coggin's

Point. Hill's failure to harry McClellan's retreat from the Peninsula prompted Lee to recommend that the Carolinian be relieved. "I fear General Hill is not entirely equal to his present position," Lee explained to President Davis. "An excellent executive officer, he does not appear to have much administrative ability. Left to himself he seems embarrassed and backward to act." Lee thought General French better suited for command of the Department of North Carolina and made the change official on August 21.[60]

These adjustments revolved around one additional officer. Major General Gustavus Woodson Smith had achieved high rank in the Confederate service early in the war—so high, in fact, that it was Smith who had succeeded the wounded Joe Johnston at Seven Pines on May 31. Smith's cameo appearance as army commander had been characterized by vacillation and confusion. This performance, and poor health, resulted in his prompt removal in favor of Lee. Suffering from an illness he described as paralysis, Smith recuperated for more than two months, all the while nursing resentment over his sudden fall from grace along with his physical ailments. By August 10 Smith had recovered sufficiently to assume command of the infantry division in Lee's army formerly led by D. H. Hill, an assignment that lasted less than a fortnight before Hill returned to his old troops.[61]

Lee's departure to confront Pope in the Piedmont left the units around Richmond without a commander. Lee opted to assign Gustavus Smith a grand military region incorporating the Department of North Carolina and the Confederate capital. French, as department commander with headquarters in Petersburg, would report to Smith's Richmond offices. Orders of August 30 and September 19 formalized these arrangements.[62]

On the surface, Petersburg's two new military leaders shared much in common. Both had distinguished records at West Point, served in the Mexican War, and resigned their commissions to enter private business. Smith, a Kentuckian, had gone north to become street commissioner for New York City at the outbreak of the war. French, a Northerner, had gone south, where he engaged in planting and married a Mississippi woman. Both had attained a general's wreath in 1861, and each man exuded confidence—along with genial (if somewhat imperious) personalities.[63]

Sam French's military responsibilities proved wider than deep. With the main focus of the war shifted to northern Virginia and then across the Potomac, southern Virginia resumed its place as a military backwater. Southeastern Virginia and eastern North Carolina drew most of French's attention. Here Federal troops conducted minor operations from their strongholds east of the Blackwater River, in Norfolk and New Bern, and along Albemarle Sound.

French's main responsibility remained the protection of the rail connection from Wilmington to Richmond, and he distributed his forces accordingly. Martin's Brigade guarded the North Carolina portion of French's department above Wilmington. A new North Carolina infantry brigade commanded by Brigadier General J. Johnston Pettigrew established headquarters in Petersburg, but the brigade spent most of its time deployed east of the city, as far as the Blackwater River, or in northern North Carolina. French also commanded small detachments assigned to Port Walthall and Fort Clifton—two Appomattox River strongpoints northeast of Petersburg—as well as at Drewry's Bluff, Prince George Court House, and along the Richmond-Petersburg Turnpike. Milligan's scouts and telegraphers remained within the department. Daniel's Brigade guarded Chesterfield County between Petersburg and Richmond.[64]

French sent troops toward Suffolk in late September, and in early November he practically stripped Petersburg of defenders to respond to Federal activities in North Carolina. On November 13 the importance of the southernmost sector of Smith's and French's military jurisdiction prompted an administrative change. Smith informed French that Brigadier General William Henry Chase Whiting would assume control at Wilmington and report directly to Smith, thus reducing French's authority. One month later Smith similarly removed the northern portion of French's department by assigning Major General Arnold Elzey responsibility for Drewry's Bluff and the Richmond defenses on either side of the James. "It is difficult to prescribe exact geographic boundaries between the commands of Generals Elzey, French, and Whiting," Smith admitted, "but even were these lines definitely drawn they would . . . be disregarded in emergency, and, in . . . active operations against the enemy, department or district lines would be set aside and a combined effort made to beat the foe."[65]

Petersburg now resembled a garrison town more than ever. On October 5 the Fifty-fifth North Carolina Infantry arrived from Wise's Forks and Kinston, North Carolina, and by the end of the month began acting as Petersburg's provost guard. Independent of any combat brigade, the Fifty-fifth took up residence at the Model Farm, where men such as the semiliterate Private James King Wilkerson found their accommodations much to their liking. "We have got splendid houses to stay in if we can stay hear. . . . Most of [the houses] is got splendid chimneys made of brake. Kitchens to, and good bunks to sleep on already made. our room will hold 96 men, only two men to a bunk . . . most of the houses is painted and some [of] them plastered and some litening rods." Major Alfred H. Belo of the Fifty-fifth considered the assignment "delightful," although the duty was not without its challenges. "Petersburg was under martial law, and to keep the city in peace and order was no small task," admitted French.[66]

Each morning about one hundred men would report for a twenty-four-hour shift. Many soldiers cooked and carried their daily rations, while others braved the outrageous prices in the Petersburg markets, where opossums sold for four dollars a piece and rabbits and squirrels cost one dollar each. "I am getting tired of walking the streets," complained one member of the regiment. "We walk them from one morning until the next nearly all night."[67]

Controlling the illegal sale of alcohol remained high on the commanders' agenda. "Men who were regarded respectable would sell liquor to the soldiers," complained French, and "to fine the offenders was useless." He decided to apply an unorthodox punishment to discourage this illicit traffic. He made it known that violating the proscription against liquor sales would result in shaving the perpetrator's head and marching him through town for two hours wearing a "barrel shirt" for ten days. "How would a dude look with his head shaved and protruding through a hole in the head of a barrel?" chuckled French. "That ended selling whiskey," at least for the time being. However, members of the Fifty-fifth North Carolina were not immune to the lure of other sinful temptations in Petersburg. The regiment reported thirteen new cases of venereal disease that fall, doubtlessly contracted in the city's brothels.[68]

The regiment also discharged the strange duty of incarcerating fellow Confederates. The armies had instituted a formal system of parole and exchange in 1862 by which prisoners would be released but remain out of active service until officially traded for prisoners from the other side. This system relieved each government from housing, feeding, and guarding enemy prisoners of war. Until parolees were exchanged, however, both the Union and Confederate armies preferred to keep them in central locations under strict observation, fearing that allowing paroled prisoners to go home would make them difficult to retrieve once their exchange had occurred.

One of these parole camps was established in mid-November at the Model Farm, which dislocated the Fifty-fifth North Carolina to new, less commodious quarters on Dunn's Hill. Flag-of-truce boats docked at City Point, where paroled Confederates disembarked for the trip to the Model Farm. General French ordered the officer at City Point, Captain W. W. Roberts, to forbid the distribution of the Richmond, Petersburg, and Raleigh newspapers to Federal officers on board the vessels in an effort to control military intelligence. The provost guard also attempted to regulate the sale of goods brought through the blockade.[69]

Despite French's measures to discourage the sale and consumption of spirits, the approach of Christmas signaled an increase in alcohol abuse among citizens and soldiers. "We find a good many drunkards now," reported a private in the Fifty-fifth North Carolina on December 16. Rounding up the inebriated was child's play compared to the most loathsome task assigned the Tarheels. They bore the responsibility for executing soldiers condemned for desertion, a grim job universally despised by Civil War soldiers.[70]

When General French assumed command at Petersburg, the Dimmock Line had been completed only as far as Jerusalem Plank Road, near Timothy Rives's farm. Colonel Stevens had laid out the line west of this point to its junction with the Appomattox River upstream from Petersburg, but French's far-flung responsibilities left him few soldiers to perform construction. Hill's black labor force had dispersed, so French requested on September 8 that 150 new laborers be provided for fatigue duty. Obtaining workers for the city's defenses would prove problematic for the rest of French's Petersburg tenure.[71]

Captain Dimmock did manage to keep several hundred blacks employed on the fortifications throughout the fall. The Virginia General Assembly authorized the impressment of slaves to build defenses throughout the state, but it limited the number that could be conscripted from counties or individual owners. Furthermore, no impressed slave could work for more than sixty days. Finishing Fort Clifton and other defenses in Chesterfield County also drained Dimmock's limited manpower. Smith assigned Lieutenant Colonel Reuben Lindsay Walker, an accomplished artillery officer, to assist in preparing gun positions, but this technical advice did nothing to solve Dimmock's primary problem—a shortage of workers. Once the threat posed by McClellan's army had been removed, the urgency to prepare for the next military emergency disappeared with it.[72]

French brought the matter to a head on December 12. He presented a letter drafted by Dimmock to the Petersburg Common Council, which both described the problem and proposed a solution:

> The early completion of the defensive works around your city must be a matter of paramount interest to yourselves. [Despite] the efforts of the state government . . . it has been found impossible to secure an immediate and adequate force to meet the demands for labor. . . .
>
> It is proposed that you secure a force of 200 negroes by such means as may . . . seem best from that character of your population in & around the city. This force to report each morning upon the work which is two miles from the city at eight o'clock to be dismissed and permitted to return home at 4 p.m. thus avoiding the nefarious discomfort and exposure of camp life.
>
> With this force for two or three weeks more could be accomplished than in as many months of the rapidly approaching bad weather.[73]

Charles F. Collier moved that this correspondence be referred to the mayor and council for immediate consideration. The next day the council instructed Mayor W. W. Townes and councilmen Benjamin B. Vaughan and David G. Potts to advertise for slave and free black laborers. Workers would be paid two dollars per day by the city, with rations provided by the Confederate government. No such man would be retained for more than twenty days and would work, in accordance with Dimmock's suggestion, from 8:00 AM until 4:00 PM, returning home each night. The council selected one of its own, the local builder Samuel Lecture, to supervise the workers, providing him a salary of five dollars per day. Although one Virginia private commented on the "powerful fortifications" around Petersburg on Christmas Day, efforts to complete the Dimmock Line would continue well into 1863.[74]

Shortly after French finished lobbying the common council, military affairs drew him away from the Cockade City. The Union commander in North Carolina, Major General John G. Foster, launched an offensive in conjunction with a new push toward Richmond from northern Virginia by McClellan's successor, General Burnside. Foster led a force of more than ten thousand men out of New Bern on December 11, targeting the important rail junction at Goldsboro. Because Goldsboro occupied a vital point between Wilmington and Richmond, French and most of his troops moved south and blocked the Federals.[75]

French's departure left Colonel John K. Connally of the Fifty-fifth North Carolina in charge at Petersburg. French would return following Foster's withdrawal from Goldsboro, but not for long. General Smith recognized that with Burnside's repulse on December 13 at Fredericksburg, the Virginia portion of his department was relatively safe. The real danger lay in North Carolina. On January 3, 1863, Smith ordered French to move to Weldon or Rocky Mount and concentrate his forces there, relying on P. G. T. Beauregard in South Carolina to reinforce Wilmington and Lee to protect southern Virginia.[76]

Troops from a distant theater would fill the vacuum that French left. The Twenty-ninth, Fiftieth, Fifty-fourth, and Sixty-third Virginia Infantry Regiments and the Twenty-seventh Battalion of Virginia Cavalry (dismounted) had served in southwestern Virginia, Tennessee, Kentucky, and in the Kanawha Valley of western Virginia in 1862. No longer needed in the mountains, and hemorrhaging men by desertion to their nearby homes, Lee ordered them to Petersburg. These western Virginians broke camp on December 16 and entrained at Wytheville for their long journey east, arriving in Petersburg about Christmas Eve. Their new commander, Brigadier General Raleigh E. Colston, had graduated from the Virginia Military Institute—where, before the war, he had served on the faculty alongside Thomas Jackson. Colston had commanded a brigade at Seven Pines, but had fallen ill shortly thereafter and did not resume active duty until December. The War Department then sent him to Petersburg to command the approximately twenty-two hundred strangers arriving there from the Virginia mountains.[77]

On New Year's Day 1863 Colston gazed on a Petersburg that had become a thoroughly military town. Although no shots had been fired in the city limits, the enemy had appeared a few miles away, and only Lincoln's lack of confidence in George B. McClellan had spared the city certain capture. Threats to Petersburg had come from Union-occupied southeastern Virginia, but in a strategic and administrative sense the Cockade City belonged to North Carolina. Petersburg's most valuable military asset remained its rail connection to the Tarheel State. While his defenses had not yet been perfected, Captain Dimmock had made a good start on turning Petersburg into a citadel. Inside the growing fortifications lay myriad government operations supporting the war, including one of the largest medical establishments in the South. By the end of 1862 Petersburg's citizens had learned to adjust their lives in keeping with a society at war.

⌐ 5 ⌐

"We Are on the Eve of Great Events"

LIFE IN PETERSBURG
JANUARY 1863–APRIL 1864

THE SIGHT OF convalescent troops from Petersburg's seven military hospitals navigating the city at liberty reminded citizens of the war's presence, despite the lack of imminent combat. "Crippled soldiers are so commonly seen in the streets now that they hardly attract any attention," testified one observer in January 1863. The patient census fluctuated with battlefield activity, but soldiers stricken by disease often outnumbered those wounded in combat.

Smallpox proved the worst of the various afflictions that plagued the army, particularly during the winter months. In January physicians at the General or Fair Grounds Hospital confined patients in an effort to contain the highly contagious disease. Smallpox victims populated every hospital, one report stating that "near a thousand cases" were present. Twenty members of the Twenty-ninth Virginia Infantry alone died of the disease during the winter. Inevitably, smallpox infected Petersburg citizens, prompting city officials to open a facility specifically for stricken residents. The Petersburg Common Council hired a physician to treat patients there and to make house calls on the poor who suffered at home. Many Petersburgers received vaccinations. The city government eventually required any dwelling that contained smallpox to display a white flag from the front window as a warning to passersby.[1]

Petersburg's Confederate hospitals treated myriad ailments and earned accolades from visitors. The army established an efficient centralized medical administration in 1863, with Surgeon John H. Claiborne presiding over all the hospitals from an office on Union Street. Physicians reporting to Claiborne had specific charge of one hospital each, most of which served a particular geographic clientele. Surgeon F. P. Porcher ran the South Carolina Hospital, which also treated soldiers from Alabama, Mississippi, and Louisiana. Dr. J. H. Pottenger superintended the Virginia Hospital. Surgeon Smith ministered to Georgians and Texans at the Confederate States Hospital. Dr. John G. Brodnax at the North Carolina Hospital and Dr. R. P. Page at the Poplar Lawn (Pavilion) Hospital treated Tarheel troops. The Fair Grounds Hospital evolved into a facility for paroled prisoners, while Dr. Martin P. Scott's new Wayside Hospital for transients, located on the eastern end of Bollingbrook Street, accepted patients irrespective of their state of origin. Whenever a trainload of the wounded or ill arrived at one of the Petersburg depots, ambulances and attendants met and transported the sufferers to their designated facility.[2]

Charles Campbell praised the Virginia Hospital in glowing terms. "Everything was clean & nice & comfortable; not the least unpleasant odor," he wrote. "The factories appear providentially to answer for hospitals almost as well as if built for the very purpose." An Alabama patient at the Fair Grounds Hospital agreed: "I have had excellent attention here, this is a nice hospittal." A Texas soldier, William W. Heartsill, was particularly effusive. "A visit to the Hospitals in Petersburg will repay any one," he advised. "To witness the perfect order, the cleanliness of every thing, then to see how punctually they are visited by scores of ladies of the city; who bring soup, wine and every delicacy that a sick or wounded man could desire."[3]

Supervising surgeons relied on African American stewards and welcomed a few intrepid ladies as volunteer aides. Soldiers detailed from their regiments also assisted the physicians with routine duties. One such man at the North Carolina Hospital ran afoul of Surgeon Brodnax, who accused him of "ungentlemanly" conduct toward female volunteers and encouraging "insubordination among the negro servants."[4]

There is little to indicate that the patients in Petersburg hospitals suffered substantially from a lack of medical supplies during the war's middle years. The records of the North Carolina Hospital, however, reveal that physicians prescribed whiskey more often than any purely pharmaceutical remedy. Fund-raisers staged for the benefit of Petersburg hospitals, such as the concert held in Louisburg, North Carolina, in December 1862, helped purchase additional supplies.[5]

Besides healing physical ailments, hospital authorities treated the minds, souls, and spirits of their patients. Volunteers visited the wards armed with spellers to help illiterate soldiers learn to read. Colporteurs distributed religious tracts. Musical entertainment lifted the morale of the sick and wounded, and the weary caregivers who attended them.

Patients arrived on trains from battlefields, from hospitals in Richmond, or directly from their regiments. They left by discharge, transfer, or through death. Hearses provided a daily reminder of the wages of war. Among the most poignant visitors to Petersburg were family members arriving to retrieve the remains of sons, brothers, and husbands who perished in a hospital. The widow of Private Thomas L. Whitefield of the Fiftieth North Carolina Infantry engaged a family friend to bring her husband's body back to their home after he died at the North Carolina Hospital of chronic diarrhea in February 1863. It is difficult to imagine her reaction when her friend returned to Person County empty-handed because he lacked funds to pay the officials at Blandford Cemetery to exhume Whitefield's corpse.[6]

Petersburg's business community faced financial problems on a larger scale. The Union blockade, evaporation of Northern domestic markets, and the shrinking buying power of Southern consumers left two primary customers for Petersburg products and commodities: the Confederate government and European patrons of blockade runners. Petersburg manufacturers, merchants, and railroads coped with increasing problems of supply and capital to maintain facilities and produce profits.

Government contracts sustained Petersburg's cotton manufacturing through 1864. Between June and December 1863 the army's Richmond Clothing Bureau purchased nearly 1.3 million yards of cotton cloth from Petersburg mills, the Battersea Mill alone providing more than 750,000 yards. The mills consumed more than six hundred bales of cotton per month to maintain this level of production. The pace continued during the first half of 1864 when the Battersea, Ettrick, and Matoaca mills shipped the government nearly 1.5 million yards of cloth. Most provided uniforms, although in August 1863 Petersburg cotton went to Charleston, South Carolina, to make sandbags. Petersburg mill owners retained agents to scour the South for spare parts and equipment to keep their aging machinery in operation. A bobbin plant in Georgia, for example, sold twenty thousand units to Petersburg mills in just two months.[7]

On March 9, 1864, the Virginia legislature authorized the governor to requisition cloth according to a quota system based on each mill's production capacity. The state promised to supply the raw cotton and compensate the mills fairly for their work. In Petersburg a conflict arose between the primacy of state and Confederate needs. The operators of the Ettrick, Battersea, and Matoaca mills protested to Governor William Smith that, except for a small quantity of cotton yarn used to exchange for employee provisions, the Confederate Quartermaster Department claimed their entire production, making it impossible to satisfy both the state's new requirements and their existing contract. John B. Dunn of the Mechanics Manufacturing Company, Petersburg's fourth cotton mill, sent a similar message to Governor Smith. He manufactured fine cloth under contract to the Confederate Subsistence Department, which in turn swapped the material to obtain soldiers' rations. Dunn explained that he was under pressure to increase his production because the Subsistence Department "are in great want . . . to barter off for meat for the army." He could not understand how to satisfy the demand from both the army and the commonwealth.[8]

The Confederacy avoided such complications in one instance by directly operating a cotton plant in Petersburg. Between January 1863 and March 1865 Captain Thomas A. Jackson of the navy leased a facility near Ettrick from Archibald McIlwaine for the production of cotton cordage that, when tarred, substituted nicely for hemp rope. Jackson relocated machinery from Isle of Wight County and employed Lieutenant S. Welford Corbin to supervise the operation. The factory produced about five hundred pounds of cotton rope each working day, eighty-four thousand pounds from April 1863 through September 1864 alone, more than the navy required. The navy sold the surplus to the army or civilians, such as coal miners involved in government enterprise.[9]

Cotton manufacturing was but one of several business pursuits that survived in midwar Petersburg. City merchants continued to carry on wholesale and retail trade, both of which relied to a great degree on blockade running. John B. Wilson, a partner with John McIlwaine in a Petersburg commission house, exemplified the relationship between the rewards of local commerce and the vicissitudes of the blockade. Wilson prospered by buying and selling consumer items throughout the South smuggled past the United States navy. Describing his operation as "a mixed business," Wilson not only retailed imported goods in Petersburg but he traveled to distant corners of the Confederacy to obtain and resell items both domestically and to international markets. One shipment that evaded the blockade at Charleston cost him four thousand dollars but yielded twenty-one thousand at retail. "Money has been made with ease," Wilson told his father in January 1863. He was proud that he had profited without dealing in "the favorite articles of traffic, whiskey & brandy." He boasted that he had declined a three-thousand-dollar commission to handle seventy barrels of whiskey bound for Petersburg. Wilson usually dealt through Nassau in the Bahamas, a favorite intermediate stop for blockade runners entering Atlantic harbors.[10]

By 1863 Wilson and other merchants confronted a growing shortage of cargo space aboard blockade runners. The Union navy grew increasingly effective at intercepting Confederate ships as the war progressed, and fewer ship owners agreed to risk their vessels. A group of prominent Petersburg businessmen led by D'Arcy Paul, a septuagenarian member of the common council, responded to this problem. They formed the Petersburg Steamship Corporation in 1863, which contracted with a British company to build a new blockade runner. Paul and his business associates named their ship the *City of Petersburg*. The new vessel measured 223 feet long, possessed a beam of 25 feet, and drew 13½ feet. She made her first transatlantic voyage in the autumn of 1863 and arrived in Wilmington on December 2, where her owners celebrated the first returns from their investment. The *City of Petersburg* brought consumer goods to Wilmington at least eight times through

August 1864, leaving the Cape Fear River on her return voyage bound for either Nassau or Halifax, Nova Scotia, laden with cotton obtained from various sources.[11]

Virtually all goods arriving in Petersburg through the blockade or from other Southern cities came by rail. Operation of the city's railroads grew ever more challenging as the war entered its third year, compounding the business community's shortage of retail merchandise. Union occupation of Tidewater Virginia east of the Blackwater River, reduced the Norfolk & Petersburg Railroad to a short-haul line traversing the thirty-five miles between Petersburg and Ivor. The Union blockade of the lower James River and Hampton Roads left the City Point Railroad commercially useless except as an alternative route between Richmond and Petersburg. The South Side Railroad fared moderately well, given the relatively modest volume of traffic moving between Lynchburg and Petersburg and the absence of occupying Union armies in central and western Virginia. The two north-south railroads, the Petersburg and the Richmond & Petersburg, suffered a steady decline as demands on their crumbling infrastructures hampered operations.

Railroads faced a variety of seemingly insurmountable problems. Rolling stock, locomotives, and tracks all deteriorated under heavy use. The South's manufacturing capacity proved woefully unable to replace equipment damaged or worn out during the war. Military shipments competed with civilian freight for space on the trains that did operate, impeding the expeditious movement of private goods to and from town. White workers left for the army in large numbers, either voluntarily or as conscripts, and African American employees and leased slaves were increasingly impressed for work on the fortifications.

Charles Ellis of the Richmond & Petersburg Railroad explained to Governor John Letcher in February 1863 the impact of losing four of his black workers to fatigue duty with the army: "If these negroes could possibly be spared without stopping our transportation to and from Petersburg, or if I could hire negroes as substitutes, I would not hesitate cheerfully to provide our quota, but these hands are absolutely necessary to load and unload our trains at Petersburg." Like cotton manufacturing, operation of the railroads encountered competing priorities, each vigorously advocated by the Confederate government, the state, and private business.[12]

Two rail improvements did occur in midwar Petersburg. A new bridge across the Appomattox River opened in late September 1863, replacing the substandard span constructed in 1861. In the spring of 1864 the Petersburg Common Council permitted a double track to be installed on Washington Street east of Adams Street to expedite north-south traffic. But neither of these modest measures could reverse the general worsening of Petersburg's rail infrastructure and its consequent impact on the city's commercial health. The deteriorating rail transportation and the tightening Federal blockade created an enormous inventory of tobacco, despite the significant reduction in production. On February 29, 1864, Petersburg's four tobacco warehouses stored an incredible 5.8 million pounds of leaf, with no practical means of moving it to market. The profits lost in this backlog defy calculation.[13]

Midwar changes in Confederate policy regarding military service also undermined Petersburg's struggling business community. The Richmond government employed a variety of measures to fill empty ranks in Southern armies, including abolishing substitution, expanding the eligible age for military service, and tightening occupational exemptions. These policies suddenly made whole categories of previously exempt employees—laborers, skilled workers, and certain administrative people—subject to military service. "The repeal of the substitute system & the probability of the repeal of many exemptions have given rise to bitter croaking," testified Charles Campbell. "It is openly declared by some that the Confederacy is 'gone' is about run out!!" New laws left boys age seventeen and men between forty-five and fifty eligible for active army service. Mandatory calls for slave labor on Confederate fortifications exacerbated employment problems for industry already weakened by the enlistment of white workers. Petersburg suffered from the same dynamics that plagued the entire Confederacy during a long war: difficulty in maintaining a viable civilian economy while prosecuting an expensive and deadly multifront war.[14]

One example of this fundamental dilemma arose in February 1864 during an exchange of correspondence between two Petersburg executives and Governor William Smith. These businessmen explained that their leased slaves "were all hired by us for the purpose of working on the railroads or at the Iron works and as we only hired enough to do the business, the roads or the works will suffer seriously if any of the labor is abstracted from them. Your Excellency is aware that the rail roads do a large amount of army transportation . . . and therefore the work of our negroes on the rail roads is in our opinion as important as it can be on the fortifications." Pointing out that the blacks working in the iron foundries spent portions of their time producing shot and shell for army contracts, the industrialists requested that the governor exempt their black workers from fatigue duty with the army.

Governor Smith rejected this logic, asserting that "there can be no reason why capital in this form should not contribute its fair proportion to the public defence. Although the roads and iron works are materially contributing to . . . the support of the war they are liberally paid for it & are doing no more than those who are making bread & meat for the army—a much more essential service." Smith explained that the same argument for exemption was made by farmers cultivating their fields. In this instance Smith decided that the prerogatives of national defense trumped the interests of business.[15]

However, this was not always the case. Pressure that influential Petersburgers applied to relieve friends and associates of military obligation grew more intense as the war progressed and Confederate conscription laws tightened. Petersburg's bankers felt particularly aggrieved by policies that deprived them of their administrative employees, and some bankers advanced strained explanations for how these men performed indispensable services.

Thomas Wallace, an attorney, former member of the House of Delegates, and Petersburg's agent for the distribution of salt, lobbied Governor Smith in January 1864 on behalf of several local functionaries, including one teller at the city's branch of the Exchange Bank. "You know the importance of a teller and the promptness, quickness, and mechanical skill that is required in the rapid manipulation of money itself is not easily acquired," wrote Wallace. "As a bank we cannot do without him and I respectfully submit that his case presents a strong case for exemption." Wallace buttressed his argument by reminding the governor that two army offices in Petersburg maintained their accounts at the Exchange Bank and that the teller's absence might threaten competent management of these funds. Governor Smith approved the request.[16]

Similar applications arrived at the governor's office from other Petersburg bank officers and on behalf of professionals such as Captain J. M. Nichols, assistant superintendent of the gas works, who had been discharged from the Petersburg Artillery because of chronic rheumatism. Nichols's proponents justified their request by reminding the governor that the gas works supplied hospitals, quartermaster headquarters, and commissary offices in Petersburg. Nichols's absence in the army, they argued, would reduce the facility's ability to deliver these vital services. The governor relented. Governor Smith also approved the common council's request in March 1864 to exempt a large number of city officials.[17]

Governor Smith did reject the exemption applications of various Petersburg tobacco inspectors. These state-appointed officials, at least two men for each of the city's four warehouses, became less necessary as the market for (and ability to transport) raw tobacco declined throughout the war. The governor cited this economic reality on February 25, 1864, when he refused categorically to exempt any man who held what had become by the war's third year little more than a sinecure.[18]

Although the draft laws undermined railroad operations, new regulations concerning blockade running also damaged Petersburg's retail trade. The Confederate government passed statutes in early 1864 controlling all foreign commerce, including space on private blockade runners. Richmond authorities now governed commodity exports and required imports to include a larger proportion of military supplies at the expense of consumer goods and luxuries. Agents of the Bureau of Foreign Supplies enforced strict quotas on nonessential items, which severely undercut what had intermittently been a lucrative, if less-than-patriotic, traffic in commercial cities such as Petersburg. "We are having an unusually dull time in business," complained John B. Wilson in April 1864, "but one vessel has come in since the regulations [regarding blockade running] went into effect." Prices for the retail goods obtained from this shipment were "very high," but by the fourth spring of the war large and consistent profits from scarce products had themselves grown scarce.[19]

Nothing damaged Petersburg's economy more than inflation, fueled in part by a shortage of commodities. Edmund Ruffin, linking the blockade directly with rising prices and shrinking inventories, confessed in February 1863 that if "the prices of the necessaries of life continue to rise above present enormous rates, I . . . cannot see how the people or the government of the C[onfederate]. S[tates]. are to support the burden." Two months later the Prince George fire-eater sounded an even gloomier note: "It seems to me that our country & cause are now, for the first time during the war, in great peril of defeat—& not from the enemy's arms, but from the scarcity & high prices of provisions."[20]

Shortage's stepbrother—speculation—also bedeviled most Petersburgers, who deeply resented the prospect of anyone growing rich by exploiting the suffering masses or at the expense of independence. "Fabulous wealth— if Confederate paper is wealth—has attended the investments of some," wrote one Rebel officer in March 1863. "Everyone who is out of the service is bit by a mania that . . . has stifled every sense of patriotism & driven them into that most hateful of vices, making haste to get rich for the sake of dazzling the eyes of more honest & less successful neighbors."[21]

Most communities across the Confederacy grappled with rising prices and shrinking inventories. A proliferation of paper currency, production shortages caused by the diversion of labor to military use, and deficit government spending created economic misery. Reduced agricultural output, combined with the effects of the blockade and deterioration of the domestic transportation network, only worsened the crisis. The catastrophic Appomattox River flood of April 1864, which destroyed newly planted crops and ruined food stored in riverfront warehouses, only exacerbated the problem in Petersburg. By mid-1863 prices had increased nearly eightfold. Salaries failed to keep pace. The result, of course, was a level of economic privation that exceeded any depression or panic endured before the war.[22]

A comparison of Petersburg prices between the winter of 1863 and the spring of 1864 illustrates the dramatic nature of inflation during the midwar months. Renting a hotel room rose from six dollars per night to thirty dollars, with commensurate increases in the costs of restaurant meals. Butter prices that brought howls from consumers at four dollars per pound in October 1863 went up to fifteen dollars per pound seven months later. Eggs grew scarce, as their price increase of nearly 1,500 percent between October and March would suggest. Flour increased from seventy-five dollars to three hundred dollars per barrel; beef from thirty cents to four dollars per pound; meal from twelve dollars per bushel to forty dollars.

In the spring of 1864 milk in Petersburg cost two dollars a quart, shad five dollars each, and turkey three dollars and bacon more than seven dollars per pound. Firewood cut and delivered demanded twenty-two dollars per cord. One soldier paid twenty-one dollars for a diary and eight dollars for a single watermelon. A pair of shoes cost sixty dollars and a tooth extraction three dollars in the late summer of 1863. Families depending on salaries that lagged grotesquely behind the cost of everyday items found themselves impoverished by the challenges of daily living. One Petersburg clergyman sold his horse, vital for his work, because he could not afford to feed it.[23]

Petersburgers responded in a variety of ways to the dearth of affordable supplies. Sources of protein unthinkable earlier in the war occasionally found their way onto Petersburg tables, government officials ensuring hungry citizens that when properly prepared, mice and rats could be as tasty as squirrels. Sheep head soup proved both palatable and cheap. Citizens accustomed to relying on ice shipped from Maine relearned the art of cutting ice from local ponds.[24]

In an effort to curb speculation and price gouging by middlemen, the Petersburg Common Council prohibited persons living within ten miles of the city from offering fresh foodstuffs at market unless grown by the sellers. "The farmers are too busy to come themselves, or send their servants," observed one local editor, so they "are compelled to keep their products until it suits them to come to town." The result, predictably, only worsened shortages and fueled price increases.[25]

"The minds of the people are now absorbed in the question of how they are to live at the present rate of prices," wrote Charles Campbell in the autumn of 1863. "Unless some remedy is provided there must be terrible outbreaks of increased disaffection." In fact, violence had threatened to erupt in Petersburg in early April. A group of women, primarily soldiers' wives, organized a protest against the scarcity of affordable food that included plans for looting stores and warehouses. Authorities discovered the scheme, hatched on April 1, and limited its impact. Similar but more disruptive episodes in Richmond, Mobile, and Salisbury, North Carolina—styled "bread riots"—demonstrated that Petersburg's muted reaction to the suffering was hardly unique.[26]

The war's economic impact shook the foundations of Southern life and compelled women to weigh all kinds of purchasing decisions more carefully. "Am afraid to buy negroes . . . in view of the uncertainty of such property in the present condition of the country to say nothing of their high price," wrote one Petersburger. Bessie Meade Callender, who was married to a cotton mill manager, thought "it was laughable to see the home made clothes used."[27]

Petersburg authorities dealt with the midwar economic crisis through various means. The common council steadily increased the welfare budget to benefit soldiers' families who otherwise relied on the meager and irregular salaries that distant volunteers sent home. In June 1863 the total monthly allocation rose 25 percent, to $5,000. This figure increased to $10,000 in October and then doubled again in February 1864. At its March 1 meeting the council appropriated $15,000 for relief, which it supplemented three weeks later with another $25,000. Inflation naturally reduced the buying power of such seemingly lavish spending, but the public dole spared many Petersburg families from starvation.[28]

In addition to providing devalued cash to the needy, the city took steps to outflank inflation by directly supplying poor families with the necessities of life, including firewood. The city purchased at least 2,700 cords of fuel for the poor and the families of soldiers during the second half of 1863. Such assistance required contracts not only with timber owners but with the railroads who hauled the wood to town, placing another burden on the overworked trains.

Buying food for the poor proved more problematic because Petersburg had to compete with the national government for scarce edibles. The Richmond authorities began meeting the growing need for army supplies by impressing foodstuffs from farmers throughout Virginia and North Carolina. Fortunately, Confederate commissary officers and municipal purchasing agents discovered that food supplies were usually adequate for both the army and the families of soldiers in Petersburg. Eventually the secretary of war gave permission to exempt all food purchased by city agents from Confederate impressment. "The common council . . . have sent out committee men to buy beef, corn, hogs & c to be sold to citizens at cost—an excellent scheme for the city," commented one resident in the fall of 1863. The council provided certificates good for five pounds of beef to the head of each needy white family once every two weeks.[29]

Such measures could not completely alleviate the suffering of Petersburg's dependent population. A number of prominent local citizens supplemented the city's efforts to sustain the poor. In early November a food distribution center, which Charles Campbell called the soup house, opened at the Virginia Engine House on West Tabb Street. The railroad president William T. Joynes, the wounded veteran Anthony M. Keiley, and the Reverend William Hoge, newly installed pastor at the Tabb Street Presbyterian Church, spearheaded the effort. The organizers hoped to purchase supplies from the city at bargain prices for free distribution to those most in need.

Residents a little more fortunate could buy tickets that provided them a discount from prevailing market prices. A quart of soup and a half loaf of baker's bread could be obtained for just twenty cents under this subsidized system.

Fund-raising lectures that the famous Richmond preacher Moses Drury Hoge (William Hoge's father) delivered at his son's church, along with private subscriptions, helped sustain the soup house. The quality of the service, unfortunately, declined over the winter as demand increased and charitable contributions dwindled. The soup prepared at the kitchen was "very hot with red pepper; has small black bugs floating in it perhaps from the cabbage & has an unsavory smell," reported Charles Campbell. Some of the poor children ungratefully (if honestly) referred to this preparation as hog wash. Nevertheless, by the spring of 1864 no fewer than seven hundred residents relied on the soup house. An estimated sixty thousand meals had been served there since November. These persons, "cut off from this source of supply, would suffer untold horrors from hunger and want," wrote the *Petersburg Daily Express*.[30]

A mass meeting on March 15 at the First Baptist Church assumed an air of desperation as the organizers sought to keep the soup house functioning. "Surely an institution which relieves the destitute, without wounding their self respect, will not be allowed to fall through for want of means!" exhorted the town's *Daily Register*. "We hope . . . that the benevolent Managers will find themselves . . . provided with ample funds that will enable them to relieve all worthy applicants, and spare the necessity of refusing food to famishing families of women and children—destitute, not through any fault of their own, but innocent victims to the direful necessities of a bloody and protracted war for the preservation of our property and our liberties."[31]

In addition to firewood and food, salt grew more precious with each passing day. The city and the state combined to relieve Petersburg citizens of a crippling lack of this irreplaceable preservative. Virginia maintained a reasonable quota system for distributing salt to various communities, but obtaining and transporting it from the salt works in the southwestern part of the state became increasingly difficult in 1863. The common council authorized the lease or purchase of ten slaves in October "to be sent to the salt works [to procure] the share of salt to be distributed to the city." Government-owned salt, like other necessities, was either provided free to the needy or sold at cost to those with means. As Union cavalry raids compromised Virginia's reliable salt supply, the city implemented a rationing program to cope with growing, if intermittent, shortages.[32]

Petersburg did not limit its welfare responsibilities to civilians. The city continued to appropriate funds to supplement Confederate supplies provided to local soldiers in the field. In February 1864 the common council spent $6,200 to purchase shoes for Petersburg units. Company K of the Twelfth Virginia Infantry, for example, received 102 pairs of socks and 51 pairs of drawers in March compliments of the city.[33]

The state and national governments also took steps to address inflation. In the fall of 1863 Confederate authorities attempted to fix prices on all items the government purchased from usual sources in Southern cities. The Virginia legislature considered similar restrictions on state procurement. Price controls predictably floundered.

In a renewed effort to defeat inflation, Congress framed legislation in February 1864 intended to increase tax collection. More revenue would presumably reduce reliance on the printing of more and more paper money, ever the fundamental source of inflation. These measures were "the exciting topics of the day" in Petersburg and seemed to learned men such as Charles Campbell to promise relief. But the new laws had no effect on the economic crisis. "The first result of the finance & tax bills has not been to lower, but to raise prices," observed Edmund Ruffin. "Provisions & articles of necessary use rose immediately." One month after the acts took effect, Campbell described prices in Petersburg as "monstrous" and noted that the new tax laws "appear to be very onerous & uniquely so upon bank & railroad stocks often the chief income of widows & orphans."[34]

Coping with privation was merely the most pervasive of many challenges Petersburgers faced during the middle of the war. Breakdowns in family life and their sad consequences resulted directly from economic crisis. The absence of soldier-fathers, mothers compelled by poverty to seek jobs in local factories, the presence of thousands of rough-hewn soldiers (removed from the gentling influence of home and family), and the interruption of the controls that rigidly regulated African Americans all contributed to a rising crime rate. Most of the felonies involved property crimes or nonlethal assaults. Among the more infamous incidents was the burning of the North Carolina Hospital in April 1863, an act that destroyed the building.[35]

Adolescents too young for military service but old enough to navigate the streets alone frequently found trouble with the law. In July 1863 two fourteen-year-old boys engaged in a vicious fight. One of the combatants, David Grimstead, died from a blow to the head administered by young Walter Quarles, an almost incomprehensible tragedy for David's mother, who had recently lost her husband at the battle of Gettysburg while another soldier-son lay ill in a Richmond hospital. Youngsters might be found on any given night loitering around the entrance to Phoenix Hall, "smoking rotten cigars and using profane and obscene language . . . while they are awaiting a chance for admittance" through cadged tickets. "A boy allowed to see the scenes and mingle with the idle and dissipated that haunt the streets of a large city at night will soon unblushingly follow the evil example and add one more traveler on the 'road to ruin,'" warned one newspaper editorial.[36]

Theft presented a constant threat. One wealthy Petersburg lady wore her jewelry whenever she left her house for fear that her gems would be stolen if left at home unattended. Less valuable property was also at risk. The *Daily Register* humorously described one incident involving the theft of ducks by a Petersburg slave. The crime was discovered when "an uproarious quacking among the ducks" alerted their owners to foul play. The thief received twenty-five lashes, but the owner failed to reclaim his ducks, they having gone "to that bourne from whence no duck ever returns."[37]

Many petty criminals were remanded to the city jail, a notoriously porous and poorly supplied facility. The Petersburg Common Council in January 1863 appropriated funds to provide "suitable bed covering and other essential comforts for the prisoners." Such amenities failed to dissuade inmates from escaping. Governor Smith expressed concern in January 1864 that jails in the Petersburg area circuit suffered from far too many breakouts. The presiding judge promised to investigate, deferring, however, to the local authorities to improve the facilities, a task made difficult by a shortage of funds and labor.[38]

Transient troops and those who served them accounted for an increasing percentage of Petersburg crime. Edmund Ruffin complained of bands of Petersburg-based soldiers who roamed the countryside plundering neighborhood farms. Drunken soldiers caused trouble on the streets, in the taverns, and in the houses of prostitution, whose employees predictably behaved as less-than-model citizens.[39]

More often than not, Petersburg crime centered on blacks. Tales of theft, burglary, and illegal congregation filled columns in local newspapers. One spring day in 1864 the *Daily Register* sarcastically reported an unusually empty docket in the mayor's court. "The darkies kept within bounds the night before, and the police had a quiet night," explained the paper. The case of sixteen-year-old Elvira, a slave girl convicted of trying to poison her mistress, certainly spoke to slaveholder insecurities that the war only served to elevate. Runaway slaves captured in the area were imprisoned by night and then used as laborers during the day until their owners claimed them, slightly reducing the demand for local impressment. Most African Americans in Petersburg, of course, avoided criminal activity. They suffered the trials of life in the wartime Confederacy with the rest of the population, although they started with far less than the whites and only grew more destitute.[40]

The sight of an idle, healthy African American in wartime Petersburg was as rare as it was despised (and implicitly feared) by white authorities. Labor shortages caused by military service opened almost unlimited employment opportunities for free blacks and provided slave owners numerous options to lease their chattels for industrial work. Black employment on Petersburg's railroads increased throughout the war. The number of African

Americans working for the Petersburg Railroad increased from 121 in 1861 to 150 in 1862 and to 191 in 1863. By 1864 the railroad engaged 265 blacks in various skilled and unskilled pursuits, ranging from tracklayers and laborers to carpenters, machine shop workers, painters, and firemen. Blacks, both free and enslaved, also found ready work at the local Confederate industrial facilities.[41]

Enterprising African Americans, particularly women, earned a living selling to Confederate soldiers stationed around the Cockade City. Obtaining vegetables, sweets, and meat in a variety of ways (most of them, presumably, aboveboard), these vendors found an eager market among hungry soldiers with money in their pockets. Occasionally, however, these independent peddlers ran afoul of their customers. In July 1863 some African Americans visited the camp of the Forty-ninth North Carolina Infantry, selling meat that they advertised as pork. Somehow the Tarheels became convinced that the flesh was canine in origin. The soldiers seized two females and flogged them thirty-nine times with a leather strap in imitation of civil justice routinely administered to slaves. "I don't think they will bring any more Dog stew to the 49th soon again," bragged one of the soldiers.[42]

Not all of the work of Petersburg's black females was voluntary. In September 1863 the Confederate government impressed fifty free black women to collect forage for animals stabled in Petersburg. They were confined overnight in the city jail to ensure their availability the next day, which reduced many of these proud, law-abiding ladies to tears. Charles Campbell observed that in general Petersburg's African Americans suffered from the same wartime anxiety and depression that whites experienced: "Laughter is much less frequent among them than formerly."[43]

The need to build and maintain fortifications imposed the war's most onerous burden on Petersburg's blacks. Legislation passed in October 1862 and amended the following spring established a quota system and strict regulations to administer the mandatory defense-building labor of Virginia slaves. Not only did this policy remove African Americans from their homes for weeks, it created inconvenience and even economic hardship for slave owners who needed the labor. Free blacks were also subject to compulsory government service, requirements made more stringent in February 1863 in response to complaints from slaveholders. Petersburg's quota numbered 100 out of 1,029 freemen required from twenty-four Virginia jurisdictions. The Confederate war effort spared no segment of its population, in Petersburg or anywhere in the South.

The first requisitions for slave labor bypassed Petersburg, although on January 22, 1863, Governor Letcher called on the Cockade City to provide 230 slaves for duty on the trenches. The absence of agricultural workers in the surrounding counties, especially during the winter, would hurt Confed-

erate productivity less than depriving Petersburg businesses of their work-
forces. Thus the slave quotas for neighboring Dinwiddie County numbered
320 and for Chesterfield County 350. Protests from slaveholders reduced
these requisitions, and as of March 23, 168 Petersburg slaves had been conscripted for military labor. The government impressed another 120 bondsmen in January 1864. The law made male slaves aged eighteen to fifty-five
liable for service, although no more than 20 percent of a jurisdiction's eligible slave population could serve simultaneously. Local courts selected
which slaveholders would provide labor in return for compensation of
twenty dollars per month. The Petersburg Common Council also appropriated funds to pay slave owners for the use of their human property.[44]

There is little testimony regarding the reaction of impressed blacks to
their compulsory service. Some did attempt an escape to Federal lines. Others suffered under unusual working conditions, often harsher than those to
which they were accustomed. The record is more fulsome regarding slave
owner resistance to impressment. Many masters resented government interference with their bondsmen as much as they did conscription. The refusal of Petersburg's slaveholding community to comply with the law in the
spring of 1864 impelled City Sergeant John H. Patterson to issue a published
warning: "Persons who have failed to send slaves to labor on fortifications as
required by the order of the Court are notified to deliver the slave or slaves
drafted to me at the Courthouse on Monday the 7th instant by 5 o'clock . . .
or I shall be compelled to seize said slaves, and the owners will be subject to
fine and costs."[45]

If the faltering economy failed to remind Petersburgers that they were a
society at war, the presence of soldiers in gray—and blue—certainly did. The
Cockade City welcomed a never-ending stream of Confederate units, some
transient and others for the local garrison, throughout 1863 and early 1864.
The early war excitement about the arrival of soldiers had long since passed.
Military strangers had become a part of everyday life, and for the most part
Confederate troops integrated into Petersburg routines. Some, such as one
Georgia soldier in March 1863, blended so well that he took a local girl for his
wife. Other out-of-town volunteers wooed Petersburg women with success, if
not to the extent of marriage. "We have a number of South Carolina officers
here, who are great ladies men," reported one Virginia soldier, "& the girls are
much exercised about them." Virginians were no less popular. "Most of the
fellows are ladies men here now," wrote one member of the Thirty-second
Virginia Infantry, "with courting & flirting they pass away the time."[46]

Less innocently, Confederate soldiers in Petersburg fell prey to the temptations typically found around army bivouacs. Brothels did a booming business in the city's commercial districts. Bored soldiers on their way through
town who did not patronize these establishments often sprawled on the

sidewalks and in the yards of residents, sometimes stealing or acting in a disorderly manner. Alcohol proved the greatest source of trouble. Charles Campbell often saw intoxicated troops wandering the streets, one even coming to his home, "too drunk to be very troublesome." Although previous attempts to prohibit the sale of liquor had failed, some Petersburgers renewed the effort to make their city dry. "You have the power to save our soldiers and young men from drunkenness & degradation, our mothers & sisters will bless you—if you will only shut up all the grog shops," wrote an anonymous resident to Governor William Smith. "The only party that will croak against you are the miserable speculators . . . our city jail and guard house will show the results of the above."[47]

Union prisoners passing through Petersburg had once attracted throngs of derisive citizens eager to taunt the humbled enemies of the Confederacy. In 1863 and 1864 Federal prisoners of war continued to trek through town, sometimes in huge numbers, but their presence no longer elicited much notice. Perhaps the novelty of viewing "live Yankees" had merely worn off, or maybe the hardships of the war taught Petersburgers a little humility in the presence of the humbled. One English observer watched in midwar as roughly 450 paroled Union prisoners marched through Petersburg heading for City Point and exchange. The men were guarded by fifty Confederate soldiers who allowed them to amble "like a mob" through town while changing trains from the Richmond depot to the City Point line. A docile, if scowling, collection of women, children, and African Americans gathered as they walked through town, and "not a word of insult was uttered on one side, or retort on the other," reported the foreigner.

Several thousand prisoners captured in the battles around Chattanooga, Tennessee, arrived in Petersburg during the fall of 1863 en route from Georgia to Richmond. Charles Campbell thought these western Federals looked "strong & robust," and he commented on their slouch hats and "Yankee impudence," evoking attitudes and adjectives used early in the war. Some of the bluecoats obligingly agreed to exchange greenbacks for Confederate dollars at a rate of one to ten, underscoring the lack of devotion in Petersburg to the national currency.[48]

From time to time a Union captive would be confined in the military prison on Bank Street, usually reserved for miscreants caught by the local provost guard. One of these Northerners managed to escape, but he was soon caught "in a negro house near the Old Market," a subtle reminder of the possible collusion between Union soldiers and local African Americans. When one Federal captive asked to attend church services in Petersburg he was permitted to visit St Paul's, where, perhaps for his benefit, the officer heard "a bitter tirade upon the North" from the pulpit. Petersburg, however, never became a prison town.[49]

Church attendance, in addition to its spiritual benefits, provided social diversion for many Petersburgers. A small, elite portion of Petersburg society managed more lavish entertainment, despite wartime hardships. The daughters of Petersburg's wealthy business leaders, abetted by the men of the class disqualified for military service by reason of age, infirmity, or exemption, assumed the lead in midwar Petersburg social life. Girls such as Mary Tabb Bolling, Molly and Anne Banister, Alice Gregory, Betty and Jean Osborne, Betty Cabaniss, Betty and Lucy Page, Sally Hardy, Nannie Cocke, Patty Cowles, and Julia, Mary, and Marion Meade tried as best they could to enjoy the heady days of youthful courtship and flirtation amid wartime privations and a dearth of local suitors.[50]

The surplus of eligible women provided amusement for younger resident officers such as Captain Charles H. Dimmock of the Confederate engineers. Dimmock loved a girl from Tidewater Virginia, and he pursued her in a spirited suit through frequent correspondence. He occasionally attempted to excite jealousy and accelerate the pace of their romance by suggesting how irresistible he had become to the Petersburg social set. "I have made many delightful acquaintances here," he boasted in one of his love letters.

Dimmock regaled his lady love throughout 1863 with tales of wonderful Petersburg parties. "I have almost broken myself down attending," he explained in January, "for you know old legs can't continue a caper as long as young ones." In addition to *soirees* hosted by the female socialites and those visiting from out of town (such as the Baker sisters from Norfolk who threw "quite an affair" at the Bollingbrook Hotel), local industrialists opened their homes for memorable celebrations. William Ransom Johnson shared his good fortune in selling what Dimmock estimated to be three hundred thousand dollars of tobacco in March 1863 by sponsoring "the grandest supper I ever attended." Johnson invited "the lofty & lowly, rich & poor, distinguished & obscure." Dimmock described the menu with shameless enthusiasm. "In times of profound peace, when the luxuries of the world were accessible, there was never a more sumptuous affair," he wrote. "Champagne seemed to have run the blockade in indefinite quantities & rockfish of admired proportions, lay amid the butter, eggs & parsley as though in their native element." Johnson rolled out successive courses featuring wild duck, turkey, and partridge "until one was disposed to lament at the advance of each new dish, having eaten so much of the one that had preceded it."[51]

Another Petersburg gala, hosted about the same time as Johnson's elaborate gathering, did not come off so well. The twenty-nine-year-old James E. Collier, a former Petersburg city collector, married one of the tobacco magnate Reuben Ragland's daughters in the winter of 1863. The proud father of the bride threw an extravagant party, inviting both local citizens and army officers. The liquor flowed. Right after the dessert table collapsed in a heap of broken crockery and glassware, two of the guests engaged in a brawl, which resulted in one of the pugilists suffering a knife wound. "These men getting drunk and fighting at [Ragland's] house will not enhance the social position of his family," wryly observed one amused Petersburger. Occasionally, officers imitated their civilian neighbors and celebrated with excess, such as the Christmas party that Dr. John Claiborne hosted in 1863, featuring eggnog and whiskey punch for all in attendance. Charles Campbell enjoyed a family Christmas menu that year of ham, turkey, pumpkin pie, dried peach pie, and sponge cake and sauce, all washed down with blackberry wine.[52]

Petersburg's debutantes were not alone in seeking male companionship. Older women in varying states of economic distress, both maidens and war widows, sought husbands to help them share life's increasing burdens. The stakes of this romantic game ran high, and the ladies resorted to every available stratagem. John W. Syme, a fifty-three-year-old Petersburg native who had edited several local newspapers before the war, returned from Raleigh in October 1863 and began publishing the *Daily Register*. Famous for his independent voice and willingness to criticize the Confederate government, Syme also had words of wisdom for Petersburg's older eligible women during the social season of 1864. He warned the ladies about using rouge to attract men, citing the health risks of such cosmetics. More pointedly, the editor reminded these women that "bachelors are a shy game and when convinced of one deception being practiced, imagine many more . . . in their alarmed imaginations."[53]

Public places of entertainment attracted city residents in significant numbers. The once popular Newmarket race track east of town reopened in November 1863, but within two weeks Charles Campbell had pronounced the season "a complete failure." More successful were performances at Phoenix Hall, particularly plays such as *The Fate of a Coquette* and *Lady of Lyon* starring the popular actress Katie Estelle. Ticket prices escalated but remained within reach of the middle class. In March 1864, for example, a gentleman and his lady could purchase two reserved seats for $3.00, a single admission for an unaccompanied man cost $2.50, and African Americans might sit in the "colored gallery" for $1.50 each.[54]

Higher-brow entertainment might often be found at Library Hall, where visiting scholars lectured on academic topics or current affairs. The Reverend Doctor Leyburn, for example, spoke in the winter of 1864 about his journeys to Palestine. Dr. John A. Broadus no doubt thrilled his audience with a discourse entitled "The State of the Roman Empire at the Opening of the New Testament History." Confederate Senator J. L. M. Curry of Alabama held forth on the topic "Political Quicksands," in the process providing (according to one listener) "an able defense of the slaveholding system" and drawing "a parallel or contrast between [Benjamin] Butler & Stonewall Jackson as types at North & South."[55]

Sometimes these presentations doubled as fund-raisers to benefit Confederate troops. Occasionally a Petersburg clergyman would open his church for a public lecture designed either as a charitable undertaking or aimed at lifting drooping spirits. In this vein, T. V. Moore lectured on General Thomas J. Jackson at the Tabb Street Presbyterian Church shortly after Stonewall's death. An average admission charge of one dollar at Library Hall and free seats with a collection at church-sponsored talks suggest that it was often cheaper to be informed than entertained.[56]

Several dignitaries visited Petersburg during the war's middle years, some with public agendas but all creating a public stir. Governor-elect William Smith came to the city in October 1863 to speak at Phoenix Hall. Earlier in the month citizens took note as President Jefferson Davis changed trains in Petersburg, en route to Georgia and the troubled high command of the Army of Tennessee. Former Vice President of the United States John C. Breckinridge, then a Confederate general, garnered attention when he spent the night at the Bollingbrook Hotel in January 1864 while on his way to the capital.[57]

Accomplished visitors of a less famous pedigree descended on Petersburg in late December 1863. The Association of Teachers in Richmond and Petersburg sponsored a statewide educational convention that drew fifty of the leading instructors in Virginia to discuss the acute educational crisis that wartime shortages created. A. J. Leavenworth, William T. Davis, and William B. Carr handled the arrangements for Petersburg, with Charles Campbell serving as the local housing coordinator. The railroads supported the convention by offering free return passage to all in attendance. The outgoing governor, John Letcher, provided the keynote address. The educators met for three days and formed the Virginia Teacher's Association, which Charles Campbell thought would "result in good effects"—a surprisingly optimistic position for a society at war.[58]

Many of these teachers would train the nascent republic's future citizens, although wartime politics offered important lessons in political socialization. Four elections—local, statewide, and national—occurred between the springs of 1863 and 1864. The Petersburg Common Council maintained its normal spring election cycle throughout the war. Voters cast ballots by ward, the top six candidates in each winning seats. As usual, Petersburg's citizens reelected most of the incumbents during the war's middle years, including the popular mayor W. W. Townes, who ran unopposed both times. The council selected its own officers, choosing from their ranks a recorder, senior alderman, and ten aldermen who served on the Hustings Court. Every incumbent alderman earned reappointment in 1864.[59]

The council's committee appointments revealed its stable power structure as well as the nature of midwar municipal services. D'Arcy Paul ran the Finance Committee, J. T. Young was in charge of the Streets Committee, and Alexander Donnan chaired the Gas Committee in 1864. Wesley Grigg, Charles Corling, and Harmon W. Siggins presided over the Public Property, Water Works, and Fire Committees, respectively. William L. Watkins took control of the Claims Committee and Samuel Lecture oversaw the Cemetery Committee, a distressingly busy job in 1864. The council also appointed trustees for the East Ward Free School, City Free School, and Anderson Seminary, as well as men to govern the Board of Health and administer aid to the poor. Although life in Petersburg changed drastically during the war, the same class of men who ran the city in 1860 continued to guide it.[60]

A special canvass took place during the summer of 1863. On July 2 William Joynes won an eight-year term as the judge of the Second Judicial Circuit. Joynes's new jurisdiction included Petersburg and seven surrounding counties. Joynes replaced Judge Thomas Saunders Gholson, who had stepped down from the bench to vie for a seat in the Confederate Congress in what turned out to be a bitter contest with the incumbent, Charles Fenton Collier.[61]

Collier had represented Petersburg and Virginia's Fourth District in the Confederate Congress since 1862, when he replaced General Roger Atkinson Pryor. The secessionist wave in 1861 had drowned Collier's prewar unionism, and he had allied himself with the Davis administration early in his tenure. By 1863, however, Collier aligned with the faction that generally opposed Davis's efforts to assert strong national power. Collier broke with the president over taxes, conscription, and impressment. Gholson, in contrast, had been an early proponent of secession while sitting as a state judge before the war, and he was viewed in 1863 as a Davis ally. Gholson enjoyed the support of the powerful James Seddon, Confederate secretary of war, who had been an unsuccessful candidate for Pryor's seat in 1862. The election shaped up as a referendum on Davis's administration.

To make matters more interesting, the Gholsons and Colliers had been political enemies prior to the war. Gholson's brother was also a judge, and Collier's father represented Petersburg in the Virginia State Senate. Bad blood between these families led to a vitriolic exchange of pamphlets in the antebellum years, so the 1863 election promised to be spirited.

Gholson won by a razor-thin margin of twenty-seven votes. Much of the judge's support came from soldiers—which prompted Collier's father, Robert R. Collier, to send Governor Letcher a twelve-page inquiry regarding the propriety of counting certain military ballots. The Colliers argued that votes from soldiers not residing in the district had been tallied in Gholson's column. They also presented a laundry list of technical irregularities that, in their view, invalidated the election. Letcher and his secretary of the commonwealth, George Wythe Munford, fielded numerous, if polite, complaints along these lines from both Colliers, the last one dated July 20, 1863—more than two months after the polls had closed. Their protests ultimately fell on deaf ears. Gholson took his seat in Richmond, and Charles Collier retired to his post on Petersburg's common council.[62]

Virginians also elected a new governor in May 1863. This contest, in contrast to the congressional campaign, elicited relatively little heat in Petersburg or throughout the state. The former governor and Confederate brigadier general William "Extra Billy" Smith triumphed, taking office on January 1, 1864.[63]

Like every newly elected governor, Smith faced a flood of requests for executive patronage, with Petersburg aspirants as numerous as those from any city. The governor dispensed with the routine appointments of bank directors: Petersburg's familiar business and government leaders filled these offices, as they had earlier in the war. The office of inspector of tobacco had similar low-stakes status, with nominees usually rubber-stamped by the governor. In 1863 these portfolios had become coveted due to their potential for earning a military exemption, but Smith's refusal to relieve tobacco inspectors from the draft reduced interest in these jobs.[64]

Military service—and how to avoid it—remained a central issue among residents eligible for the army. Duty in the militia frequently interrupted civilian pursuits, while impressed blacks continued to march off periodically to work on the fortifications around town. Rarely was compulsory service viewed kindly by those expected to perform it. "The calling out of the militia gives rise to much complaint & grumbling," observed Charles Campbell in August 1863. "Croakers are busy & many persons are desponding if not despairing of the Confederate cause." Officers sometimes went door-to-door to collect militiamen who failed to report for musters. In June the seizing of African American factory workers for fatigue duty around Butterworth's Bridge southwest of town elicited similar resistance. Several of these men risked severe punishment by attempting to escape, while Charles Campbell watched "a negro woman crying probably because her husband had been impressed."[65]

An examination of the efficacy of conscription in Virginia's Fourth Congressional District during the late spring of 1863 reveals both the limited results of the draft and the means by which men avoided military service. Approximately 1,449 names appeared on the conscription rolls at this time, but only 488, about one-third, entered the Confederate military. Nearly 30 percent of the draftees provided substitutes; 13 percent received exemptions based on their employment on the railroads; 14 percent avoided service because they managed twenty or more slaves; and 11 percent held government jobs that relieved them of army duty.[66]

The growing need for army manpower as the war approached the end of its third year prompted a patriotic New Year's Day editorial from the *Army and Navy Messenger*, a publication sponsored by the Evangelical Tract Society of Petersburg to circulate "the pure word of God." The editor complimented Congress on abolishing substitution by which "a man was enabled to sell a negro, a bale of cotton or barrel of whiskey, buy a white man, and thus remain at home to acquire a fabulous fortune." He also suggested several means of increasing the pool of eligible men, including the revocation of details and exemptions for youthful government functionaries, the enlistment of refugees from Europe or the North who were engaged in profiteering, the arrest of all "deserters and skulkers," and "conscription of all vagabonds, black-legs, pimps, and *sans-culottes* of the cities (plug-uglies, garroters and blood-tubs, admirable 'food for powder' who ought to be fond of martial exercises)."[67]

While most draft-aged men in Petersburg sought to avoid military service (after the early war rush to volunteer), there were exceptions. The Reverend William Henry Wheelwright, a Methodist minister, had resigned his commission in the Twenty-sixth Virginia Infantry in 1862, and by virtue of his clerical tasks was no longer liable for active service. "Realizing the weighty issues pending and acknowledging in mind and heart the duty of every one to contribute his part to our country's cause, I feel anxious to put myself in the way to be used as Providence may indicate," Wheelwright wrote the governor. Smith informed the minister that he had no suitable place for him, but ultimately Wheelwright took the field as a chaplain in the Ninth Virginia Cavalry.[68]

In April 1864 the citizens of Petersburg unknowingly balanced on the cusp of momentous change. Within weeks the full fury of military combat would descend on them, changing their lives in ways they could hardly imagine. Through the war's middle years, though, they coped with social, economic, and political issues only indirectly related to hostile fire. Morale in town rose and fell largely in proportion to the success of the Confederate military, particularly the Army of Northern Virginia, in which so many local soldiers served. Petersburgers gleaned their information about the war from Union prisoners, newspapers (including Northern periodicals obtained in a variety of ways), and witnesses who had visited the front lines.

General Robert E. Lee's victory at Chancellorsville in May 1863, tempered as it was by the death of Stonewall Jackson, propelled the Army of Northern Virginia north, where it came to grief near Gettysburg, Pennsylvania. Ironically, preliminary reports from Pennsylvania and Mississippi, where the fate of Vicksburg hung in the balance, had generated great optimism in Petersburg. Rumors of forty thousand Union prisoners at Gettysburg and victory at Vicksburg filled the streets. Reports of a Yankee retreat toward Baltimore and the Confederate liberation of Maryland all too soon gave way to a more accurate accounting of Confederate misfortunes. By July 11 Petersburgers knew the grim truth about Lee's disastrous Pennsylvania campaign and the fall of Vicksburg.

From this point on Petersburgers exhibited diminishing optimism about the war. Fantastic stories about drafting old men in South Carolina, a by-product of the unpopular expedient of conscription, further depressed sagging spirits. Even the news in September 1863 of Confederate victory at the battle of Chickamauga produced little elation in Petersburg. Some linked Confederate military reverses to "covetousness, avarice & selfishness" among civilians, and men such as Charles Campbell began to see the origin of ultimate defeat in the behavior of the citizens at home, indications of cracks in the national resolve that appeared elsewhere in the South.[69]

Despite this perception of Confederate decline, the spring of 1864 brought a renewal of hope both to Lee's army and to Petersburgers. Winter snows gave way to warm breezes and the promise of bountiful gardens and military victories. Confederate armies in North Carolina had campaigned successfully during the winter; Lee's forces had recovered from their Gettysburg defeat and were ready to take the field in northern Virginia; and Dr. Claiborne, from his office in Petersburg, thought that "things are still bright for our sky . . . and a glorious peace in the perspective. . . . The people are cheerful, seem to have no fear of failure in our spring campaign." Charles Campbell felt less sure. "We are on the eve of great events," he wrote on April 29, 1864. The Civil War knew no truer prophecy.[70]

⌐ 6 ⌐

"I Must Confess That I Am More Concerned for Petersburg Than for Richmond"

THE CONFEDERATE MILITARY IN PETERSBURG
JANUARY 1863–APRIL 1864

THE PETERSBURG headquarters of the Department of North Carolina bustled with activity during the first week of January 1863, animated by two threats from numerically superior Union opponents. The department commander, Samuel G. French, believed that as many as forty thousand Federal soldiers around New Bern, North Carolina, two hundred miles south of Petersburg, had plans to disrupt the vital rail connection between Petersburg and Wilmington. Protecting these communications was French's primary mission. At the same time five thousand bluecoats drilled around Suffolk, Virginia, within two days' march of an alarmingly vulnerable Petersburg. French deployed his thirty-three thousand troops, more than one-third of whom defended Wilmington, as best he could to meet these dangers. French left Petersburg for North Carolina on January 5 to confront the anticipated Union offensive from New Bern. He also wired Secretary of War James Seddon, requesting up to fifteen thousand reinforcements for his department.[1]

Brigadier General Raleigh E. Colston now assumed command in Petersburg. Colston had recently arrived at the head of a brigade of Virginians from the western portion of the state. The general and all but one regiment of his brigade promptly left Petersburg, however, marching forty miles southeast toward the Blackwater River defense line, which marked the military frontier separating the Union forces at Suffolk from Confederate-held territory to the west. The local commander along the Blackwater, Brigadier General Roger A. Pryor of Petersburg, had dispatched his forces to North Carolina to help French deal with the brewing crisis south of the state line, leaving his bailiwick defenseless. Colston assigned his regiments to Pryor and promptly returned to Petersburg, where only Captain James F. Milligan's handful of scouts and signalmen, the Fifty-fifth North Carolina In-

fantry acting as the municipal provost guard, his Twenty-ninth Virginia Infantry, and an unfinished ring of fortifications guarded the city.[2]

The absence of an adequate garrison at Petersburg inspired state and
Confederate authorities to take urgent action. The War Department requested that Governor John Letcher activate the militia in Southside Virginia, should the Federals advance from North Carolina or Tidewater. On
January 8 Letcher issued a proclamation calling on men aged forty to forty-
five who were not subject to national conscription and who resided in Petersburg, Lynchburg, or one of fourteen neighboring counties to report to
Petersburg immediately for active service not to exceed six months. The governor specified the manner in which commanders would be selected, anticipating an excess of officers relative to the numbers in the ranks. The state
would bear all travel expenses and provide the militiamen with arms and
ammunition—but not uniforms—once they had been mustered. Letcher
specifically noted that bank officers and employees of transportation companies were exempt from the call.[3]

Although the prewar paper strength of these militia outfits amounted
to more than twenty thousand men, Letcher's January summons yielded far
fewer. Most white males of the proper ages in these Southside jurisdictions
pursued occupations that exempted them from military service. Only eighty
officers and men reported for duty, eliciting scant attention from either the
citizens and press of Petersburg or the local Confederate commanders. They
were employed primarily in guarding paroled prisoners awaiting exchange.
When regular units returned to Petersburg, the militia received their discharge effective March 30, 1863.[4]

To Colston and the civilian authorities, completion of the line of forts,
batteries, and infantry works bracketing three sides of the city was as important as strengthening the Petersburg garrison. The Petersburg Common
Council tried to provide the engineer officer Charles H. Dimmock with the
labor necessary to finish his work on these fortifications, getting a boost
from the late January conscription of African American laborers. As a sop
to begrudging slave owners, the War Department agreed to improve the
rations issued to slaves. The army had been dispensing a soldier's daily allotment to impressed slave laborers—one and one-half pounds of flour or
one and one-quarter pounds of meal, plus one-half pound of salt meat or one
pound of fresh meat per day. Dimmock and other officers received instructions to increase this ration, a small comfort to the workers, no doubt, but
not nearly enough to mollify most slave owners, whose absolute control of
their human property usually trumped their patriotism.[5]

In addition to managing increased manpower in the camps and on the
construction line, Colston also stepped up vigilance against a waterborne in-

vasion of Petersburg and the Virginia interior. In January he ordered Captain W. W. Roberts at City Point to establish a line of pickets along the James River shore in Prince George County. The Twenty-ninth Virginia Infantry and the Halifax (Virginia) Artillery took position around Coggin's Point to contest enemy landings.[6]

All these precautions proved unnecessary. The Federals launched no winter offensives in the Tarheel State or up the James. General Pryor initiated the only hostilities along the Blackwater River line, resulting in a spirited if strategically meaningless skirmish near Suffolk on January 30. Indeed, the most important military matter affecting Petersburg during the war's second winter involved the influence of two unhappy officers on the administrative command structure.[7]

Daniel Harvey Hill, the ranking officer at Petersburg the previous summer, had returned to the Army of Northern Virginia in August 1862. He gallantly led his division at South Mountain and Sharpsburg, Maryland, in September and at Fredericksburg in December. On January 1, 1863, Hill startled the army by submitting his resignation. "My strength and health are not sufficient for the proper discharge of my responsible duties," Hill explained. "I have been in service more than twenty months and have been habitually at my post, though I [have] never been free a single moment from pain . . . often of the most excruciating character." Hill's explanation possibly masked the real motivation for his resignation—disappointment with the government's decision to bypass him for promotion to lieutenant general.[8]

General Robert E. Lee hoped that his unhappy subordinate might be retained in service even though he was not particularly partial to the quarrelsome Carolinian. Perhaps a transfer to North Carolina as department commander would suit the purpose. Secretary of War Seddon, sharing Lee's desire to keep Hill in uniform, persuaded the general to repair to North Carolina on leave. Once rested he might be enticed to retake the field as commander in the Tarheel State. To this end, on January 17 Seddon informed North Carolina Governor Zebulon Vance in Raleigh that Hill was en route to recuperate and that the governor would be wise to seek his counsel on current military problems.[9]

Richmond's dissatisfaction with Major General Gustavus W. Smith—who, since September 1862, had exercised overall command of the vast territory between Richmond and Wilmington—also fueled interest in assigning Hill to the Department of North Carolina. Smith continued to sulk over his failure to receive promotion, muting his resentment even less than Hill. Smith went so far as to imply that he, rather than Lee, should have been named to command the Army of Northern Virginia when he returned to active duty the previous summer.

Smith's absurd hubris hardly endeared him to the authorities. The situation worsened in late January when an officer in North Carolina, where Smith had journeyed to advise French on the strategic landscape, privately conveyed to General Lee grave concerns about Smith's competence. Lee just as discreetly passed along these misgivings to President Jefferson Davis, indicating that he shared them. When Smith complained that his exertions in the field had impaired his health, Davis had the excuse he needed to recall the unhappy commander to Richmond. French resumed control of the troops in North Carolina, while Seddon lobbied with Hill to accept formal command of the state.[10]

Smith seethed under the perceived injustice of his situation, finally submitting his resignation on February 7. Davis eagerly accepted it. The same day the War Department named Hill as the head of the Department of North Carolina, including Petersburg, to which General French was once again assigned as local commander, supplanting Colston. Hill's authority as ranking departmental officer would be short-lived, as General French would remember: "I returned to Petersburg on [February] 23d. Gen. D. H. Hill, having no troops, was put in command of those in North Carolina, leaving me Southern Virginia. I found in Petersburg Lieut. Gen. [James] Longstreet."[11]

Strategic matters, not politics or personalities, brought the famous commander of the First Corps of the Army of Northern Virginia to Petersburg. General Lee had learned on February 14 that the Union Ninth Corps had boarded transports bound for Hampton Roads to reinforce the Federal Department of Virginia, commanded by Major General John A. Dix. With the muddy roads around Fredericksburg immobilizing the armies there, Lee decided to detach elements of Longstreet's corps to counter the Union shift.

Lee selected the divisions of Major Generals George E. Pickett and John Bell Hood for the mission, and he instructed Longstreet to accompany them as their immediate commander. Pickett's Division left the Rappahannock River on February 15 and Hood's followed shortly thereafter. Longstreet and his staff boarded trains bound for Richmond on the nineteenth and spent four days in the capital, meeting with the secretary of war and learning from him of the resignation of General Smith. From the moment he arrived in Richmond, authorities referred to Longstreet as the commander of the Department of Virginia and North Carolina. His official assignment to this new post occurred on February 25, two days after he established headquarters in Petersburg. Longstreet formally announced his appointment the following day.[12]

The military situation in early March complicated Longstreet's assignment, and considerable confusion existed regarding his administrative status. Although Longstreet communicated directly with the War Department in Richmond as befitting a department commander, Lee still considered his senior lieutenant and the divisions of Pickett and Hood as part of the Army of Northern Virginia and subject to his orders. Some organizational matters were clear: Major General William Henry Chase Whiting in Wilmington reported to Longstreet on paper, as did Hill in east-central North Carolina, French in Petersburg, Pryor along the Blackwater River, and Major General Arnold Elzey in the defenses of Richmond. The vague boundaries among these five officers' specific jurisdictions posed less of a problem for Longstreet than did his command relationship with Lee.

More troubling still, Longstreet faced conflicting responsibilities. Clearly, he was to defend Richmond and Petersburg from any offensive up the James River emanating from Fort Monroe—the Union base on the Peninsula. Lee also expected Longstreet to position Pickett and Hood for quick returns to the Army of Northern Virginia, in case Federal forces north of the Rappahannock should resume the offensive, while the War Department required Longstreet to gather foodstuffs in southeastern Virginia and northeastern North Carolina for the hungry troops in northern Virginia. He had to do all of this as he was assuming the core responsibilities of French's old command: protecting the line of the Blackwater River and the rail communications between Wilmington, Petersburg, and the Confederate capital. Although Petersburg served as a convenient logistical hub from which Longstreet might orchestrate his problematic command, the city was not his primary focus of attention. Not until April 1, when General Orders Number 34 spelled out the geographic limits of Longstreet's authority and named Lee as Longstreet's immediate superior, did the command uncertainties dissipate.[13]

French's newly designated Department of Southern Virginia included eight thousand officers and soldiers present for duty in early March, mostly deployed along the Blackwater River under Colston and Pryor. Colston's Twenty-ninth Virginia Infantry continued to watch the lower James River and support various artillery batteries positioned in key places east of Petersburg. Captain John H. Thompson took command of the forces at City Point, replacing Captain Roberts. Thompson had formerly led two hundred troops guarding the Model Farm on Petersburg's western outskirts, where paroled prisoners awaited exchange. Milligan's signal corps numbered approximately 130 men scattered in various posts, including Petersburg. French and Longstreet relied on only twenty-eight cavalrymen to patrol the entire Petersburg area.[14]

Pickett's Division passed through Petersburg on March 1 and encamped east of town, along the City Point Railroad at a place dubbed Camp French, and near Prince George Court House. Pickett added nearly seventy-five hundred men to the immediate defense of Petersburg. Hood's Division bivouacked north of the city.[15]

Routine military matters marked the early weeks of Longstreet's Petersburg tenure. He established a military court by February 26 to hear cases in-

James Longstreet (1821–1904). General Longstreet briefly commanded in Petersburg during the late winter and early spring of 1863, when he used the city as a
springboard for his Suffolk campaign. Longstreet returned to Petersburg during
the 1864–65 campaign and was with General Lee on April 2, 1865, the last day
Petersburg remained in Confederate hands. (Courtesy of Valentine Richmond
History Center)

volving desertion, drunkenness, and incompetence among his officers. Captain Charles M. Blackford presided over these proceedings at a building on
Bollingbrook Street.[16]

Soldiers in camp pursued their usual vices. Captain Virgil Parks of the
Seventeenth Georgia Infantry labored mightily to eradicate the pervasive
gambling games of "Kenos, Rouletts, 'Feather and Anchor', Chuckaluck,
Mexico, Flying Jinny, Seven up and Poker," which he thought undermined

the morality of his company. When he extracted a pledge from his men to forsake wagering, Parks became "unspeakably happy" and declared that there was not "a bad man" in his company. "I would that as much could be said of all Georgia troops," he added candidly. Longstreet's staff also confronted the high prices that plagued Petersburg citizens. The staff lieutenant Thomas J. Goree informed his mother on March 13 that he was boarding with a local family for seventy-five dollars per month. "You no doubt think this an enormous price, but it is less than is generally charged, and we find it cheaper than keeping up our mess with the present enormous prices of provisions," he wrote.[17]

Although General Longstreet prepared for offensive operations, he did not neglect the protection of Petersburg. The recent (and pending) requisitions of black labor pleased Captain Dimmock, who confirmed that the general had pledged to complete the defense line to the Appomattox River upstream from Petersburg—a two-month task according to Dimmock. "Our breastworks are quite formidable," the captain wrote his future bride, Elizabeth Lewis Selden, on March 8, "but . . . your addition to the Engr. Department & location in Petersburg would be an inducement to increase their strength." Miss Selden's motivational attributes notwithstanding, Longstreet's presence provided an important impetus toward finishing the fortifications that would prove so important in the coming year.[18]

In early March, Secretary Seddon pressed Longstreet to address Lee's increasingly severe supply shortage by venturing into southeastern Virginia and northeastern North Carolina on a grand foraging expedition. General Lee approved this mission by the middle of the month, although he worried that it might interfere with Longstreet's return to the Rappahannock should the Army of the Potomac begin to stir. Reinforced by troops from Wilmington and Petersburg, Hill would support Longstreet by moving against New Bern. The bulk of Pickett's and Hood's Divisions would march southeast, toward the Blackwater River and Suffolk, to join the troops already deployed there under Brigadier General Micah Jenkins, a young South Carolinian who had replaced Pryor and Colston. While the operation's primary purpose would be to gather supplies, Longstreet explained that he would seize any opportunity to defeat the Federal army around Suffolk.[19]

Longstreet's soldiers in Petersburg awoke before daylight on April 8 to the "rolling of drums, the shrill piping of the fife, and the sweeter, richer music of horn bands." The commotion signaled the beginning of the largest military operation originating in the Cockade City thus far in the war. Accompanied by artillery, the bulk of Pickett's and Hood's veteran divisions set out for the Blackwater River, covering twenty-one miles their first day. Longstreet departed that evening for Franklin, Virginia. Hill, whose campaign against New Bern had already floundered, now operated near Washington,

North Carolina, in position to cooperate with Longstreet and discourage the Federals from shifting troops north to Suffolk.

Longstreet had pointedly ignored General French during the strategic planning for the campaign, leaving the unhappy department head without a meaningful command. Unwilling to stand idly on the sidelines, French left a staff officer in charge of his Petersburg headquarters and rode toward the Blackwater to assert his authority as a division commander and Longstreet's senior subordinate in southern Virginia. Longstreet parried French by assigning him to direct the artillery, thereby marginalizing his involvement in the offensive.[20]

The campaign for Suffolk proved to be more laborious than sanguinary. Deprived of the naval support he believed he needed, Longstreet resorted to siege tactics that minimized casualties and allowed him to collect the abundant supplies available in this quadrant of Virginia. Hill failed to capture the Union garrison at Washington, but his presence occupied the Federal defenders and allowed foragers to exploit the region's livestock and crops. The operations concluded in late April when Major General Joseph Hooker crossed the Rappahannock and Rapidan Rivers near Fredericksburg at the head of the Army of the Potomac. Hooker's threat prompted Lee to summon Longstreet back to his imperiled army. As it turned out, Longstreet, Hood, and Pickett arrived too late to participate in the battle of Chancellorsville, which Lee and Stonewall Jackson managed to win without them.[21]

The departure of French's, Hood's, and Pickett's Divisions for the Blackwater River stripped Petersburg of all but eighteen hundred soldiers—more than half of whom, as paroled prisoners, were prohibited from fighting. The Thirty-second Virginia Infantry, 111 strong, had become the provost guard for the city. Fewer than three hundred artillerists manned batteries around town. Milligan's Independent Signal Corps, now roughly 150 men, continued to operate its system of observation posts and helped procure Northern newspapers that arrived on the Federal flag-of-truce boats that transported exchanged prisoners back to their regiments. Each of these units operated independently, because French declined to assign a temporary Petersburg commander while he served under Longstreet around Suffolk.[22]

Two local independent infantry companies, the Hargrave Blues from Dinwiddie County and the Confederate Guard from Petersburg, policed nine hundred and twenty paroled prisoners at the Model Farm. Confederate parolees confined there complained that facilities at the camp were worse than those at Northern prisons. Their voices received a hearing in Petersburg. "We are informed that [the prisoner quarters] very strongly resemble hog pens in point of cleanliness, instead of neatly kept apartments for the accommodation of human beings," editorialized the *Petersburg Daily Express.* "We appeal to the Commanding Officer of the Model Farm Barracks to use his authority to keep the buildings in better order . . . else we fear that when this war is ended, the name of the Model Farm will be one of reproach and infamy throughout the South."²³

William W. Heartsill, a paroled prisoner from Texas, provided a different perspective on life at the Model Farm. "We draw rice, sugar, and salt and are as a general thing doing finely," he wrote in April. Heartsill documented the frequent arrival and departure of paroled men, including large numbers from the western Confederacy. He and his comrades passed the time playing ball and visiting friends at the military hospitals while awaiting a return to active duty. They were released on May 4 and, like many others exchanged in Petersburg, shouldered weapons from the local armory before boarding trains bound for Richmond.²⁴

Petersburg's streets filled once again with Confederate soldiers in early May as Longstreet's troops headed north to rejoin Lee's army. Many of the men stopped in town to enjoy a hotel meal or to admire "the pretty girls after all the isolation of a backwoods campaign." Some of the soldiers visited acquaintances in the city or comrades in the hospitals, but within days they had passed through and the bustle subsided.²⁵

Longstreet's return to the Army of Northern Virginia restored General French as the ranking authority in Petersburg. Neither French in Virginia nor Hill in North Carolina remained subordinate to Longstreet, receiving instructions on May 8 to communicate directly with the War Department. On May 10 French reported 6,368 officers and men present for duty in the Department of Southern Virginia, the bulk of them in Jenkins's Brigade and the Mississippi brigade of Brigadier General Joseph R. Davis. Ten days later this number had swelled to more than seventy-six hundred, including troops at Fort Powhatan on the lower James River, the military policemen of the Thirty-second Virginia Infantry, and the captives interned at the Model Farm.²⁶

As it turned out, French's days in Petersburg were numbered. His promotion to major general postdated Hill's, making French subordinate to Hill. Longstreet and Hill enjoyed a strong personal and professional relationship, having been classmates at West Point, while Longstreet clearly thought little of French, as illustrated during the Suffolk operations. Many in the ranks shared Longstreet's low opinion of French. "Yanks were too strong for our 'old Granny' (Gen. French)," wrote one Virginia artillerist on May 24. "If he remains in this department much longer he will ruin us." Longstreet sought to enhance Hill's authority at the expense of French. "I have suggested that . . . you have command of Petersburg and everything south of that and north of South Carolina," Longstreet wrote from Fredericksburg on May 12. One week later Lee agreed, recommending to the secretary of war that Hill be given command of the department "between James River and the Cape Fear."[27]

The reorganization of the Army of Northern Virginia following Stonewall Jackson's death on May 10 complicated the command imbroglio in Petersburg. Two equally qualified North Carolina brigadiers, William Dorsey Pender and Robert Ransom, competed for division command in Lee's army. Promoting only one of these men would have caused political repercussions, and Sam French became the odd man out. On May 28 Harvey Hill formally took command of an expanded Department of North Carolina that included "the Department of Southern Virginia as far north as to embrace the city of Petersburg and its environs, and including the Appomattox River." The same order that abolished French's department sent him to Mississippi to serve under Joseph E. Johnston. Ransom rose to major general in Hill's jurisdiction, taking French's old division in his Petersburg-based department, while Pender assumed division command in the Army of Northern Virginia.[28]

French left Petersburg on June 3 largely unmourned, although Charles Dimmock believed that "our people here do not seem to appreciate his loss." Dimmock's low opinion of Hill no doubt influenced his sentiments. "[Hill] has no amiable feelings toward me, but I hope not to come in contact with him," he wrote. As it turned out, Hill was too busy protecting the administrative integrity of his department from Robert E. Lee to take much notice of the young captain of engineers.[29]

Lee's decision to launch an offensive into Pennsylvania (an operation Hill thought "very hazardous . . . and one that must prove fruitless if not disastrous") prompted his desire to reinforce the Army of Northern Virginia with every available soldier in the eastern theater. Lee particularly coveted Hill's twenty-two thousand men in the Department of North Carolina. Hill's three best brigades, those of Major General Robert Ransom and brigadier generals Micah Jenkins and John R. Cooke, had all once served with Lee's army, and "Marse Robert" considered them detachments subject to immediate recall.

Spirited and at times discordant correspondence in late May and early June flew among Lee, Hill, President Davis, and the War Department regarding the disposition of Hill's forces. The Petersburg commander resisted Lee's efforts to weaken his department by enumerating the threats to Richmond and Petersburg from the Tidewater area and in all the usual strategic places in North Carolina. "The Yankees are massing a large force at Yorktown with the view of taking Richmond during Genl Lee's absence," Hill informed his wife in June. "We may have some very hard fighting here." After protracted debate, Lee added the brigades of Junius Daniel, Joseph R.

Davis, and J. Johnston Pettigrew to the Army of Northern Virginia from Hill's department, while the Carolinian retained Ransom, Jenkins, and Cooke. Hill assigned these brigades, numbering about eight thousand effective officers and men at the beginning of June, to the Virginia portion of his command.[30]

Hill had appreciated Petersburg's strategic significance earlier than any ranking officer in the Confederate army. In June a new threat appeared from more than twenty thousand Northern troops under General Dix, who had moved up the Peninsula from Fort Monroe to a point twenty-five miles east of Richmond. Dix had orders to maintain pressure on the Confederate capital and exploit any opportunity offered by the absence of the Army of Northern Virginia. General Elzey bore direct responsibility for Richmond's defense, but Hill's larger force would inevitably assist against any sustained offensive that Dix launched. Hill predicted that although the Federals might move north of Richmond and cut the railroads running north and west of the city, he thought it more likely that "they will land at City Point, and isolate Petersburg, crossing the Appomattox between its mouth and [Petersburg]." Such a strategy would "be a very serious one for us," wrote Hill. "It is entirely practicable . . . and cannot be resisted by us."[31]

Hill hurried Jenkins's South Carolinians from the Blackwater River line to Petersburg, and he sent Ransom's Brigade, now commanded by Robert's older brother, Matt, to Drewry's Bluff between Petersburg and Richmond. Secretary Seddon did not share Hill's anxiety for Petersburg, thinking it unlikely that the Federals would expose their supply depot at Yorktown by crossing to the south side of the James. Seddon thus encouraged Hill to use both Ransom and Jenkins in the defense of Richmond should Dix's army approach the capital's defenses north of the river.

While Hill continued to believe that "an approach on this [the south] side is to be much more apprehended," he pledged to employ all his available troops to protect Richmond if necessary. In the meantime, Hill asked the Engineer Department to send more slave labor to finish the Dimmock Line, which still fell more than one mile short of completion and included "many troublesome problems in regard to their defense." Colonel Jeremy Gilmer, chief of engineers, told Hill that no slaves could be spared and recommended that Hill employ his own thinly stretched troops on fatigue details.[32]

Not much is known regarding Hill's daily activities in Petersburg. He informed his wife that he was "messing alone," instead of sharing meals with other officers, and he provided only a glimpse of his routine: "I come to my office soon after 6 [AM] and stay till 12 in the afternoon. I ride around and visit the troops and the fortifications. . . . Excited dispatches come at all hours, day & night." Hill's troops purchased items in town and enjoyed meals in local hotels, if they could afford them. The artillerist James W. Albright was amused by "a free fight of officers," which resulted in no serious injuries because "no guns or knives were used." Other officers visited friends and courted local ladies, much as they and others had done earlier in the war.[33]

Hill thought that Confederate strategy should concentrate on lifting the siege of Vicksburg, Mississippi, instead of conducting a campaign into Pennsylvania. Nevertheless, he responded in a thoroughly professional manner to the threats to Richmond and Petersburg that Lee's offensive made possible. Hill utilized the information that Captain Milligan provided to keep abreast of Union movements along the James, and by the 4th of July he had begun to doubt Dix's commitment to testing the capital's defenses. "The Yankees are . . . fond of clap-trap," Hill wrote the secretary of war. When General Elzey requested a position with Lee's army in early July, Hill inherited command of the Richmond forces in addition to his responsibilities south of the James. He worked diligently to improve the capital's fortifications on the east and north, but he showed his disdain for the Federals by referring to them as the "Monkey Army," a sarcastic play on words derived from the Pamunkey River, where Dix's men established their base.

As late as July 7, Hill told Seddon, "I must confess that I am more concerned for Petersburg than for Richmond, and always have been." In truth, he need not have worried about either city. Dix had conducted a council of war on June 29 at which he and his officers agreed to risk no attacks but merely to conduct demonstrations and raids to keep the Confederates in Virginia off balance.[34]

Hill discerned Dix's intentions as early as July 5. "Where have the Yankees gone?" Hill rhetorically asked the secretary of war. "The design on Richmond was not a feint but a faint." Four days later Hill pronounced that "there can be but little doubt that the Yankees are moving rapidly back. A small force may be kept under cover of their works and gunboats for days and even weeks at White House for the purpose of deception."

Having declared the crisis around Richmond and Petersburg over, Hill was now free to follow in French's footsteps and accept a transfer to Mississippi to serve under his old comrade Joseph Johnston. In mid-June, Hill had expressed his desire to move to the western theater, a suggestion that President Davis agreed to consider once circumstances in the Department of North Carolina permitted. The president acted on Hill's request on July 12 and ordered him to report to Jackson, Mississippi, endowed with the new rank of lieutenant general. Major General Robert Ransom succeeded to Hill's command, including jurisdiction over Petersburg.[35]

Ransom enjoyed a tenure of less than twenty-four hours as the ranking officer in the Department of North Carolina. His assignment to department command on July 13 surprised even Secretary of War Seddon, who had been equally unaware of Hill's promotion and transfer to Mississippi. To complicate the command situation further, within hours of Ransom's ascendance, Special Orders Number 166 of July 14 named General Whiting commander of the Department of North Carolina, including Petersburg, with headquarters in distant Wilmington. "Shall not be surprised if I have to command in Richmond," wrote Whiting, who had become a fixture in the Tarheel metropolis, "but shall be very sorry." Ransom, who that day had corresponded under the signature "Major-General, Commanding Department," reverted to a subordinate position under the temporary direction of General Elzey in Richmond.[36]

In the midst of these administrative adjustments, a Union sortie near Lower Brandon Plantation on the James, some twenty miles below Petersburg in Prince George County, attracted attention in the Cockade City. A flotilla of Northern ships and troop transports appeared in the predawn hours of Sunday July 12, sending small boats filled with soldiers to the shore. Colonel Edgar B. Montague of the Thirty-second Virginia Infantry and a handful of Georgians, perhaps five hundred men all told, were the only regular troops around Petersburg to contest this incursion. Secretary Seddon urged Montague to call on Mayor Townes to organize the Petersburg militia, while Ransom's Brigade hurried from Richmond to Petersburg to protect the city.[37]

Throughout most Petersburg churches, clergymen interrupted their services to announce that men enrolled in the militia were to muster at the post office. Charles Campbell speculated that when combined with convalescents at Petersburg's military hospitals, fifteen hundred emergency soldiers could be gathered to confront the enemy. Three cannon shots fired during the afternoon signaled the militia to report to Poplar Lawn prior to marching east. That evening hundreds of citizen-soldiers passed an uncomfortable night without tents along the city's eastern fortifications. Petersburg, reported an observer, was in "great excitement" at this latest threat. Had Hill's warning about the city's vulnerability come home to roost? In the end, the scare proved needless. The Federals reboarded their ships, the militia went home, and Robert Ransom departed the scene, having applied for sick leave on July 18.[38]

Petersburg now straddled both Whiting's Department of North Carolina, to which the city administratively belonged, and Elzey's Department of Richmond. With the exception of the Thirty-second Virginia Infantry, Petersburg's provost guard, the city had no organic troops. Ransom's Division, now consisting of just Matt Ransom's North Carolina brigade and Micah Jenkins's South Carolinians, remained temporarily assigned to Elzey's department, but their proximity to Petersburg made it logical that they respond to such threats as the Lower Brandon raid, rather than Whiting's units in distant North Carolina. Whiting exercised little practical authority in Petersburg, and this confusion might have caused considerable difficulty if a lull in Union activity had not followed the episode at Lower Brandon. Ransom's Tarheels eventually encamped around Petersburg, while Jenkins remained near Richmond.[39]

Jenkins desperately wished to return to duty with the Army of Northern Virginia, feeling keenly the Gettysburg losses of his old division—George Pickett's. "In the past campaign we fought side by side with the gallant men who sealed their devotion with their lives on the field of Gettysburg," Jenkins pleaded with the War Department, "and I now respectfully beg to be permitted, at the earliest moment allowed by the good of the service, to rejoin my division, and recruit its shattered ranks with my rested brigade." Robert Ransom endorsed this request before he left on sick leave, and Elzey concurred, but it would be several months before Jenkins realized his ambition. Meanwhile, Captain Dimmock continued to build a new railroad bridge across the Appomattox eight hundred yards east of the defective bridge constructed in 1861, and he fretted about the still unfinished works that had occupied his professional attention for many months. "The defenses of the city are not entirely completed," Dimmock confessed, "but sufficiently so for all defensive purposes."[40]

Two dispatches on July 27 triggered some activity in the otherwise quiet Petersburg. In North Carolina, General Whiting reported a Union movement from Plymouth toward Weldon and the vital railroad connection linking Wilmington, Petersburg, and Richmond. Elzey responded by ordering Ransom's Brigade at Petersburg to board the cars immediately and prepare to defend Weldon. At the same time, Captain Nathaniel W. Small of Milligan's Signal Corps warned that Federal advances from Portsmouth toward Suffolk suggested the possibility of raids against Petersburg. Elzey reacted by sending Jenkins to Petersburg, along with Major James R. Branch's artillery battalion, to "assume command of all the troops at that place and the direction of the military operations against the enemy advancing from Portsmouth."

Jenkins promptly boarded his brigade of roughly twenty-four hundred men on the Richmond & Petersburg Railroad, arriving the next day. He marched to the West End, establishing camps at the fairgrounds and near the Model Farm. The South Carolinians entered Petersburg with much fanfare, accompanied by the music of two military bands, each regiment "preceded by 6 or 8 drums beaten by boys."[41]

While Matt Ransom handsomely repulsed the Union raiders near Weldon, Jenkins detected no suspicious movement toward Petersburg from either Portsmouth or Suffolk. He did, at Ransom's request, send elements of his brigade to guard the bridges on the Petersburg Railroad as far south as Hicksford. Jenkins also sought clarification from Elzey about both his re-

Micah Jenkins (1835–64). General Jenkins, a dashing young South Carolinian, earned praise as Petersburg's reluctant commander during the summer of 1863. Jenkins died at the battle of the Wilderness on May 6, 1864. The deadly volley that claimed Jenkins, mistakenly aimed by other Confederates at Petersburg's Twelfth Virginia Infantry, also severely wounded General Longstreet. (Courtesy of Valentine Richmond History Center)

sponsibility for Ransom's Brigade, seeing that he was senior to the North Carolinian, and a possible offensive with Ransom in North Carolina. Jenkins also directed a message to General Lee from Petersburg on July 30. "I am here temporarily to guard against raiders," he wrote, "but do not think the place in danger." Telling Lee that his unit was "pronounced by all officers in unsurpassed condition," Jenkins again requested that his place be taken by "some shattered brigade to rest and recruit," allowing him to rejoin Pickett's Division.[42]

General Jenkins had not yet reached his twenty-eighth birthday. Born on one of the South Carolina sea islands to a wealthy planting family, Jenkins pursued a military career, graduating first in his class at the South Carolina Military Academy and founding a new military school in the state's up-country. He earned the praise of all his superior officers as he rose from regimental to brigade command, and on August 13 Daniel Harvey Hill wrote the adjutant general that he knew of "no Brigadier in the service more worthy of promotion. He has all the qualities necessary to make him a most efficient division commander." A fellow officer called Jenkins "a remarkable man, full of spirit and enthusiasm and as full of the most resolute courage. He could lead a charge as dashingly as Murat and repel one as stubbornly as Ney." Although a North Carolina colonel thought Jenkins's Brigade "remarkable for dressing like Yankees, for being most ordinary & stolid in appearance & the most homely [brigade] we have seen," most observers considered the Carolinian and his five regiments superb specimens of Confederate military prowess.[43]

August proved to be another quiet month around Petersburg, but the constant threat of Union raids against the railroads or incursions from southeastern Virginia kept Jenkins on his toes. Because Jenkins's Brigade was liable to be called away at a moment's notice, Secretary of War Seddon instructed Governor Letcher on August 3 to activate Petersburg's Second Class Militia to defend the city if and when the South Carolinians were needed elsewhere. By the fifth, Petersburg's eligible old men and young boys gathered in town. "There is a great Pow Wow among the militia," wrote Warner Lewis Baylor, assistant surgeon at the Confederate States Hospital. "What point they will be sent to, or whether they will be sent at all is a matter of doubt."[44]

Jenkins had these part-time soldiers drill in the Grove, a pleasant campground west of the city. The men slept in planked tents and mixed their training with pastimes such as reading, watching dress parades that Jenkins's regulars conducted, or listening to band concerts. After ten days without much cause to warrant their continued employment, the War Department directed the militia to return to their homes at night after conducting a daily drill at 5:00 PM.[45]

Jenkins's men enjoyed their weeks in Petersburg immensely, despite the restiveness of their combative commander. "We are camped in the edge of Petersburg and we are having a glorious time," wrote Private William E. Hardy. "Hundreds of pretty girls visit our Regiments every evening to see the dress parades. I have formed the acquaintance of several, and . . . am willing to remain here until the war ends." Petersburgers thought equally highly of the South Carolinians. Charles Campbell found the performance of Jenkins's regimental bands "well-nigh better than most of those in the Confed. army," while another observer reported that "Jenkins Brigade are amusing the young ladies of Petersburg by concerts. They have an amateur troupe of negro minstrels. The performances are very much admired."[46]

Preceded by three bands playing "The Bonnie Blue Flag" and other stirring tunes, on August 20 the brigade moved with some pomp from the Grove to the east side of town. Elzey warned Jenkins of suspicious activity along the Blackwater River, but the month passed without disturbance. "I have had a very pleasant time indeed," Jenkins confessed to an officer on Longstreet's staff. "The hospitalities of . . . this city having been unsparing. We have made most charming lady friends, and . . . could not have been situated more to my pleasure." Still, Jenkins longed to be reunited with his corps. "Have you all forgotten us? If not, cannot another effort still bring me to you?" Advancing the work on Dimmock's fortifications and entertaining the local citizens were not enough for the restless Jenkins.[47]

Circumstances in northern Virginia and eastern Tennessee would finally gratify Jenkins's wishes. Following its defeat at Gettysburg in July, Lee's army returned to the Old Dominion and assumed defensive positions along the Rapidan River. The Federals did little to disturb them. No such calm prevailed around critical Chattanooga, Tennessee, a rail junction with strategic value to Georgia, Tennessee, and Alabama akin to Petersburg's importance to Virginia and North Carolina. A late summer Union offensive threatened Chattanooga and the heartland of the Confederacy to its south.

General Longstreet lobbied successfully to shift his corps toward Chattanooga, and he suggested that Jenkins's Carolinians join him for the movement south. Lee approved this plan on September 9. He noted that Pickett's Division, depleted terribly at Gettysburg, should remain in the Richmond and Petersburg area in place of Jenkins and Elzey's other available brigade, Brigadier General Henry A. Wise's Virginians. Longstreet's men would pass through Petersburg, since the railroad directly connecting Virginia with eastern Tennessee had been captured by the Federals.[48]

The new railroad bridge across the Appomattox started carrying trainloads of Longstreet's men through Petersburg on the night of September 9. Some soldiers knocked out the sides of the cars to improve ventilation, while others rode on top to enjoy the views. Although the trains could now pass directly through town without stopping, most of them paused at the Southern depot, affording the soldiers a chance to explore Petersburg. "Have spent the evening very pleasantly strolling over the city," wrote one Mississippian on September 11, with a sentiment typical of Longstreet's transients. "Petersburg is a very nice & pleasant old city."[49]

From September 10 through 14, thousands of Confederate soldiers filled the streets of the Cockade City en route to General Braxton Bragg's army outside Chattanooga. Bands played impromptu concerts; troops bought pies, cakes, and fresh fruit from Petersburg markets and vendors; proselytizers distributed religious tracts; and the soldiers gambled, drank, and ran foot races through the streets, to the delight of onlookers. Charles Campbell watched as Longstreet's men threw firecrackers and played practical jokes at the expense of gullible children and blacks. The veteran Confederates exuded optimism and high morale. "I never saw men in finer spirits than mine are this morning," recorded General Wise on September 15. "They are sportive as kittens and cheer everything along the road."[50]

Some of the ebullient behavior proved less than kittenlike. "Much trouble was occasioned by the men becoming too familiar with John Barleycorn, Esq.," wrote one member of the Forty-sixth Virginia Infantry. "Women and wine frequently produce the sensation of a full grown 'nightmare' upon the male population."[51]

Campbell sold a Mississippi soldier some okra out of his kitchen garden and noted that this man expressed regret at leaving Virginia, an emotion not shared by Micah Jenkins. On September 11, Special Orders Number 216 officially attached Jenkins to John Bell Hood's Division of Longstreet's corps, and the South Carolinian and his brigade, beloved by Petersburgers, left the Cockade City. Another familiar unit also departed at this time. The Thirty-second Virginia Infantry, the small regiment that had done provost duty in town for much of the year, received an assignment north of the James River. "Their service both to the Government and the city deserve a remembrance," editorialized a Petersburg newspaper, "and speaking for the latter, we can assure the men of this command, that they will not be forgotten."⁵²

A well-known figure from the Army of Northern Virginia filled the void in Petersburg. George Edward Pickett finished at the bottom of his West Point class, served with distinction in the Mexican War, and remained in the army until the summer of 1861, when he resigned his commission and journeyed from the Pacific coast to his native Richmond. He rose through Confederate ranks, winning a brigadier general's wreath in early 1862 at age thirty-seven. Pickett earned accolades for his leadership during the Peninsula campaign, where he sustained a wound that incapacitated him through the summer. In the fall of 1862 Pickett received promotion to major general, inheriting Longstreet's old division when that officer assumed corps command. Pickett's Division played a minimal role at the battle of Fredericksburg and missed the carnage at Chancellorsville due to its participation in the Suffolk operations. At Gettysburg, however, Pickett's renowned attack against Cemetery Ridge on July 3 so shattered his three brigades that Lee and Longstreet thought it prudent to leave them in a rear-echelon area rather than send them to Georgia. The flamboyant Pickett thus arrived in Petersburg as the city's ranking officer in mid-September, still nursing resentment over the destruction of his command at Gettysburg.

Pickett arranged a dramatic introduction. On September 15 he married the young LaSalle Corbell of Nansemond County at St. Paul's Episcopal Church. The bride would remember that a crowd of "thousands" cheered the marriage and that a "salute of guns, hearty cheers, and chimes and bugles" signaled their departure for a Richmond honeymoon. Contemporary evidence describes a similar if more subdued scene. "Yesterday Major Genl Pickett was married in the town at St. Paul's Church to a Miss Corbell," recorded the observant Charles Campbell. "The church bells chimed in honor of the occasion & a salute of 12 guns was fired on Dunn's Hill." Captain Dimmock confirmed that Pickett and his bride left Petersburg after the nuptials and attended several parties in Richmond.⁵³

In accordance with Special Orders Number 226 of September 23, Pickett assumed command of the Department of North Carolina the next day. He took responsibility for the territory between the Appomattox and Cape Fear Rivers, with headquarters in Petersburg, and thus ended the administrative fiction that General Whiting commanded Petersburg from Wilming-

George Edward Pickett (1825–75). Pickett's marriage in Petersburg's St. Paul's Episcopal Church on September 15, 1863, and his management of the city's defense in
May 1864 provided highlights of his otherwise undistinguished eight-month stint
as Petersburg's commander. (Courtesy of Valentine Richmond History Center)

ton. The general and his bride set up housekeeping at the palatial Robert
Dunn McIlwaine residence, "a beautiful home with a large yard and tall
trees and flowers, green grass and fountains" on the southwest corner of
Washington and Perry Streets. Major Robert Taylor Scott of Pickett's staff
reported that Pickett's army family was also "comfortably fixed," and he
hoped that the general would remain in Petersburg for an extended stay.[54]
    The force Pickett brought with him to garrison Petersburg represented

but a fraction of his Gettysburg command, and a broken fraction at that. Lewis Armistead's Brigade had lost its commander and nearly half its men on July 3. Colonel William Aylett of the Fifty-third Virginia Infantry, although wounded during the charge, now led the brigade, which numbered barely one thousand effective men in five depleted Virginia regiments. Aylett boarded with the Hugh Nelson family at the West Hill estate on Tabb Street while his troops bivouacked astride Jerusalem Plank Road south of town.[55]

Pickett's other two brigades encamped north of the James River, with the exception of the decimated Eighteenth Virginia Infantry of Brigadier General Eppa Hunton's Brigade, which replaced the Thirty-second Virginia Infantry as Petersburg's provost guard. This regiment "looked like a company[,] so much had it been thinned at Gettysburg," thought Charles Campbell. Their numbers shrank even more when two companies went to City Point to superintend the transfer of paroled prisoners. Pickett also benefitted from the presence of Major Benjamin F. Eshelman's Battalion of the Washington Artillery of New Orleans, which, due to transportation problems, did not accompany the corps on Longstreet's movement to Georgia. These men initially went into bivouac at the Grove. Other artillery units occupied positions along the lower Appomattox River.[56]

Pickett quickly embraced his new responsibilities. The staff officer Scott thought his commander had become "quite domesticated" under the influence of "Cousin Sally," whom he described as "quite sprightly and handsome and very much in love with [Pickett]." Several administrative changes marked Pickett's first fortnight in command. He named Major George C. Cabell of the Eighteenth Virginia Infantry, a former Danville lawyer and newspaper editor, as provost marshal of Petersburg. More important, Brigadier General Seth M. Barton, captured at Vicksburg and recently exchanged, became the new commander of Armistead's Brigade.[57]

Within forty-eight hours of Barton's ascension, the brigade boarded trains for Weldon and eventually Kinston, to engage in another of the numerous minor affairs that characterized the war in North Carolina. Barton's Brigade would spend much of the fall and winter shuttling between Petersburg and various posts in the Tarheel State. Brigadier General Montgomery Corse's Brigade, detached from Pickett during the Pennsylvania campaign, traveled from southwest Virginia to rejoin their old command briefly in October, only to return a short time later. In the absence of a threat from the Blackwater River or the Peninsula, Pickett's troops could be assigned away from Petersburg without endangering department headquarters.[58]

The artillery units in Petersburg shifted locations less often and thus had a better opportunity to settle into city life than did their infantry counterparts. The Virginia cannoneer James Albright pursued the suit of two local girls, Mattie Purvis and Lucy Brittain, and had pictures made of both his sweethearts. The Washington Artillery moved its camp to the east side of town and entertained themselves and locals with horse racing at the New-market course. The Louisianians also organized a thespian society and pre-sented plays at Phoenix and Mechanics Halls. One of their more popular shows was the burlesque "Po-ca-hon-tas or Ye Gentle Savage."[59]

A new unit, the Petersburg City Battalion, also known as the Forty-fourth Battalion of Virginia Infantry, organized at this time. Composed of boys aged sixteen to seventeen and men over forty-five and organized in three companies, they began to drill in late September under the command of Major Peter V. Batte. The City Battalion assisted the Eighteenth Virginia Infantry with security in town, including escorting as many as five thousand prisoners of war, many captured at the battle of Chickamauga, in which Longstreet's divisions played a conspicuous role. Captain Milligan sought to use some of Batte's men as mounted scouts to supplement his signal corps, although there is no record of Pickett acting on this suggestion.[60]

Pickett's primary military challenge during November 1863, like that of his predecessors, remained the execution of a strategic juggling act, neu-tralizing multiple threats with inadequate manpower. The Union occupiers of eastern North Carolina constantly demanded vigilance, as did the Federal presence east of the Blackwater River. Renewed sparring between the main armies in the northern Piedmont worried the Confederate War Department because Longstreet's departure for the West had so weakened Lee. When Lee's army had needed reinforcements in the past, the Richmond authori-ties had looked to Petersburg for help. Pickett justified the retention of his manpower by shifting his troops back and forth between the far-flung cor-ners of his department, responding to dangers, perceived and real.

Union operations in northeastern North Carolina early in November prompted Pickett to accompany Barton's Brigade to Weldon, while Ran-som's troops sought to repel the Federals moving toward the Wilmington & Weldon Railroad. Less than one week later Secretary of War Seddon in-formed Pickett that Northern newspapers predicted a sudden dash against Richmond. He suggested that a brigade be returned to Petersburg immedi-ately to counter this possibility. When the maneuvering around Mine Run in Orange County, Virginia, late in November, foretold a major Union offensive by the Army of the Potomac, Seddon looked again to Pickett to provide pro-tection for Richmond and support for Lee.[61]

Pickett's resources could not stretch to cover all the threatened points for which he was responsible, let alone serve as the strategic reserve for the Army of Northern Virginia. Matt Ransom's twenty-three hundred men were in North Carolina watching the railroad between Wilmington and Weldon. Barton's Virginians, only twelve hundred strong, shuttled between Weldon and department headquarters in Petersburg, watching both North Carolina and the Blackwater River line. In Barton's absence the Cockade City lacked any permanent garrison save for the militia and provost guard. The rest of Pickett's old division served outside his departmental authority—James L. Kemper's and Hunton's Brigades in the Richmond defenses and Corse's Brigade entirely out of reach in eastern Tennessee.

Pickett pleaded with Secretary Seddon to unite his division before committing him to major combat, citing Gettysburg as the painful wages of a fractured command. He also warned Seddon against stripping the Department of North Carolina in order to reinforce Lee, the same advice that Hill had offered during the summer. Pickett thought it likely that any offensive against Lee in the Piedmont would be accompanied by a movement from Tidewater up the Peninsula toward Richmond or against Petersburg and that it would be reckless to leave these areas defenseless.

Pickett's department mustered fewer than eighty-seven hundred effective troops of all arms in late November, including seventeen hundred artillerists and infantry around Petersburg and Barton's gypsies, who frequently traveled in and out of the city. On the twenty-eighth Seddon directed Barton to move to Hanover Junction, twenty miles north of Richmond, where his men could shift either west or north, depending on Lee's needs along Mine Run. Ransom's Brigade from North Carolina would replace Barton in Petersburg, and Brigadier General Thomas Clingman's Brigade would be detached from General P. G. T. Beauregard's command around Charleston to cover the territory in northeastern North Carolina that had been Ransom's responsibility. Thus elements from three Confederate departments continued to dash across the strategic chessboard in Virginia and the Carolinas (not to mention the western theater) as the Confederacy attempted to cope with increasingly lopsided logistical arithmetic.[62]

A personal misfortune complicated these tense times for Pickett. In the middle of the month as he and his wife were returning to Petersburg from the races at Newmarket, their carriage tipped over in an accident caused by a drunken driver. Pickett escaped without serious injury, but LaSalle had to be cut out of the vehicle and suffered several fractured ribs—an emotional blow to her new husband.[63]

The contretemps in northern Virginia came to naught, and Barton's Brigade returned to Petersburg on December 10, only to be sent south to Kinston the next day. Clingman's Brigade rather than Ransom's began to arrive on the fourteenth to replace Barton, bivouacking first in the streets but ultimately a few miles east of town on Hare's Hill. Pickett's Petersburg defenders by year's end included most of Clingman's Brigade, the Eighteenth Virginia Infantry as provost guard, fifteen hundred artillerists with sixty-five guns, and the Forty-fourth Virginia Battalion, for a total of thirty-six hundred men. Barton's Brigade lay at Kinston, Ransom's at Weldon, and small detachments of infantry and cavalry patrolled the Blackwater River near Franklin and Ivor.[64]

Pickett reported a possible Union cavalry offensive and "a negro expedition" up the James and the Peninsula on New Year's Eve, and he sought additional troops to confront it. He also corresponded with Secretary Seddon regarding plans to create a new brigade to occupy eastern North Carolina under the command of Colonel William J. Clarke of the Twenty-fourth North Carolina Infantry. Outnumbered and continually threatened from several directions, 1863 ended for Pickett under strategic circumstances identical to those he inherited in Petersburg. Still, the Virginian enjoyed the city's comforts and the company of his young wife, who quickly recovered from the injuries sustained during her carriage mishap.[65]

Life in Petersburg possessed its simple charms for Pickett's soldiers, as well. The Louisianians of the Washington Artillery shifted from camps on the Friend farm east of town to the Jones farm southwest of Petersburg and eventually to the Model Farm. The enlisted men occupied the barn there, which Private David W. Pipes remembered as "cold and bleak," devoid of a fireplace, mattresses, or much bedding. The officers enjoyed better quarters in the nearby cottages, while headquarters was established in the superintendent's house. The men passed the time playing ball and drilling. Pipes fondly recalled the morning when a Petersburg miller, James M. Venable, appeared in camp and witnessed three cannoneers eating a spartan breakfast of a single hoecake and three strips of bacon. Refusing the soldiers' offer to share their meager repast, Venable told them, "Boys, I have a mill which grinds every Saturday and if you will send to the mill you will not suffer for lack of bread as long as you camp in Petersburg." Pipes and his comrades gratefully accepted Venable's generosity.[66]

Other Confederates, such as James Thomas Perry of the Seventeenth Virginia Infantry, found quarters in town, where they became patrons of the Library Association and attended worship services. In late January, Colonel James Dearing, a Virginia cavalryman, was married at St. Paul's Church, in another notable military wedding that the Reverend William H. Platt conducted. In addition to the rest of the Confederate facilities functioning in Petersburg, the Confederate States Wagon Shop opened in the Blandford section of the city in January 1864. Stables, a blacksmith's forge, woodworking shops, and wheelwright facilities comprised this complex, which employed about thirty workers, many of whom were African Americans. The repair and fabrication of wheels, harnesses, wooden vehicle components, and iron work occupied workers from dawn until well after dark.[67]

General Pickett began 1864 with predictions of imminent Union offensives in the Carolinas. True to form, he requested more men and suggested sending the reinforcements to Goldsboro, North Carolina, where the railroad split—one line leading east through Kinston toward the Federals at New Bern and the coast and the other continuing south to Wilmington. He explained that from Goldsboro the troops could easily travel either to Kinston or Wilmington "or would form a nucleus, should the enemy . . . have pushed us, around which to gather troops from Weldon, Petersburg, and such other points as could best spare them." Pickett strongly recommended that Kinston be held, both to protect the ironclad gunboat under construction there and as the most forward defense against an advance from New Bern.

The Richmond authorities concurred and ordered Pickett to send Clingman's Brigade back to North Carolina, while Kemper's Brigade at Hanover Junction would replace the Tarheels in Petersburg. Pickett objected. Citing Clingman's concern that his dispirited soldiers not be sent near their homes for fear of mass desertion, the department commander suggested that Kemper's Virginians simply continue through Petersburg and on to Goldsboro. The War Department agreed, and Kemper's Brigade, under the temporary command of Colonel Joseph Mayo while Kemper languished in a Union prison, began filing through Petersburg along Sycamore Street on January 9, "the band playing, the muskets glittering in the sun." By January 10 the Virginians were en route by rail to Goldsboro.[68]

General Whiting at Wilmington also anticipated trouble from the Federals, and on January 14 he sent a coded message to Pickett requesting help. Pickett sought clarification from the War Department. Should he send Clingman's or Kemper's Brigade to Wilmington? Who would occupy Goldsboro? What troops would defend Petersburg and the Blackwater River, an area that also promised Union aggression, where Clingman had detached his Thirty-first North Carolina Infantry?[69]

Pickett did not know that while he struggled with constructing the best defensive arrangements in his department, Robert E. Lee and Jefferson Davis were plotting to assume the offensive in North Carolina. Lee had informed the president on January 2 that "the time is at hand when if an attempt can be made to capture the enemy's forces at New Berne it should be done." Citing the strategic stagnation along the Rapidan River imposed by winter roads, Lee indicated that he could detach troops for a campaign against New Bern that, combined with Pickett's forces, "will be sufficient if the attack can be secretly & suddenly made." Not until January 20 did Lee inform Pickett of his scheme, a move reminiscent of the Suffolk campaign the previous winter.

Lee ordered Pickett to accomplish his mission using Barton, Kemper, and Ransom along with Corse's Brigade (which would be sent to him from southwestern Virginia) and Brigadier General Robert F. Hoke's Brigade from Lee's army. Although Lee politely invited Pickett to modify the plan he had developed, it was clear that Marse Robert felt uneasy about entrusting the details of such an offensive to Pickett's "good judgment" alone. Hoke arrived in Petersburg on January 23 as Lee's strategic emissary and discussed with a skeptical Pickett the blueprint for capturing New Bern. Corse's Brigade began to arrive on the twenty-seventh, and by January 29 Pickett was en route from Petersburg to North Carolina to lead the operation. He left Clingman and his desertion-prone brigade behind to deal with another minor Union raid against Lower Brandon.[70]

Pickett returned to Petersburg on February 9, probably wishing he had never left the Cockade City. Operations around New Bern failed, and Pickett received the blame for the botched affair. When the War Department launched another offensive in North Carolina two months later, this time against Plymouth, General Hoke commanded the expedition, while department chief Pickett remained in Petersburg as little more than a figurehead.[71]

Nothing of strategic importance disturbed Pickett's idleness during the remainder of the month. While quiet reigned at department headquarters, socially energetic officers such as Captain W. H. S. Burgwyn of North Carolina simultaneously courted several young Petersburg women, and other Confederates attended performances at Phoenix Hall or lectures at various churches. "As far as we now know, will remain here for some time yet," wrote the quartermaster Robert Taylor Scott. "There is nothing that indicates a move."[72]

By the end of February, Pickett commanded nearly thirteen thousand effective men (including the infantry brigades of Clingman, Corse, Ransom, and Hoke) and eighty-three pieces of artillery from his headquarters at the Petersburg Customs House. Major Milligan counted 241 officers and signalmen in his command, which stretched from Drewry's Bluff to Fort Boykin on the lower James and along the Appomattox from City Point to Petersburg. Barton, whom Pickett blamed for tactical errors at New Bern, had been transferred with his brigade to the Department of Richmond. Clingman's Carolinians remained posted in and around Petersburg, along with twenty pieces of artillery, although General Clingman was absent on leave in early March.[73]

Pickett's nerves were tested at this time by frantic messages from Richmond demanding reinforcements to counter a Union cavalry raid and an operation up the Peninsula, both targeting the Confederate capital. On March 3 the War Department called on Pickett to "send without delay . . . the nearest brigade of your command." Pickett dispatched approximately fourteen hundred of Clingman's veterans along with some field artillery—all the troops then at Petersburg—to meet the crisis. The panic soon subsided as Union troopers under Brigadier General Judson Kilpatrick and Colonel Ulric Dahlgren bypassed the city and headed for safety on the Peninsula.

Pickett had called out the Second Class Militia to defend Petersburg in the absence of the regulars, "a motley crowd" in the opinion of Charles Campbell, consisting of "old gray beards [and] smooth-faced striplings." Rumors of the latest Yankee raid gave Petersburgers a day of "great confusion," but just as soon as the excitement appeared, it dissipated. Kilpatrick and Dahlgren never seriously threatened the city.[74]

The rest of March passed quietly in Petersburg. The new chief military advisor to President Davis, the otherwise discredited Braxton Bragg, visited the city on March 13 and reviewed the situation with Pickett. Some South Carolina cavalry en route to Charleston clattered through town late in the month, stimulating Charles Campbell with "a feeling of patriotic delight, when I think of the heroism of our armies in this bloody war." The troopers talked about their snowball fights that winter, conversations Campbell thought "very diverting to the soldiers." Snow swirled in Petersburg as late as April 2, but soon spring would harken another campaign season.[75]

By then Federal strategists were perfecting their plans to make 1864 the climactic year of the war. Confederate commanders across Virginia, including Pickett, presumed as much, and they were aware of Union troop concentrations in northern Virginia; Tidewater Virginia; Annapolis, Maryland; and eastern North Carolina. Determining where the Federals would strike dominated Confederate military thinking as winter gave way to the tardy spring of 1864. Pickett learned on April 12 of Hoke's mission against Plymouth—a slight to Pickett's ego softened only marginally by Braxton Bragg's transparent assurance that "the conduct of this expedition is intrusted to Brigadier General Hoke, so as not to withdraw you from a supervision of your whole department at this critical time." Ironically, Hoke's departure with virtually all of Pickett's infantry left Petersburg dangerously vulnerable to a waterborne offensive up the James.[76]

Pickett, like Hill, had always considered Petersburg a logical target. The city's relationship to Richmond and its critical location on the railroad network connecting the capital to Wilmington suggested to the beleaguered department commander that, sooner or later, the Federals would try to capture the Cockade City. Mid-April reports of Union troop and naval buildups in southeastern Virginia and menacing movements toward the west seemed to Pickett the prelude to the long-expected Union offensive (as indeed they were).

On April 11 Lee validated Pickett's concerns. "The defenses at Petersburg should be strengthened immediately to their fullest extent," Lee told the Virginian. Bragg instructed Pickett three days later to keep the War Department advised of all movements in southeastern Virginia, and Pickett did so to a fault. Rather than analyzing the numerous and sometimes contradictory intelligence reports forwarded by spies and scouts along the lower

James and on the Peninsula, Pickett simply passed them along to Bragg verbatim. A frustrated Bragg told Pickett that crediting "exaggerated or unreliable reports" was potentially "useless if not injurious" to command decisions. Pickett bristled at this criticism. "The tone [of your letter] is as harsh as the inferences to be drawn are unmerited," Pickett scolded his superior. He added that by providing the information to Bragg as it arrived in Petersburg "would enable you to form your own conclusions."[77]

This exchange occurred as rumors circulated in Petersburg of Pickett's fondness for alcohol. Charles Campbell, for example, recorded that a young black man had seen Pickett so drunk "that he could hardly get off from his horse." These tales might have reached Richmond. More important, Pickett's unapologetic refusal to take responsibility for strategic policy at Petersburg, added to his lackluster campaign at New Bern, ended his tenure in command of the Department of North Carolina.

The day after Pickett's petulant letter reached Braxton Bragg in Richmond, Special Orders Number 90 announced that Whiting's District of Cape Fear had been united with the Department of North Carolina into one jurisdiction commanded by General Beauregard, then in charge at Charleston, South Carolina. On April 23, from temporary departmental headquarters in Weldon, Beauregard formally assumed his new duties and declared that his command would be known as the Department of North Carolina and Southern Virginia, embracing the Tarheel State east of the mountains and the Old Dominion south of the James and Appomattox Rivers. Pickett would remain in district command at Petersburg, his authority and responsibility more restricted than it had been since his days as a brigade commander in the Army of Northern Virginia.[78]

If Pickett felt shame or disappointment in his loss of departmental command, the record does not reveal it. Harried by what he perceived as a looming crisis at Petersburg and desirous of returning to the field, Pickett immediately sought a return to Lee's army at the head of his old division. His military patron, James Longstreet, endorsed this request, and on May 4 Pickett received orders to move to Hanover Junction and rendezvous with his brigades. Circumstances at Petersburg, however, would delay this change and expose Pickett to some of the most critical days in the city's wartime history. Petersburg's long nightmare was about to begin.[79]

⌐ 7 ⌐

"The Hurly Burly Produced by the Descent of the Yankees"

APRIL 20–JUNE 18, 1864

EVENTS IN PETERSBURG during the last days of April 1864 proceeded with a deceptive normality, as if no one anticipated the military crisis that would engulf the city in the coming weeks. Captain William H. S. Burgwyn of the Thirty-fifth North Carolina Infantry thought more about Petersburg women than Petersburg's enemies, making social calls on four local belles in one day. "We are still getting on pretty well," confirmed Dr. John H. Claiborne on the twenty-fourth. "No fear of the Yankees here."[1]

General George Pickett lent an international flavor to the city's society when he hosted a dinner on April 19 for the officers of two French ships anchored at the mouth of the Appomattox River. (The French had negotiated an agreement with the Lincoln administration to retrieve a quantity of Confederate tobacco at City Point.) Some Petersburgers optimistically believed that the presence of foreign warships promised military resistance to any Union expedition up the James River. Fantasies of intervention died on April 23 when Major General Benjamin F. Butler, Union commander of the Department of Virginia and North Carolina headquartered at Fort Monroe, sent an officer to the French with instructions for the ships to return to Hampton Roads as previously stipulated. Five days later the French complied.[2]

Although most of Pickett's combat troops were in North Carolina, Petersburg retained a substantial Confederate presence. Government hospitals continued to register new patients brought almost daily by ambulance from the Richmond depot. Some of the wounded and sick went to one of Petersburg's seven hospitals, while others continued to the Petersburg Railroad station for transportation farther south. Dr. Claiborne supervised the military medical community from his headquarters opposite the post office on Union Street.

A number of other Confederate administrators conducted business in Petersburg. Major Robert Tannahill superintended Pickett's subsistence department from a building at the foot of Sycamore Street. Major Edward B. Branch ran the quartermaster and transportation operations from chambers at the corner of Sycamore and Old Streets. Captain Archibald W. Dunn managed the forage and stable responsibilities from his desk on Lombard Street. The provost marshal's office could be found on Bank Street, while Major Charles S. Wallach opened his paymaster's window on Sycamore Street near Lombard. Captain Charles H. Dimmock continued to oversee improvements to the city's completed perimeter defenses, rising at a distance of two to three miles from his headquarters on Old Street. We "work every other day A thrain [throwing] up Brest works," reported Private A. H. Massey of the Thirty-first North Carolina Infantry. "We don't have to dril as long as we have to work." A destructive fire on the morning of April 30 consumed the barn and stables at the Model Farm, one of Petersburg's Confederate landmarks, and displaced elements of the Washington Artillery who had quartered there over the winter.[3]

A newly elected Petersburg Common Council met during the first week in May under intense criticism. Not only did the press publish sarcastic editorials lampooning the invisibility of these officials but Thomas Branch, former delegate to the state convention and one-time unionist, claimed that "large sums of money & a quantity of liquor was . . . efficacious in getting conscripts (young men) elected." Branch wrote Governor William Smith suggesting that he strip these alleged shirkers of their military exemptions. The governor decided to leave the councilmen to their civic duties.[4]

Safe for now in their elective offices, the councilmen considered an increase in the appropriations for support of the city's poor, which now numbered 2,416. An estimated thirty-five thousand dollars per month was now required, but the cost-conscioius council only authorized thirty-one thousand dollars. Inflation continued to devour the municipal budget as well as the buying power of individuals. A riding horse, for example, now cost two thousand dollars.

The city's leaders spent their time attending to prosaic affairs, such as debating the need for repairs on the Pocahontas Bridge, giving little hint of the impending martial storm. An article in the May 4 edition of the *Petersburg Daily Express* did sound a more ominous note. The paper warned that all white men aged sixteen through fifty-five must report for drill with the Second Class Militia or face immediate conscription into the regular Confederate army. "Nothing but absolute physical disability will excuse a man from the call." Little did the citizens of Petersburg understand how timely this order would be.[5]

While Petersburg's military and civilian officials handled such routine business, seventy-five miles east of the city at Fort Monroe, General Butler put the finishing touches on a bold plan. In early April, Butler had consulted with the new Union general-in-chief, Lieutenant General Ulysses S. Grant, on a campaign against Richmond and Petersburg. Butler's operations would comprise one element of Grant's three-pronged offensive in Virginia. Major General George G. Meade's Army of the Potomac would hammer Robert E. Lee's forces along the Rapidan River while another blue-clad army moved south through the Shenandoah Valley toward the Virginia Central Railroad. Butler would advance simultaneously up the James River with nearly forty thousand soldiers and take possession of City Point and Bermuda Hundred, the peninsula between the James and Appomattox Rivers. From there he could sever the railroad connecting Petersburg with Richmond. Butler understood that his primary mission entailed a rendezvous with the Army of the Potomac somewhere around Richmond, with Petersburg a secondary target.

General Pickett divined that Butler had some sort of offensive in the works. Beginning in late April the Virginian submitted several warnings to Braxton Bragg, President Davis's military advisor in Richmond, and to General P. G. T. Beauregard, Pickett's immediate superior at Weldon, North Carolina. On May 4 Pickett reported a huge Northern buildup on the Peninsula and the arrival of a large fleet near Fort Monroe. Like the rest of his messages, this information made little impact. Beauregard had convinced himself that Lee's army, not the Department of North Carolina and Southern Virginia, would be Butler's target. An exhausted and exasperated Pickett now looked forward to washing his hands of responsibility for Petersburg and rejoining his division in Lee's army, but Butler's next move would postpone Pickett's departure.[6]

The Union fleet left the mouth of the James River about 6:00 AM on May 5. By late morning Confederate observation posts along the riverbank spotted the Northern vessels and informed Pickett of their menacing progress upstream. The Petersburg commander sent a series of telegrams to Richmond, ten in all, alerting the War Department of the enemy advance. Pickett's credibility in the capital had declined so severely, however, that Bragg failed to even acknowledge receipt of these increasingly frantic messages. Fortunately, Beauregard in Weldon took Pickett's warnings more seriously. The Creole general told Pickett to remain in Petersburg for the time being and authorized him to halt a brigade of Richmond-bound reinforcements once it reached Petersburg. Meanwhile, Beauregard directed his troops operating in North Carolina to return to Virginia.[7]

Until these fresh units arrived, or the Richmond authorities sent him manpower from the capital, Pickett would have to rely on his meager forces to protect Petersburg and its railroad connections north and south. He ordered his only regular infantry, five hundred men of the Thirty-first North Carolina Infantry, into the fortifications east of town guarding the road from

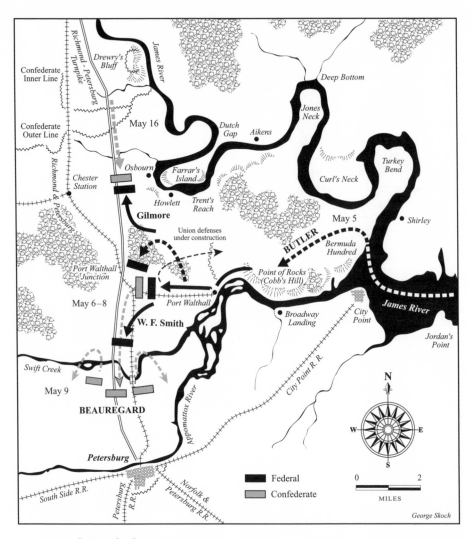

Bermuda Hundred, May 5–16, 1864

City Point. Soon thirteen guns of the Washington Artillery arrived in support. The cannoneers used "horses belonging to omnibuses, express-wagons, buggies,—in fact, any animal that can help haul a gun" to move the artillery through town and out to the works.

The courthouse bell began to ring in the afternoon, summoning the militia to gather on Union Street. "The turn out was . . . larger than . . . the day before," testified Charles Campbell. As many as six hundred emergency soldiers, organized as Companies A and B of the Second Class Militia of the city of Petersburg under Captains Owen H. Hobson and James E. Wolff, marched to the ordnance depot on Old Street to draw ammunition and firearms. They were joined by Major Fletcher H. Archer's Petersburg militia battalion. Once equipped, these citizen-soldiers also headed east to bolster the North Carolinians and Louisianians, giving Pickett a force of perhaps fourteen hundred men. This concentration came none too soon. By 4:00 PM Butler's infantry began landing at City Point. "I have sent you numerous telegrams," Pickett pleaded to the War Department, "and fail to obtain an answer. The emergency is so great that I send a courier by train, to say that the enemy in force are coming up the river. . . . You had better, if possible, either send troops or have trains ready to reinforce this point."[8]

Pickett faced threats from three directions—City Point, Bermuda Hundred, and the Blackwater River. As Butler's divisions disembarked both at City Point and Bermuda Hundred, Pickett recalled the Fifty-first North Carolina Infantry and their brigade commander, Thomas Clingman, from the Blackwater line to strengthen the thin Petersburg defenses. Beauregard was too ill to come immediately from Weldon, so Pickett retained interim responsibility for stopping Butler. The most Beauregard could do was to send Petersburg's former commander Daniel Harvey Hill to the city. Hill, currently without an official assignment, would serve as a volunteer aide and advisor.[9]

Butler's timid corps commanders kept the Federals from advancing west on the night of May 5–6, buying Pickett a few more hours to prepare his defense. The Fifty-first North Carolina Infantry arrived by rail from Ivor early on May 6. Pickett sent them across the Appomattox River to Fort Clifton, supported by a battery of the Washington Artillery. More militia appeared from surrounding counties, although some of these second-tier soldiers treated the situation with less gravity than it deserved. These inexperienced and poorly armed men would provide little help. Pickett continued to correspond with both Beauregard in North Carolina and Bragg in Richmond, seeking aid from both directions. In the absence of fresh brigades, he cleverly ran locomotives in and out of town to create the audible illusion of arriving reinforcements.[10]

The first actual help from outside Virginia, advance regiments of Brigadier General Johnson Hagood's South Carolina brigade, began to arrive from the south on May 6. Pickett stationed them near Port Walthall Junction, an intersection on the Richmond & Petersburg Railroad eight miles north of Petersburg where a spur line led to docking facilities on the Appomattox River. If Butler's soldiers intended to break Petersburg's railroad connection to Richmond, Hagood's troops would be ready to stop them. The Federals had begun a ponderous advance toward the tracks, promising a clash of arms before sunset. Citing the faulty Confederate strategy that had left Petersburg so vulnerable, a Confederate soldier, James Thomas Perry, wrote in his diary that "Bragg or somebody else is criminally to blame in the matter. But Providence I trust will take care of Petersburg."[11]

As refugees poured in from Prince George County and worried wives of militiamen wrung their hands in anxious despair, Petersburg's common council stiffened its collective backbone during an emergency session on May 6. On a split vote, they passed a defiant and bravely worded resolution, at once sincere and ironic given the city leaders' history of seeking military exemptions for themselves and their cronies:

> Believing that the war in which we are forced by an unrelenting foe . . . is just and holy . . . and knowing that the enemy is now in our vicinity . . . this City [should] be defended under all circumstances and to the last extremity . . . that the Mayor . . . be instructed under no circumstances to surrender . . . but if the miserable Yankees by force can take it . . . [we] must surrender our wives and children and noncombatants to their tender mercies . . . that the Grate State of Virginia . . . ought to be . . . free and independent . . . that our people have entire and implicit confidence in our able and gallant commander . . . George E. Pickett, and . . . we hereby tender [thanks] to that General for the distinguished ability and gallantry displayed in the administration of its affairs both military and civic.

The lack of unanimity, however, weakened the moral impact of these resolutions.[12]

Meanwhile, a brigade of Butler's army near Port Walthall Junction tentatively attacked a small body of Hagood's men. The Southerners prevailed despite odds of more than four to one. Throughout the night fresh brigades—at last—streamed to the makeshift Confederate line from both Richmond and points south. "Heavy reinforcements . . . were arriving hourly yesterday and all through last night," reported the *Daily Express*. "Their sturdy shouts, as they passed through our streets, was [*sic*] indeed *music*, such as our people delighted to hear." The editor echoed the city council's esteem for Pickett and urged the citizens to be "hopeful, cheerful, prayerful. Petersburg will never fall into the hands of the brutal oppressors."[13]

May 7, the third day of peril for the beleaguered George Pickett, brought a new challenge. Butler's cavalry under Brigadier General August V. Kautz rode southwest through Prince George County, reaching Stony Creek depot on the Petersburg Railroad, nineteen miles south of Petersburg. The Union troopers burned the railroad bridge there, breaking the vital rail link on which Petersburg relied for reinforcements from North Carolina. Pickett also learned that Beauregard remained too ill to venture northward, leaving him only the unofficial counsel of Hill to manage affairs for another day. Although Butler's stumbling subordinates failed again to disperse the Confederates at Port Walthall Junction, they did manage to cut the telegraph line connecting Petersburg with Richmond. Kautz also snipped the wires south of the city, leaving an increasingly unnerved Pickett isolated and out of touch.

Despite his success in thwarting Butler, Pickett issued orders to the commander at Port Walthall Junction on the night of May 7 to retire south behind Swift Creek, an Appomattox tributary three miles north of Petersburg. This shift, reasoned Pickett, would place his troops in a consolidated position, enabling them to better meet possible attacks both north and east of town, at the cost of ceding the Richmond & Petersburg Railroad to Butler. Pickett clearly considered the defense of Petersburg, not Richmond, his top priority. By 3:00 AM on May 8, nearly five thousand Confederates began moving south of Swift Creek, supported by eighteen pieces artillery.[14]

George Pickett approached his psychological breaking point on the morning of May 8. "Such a week of anxiety as the General passed, only he can know who holds in his hand the homes, the lives, the honor, of men, women, and children," wrote his sympathetic wife. Pickett, according to his bride, had hardly slept since May 5, and his meals were limited to the soup, bread, and coffee that LaSalle Pickett carried to him. Fortunately for Pickett, Butler decided to fortify on May 8 instead of pushing forward to break the railroad. This day Beauregard at last felt healthy enough to start the trek from Weldon to Petersburg. Because of the Federal cavalry around Stony Creek, the sixty-mile hop from Weldon to Petersburg turned into a sojourn of thirty hours via Raleigh, Greensboro, Danville, and Burkeville Junction.[15]

The new militiaman Charles Campbell had no knowledge of these developments. He simply reported to the Jordan farm to help guard the city's eastern approaches. Major Archer had deployed his volunteers in a thin line from Battery Five southward to Battery Ten. "We are here quietly awaiting the approach of the enemy," Archer wrote his new wife at their Petersburg home, "but I have comparatively little anticipation of them attacking this position." Only minor cavalry skirmishing along City Point Road belied Archer's prediction on the eighth.[16]

General Butler resumed his offensive on May 9, instructing most of his army to march west and mangle the tracks linking Petersburg with Richmond. As a part of the day's operations, the Union commander also ordered a demonstration against Petersburg. Because he feared that a direct assault would complicate his ability to achieve his primary objective—linking with Grant near the Confederate capital—Butler decided to forgo anything more than a show of force against the outnumbered Pickett.

The Federal infantry struck the Richmond & Petersburg Railroad near Chester Station, ten miles north of Petersburg, and at Port Walthall Junction, where they destroyed miles of track. Laboring in temperatures that topped one hundred degrees, the unionists turned south by midafternoon and approached Pickett's defense line at Swift Creek. Hagood's men sallied out to meet them. A bloody if "most useless and disastrous reconnaissance in force" ensued, costing Hagood 137 needless casualties.

In the meantime, east of Petersburg, elements of the African American division of Brigadier General Edward W. Hincks pushed westward from City Point, coming under fire from Fort Clifton across the Appomattox River. Hincks withdrew late in the afternoon, ending what—if Butler had so chosen—could have been the day that Petersburg fell to enemy forces. Instead, Butler kept a strategic eye peeled to the north, hoping to cooperate with Grant and Meade (who were fifty miles from Richmond, near Spotsylvania Court House) to sandwich the Confederate capital between his army and theirs. Butler would still move against Petersburg, should circumstances allow.[17]

Butler met with his subordinates late in the afternoon of May 9 to discuss the next day's activities. Having heard nothing from Grant to indicate his proximity to Richmond, Butler decided to attack Petersburg the following morning. By advancing both from the north and east, Butler expected to overwhelm Pickett's defenders at Swift Creek and the Dimmock Line without entangling his troops in a prolonged battle. Information received from Secretary of War Edwin Stanton that evening caused Butler to cancel this promising operation. Stanton reported that "Lee's army fell back . . . yesterday [and] were in full retreat for Richmond." This inaccurate dispatch prompted Butler to return to what he understood to be the object of his campaign: to threaten Richmond from the south in cooperation with Grant and Meade. Thus the Cockade City again escaped almost certain capture.[18]

Coincident to Butler's decision to spare Petersburg, General Beauregard finally arrived in the city about 9:00 AM on May 10 and assumed command. "Will take the offensive as soon as practicable," Beauregard blustered, although his primary mission at Petersburg was clearly defensive. Thousands of reinforcements from Weldon streamed into the city shortly after Beauregard's appearance—Kautz's cavalry having returned to City Point—raising the Confederate strength to seven brigades and reminding one witness of "scenes which would have brought back the first days of the war." "Beautiful ladies showered bouquets of flowers upon us as we marched the streets," reported Private James C. Elliott of the Fifty-sixth North Carolina Infantry.

The Tarheels established camp at Poplar Lawn, where, according to Elliott, "white ladies and colored aunties began to pour in upon us with great baskets of everything good to eat and gave us a bountiful feast." Dr. Claiborne paused from his medical duties to take note of the Petersburg women who would "rush out to cheer the soldiers as their deliverers," and he re-

Pierre Gustave Toutant Beauregard (1818–93). Beauregard's outstanding generalship in May and June 1864 prevented Petersburg from almost certain capture. Once the Army of Northern Virginia arrived in Petersburg, Beauregard ceded practical responsibility for the city's defense to General Lee. (Courtesy of Valentine Richmond History Center)

ported that "the working of handkerchiefs & shouts of the soldiery and the Marshall [sic] music stirred the blood of the coldest." Other women delivered freshly baked bread to the troops in the trenches at Swift Creek. The appearance of so many Confederate soldiers buoyed the militia, who had faced daunting odds for nearly one week. "With the reinforcements we have received I am entirely hopeful of success," wrote Major Archer from his post on the Jordan farm.[19]

Word arrived that afternoon at the Customs House, Beauregard's Petersburg headquarters, that a large Union cavalry force under Major General Philip Sheridan was approaching Richmond. "This city is in hot danger," reported Secretary of War James Seddon from the capital. "It should be defended with all our resources to the sacrifice of minor considerations," presumably including the defense of Petersburg. Beauregard received instructions to move north against Butler's rear while the Richmond garrison both blocked Butler's advance from the south and Sheridan's looming threat from the north. The Louisiana general, despite his bellicose pronouncement earlier in the day, proved in no particular hurry to take the field. He informed Braxton Bragg that he would not be ready to move north until the evening of May 11.

In preparation for the advance he divided his army into two divisions commanded by Pickett and Robert F. Hoke, recently promoted to major general. Pickett, however, exhausted by the strain of orchestrating Peters-

burg's hairbreadth escapes from disaster, collapsed and took to his bed under the solicitous care of his adoring wife. "Gen. Pickett deserves much
credit for having successfully defended with a very small force the town [un-
til] the arrival of reinforcements," thought Lieutenant Colonel Henry Carrington of the Eighteenth Virginia Infantry. In truth, Stanton's misunder-
standing of the military situation in distant Spotsylvania County, combined
with Butler's overcaution and strategic focus on Richmond, spared Petersburg more than Pickett's competence. Beauregard named Brigadier General
Matt Ransom to lead Pickett's brigades while the Virginian recuperated.[20]

Of course, the finer points of military strategy and maneuvers remained
a mystery to the residents of Petersburg. "To our readers at a distance, it may
seem very strange that we cannot speak definitely of what is transpiring so
near to us, in fact in our close neighborhood," admitted the *Petersburg Daily
Register.* "But in fact, unless we 'lie, like a rumour' we cannot . . . do anything
more than . . . vex the public ear and foment disputes as to what is probable,
or improbable true or false."

Although reliable information may have been in short supply, there was
no lack of excitement in a city that had not known the presence of such a
strong enemy army since the American Revolution. "We are still in the midst
of the hurly burly produced by the descent of the Yankees upon City Point
and Bermuda Hundred," reported the *Daily Express.* "For the last six days
we have had the war at our own doors, and our people know what it is to be
troubled by the proximity of a vandal enemy."

Morale in Petersburg remained surprisingly high, nurtured perhaps by
the inability of the citizens to understand how close they had come to disaster. "We have never witnessed more firmness and composure than are to
be seen throughout our city," testified the editor of the *Daily Express.* "No
one is at all disquieted by the stirring military scenes which are enacting in
our vicinity." Dr. Claiborne agreed: "We eat little—live on excitement—and
don't get hungry. . . . Everyone is quiet—cheerful and determined," a sentiment echoed in the *Daily Express:* "Better to subsist on dry bread, than be
ruled by the most detestable race of human beings that ever libeled humanity." Claiborne rejoiced that Beauregard's fresh troops clamored for a chance
to strike "the first blow at the craven foe which had been hovering around
our doors. . . . I have never seen so much enthusiasm amongst the troops as
now. There is no way to whip them but kill them all."[21]

Amid this chest-thumping and civic bravado, Beauregard issued orders
on May 10 reorganizing his department. In addition to naming division
commanders Hoke and Ransom to lead his troops in the field, the Creole selected General Henry A. Wise to succeed Pickett as administrative chief of
the First Military District, with headquarters in Petersburg. "Genl. Beauregard has placed me in command of the entire district south of the James &

Appomattox rivers to the Roanoke river," Wise told his wife, "and I am very busy. All now is safe."[22]

This was certainly not true in Richmond. New orders arrived on the morning of May 11 responding to the threats to the capital that Sheridan and Butler posed. Beauregard was to march north with as many troops as possible to reinforce Major General Robert Ransom, commander at Drewry's Bluff eight miles south of Richmond. Beauregard's presence would release some of Ransom's troops to move north of the James to confront Sheridan. Beauregard made plans to start later in the day. He also sent word to Major General W. H. C. Whiting in Wilmington, recently the de jure commander of Petersburg and a trusted friend, to come to the Cockade City to consult with him as a senior advisor. Beauregard summoned two additional infantry brigades and Brigadier General James Dearing's cavalry brigade from the Carolinas to protect Petersburg while Hoke's and Matt Ransom's Divisions marched north.[23]

Hoke reached Drewry's Bluff on the evening of the eleventh, while Butler's forces slipped between there and Petersburg astride the turnpike and railroad. At Petersburg, as fresh troops rolled in from the south on May 11 and 12, Beauregard waited for General Whiting despite the War Department's wish that he proceed immediately to Drewry's Bluff. Whiting finally appeared on the train from Weldon about 10:00 AM on May 13. He met briefly with Beauregard, who asked him to remain in the city while the department commander at last rode north to Drewry's Bluff to seek the honor of defeating the despised Butler. Beauregard left Petersburg about noon and, following a circuitous route to avoid Butler's army, arrived at Drewry's Bluff before dawn on the fourteenth.

Within hours the visionary Beauregard had concocted a fantastic strategic plan to combine Lee's army, the forces around Richmond, Whiting's men at Petersburg, and his own troops at Drewry's Bluff to deliver sequential blows against Butler and then Grant and Meade. President Davis, who journeyed to Drewry's Bluff to meet with Beauregard, rejected this impractical scheme and ordered Beauregard to bring Whiting to Drewry's Bluff and together confront Butler's menace. By then Sheridan's cavalry had veered to the east and no longer posed a strategic threat to the capital.

Beauregard reluctantly agreed, or so he made the president believe. In reality he clung to the portion of his strategy that envisioned a two-pronged assault against Butler. While Beauregard's troops would attack the Federals from the outer works at Drewry's Bluff, Whiting would lead portions of three brigades, the bulk of the Petersburg garrison, northward and assail Butler's rear. In such a fashion the Yankees would be hammered from two directions, separated from their base of supplies, and destroyed. Beauregard set May 16 as the date for his assault.[24]

On the day of the proposed offensive, Dr. Claiborne wrote his wife from Petersburg that "our affairs are approaching a crisis. There will be an end of this whole matter soon. I look for a happy issue." Claiborne's prediction proved at least partly accurate. Beauregard attacked Butler on May 16 and, in a clumsily fought battle in the fog, drove Butler back. He paused expectantly for the sounds of Whiting's guns that would announce that the fleeing Federals had run into the second half of his fatal pincers. He would wait in vain the entire day.

Whiting had arrived in Petersburg complaining of illness. Following Beauregard's departure the military circumstances Whiting perceived only exacerbated his poor health. Whiting knew next to nothing about the situation in Petersburg—Beauregard had briefed him for an hour or so on the thirteenth before he left for Drewry's Bluff. The city streets confused him, and troop dispositions befuddled him more. Butler left small units north of Swift Creek and near City Point, and General Kautz launched another cavalry raid on May 12 that severed Whiting's communications with Richmond via Burkeville. Like Pickett the week before, Whiting sensed danger from every direction and became convinced that Petersburg, not Richmond, was Butler's actual military objective. With such a mindset Whiting deemed a march north to attack Butler as unduly risky. He advanced two brigades as far as Port Walthall Junction, encountered two regiments of Butler's rear guard, and halted despite the imprecations of Harvey Hill and Henry Wise, both of whom recognized the folly of Whiting's timid generalship. By nightfall the emotionally and physically drained Whiting had returned to Petersburg, Butler had escaped Beauregard's snare, and the Federals limped back unmolested behind their fortifications in Bermuda Hundred.[25]

The battle of Drewry's Bluff, in spite of its imperfections and missed opportunities, temporarily relieved Petersburg of the immediate threat of capture. Beauregard, the army, and Petersburg's citizens, however, had expected nothing less than the destruction of the Federal host. Whiting served as the natural scapegoat for their disappointment. "The people are greatly excited & offended at Genl. W[hiting]," wrote Claiborne. "Had Genl. Whiting pressed the enemy from here as he was ordered to do the rout would have been complete & we should have captured nearly the whole of Butler's forces. . . . Liquor is said to have been at the bottom of the whole affair."

Although it is doubtful that Whiting's notorious fondness for drink explained his incompetence on May 16, his leadership had been so flawed that some subordinates refused to serve under him any longer. He asked to be relieved, a request Beauregard was only too glad to honor. Beauregard named Hill to act in his place, thus giving this officer command of Petersburg for the third time. "The people of Petersburg express great gratitude for my labor of love," Hill informed his wife. Whiting returned to Wilmington a few days later, unmourned in the Cockade City.[26]

Petersburgers had little opportunity to celebrate their deliverance. Crews busily repaired Kautz's damage to the South Side Railroad, and service from the west resumed on May 18. Not until May 26 would trains begin running between Richmond and Petersburg again over the line Butler had disrupted.[27]

This lack of rail service added to the strain that the Meade and Beckwith families experienced as they arranged for the funeral of their kinsman by marriage Julian Ruffin, killed in the fighting near Drewry's Bluff. Dr. Thomas Stanly Beckwith, Julian's brother-in-law, recovered the body from the battlefield, but he had to ship it first by water to Richmond, then on the Richmond & Danville Railroad to Burkeville, and finally into Petersburg on the South Side Railroad, a five-day ordeal. Julian's father, Edmund Ruffin, did not learn of his son's death until May 24.[28]

Petersburg's hospitals filled with wounded from the recent fighting and appeals rang out to the townsfolk to provide all manner of food and supplies. This proved no easy task, for Petersburg's markets had been nearly empty since the commencement of Butler's campaign. So great were the logistical problems that the army asked to borrow shovels from citizens so that the city's defenses might be improved.[29]

The alarm of mid-May interrupted Petersburg's customary wartime routine only briefly. During the fortnight after Beauregard's victory at Drewry's Bluff, the indefatigable Captain Burgwyn resumed his romantic endeavors. Other Confederate officers found diversion attending Petersburg church services or strolling through the streets with local belles clutching their arms. Editorials in the local press dismissed their Union tormentors as "Grant's ruffian host." Observing that "the fewer Lincoln-Abolition Yankees there are upon the earth the better," the *Daily Express* celebrated Grant's battle casualties as a "service" rendered to the world. The *Daily Register* praised the equanimity with which Petersburgers pursued their usual habits, declaring that "a calm confidence pervades all classes, and the daily routine of city life proceeds as quietly as if the mortal struggle, for all that is dear to men and patriots was a thousand miles off, instead of at our doors."[30]

Despite this brave optimism Petersburg struggled with various municipal problems during the late spring. "Every thing is in a disordered condition," complained one soldier, "we are in the dark shadows here." A spectacular jail break involving seven slaves occurred on May 31, resulting in the mortal wounding of one of the escapees at the hands of the assistant jailer, W. H. Boisseau. The previous day 180 toughs from gangs in the South and West Wards, boys too young for military service but old enough to cause serious trouble, engaged in a vicious street fight, using firearms among less lethal weapons, until the police arrived to restore order. The Petersburg Common Council met in early June to pass resolutions increasing aid to the growing number of families that spiraling prices were making desitute. Providing an ominous background to this social chaos, Butler's army crouched in its trenches in Bermuda Hundred and around City Point, an easy day's march from the Cockade City.[31]

Through late May, Beauregard continued to organize his department and adjust his defense of both Chesterfield County and Petersburg. On the twenty-first, Special Orders Number 10 relieved General Hill of his temporary command and returned him to a ceremonial position on Beauregard's staff. Hill's long-standing feud with President Davis, and the refusal of either man to take a conciliatory step, deprived the Confederacy of one of its better field commanders. The order also named Brigadier General Bushrod R. Johnson, soon to be promoted to major general, to command a division. A few days later Beauregard chose Colonel William Butler of Johnson's staff to command the garrison at Petersburg and the territory between the city and Swift Creek. General Wise was reconfirmed as commander of the First Military District of Beauregard's department, embracing all the territory south of the James and north of the Roanoke Rivers. Beauregard counted 14,530 soldiers of all descriptions around Petersburg, including a detachment of Georgians serving as the municipal provost guard.[32]

A portion of the manpower available to Beauregard included the Virginia Reserves, commanded by one of Pickett's former brigadiers, James L. Kemper. Kemper received orders on May 16 to reorganize the Reserves statewide, including some of the militia units serving in Petersburg. Major Peter V. Batte's Forty-fourth Battalion became a part of the new organization, as did Fletcher Archer's command, soon designated as the Third Battalion of Virginia Reserves, which incorporated companies from Prince George and Dinwiddie Counties. Major William Hood commanded companies of Reserves manned primarily by employees from Petersburg's heavy industry. These units, such as the Petersburg & Weldon Railroad Company, the Ettrick Cotton Works Company, and the Southside Rail Road Guards, would be called into active service only under emergency conditions.[33]

Some in Petersburg, such as the disabled veteran Anthony M. Keiley recently elected to the Virginia legislature, believed that the militia should be discharged from active duty. He wrote the governor on June 1 arguing that the militia's "presence in the field . . . with but few hostile troops South of the Appomattox cannot be very important." Keiley could not know that Beauregard would soon need every man he could muster.[34]

The politically ambitious Benjamin Butler had not considered the outcome at Drewry's Bluff fatal to his campaign, for either Richmond or the White House. General Grant, however, believed that Butler's withdrawal behind earthworks in Bermuda Hundred and the requirements of Meade's army north of Richmond suggested that a portion of Butler's troops might be better employed as reinforcements for the Army of the Potomac. Butler sought to forestall the dismantling of his army by conducting an offensive against Petersburg. By May 27 he had perfected his plans. He would send Major General William F. "Baldy" Smith with eleven thousand infantry across the Appomattox River to reinforce the black troops under General Hincks, who still occupied City Point and the area immediately to its west. According to the plan, Hincks and Smith would surprise the Confederate pickets east of the city at dawn on May 29 and dash into Petersburg, thereby achieving a significant strategic victory and nullifying Grant's intention to detach Smith.

General Beauregard detected unusual activity in the Federal camps, but he could not fathom Butler's intent. His own forces had been depleted by General Lee, who needed to replace soldiers lost in the bloodbaths of the Wilderness and Spotsylvania Court House. Charged with watching the unionists in Bermuda Hundred as well as guarding Petersburg, Beauregard deployed a paper-thin line of soldiers in the fortifications east of Petersburg on May 28—perhaps two thousand men—including the inexperienced Virginia Reserves. The situation beckoned Butler's veterans to overrun Petersburg's defenses and storm the city.

Once again extraneous circumstances saved Petersburg. Sufficient water transportation arrived on the afternoon of May 28 to shift General Smith's men to Meade's area of operations. A few hours later Butler canceled the orders for his movement against Petersburg. "I grieve much that this weakness of the Army of the Potomac has called the troops away," lamented Butler, "just as we were taking the offensive, and that the attack on Petersburg . . . must be abandoned."[35]

General Smith's departure prompted the dispatch of Hoke's Division to Lee as a countermeasure a few days later. Both of these forces would fight on June 3 a few miles northeast of Richmond at the horrendous battle of Cold Harbor. Meanwhile, the stalemate at Bermuda Hundred continued to vex Butler, who still controlled considerable resources—including Hincks's African American infantry that moved freely around City Point. The presence of these black troops struck a nerve with John W. Syme, editor of the *Daily Register*. Using blunt language, Syme reflected the feelings of many white Southerners who deeply resented the use of black troops—many of them former slaves—as occupiers in Confederate territory. "It is hard that a sett [*sic*] of stinking, thieving 'niggers' should rule with a high hand, and high head, almost within sight of the steeples of this city," snarled Syme. "A force of a thousand men properly stationed, could either keep these aromatic sons of Ethiopia in their fortifications, or make them pay dearly for exposing their odoriferous carcasses outside of them, or popping their wool over their breastworks."[36]

Butler now determined to use these soldiers, and August Kautz's weary

cavalry, to burn the Appomattox bridges and destroy the public buildings in
Petersburg, but a skirmish that Beauregard initiated on June 2 at Bermuda
Hundred caused Butler to postpone the raid. In the aftermath of Cold Harbor even more of Beauregard's troops trekked north of the James, leaving
him with fewer than six thousand soldiers in three brigades. Beauregard distributed twenty-two hundred men in the Petersburg defenses and left the
rest in the lines blocking an advance from Bermuda Hundred. The weakened Confederate positions encouraged Butler to dust off his Petersburg
attack plans on June 8, as did the anticipated shifting of a part of Meade's
forces south of the James. Meade's pending arrival suggested to the
headline-hungry Butler that time for an independent victory was running
out. He began perfecting an attack that would provide Petersburg one of its
most memorable days.[37]

Although Butler had only ten thousand men at his disposal between
Bermuda Hundred and City Point, he knew from a captured map, testimony
from runaway slaves, and a trickle of deserters that the lines east and south
of Petersburg were in poor condition and weakly held. His attack plan envisioned three simultaneous assaults: two with infantry along City Point and
Jordan Point Roads and a cavalry dash northward on Jerusalem Plank
Road. All told, Butler committed roughly forty-six hundred soldiers to the
raid, including fourteen hundred veteran troopers under General Kautz.
"The advantage [of seizing Petersburg] would be cheaply purchased at 500,
and not too dearly with the sacrifice of 1,000 men in killed and wounded,"
observed Butler.[38]

Butler's intelligence described the Confederates' situation at Petersburg
on June 9 quite accurately. Despite Captain Dimmock's efforts, the earthen
walls of his vast fortifications had eroded during the winter and spring.
More important, by then General Wise had even fewer troops to defend his
works than earlier—perhaps twelve hundred in all—many of whom were
Virginia Reserves.

Hood's and Batte's Reserve units took position between Batteries Two
and Seven east of town, supported by artillery. To their right five hundred
veterans of the Forty-sixth Virginia Infantry extended as far southwest as
Battery Sixteen, where four heavy guns anchored the right flank of Wise's
continuous line of defense. To the west, across one mile of nearly empty
fortifications, stood two guns of Sturdivant's (Virginia) Artillery; in Batteries Twenty-six through Twenty-eight, the men of Archer's Reserve battalion
guarded Jerusalem Plank Road. A thin screen of cavalry deployed east of
town augmented this skeleton force. General Wise commanded the entire
military district, but on June 9 Brigadier General Raleigh E. Colston, who
had informally assumed command of the Post of Petersburg while awaiting
a permanent assignment, was the ranking Confederate officer in the Cockade City.[39]

Butler reluctantly agreed to entrust command of his operation to Major General Quincy A. Gillmore, his senior subordinate south of the James but a man in whom Butler placed little confidence. Gillmore proceeded to justify Butler's skepticism by conducting a tardy march during the night of June 8–9, causing his expedition to fall behind schedule. He attempted to make up lost time by denying his infantry the chance to rest prior to their attack. When the enervated Federals ran into Confederate cavalry skirmishers east of the Dimmock Line, the sun had risen well into the eastern sky, and whatever element of surprise Butler hoped to achieve had vanished.[40]

A courier from the Forty-sixth Virginia Infantry dashed to Major Archer in the sagging works along Jerusalem Plank Road and warned the aging officer of the impending Union assault. By 9:00 AM word reached Petersburg as well. "All the available bell metal in the corporation broke into chorus with so vigorous a peal and clangor . . . as to suggest to the uninitiated a general conflagration," remembered Anthony Keiley. The citizens responded to the unexplained emergency by rushing from their homes and offices into the streets, where anxious questions yielded news of the Union approach. Almost immediately "greyhaired men, and beardless boys," exempt by virtue of age, occupation, or disability, "hastily kissed the dear ones at home, seized their muskets, and rushed out to [Archer's] lines to assist in protecting their firesides against the advancing hosts," wrote one Confederate soldier.[41]

General Wise delegated local command to Colston about 9:30 AM, while he hurried north to inform Beauregard of the brewing crisis. Colston hustled toward Battery Sixteen. Happily for him and the defenders on Petersburg's eastern outskirts, Gillmore's infantry attack sputtered almost immediately, then died. Rifle and artillery fire from Batteries Four and Five halted the Federals along City Point Road. One mile south the black troops under General Hincks took enfilading fire against both flanks as they deployed opposite Battery Nine. The Confederate line between Batteries Four and Seven comprised an eastern-thrusting salient that separated Gillmore's two infantry wings and prevented easy cooperation between the Union columns. A more aggressive officer than Quincy Gillmore would have pressed the thin Confederate line harder, but by 10:00 AM he stopped even prodding. Three hours later Gillmore ordered the infantry to withdraw. "I found the enemy prepared for me," he lamely explained, and "the works are as strong . . . as our own. . . . In my opinion, they cannot be carried by the force I have." Thus thirty-three hundred infantry had been blunted by approximately nine hundred militia and regulars supported by a handful of artillery. Now Butler's hopes rested solely with his cavalry.[42]

General Gillmore mentioned the sound of fighting to his left, indicating that "Kautz finds himself opposed." Indeed, the Union cavalry commander had run into what would become the war's most renowned defense

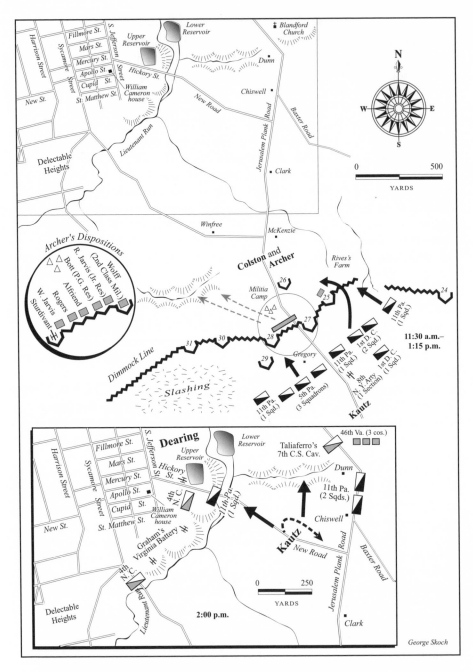

The Battle of Old Men and Young Boys, June 9, 1864

by amateur volunteers. Fletcher Archer's Battalion of Virginia Reserves, composed primarily of the professional and businesses classes of the city, had been shifted weeks earlier to Batteries Twenty-six through Twenty-eight, on the Timothy Rives farm, from their original positions around Battery Five. In early June, as Butler's army lolled in Bermuda Hundred and City Point, Archer's militiamen traveled freely between their camps and town, tending to personal business while military responsibilities seemed only theoretical. When all of Archer's men mustered, the major could count perhaps 125 emergency soldiers. Archer enjoyed virtually no flank support on June 9—the nearest troops on his left lying one mile away, while four miles of empty trenches stretched to his right. An overturned wagon and some fence rails blocked Jerusalem Plank Road where it passed through the works. By midmorning Kautz approached Archer's meager defenses with three experienced regiments supported by a few cannon.[43]

Anthony Keiley was among the volunteers who left his office for the front, but he departed without a weapon. He reached Archer's line, where, after he examined some spare muskets that proved hopelessly inoperable, someone handed him a serviceable rifle, and he took his place in the ranks. Others among the volunteers who reinforced Archer that morning included the fifty-nine-year-old bank officer William C. Banister; three members of the Petersburg Common Council—Robert A. Martin, Charles F. Collier, and James Boisseau; and the mill manager David Callender, who had been awake all night guarding prisoners in town when the alarum aroused him out of bed.

Archer placed these new arrivals in position, "and what a line it was!" recalled the major. "In number scarcely more than sufficient to constitute a single company. . . . In dress nothing to distinguish them in appearance from citizens pursuing the ordinary avocations of life. In age many of them with heads silvered o'er with the frosts of advancing years, while others could barely boast of the down upon the cheek. . . . In arms and accouterments such as an impoverished government could afford them." Archer's men—Colston estimated them to number between 150 and 170—occupied portions of Batteries Twenty-five through Twenty-nine, but they had no artillery and faced odds of better than eight to one.[44]

About 11:30 AM the Eleventh Pennsylvania Cavalry conducted an unscripted charge straight at Battery Twenty-seven. The Reserves, maintaining discipline worthy of combat veterans, waited until the range had closed to fifty yards: then they loosed a ragged but telling volley. A few Pennsylvania saddles emptied, and the Federals retreated, paying a sharp price for such an impetuous attack. General Kautz then arrived and adopted a more professional, if overly cautious tack. Dismounting most of his men, the Union commander spent considerable time reconnoitering the Confederate position. By then General Colston had assumed tactical control from Archer, dragging with him one twelve-pound howitzer from Sturdivant's Battery to strengthen the position. The Federals approached again, but, aided by their cannon and a determination born of the desire to defend their homes, the Confederates repulsed this second assault. For nearly an hour the two sides exchanged shots. The Confederates resisted so stoutly that one of Kautz's brigade commanders estimated Confederate strength at fifteen hundred infantry and three cannon.[45]

The defenders endured withering blasts from Kautz's artillery, which Colston knew would eventually tip the balance of firepower in favor of the Federals. He called for a volunteer to ride to General Wise with a plea for immediate aid. Wales Hurt, a lieutenant barely eighteen years of age, answered the call. With bullets singing around him, Hurt galloped northward on Colston's borrowed horse in search of Wise and salvation.

By this time General James Dearing and Captain Edward Graham were already leading fresh troops into Petersburg. Soon after Gillmore's appearance Wise had reached Beauregard's field headquarters a few miles north of the city, near Dunlop Station on the Richmond & Petersburg Railroad. Responding to Wise's pleas for help, the department commander released Colonel Dennis D. Ferebee's Fourth North Carolina Cavalry of Dearing's Brigade and Graham's Petersburg Artillery from their camps seven miles north of Petersburg. Dearing assumed overall charge of these modest reinforcements. Petersburg's fate now depended on the ability of Archer and Colston to hold at the Rives farm long enough for Dearing's troopers and Graham's cannoneers to arrive from Chesterfield County.[46]

Dearing and Graham thundered over the Pocahontas Bridge, headed up Second Street to Lombard Street, and turned eastward, assuming that they would be needed at Battery Five. Informed by a staff officer that the danger lay south and west of the city, Dearing turned left on North Main Street through Blandford then left again on Bollingbrook Street. By doubling back west to Sycamore Street, he could follow this thoroughfare south to their destination.

The column careened through Petersburg's streets at breakneck speed, almost trampling one local lady, Lossie Hill, in the process. "Get out of the way," screamed Graham. "Damn the women! Run over them, if they don't get out of the way!" Graham's four guns, followed by the North Carolina cavalry, turned south in the heart of Petersburg's business district, where some of the citizens joyfully recognized their hometown unit. With shouts of encouragement ringing in their ears, Dearing's troopers pushed their horses at full gallop.[47]

By then, however, the final drama at the Rives farm had played out. Kautz's artillery continued to exact a toll on the outnumbered defenders, as dismounted soldiers from the Eleventh Pennsylvania Cavalry and First District of Columbia Cavalry crept around the Confederates' left flank—and into the rear of Batteries Twenty-five and Twenty-seven. Colston shifted the Reserves so they could return fire toward the rear, buying a few extra minutes for the reinforcements he hoped would appear. Finally, as the old men and young boys began to fall with alarming frequency, Colston told Archer to withdraw his battalion. "We were now hemmed in on three sides, and only a narrow path leading through an abrupt ravine offered a way of escape," remembered Colston. The intrepid but inexperienced Reserves fell back, every man (and boy) for himself.

Union troopers flooded into the works, capturing some defenders and shooting others as they attempted to escape. The elderly William Banister, either through stubbornness or failure to hear the command, refused a demand to surrender and kept firing until a bullet through the head killed him on the spot. Anthony Keiley paused to help a wounded neighbor, the dentist William Bellingham. The delay proved his undoing, as a Union soldier "presenting his loaded carbine, demanded my surrender with an unrepeatable violence of language that suggested bloodshed," related Keiley. "I yielded with what grace I could to my fate, captive . . . of a hatchet-faced member of the First District Cavalry, greatly enamored of this honorable opportunity of going to the rear." Archer's lone artillery piece positioned in Battery Twenty-eight fell to the Federals as the surviving militia rushed to the west, out of harm's way. Councilman Robert Martin turned to fire the last defiant shot at the victorious Federals at 1:15 PM. Archer's men had held their ground for nearly two hours, but now the road to Petersburg lay open.[48]

Although the horse holders promptly brought mounts forward to the captured works, General Kautz wasted valuable time interrogating prisoners, looting the abandoned Confederate camps, and burning the Rives house. After this needless delay he ordered the Eleventh Pennsylvania Cavalry to ride north on Jerusalem Plank Road. Some of the Pennsylvanians turned west at the intersection with New Road, aiming toward the heights at the south end of town, while other troopers continued due north toward Wells Hill and Blandford Cemetery. Accompanied by one gun, the troopers on New Road descended toward Lieutenant Run. As they crossed the little stream and cantered up the opposite slope, flashes from artillery and small arms erupted in their faces at a range of about one hundred yards. The Union commander Colonel Samuel P. Spear believed his troopers had encountered a strongly defended stockade. "Had the enemy reserved this fire for a few minutes longer the most fearful results to my command would have ensued, and I was compelled to fall back under cover immediately," explained Spear.[49]

Spear's stockade was in reality the berms of a city reservoir. Graham had dashed ahead to find the best place to unlimber his guns. When the teams arrived, the Petersburg cannoneer led one section to the south side of the reservoir and sent another to the end of Sycamore Street, just west of the tobacconist William Cameron's mansion, all under the anxious eye of large numbers of curious women and children. It had been a close affair. A few minutes more and the Union cavalry might have gained the crest of the heights and entered the city's streets, where buildings would have neutralized the power of artillery. As it was, Graham's guns froze the Federals, aided by the brave survivors of the fight at the Rives farm and portions of Dearing's cavalry. The rest of the North Carolina troopers charged straight ahead toward the shocked bluecoats. Spear saw no alternative but to retreat.

The portion of Kautz's cavalry that had ridden north toward Blandford encountered a motley collection of "patients and penitents"—convalescents gathered from the city's military hospitals, along with Confederate prisoners whose bad behavior had landed them in jail. The withdrawal of the Union infantry east of town allowed several companies of the Forty-sixth Virginia Infantry to march to the aid of the extemporized battle line on Wells Hill. Their arrival, along with elements of Dearing's cavalry that had not ridden to the reservoir, convinced the Federals that here, too, they had run into an insurmountable force, and these troopers also withdrew. Kautz now reasoned that the probability of more Confederate reinforcements and the lack of infantry support on his right ended any hope of seizing Petersburg and burning the bridges across the Appomattox. By 3:00 PM Kautz began to retire toward Bermuda Hundred. One historian called the Union actions on June 9 "the sorriest performance ever turned in by the Army of the James."[50]

"The hand of Providence was with us," thought a grateful Margaret Stanly Beckwith. No Union soldiers had entered the city limits. As more of Beauregard's soldiers streamed into Petersburg, the danger of sudden capture and depredation faded. The relieved citizens now turned to assess the cost of their salvation. Archer's losses amounted to seventy-eight citizen-soldiers, more than half of his total complement. Fifteen of Petersburg's defenders were either killed or mortally wounded, including the aged William Banister and the youthful Wales Hurt, who had been shot when returning from his duty as a courier. Eighteen additional men sustained wounds, and forty-five were captured. Among the latter were Councilman James Boisseau and Timothy Rives, former delegate to the state convention, on whose farm the battle had been fought.[51]

The teenaged Anne Banister watched as her uncle drove up with her father's lifeless body in the back of a wagon. "My precious mother stood like one dazed," the girl recalled, "but in a few seconds she was kneeling by my father in such grief as I had never seen before." Similar scenes rent neighborhoods throughout the city. One by one, ambulances brought dead or mangled men into town to be greeted by mourning family and friends. The toll had been too great to permit Petersburgers to celebrate their deliverance from disaster. "Night closed in, and we sat down face to face with our woe," wrote one resident, "some to watch the dying, others to keep sad vigil beside their dead; while numberless hearts agonized in prayer for loved ones torn from home, and now on their way to pine, and perhaps die, in some Northern prison."[52]

Bessie Meade Callender deemed June 10, 1864, as "the saddest day that ever dawned on Petersburg." Funerals commenced in the morning and continued into the next day, most of the city's churches and some homes providing the venues for these poignant affairs. "It was a day of mourning for all," recalled Mrs. Callender. The common council met in emergency session and passed a resolution calling on the Confederate government to arrange for the speedy exchange of prisoners taken on the Rives farm, such as their colleague James Boisseau, the city chamberlain John B. Stevens, and Keiley. Petersburg's close call persuaded the War Department to shift a brigade from the Richmond defenses to aid Beauregard south of the James, who in turn sent more troops to Petersburg. "I have my entire brigade here now and don't fear another attack," General Wise informed his wife from Petersburg on June 12. Wise issued congratulatory orders that day, honoring "a mere handful of citizen soldiers, who stood firmly and fought bravely as veterans . . . consecrating with their blood the soil of the homes they defended."[53]

In the years after the Civil War, Petersburgers would choose June 9 as the day to commemorate their wartime sacrifice and valor. During the second week of June 1864, however, city residents had no idea that their worst days still lay before them. General Grant, having exhausted his alternatives north of the James River, determined to continue his campaign on the south side. Even as Petersburgers buried their loved ones killed on June 9, Grant's engineers prepared the approaches for a massive pontoon bridge spanning the James. At the same time Baldy Smith's corps embarked on transport ships heading back to Bermuda Hundred and City Point. Butler had chosen not to capture Petersburg in May, and Kautz and Gillmore had intended only to raid the city on June 9; but Grant's new strategy anticipated isolating Richmond from its supply lines to the south by conquering the Cockade City. He would wield the entire weight of the Army of the Potomac to achieve his objective.[54]

Grant took great pains to mask his shift south of the James from General Lee, and the ruse worked. The Confederate commander continued to believe that Meade's army, including Smith's corps of the Army of the James, still faced him east of Richmond. One Confederate did accurately predict Grant's course of action. D. H. Hill, still serving without a command because of his enduring clash of egos with Jefferson Davis, had always considered Petersburg the strategic avenue to Richmond. On June 11 Hill encouraged

Beauregard to shift all his forces to the Cockade City and appeal to the War Department for additional troops to watch the lines in Bermuda Hundred. "It is arrant nonsense for Lee to say that Grant can't make a night march without his knowing it," declared the outspoken Hill. "Has not Grant slipped around him four times already?" Stating plainly that the loss of Petersburg "surely involves that of Richmond—perhaps of the Confederacy," Hill warned of "a terrible disaster" should Petersburg remain so vulnerable. Beauregard concurred, but he despaired of convincing the War Department to look south for the key to Richmond's defense: "I shall continue to hold 'the lines' as long as there is the slightest hope of being able to do so with success and without endangering Petersburg."[55]

In Petersburg, Dr. Claiborne admitted uncertainty on the eve of Grant's new offensive as mundane matters continued to arrest the attention of citizens. "I hope the authorities have determined to make a stand here even against any force," Claiborne wrote. "We are still in the dark in reference to Grant's movements & until they are developed we shall not know our fate." On June 14 the *Daily Register* reported not the impending advance of a strong Union force but the arrest of seventeen free blacks on High Street, "the elite of the city's colored community," for gathering in numbers large enough to constitute an unlawful assembly. The next day's edition likewise omitted mention of the Federal approach, the editor expressing complete confidence in the city's security. Beauregard was not so sanguine: scouts and deserters informed him of the proximity of Smith's corps, and on June 14 he asked Lee to return the troops he had loaned him for the fight at Cold Harbor.[56]

Wednesday, June 15 dawned as bright as any other early summer day. When word reached Petersburg that Union soldiers had been spotted, no one could know that this was not simply another of the intermittent threats that had plagued the city since early May. At 7:00 AM Beauregard wired General Bragg in Richmond that the appearance of Butler's soldiers "renders my position more critical than ever; if not re-enforced immediately enemy could force my lines at Bermuda Hundred . . . or take Petersburg." Beauregard continued to bombard Richmond with status reports and requests for help throughout the morning. Fortunately, Hoke's Division hurried south to reinforce the twenty-two hundred men of Wise's Brigade and the militia, who defended four miles of the Dimmock Line east and south of town.[57]

"Cannonading and musketry are distinctly heard from the city," reported one North Carolina soldier on June 15. At 7:00 AM the skirmishing east of town prompted the city's bells to toll their warnings. Complacency borne of repeated alarms led most citizens, unaware of the unprecedented peril, to pursue their usual routines. Charles Campbell joined a number of schoolgirls and women on the roof of the Iron Front Building on Sycamore Street.

From there he spotted blue-clad troops to the east. As the cautious Federals slowly neared the city's outer defenses, Campbell observed elements of Bushrod Johnson's Brigade march through town, dispatched by Beauregard as reinforcements from the lines at Bermuda Hundred. Major Giles Buckner Cooke of Beauregard's staff, acting as a courier between Wise and Beauregard, informed Wise that help was on its way from north of the Appomattox. This help, as it turned out, would arrive too late to save the city's eastern ramparts.

Early in the evening—after an unconscionable delay by Smith, who may have been haunted by recent memories of Cold Harbor—a Union assault easily overwhelmed the outnumbered defenders from Batteries Three to Eleven. One and one-half miles of the Confederate line crumbled with barely a struggle. Smith captured about two hundred and fifty Confederates and sixteen pieces of artillery, killing and wounding uncounted others; Major Peter Batte was among the prisoners. Darkness blunted further Union gains, but not nearly so effectively as Smith's timidity. Worried about possible Confederate reinforcements and the exhaustion of his troops, Smith decided against a night advance, thus affording Petersburg a reprieve from certain capture.[58]

Beauregard had arrived in Petersburg about 6:00 PM, thus learning firsthand of the collapse of his lines. Using the fresh levies from Chesterfield County, he formed a new defensive front that incorporated Batteries One and Two and then followed the western bank of Harrison's Creek south, rejoining the original Dimmock Line near Battery Fifteen. More troops from both armies poured into the Petersburg area on Thursday June 16. In his quest to capture the city, Grant sent reinforcements as fast as possible from north of the James. Beauregard stripped his defenses at Bermuda Hundred and continued to beg Lee to move his army to Petersburg, but Lee still doubted that Grant's primary target lay south of the James.

The armies skirmished before Petersburg throughout the day, with cannon fire audible as far away as Lunenburg County. Charles Campbell watched as a few artillery shells landed in Petersburg. Just as one week earlier, every able-bodied man in town, and some of the ill and walking wounded, had taken positions near the front lines—many at the south end of Sycamore Street. Major Cooke scurried to and from Beauregard's headquarters at the Customs House, carrying messages and directing troops to their assigned positions. After dark, Cooke attended the funeral of a comrade, Captain John C. Pegram, mortally wounded in the day's fighting. With the angry sounds of big guns as a backdrop, the Reverend William H. Platt presided over the service at Blandford Cemetery, where Cooke helped bury his young friend by moonlight.[59]

Only hours before, Meade's forces had attacked Beauregard's new line and captured three additional batteries before darkness ended their assault.

Robert Edward Lee (1807–70). Lee's presence in Petersburg from June 1864 until the city's evacuation on April 2, 1865, inspired the local residents. He frequently attended services at St. Paul's or Grace Episcopal Churches and dined with various Petersburg families. (Courtesy of Valentine Richmond History Center)

This Union success prompted Beauregard to constrict his defenses again. He withdrew to another line even closer to Petersburg. As soon as the Confederates assumed their new positions on June 17, a predawn Federal attack southeast of town overran portions of Beauregard's works, signaling the beginning of a long, brutal day of combat.

The Confederate high command remained confused about the identity and whereabouts of the Union legions. Lee still refused to significantly weaken his defenses north of the James to defend Petersburg, although with each Yankee lunge it became more apparent that a substantial portion of Grant's force had shifted south of the Appomattox. Beauregard struggled with the quality of his military intelligence, at one point recommending by telegraph an attack to drive away what he thought might be a numerically inferior body of Federals. Lee rejected such an unsound tactic, allowing Meade to resume the initiative at dusk. Assaults and countercharges occupied the troops south and east of Petersburg until well after dark, resulting in massive casualties for both armies. Hundreds of Union prisoners marched into Petersburg, providing diversion for the anxious citizens. In the end the Confederate lines held, but not without more gains by Meade and expressions of doubt from Beauregard that he could continue to defend Petersburg without substantial immediate help.[60]

These gains allowed the Federals to mount field artillery in the captured positions close enough to shell the city with ease. For the first time in the war, Petersburgers experienced a sustained bombardment that claimed lives and damaged property. The shelling initiated a dislocation that would define Petersburg's way of life for the next nine months.

The first projectiles landed along Bollingbrook Street and near the courthouse. In Blandford a white resident fell wounded in the head, and two slave children sustained serious injuries near the city gas works. More intense cannonades accompanied the battles fought after sunset. Incongruously pleasant evening air carried the distant sounds of military serenades to residents who gathered on their porches in the moonlight. Suddenly shells began to burst, exploding so near to some townsfolk that they fled to the west, out of range. "Oh, what sad weary hours were those as we lay listening to the fearful sounds that seemed to threaten us every moment with destruction," remembered one Petersburg woman.[61]

Margaret Beckwith followed the nighttime infantry action through the distinct echoes of the "Hurrah! hurrah! hurrah!" of the Union assaults and the answering "Rebel Yell" of Confederate counterattacks. "For a few minutes the sound of musketry & shell was horridly near and deafening," she remembered, but eventually the cacophony of war receded and the frightened citizens relaxed a little amid the random bombshells, knowing that their city had escaped capture for at least another night.

The combat completely unnerved Mrs. Callender, prompting her to summon her husband, David, from his Reserve duties nearby. The mill executive gently admonished his panicky wife and encouraged her to show fortitude in these desperate hours. Although her husband's words provided some comfort, Mrs. Callender sought additional strength in a draught of whiskey, "about a wine glassfull . . . in a tin cup, which I drank without sugar." This seemed to do the trick. "I never felt fear again."[62]

The Federals' progress and evident determination to continue their assaults persuaded Beauregard to readjust his defenses a third time. After midnight the Louisianian ordered his troops to fall back to what would prove to be Petersburg's axis of defense for the remainder of the campaign. Located between five hundred and eight hundred yards west and northwest of the line established on the night of June 15, the new works stretched from the Appomattox River south, behind the Newmarket race track, and continued south and west until they intersected the original Dimmock Line at Battery Twenty-five on the Rives farm. This position, which the soldiers furiously improved overnight, was supported by more than forty pieces of artillery. Lee released portions of his army to reinforce Beauregard's defenders as Grant's intentions became more certain. By dawn June 18 Lee at last acknowledged that Petersburg, not Richmond, required his primary attention; he headed south to take control of the situation even as his veteran brigades marched toward the Cockade City.[63]

Lee's reinforcements included Petersburg's hometown regiment, the Twelfth Virginia Infantry. Rumors of its approach reached the city, enticing throngs of friends to gather on almost every downtown corner, laden with refreshments to share with their returning loved ones. The wealthy businessman Reuben Ragland parked a wagon on Sycamore Street loaded with a hogshead from which he dispensed coffee to the troops. Cheering supporters tossed twists of chewing tobacco from perches on the Iron Front Building. "As we marched up Sycamore Street our march was almost blocked by . . . relatives and friends," recorded Sergeant James E. Whitehorne. "It was pathetic to witness the meeting of wives & husbands, mothers and sons, and quite refreshing the greetings between beaux and lovely lasses." One Petersburg woman, searching for her son, thought the local soldiers appeared "worn with travel and fighting, so dusty and ragged, their faces so thin and drawn by privation that we scarcely knew them. It made one's heart ache to look at them." The soldiers made their way through the crowd from Sycamore Street to Halifax Street, then turning due south toward the lines.[64]

A group of Ottawa Indians from a Michigan regiment was among the hundreds of Union prisoners seized during the fighting of June 18. Charles Campbell led a group of children to the foot of Market Street, where the captives were gathered, and conversed with the unfortunate soldiers, treating them like carnival freaks. "They were tawny with dark straight black hair, black eyes high cheek bones & taciturn & very grave looking robust men," noted Campbell. Their guards, less fascinated with the anthropology of their charges, laughed at the Indians, deriding the ethnic composition of the Union army.

Lee reached Petersburg about 11:30 AM. He repaired to the Customs House, where Campbell joined a crowd craning for a glimpse of the Confederate hero. The general, who reminded Campbell of "my idea of Washington," waved to the citizens and then rode with Beauregard to the reservoir to assess the situation. Rejecting Beauregard's seemingly perpetual suggestions to attack, Lee remained content to await further Yankee assaults against what he now deemed to be a very strong position. His judgment proved accurate. For the fourth consecutive day the Federals hurled themselves with uneven degrees of élan and coordination against the raw earth of Beauregard's shield. The futile assaults continued all afternoon but failed to penetrate the Confederate defenses at any point. Credit for Petersburg's salvation belonged almost exclusively to Beauregard, whose troops had repulsed every enemy prior to Lee's army's arrival. By 6:30 PM the last gun had fallen silent.[65]

The fighting between June 15 and 18 cost between ten and eleven thousand Union casualties—a toll equal to some of the worst Civil War engagements. Beauregard suffered four thousand killed, wounded, and missing. The outcome might have been much different. "I do not think there is any doubt that Petersburg itself could have been carried without much loss," thought General Grant.

As had been the case since Butler's arrival at City Point and Bermuda Hundred on May 5, Union strategic choices and tactical blunders had contributed as much to Petersburg's deliverance as had Confederate bravery and fortitude. Beauregard found himself outnumbered at least three to one, and often five to one, between June 15 and 18. The Confederates' high morale and sound defensive positions mattered during these critical days, but Union exhaustion, poor staff work, and weak leadership counted more. Grant now settled down to a deliberate campaign, targeting Petersburg's remaining supply lines rather than relying on frontal attacks to overwhelm Petersburg's defenders—who now included the Army of Northern Virginia. "Far better that every house be battered and not one stone be left standing upon another than that Yankee footsteps pollute [Petersburg's] beautiful streets," vowed one determined Virginian. The next nine months would testify to the sincerity of this pledge, but the coming weeks would also subject the citizens of Petersburg to a trial matched by few Confederate cities.[66]

⌐ 8 ⌐

"Enough to Move the Heart of Any Man"

JUNE 19–OCTOBER 1864

JUNE 19, 1864, MARKED the beginning of a new phase of the campaign for Petersburg. Having failed to capture the city during the bitter fighting of the previous four days, Ulysses S. Grant now devoted his energies to isolating it—and by extension the Rebel capital at Richmond—from the rest of the Confederacy. He reasoned that by choking off the flow of supplies into Petersburg, he could deny the food, fodder, munitions, and medicine necessary to sustain Richmond's citizens and Lee's army. Only the Richmond & Danville Railroad served the Confederate capital without first passing through Petersburg; the Cockade City now stood as the Confederacy's most important transportation hub.

In Petersburg concerns about survival trumped musings on strategy. The Federal shelling that commenced on June 16—which some had hoped would only be incidental to the combat along the Confederate lines—continued after Grant halted his frontal assaults. The Union bombardment would never reach the level of a formal tactical operation, but as a form of terror and a source of disruption the Federal shells left an indelible impression on the city and its residents for the next four months.

Most Petersburgers considered the random shelling of a civilian population barbaric. Even when military necessity required the reduction of a town, the courtesies of war demanded that the attackers notify noncombatants of their intent and provide a reasonable time for them to remove themselves and their personal property from harm's way. When Grant's cannoneers fired projectiles into the city after the battle lines fell quiet, soldiers and townsfolk alike therefore considered the practice abhorrent. "The yankees throw an occasional shell on the town which I think, very inhuman," read a typical assessment. "Vandals shelling city again," recorded one Virginia artillerist, "almost a daily sport for the Yanks. It is distressing to see the women and children leaving their homes. It is hard on all—but to see a poor woman, with a child on one arm and little bundles on the other is enough to move the heart of any man—save a Yankee." One Confederate suggested that the government execute a captured Union officer "for every citizen who is killed or wounded by their shells."[1]

Dr. John Herbert Claiborne, administrator of Petersburg's military hospitals, was among the first affected by the Union bombardment. Claiborne ordered the more ambulatory patients from the hospitals in the eastern half of Petersburg removed either to facilities in the city's West End or outside Petersburg altogether. Citizens opened their homes to wounded and sick soldiers dislocated from their wards at the Pavilion Hospital in Poplar Lawn, the South Carolina Hospital, and the Virginia Hospital. Most of the patients in these vulnerable buildings had been moved by June 20, and General Lee urged Claiborne to evacuate the rest.[2]

Major Giles Buckner Cooke of General P. G. T. Beauregard's staff visited Mayor W. W. Townes on June 20 to encourage the city government to relocate citizens living in the most shell-prone neighborhoods, generally east of Sycamore and north of Washington Streets. The Petersburg Common Council consulted with Beauregard and met in emergency session to debate his recommendation. Ultimately they opted not to institute mandatory removals, in part because the city lacked the necessary transportation.[3]

Many residents, however, required no official imprimatur to seek safety, employing "everything that could run on wheels, from a dray to a wheelbarrow." Panic gripped people moving west on Washington Street, even as commissary wagons rolled in the opposite direction to supply defenders on the city's eastern ramparts. The old fire-eater Edmund Ruffin observed that the shelling was steady but desultory and seemed aimed at the railroad bridge across the Appomattox River. "The bomb-shells have not yet done much damage in Petersburg," Ruffin explained. "Some 6 or 8 persons have been struck, & these all women or children & nearly all negroes." Newspaper editorials reassured readers that they had little to fear from Union missiles, but by June 22 Lieutenant William Clopton of the Fayette (Virginia) Artillery concluded that the "city is pretty much deserted by the women and children but many still remain as targets for the shells of the barbarians."[4]

The Union bombardment continued through the remainder of June, steadily eroding Petersburg's wartime routines. Travel across the Pocahontas Bridge was restricted; daytime funerals at Blandford Cemetery became too dangerous, so the dead were interred first at night and then away from Blandford in the yards of churches and elsewhere; Confederate support facilities, such as the army wagon shop in Blandford and headquarters offices in the business district, closed or relocated to the West End. Even the common council moved its meetings to the South Ward Engine House on Halifax Street, to avoid the possibility of a ballistic interruption. Churches

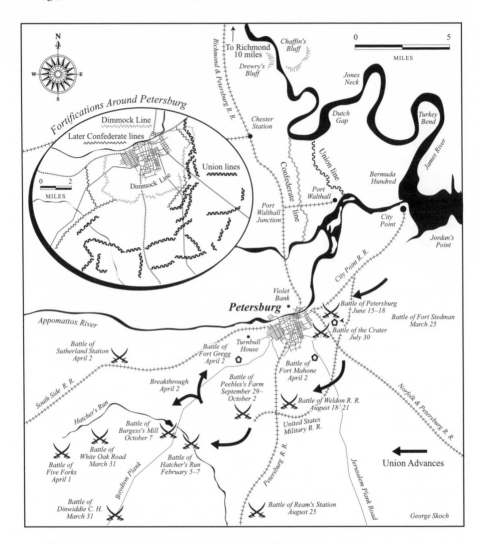

The Petersburg campaign, June 15, 1864–April 2, 1865

sustained shell damage, their steeples providing handy range finders for Northern artillerists. Civilians died—one on June 23, another on the twenty-sixth, and two more on June 30. One woman was struck in the head near Blandford on June 24, "breaking the skull and leaving the brains protruding." An early summer heat wave only added to the city's misery.[5]

After nearly two weeks of slow but constant shelling, those who remained in town developed a fatalistic callousness. General Henry A. Wise noted on June 27 that "crowds of people are passing & grouped on the streets and seem indifferent to the siege." Charles Campbell strolled about town picking up shell fragments as souvenirs. An editorial in the *Petersburg Daily Register* adopted a tongue-in-cheek attitude toward the bombardment and poked fun at citizens' efforts to avoid being struck. Declaring "Conchology— the study of artillery shells"—as a new science in Petersburg, the *Daily Register* praised its readers' grasp of the art of dodging: "As the student seldom moves in a right line but practices eccentric curves around corners, forms obtuse angles, and always prefers the hypotenuse to the base or the perpendicular, we must rank 'dodging' as a branch of higher mathematics." The editor sarcastically marveled at the "rheumatic patients [who] dart down alleys like carrier pigeons, and accomplished gentlemen [who] make unannounced entrances into private homes, without the slightest apology or acquaintance." Campbell encapsulated Petersburg's plight by writing, "We have now war at the door." By June 29 the *Daily Register's* editor adopted such a sanguine outlook that he declared one had to be "dunderpated and pigeon-livered" not to recognize that "the day of final triumph is at hand."[6]

Events on the battlefields made such statements ring hollow. Grant ordered two of Major General George G. Meade's infantry corps and some fifty-five hundred cavalry to move west in unison, cross Jerusalem Plank Road, and then target the Petersburg Railroad south of the city. The horsemen, under brigadier generals James H. Wilson and August V. Kautz, would range much farther south and west, toward the South Side and Richmond & Danville Railroads. Grant's offensives commenced on June 22, but in two days of pitched combat, the Federal infantry encountered a Confederate blocking force that limited its progress. The bluecoats failed to effect a permanent lodgment on the Petersburg Railroad, although they did hold Jerusalem Plank Road. The Union cavalry succeeded in damaging both the South Side and Richmond & Danville lines and attracted hundreds of runaway slaves before being turned back at the Staunton River Bridge on the Danville route. Southern forces punished Wilson and Kautz on their return trip to Federal lines, while repair crews restored the damaged tracks.[7]

These engagements revealed Grant's determination to slug it out at Petersburg as long as his armies could sustain their offensive punch. The capture of more than two thousand Union troops, however, provided hope for Lee and the citizens of Petersburg that Grant's efforts might ultimately fail. Residents watched as long lines of Northern prisoners marched from Jarratt's Hotel down North Sycamore Street to the Old Market and then across the Appomattox River to Ettrick. From there the Federal captives moved on to remote locations less threatened by Union armies.[8]

Along with captured Northern soldiers, Confederate horsemen rounded up numerous runaway slaves abandoned by Wilson's and Kautz's desperate troopers as they dashed for safety within Union lines. One Confederate sol-

Blandford Church sits atop Wells (Cemetery) Hill east of Jerusalem Plank Road. Built in the 1730s and abandoned before the Civil War, Blandford's adjacent cemetery contains the graves of many of Petersburg's prominent nineteenth-century residents as well as thirty thousand Confederate soldiers. (Courtesy of the Petersburg Museums)

dier described these unlucky people when they arrived in Petersburg: "I saw the negroes . . . huddled together in a tobacco factory and such a conglomerate mass of humanity I have never seen before or since. They were of all ages and sizes, and of both sexes, ranging from babies to stalwart six-footers. The babies were squalling, the larger children were playing, men and women singing camp meeting hymns or plantation songs, some whistling, others clapping, dancing and cutting all kinds of antics. They were happy at getting out alive from that fight which had been going on around them." It is doubtful, of course, that these people looked forward to returning to the servitude from which they had temporarily escaped.[9]

Grant's battlefield failures emboldened John W. Syme of the *Daily Register* to unleash his caustic pen against the most despised Yankee in the neighborhood, Benjamin F. Butler, commander of the Army of the James. Citing the inability of Union forces to capture Petersburg, Syme observed that the Confederates had

> a peculiar objection to Beast Butler's miscegenators and [are] therefore determined to keep them out in the cold, unless they come in . . . broken doses of from one to fifteen hundred at a time. The Beast must feel the delay the more keenly, as he is an excellent connoisseur in the fine arts, and is anxious to compare the contents of the plates, charts, and sideboards of Petersburg with similar articles picked up in New Orleans and Norfolk. . . . Yet with all his sagacity and industry in packing up the silver . . . belonging to the rebels, he will fall short in his calculations around Petersburg.[10]

As a stifling June gave way to an even more oppressive July, a strange dichotomy characterized life in Petersburg. Some citizens adapted to the relentless bombardment with a nonchalance that impressed Confederate soldiers. "The people of the place, ladies and all, bear this outrage upon their pleasant homes with great fortitude and dignity," thought Brigadier General William Nelson Pendleton, Lee's chief of artillery. "I have never known a braver or more patriotic people," wrote another observer. Other Petersburgers could simply endure the shelling no longer, although it primarily continued as a source of nonlethal annoyance. "Most of the families on Market Street have moved away," recorded Charles Campbell on June 29.[11]

Campbell also noted an ironic reverse flow of refugees from surrounding counties streaming into town from areas that the Union army occupied. These people inhabited dwellings recently abandoned by their frightened owners or tenants. "The whole town is in a sort of trans migration state . . . which gives rise to many strange combinations," Campbell wrote. The cannoneer William Clopton spoke for most of Lee's soldiers when he condemned the "vandals" who would fire on innocent civilians no matter what their identities, and he prayed that "God may heap retribution" on the Federals.[12]

The citizens who decided to stay did so either out of stubborn determination or, like Petersburg's free black community, because they had no alternative. Lacking the economic means to find new dwellings and racially restricted in their movement, most African Americans survived as best they could in the city's eastern precincts, the neighborhoods most vulnerable to bombardment. Some free blacks did relocate to gentle hillsides in the West End, burrowing out small shelters in the soil. Domestic slaves enjoyed even

These buildings on the south side of Bollingbrook Street are but a few of the more than six hundred Petersburg structures damaged by Union artillery. This view is looking southwest with the Petersburg courthouse at the far left. (Courtesy of Library of Congress)

less mobility. Most remained in their masters' homes even if their owners fled. "A negro thinks that when hidden he is protected, so an inch plank gives a sense of the security of a Bomb Proof," observed Captain Charles H. Dimmock, dismissing African American bravery as simple ignorance. Conditions were little better for poor whites, although some retreated to western Petersburg, beyond Union artillery range, sleeping on church pews or in vacant beds at the Fair Grounds Hospital.[13]

Numerous Petersburg citizens of greater means rejected the idea of abandoning their homes. "I . . . very much fear we shall be obliged to leave town," wrote one local woman, "as my Father's house is in the midst of the shelled district. I shall regret the necessity very much & still hope something may turn up to make it unnecessary." During particularly intense bombardments, people sought shelter in subterranean public spaces, such as the basement of the Tabb Street Presbyterian Church. Residents also transformed their own cellars into bombproofs, with cotton bales stacked outside for protection and mattresses, matting, or benches for seating. Charles Campbell furnished his coal cellar with rugs and lounge chairs. Other citizens dug holes in their yards eight feet deep and ten feet square, roofed with several layers of logs and then covered with earth, just as the soldiers behind the trenches had learned to do. "Some of these bombproofs were made quite comfortable," recounted Dr. Claiborne, "and ladies could take a book or their sewing into them."[14]

In late June and early July, Union gunners occasionally intensified their rate of fire against the city. "Grant is doing the meanest sort of fighting," wrote General Wise on July 1. "He is shelling this city now with barbarous inhumanity, without regard to age or sex, God or man." One Confederate soldier recorded on July 2 that "the Yankees throw some shell into Petersburg every day, and from the way the cannons boomed in that direction they doubled the dose to-day," while an artillery officer thought that "the bursting of shells & falling bricks in some parts of town are scarcely less frequent than the cries of melon sellers used to be." A member of General Lee's staff reported that church services were canceled at St. Paul's Episcopal Church on the first Sunday of July because "the firing on this city has been so serious." Actually, the Reverend William H. Platt moved the services to the church basement "for the benefit of such soldiers and citizens who might venture out," but he declined to ring the church's bells "for fear Gen. Lee might be tempted to come over from his headquarters across the river, and it is too dangerous for him to be riding about the streets."[15]

It is difficult to determine whether these heavier bombardments or simply the accumulated effects of more than a fortnight of constant shelling persuaded so many residents to flee their homes. In either case, an urban metamorphosis was underway by the first week of July. "Went to town and was mortified to see how much distress was caused by this barbarism," wrote the artillerist James W. Albright on July 2. "Everybody is leaving that can do so." Charles Campbell observed that the people departed "by a sort of contagious instinct of danger," and he predicted that at the prevailing pace Petersburg "will soon be in the main evacuated of its inhabitants." Most refugees were women and children. Jennie Friend, daughter of the businessman and planter Charles Friend, remembered seeing "people pouring out of town, with such clothing and provisions as they could carry but not knowing whither they were going." One staff officer reported on July 4 that the army provided transportation to families and assisted moving household effects, so that "everybody has left the city who could. It makes my heart bleed when I think of the suffering and torture of the poor citizens." Rumors that General Grant intended to burn Petersburg on July 4 in celebration of Independence Day and the first anniversary of his capture of Vicksburg hastened the departure of some.[16]

Dr. Claiborne estimated that two-thirds of the residents had abandoned Petersburg by the second week in July. One private in the Thirty-fourth Virginia Infantry told his sister that the city looked "forsaken," and Sycamore Street had grown so quiet that it reminded one officer of "Goldsmith's Deserted Village." Charles Campbell rambled through town on one of his informal inspections on July 8 and discovered "the factories and stores closed [and] business discontinued," giving the city a "deserted" appearance. One North Carolina soldier, assessing the forlorn face of the once beautiful and vibrant city, told his uncle that " I never knew what hard times were untill [*sic*] this campaign set in." Another Tarheel admitted that "our people in NC know nothing of suffering in comparison to the people here."[17]

The Beckwith family joined the exodus in early July. They had connections at General Beauregard's headquarters, and they borrowed the general's wagons and ambulances to move household belongings into the country. For many refugees, leaving Petersburg to avoid the Yankee missiles merely traded one hardship for another. Residents with relatives in either Chesterfield or Dinwiddie Counties could board with their country cousins, but the majority of evacuees had no place to go. "The people . . . are scattered & camping in fields and woods," reported Dr. Claiborne. "They suffer and I fear, unless the Government interposes, will suffer more." Some lucky people crowded into abandoned farmhouses or lodged with strangers. Others sought shelter in tents pitched north or west of town, often sharing space in army bivouacs or even with horses and mules.[18]

Mrs. John Knight, a widow residing at Indiana, just outside the city's western limits, allowed soldiers and civilians to erect tents in her yard and accommodated refugees in five rooms of her home. More than one dozen homeless camped in the yard of Grassland in Chesterfield County, while the house filled with other temporary boarders. The least fortunate had to improvise shelters out of blankets, rugs, and quilts to protect themselves from the sun or the drought-breaking rain that fell in mid-July. Some destitute families enjoyed no shelter at all. "The woods and all the country is filled with women, from old gray haired mothers down to the infant, driven from their homes without a change of dressing, thousands of them in the wood without any shelter or protection," wrote one sympathetic Georgia soldier.[19]

All the refugees had trouble obtaining sufficient food, isolated from the Petersburg markets or government welfare on which they relied. One woman subsisted in her Chesterfield haven on blackberries and huckleberries gathered in the forests. The situation grew so bad for some refugees that in late July they began to return to their Petersburg homes rather than continue a precarious existence in the counties.[20]

The relentless Union cannonade dominated the daily lives of Petersburgers who remained in their homes. Avoiding being killed by a stray projectile ranked as everyone's top priority. Before her family fled for the country, the teenager Margaret Stanly Beckwith employed various personal strategies when confronted with incoming ordnance. "We learned when going down Sycamore Street to make any needed purchase to fall flat on the pavement when we hear a shell coming our way and remain there until after the explosion," she remembered. But, she added, "it was really fun to dodge." The residents also discerned the firing patterns of Northern gunners and took advantage of predictable quiet times to go about their affairs.[21]

Soldiers and civilians alike told of brushes with death as shells exploded perilously close. "These narrow escapes are of such common occurrence that we become indifferent to them," wrote Major Cooke. One Alabama surgeon admired the bravery of citizens who were "utterly indifferent . . . to passing shells. As I rode along, a huge one bursted about a hundred yards from two ladies who were crossing the street. I expected to see them faint, scream, run, at least dodge, but . . . they only looked at it and went on without even quickening their pace." The parents and sisters of one sergeant in this physician's regiment lived in Petersburg. The women "hooted at the idea of being driven from their home by the shells of the vile Yankees. Seem to think it unpatriotic and beneath a Southern woman to manifest fear on such an occasion."[22]

Mrs. Roger A. Pryor, who found inner peace through her belief in predestination, recalled that frightened children were encouraged to remain stoic amid even the fiercest barrage. Anne Banister shared the basement of her home with her widowed mother, nursing her sick brother as best she could. The family relied on the heroic actions of a friend who three times each week delivered food and medicine to the housebound women and children. An editorial in the *Petersburg Daily Express* referred to the Northern artillerists as "vile" and proclaimed that "the almost universal sentiment of our community is, that rather than the city should be surrendered, they are willing that every brick in it shall be battered to the ground."[23]

Projectiles damaged the gas works in mid-July, and citizens feared that the water works would be the next victim. Fire bells frequently echoed through town as exploding ordnance set a home or commercial building ablaze. "The Yankees appear to be throwing incendiary shell into the city," speculated James Albright, "as some five buildings were on fire at one time from shell thrown into different parts of the city." The common council created an auxiliary fire brigade of twenty-four men and requested that the army supplement civilian firefighters with military personnel. Some militiamen objected to serving as ersatz firemen, "thinking it too perilous as the Yankees . . . will shell the light of the conflagration."[24]

In addition to the movement of patients from the city's military hospitals, authorities shifted the post office to the West End on Dunlop Street and

The Petersburg Gas Works off Lombard Street just west of Lieutenant Run stood within easy range of Union cannons east of Petersburg. Severe shelling interrupted gas service in July 1864, but the utility's employees worked tirelessly to restore municipal lighting. (Courtesy of Library of Congress)

the telegraph office to western Old Street. Captain Dimmock remained at his downtown address "until all the departments around me had been a week removed & Head Quarters had taken its departure beyond the hurtling of the shell. Most of the houses about me had been struck . . . & a man killed in my back yard." Trains from Richmond now stopped at Dunlop Station three miles north of Petersburg, while the South Side Railroad stopped running east of Campbell's Bridge to stay beyond Federal artillery range. Danger to parishioners curtailed church services: at one point only Grace Episcopal and Second Presbyterian continued to hold regular worship. Platt at St. Paul's appealed to the Union high command to cease shelling during normal Sunday church hours in the spirit of Christian decency—a request that General Meade eventually honored.[25]

During this difficult summer, looters tarnished Petersburg's reputation for noble endurance. Houses abandoned by refugees offered inviting targets for thieves, in and out of uniform. The situation grew so intolerable that the common council requested an additional provost guard to deter crime. During periods of heavy cannonading, when the military police took shelter like the rest of the residents, bold burglars plundered vacant houses and stores with impunity.[26]

The volume of iron hurled at Petersburg began to diminish toward the end of July. "Fewer shot have been fired in the last three days than have been fired since Lee's army came amongst us," wrote Dr. Claiborne on the twenty-seventh. "It really seems strange to hear no cannon, no shell bursting and no puttering of musketry—so accustomed are our ears to these peaceful sounds." This respite allowed Petersburgers to focus on their other most serious hardship of the early summer: the lack of affordable necessities.[27]

Inflation and shortages exacerbated by the presence of Lee's army turned grocery shopping into a frustrating ordeal. "The scarcity of provisions great & increasing," grumbled Charles Campbell, "scarcely any to be got for love or money." As Virginia's deteriorating railroads struggled to move supplies into the city, and the army monopolized production at Petersburg's grain mills, Confederate troops relied on local civilians to supplement their spartan army diets. "Soldiers are continually calling to ask or beg for vegetables, bread, milk, & c," remembered Campbell. "Soldiers are continually stealing from gardens." The *Daily Register* attempted to make light of this petty, if annoying, theft in an article entitled "Migratory Vegetables" published in late June. The editor called on authorities to halt the "nightly vegetable exodus" that plagued many Petersburg neighborhoods, particularly the Blandford section of town adjacent to the front lines.[28]

Hungry and innovative soldiers adopted other tactics to augment their scanty rations. Some collected shell fragments that they sold to the Ordnance Department for a few cents per pound, using the money to buy something to eat. Others raised meal money by selling their shoes, demanding as much as fifty dollars per pair. "This may account in some instances . . . for their being barefoot," explained Campbell. The more unscrupulous troops participated in looting or burglary to obtain money to buy food and liquor.[29]

Competition with the army and overtaxed railroads provided only a partial explanation for Petersburg's food shortages and prices that exceeded even those in Richmond. As usual, retailers bore the brunt of the blame. "The extremely poor are provided for by the city charity, but the middling classes . . . are suffering keen privations so that another class may reap extortionate profits," railed the *Daily Register*. The editor recommended that the common council purchase "a supply of conscience and distribute it . . . among the sellers and dealers in the Old market; there is evidently a great scarcity of that commodity." Even consumers with means often had little from which to choose. Local farmers south and east of Petersburg, hampered by the presence of Grant's forces, could no longer bring their produce to town. "We can get nothing that we have to sell to market," complained one

Southampton County grower. "Nothing now sold at Old Market & not much at the new," a glum Petersburger noted. A months-long drought retarded the growth of food crops, adding to the general deficit. "The dust is over everything & the corn looks wilted," testified Charles Dimmock.[30]

What did arrive in Petersburg's markets fetched exorbitant prices. Butter that drew Charles Campbell's wrath at ten dollars per pound on June 12 could not be had for less than fourteen dollars per pound a few weeks later, and that "as strong as wagon grease." Chickens rose at precisely the same rate. The purchase of two pounds of pork or beef would consume a month's pay for a private soldier. Petersburgers foraged for berries, and children collected corn spilled from quartermaster bags, tediously cleaning it before bringing it home to share with their families. Petersburg's African Americans made a few dollars selling homemade meat pies and stews to soldiers and civilians, but Mrs. Pryor balked at indulging in these delicacies. "I saw a dead mule lying on the common, and out of its side had been cut a very neat, square chunk of flesh," she explained.[31]

At no time during the previous three years had Petersburg's standard of living been worse. Yet the residents and their soldier neighbors did manage to find some diversion amid the chaos of bombardments and the struggle to maintain a full stomach. The public library opened periodically between shellings. Henry Wise and the artillerist Lieutenant Colonel Willie Pegram were among its patrons, although Charles Campbell reported that "the books . . . are in some danger from the shells." Soldiers could check out books for one dollar per volume. Military bands provided many pleasant hours for soldiers and civilians. "The strains of music near and distant have rendered the city very lively for some nights, and the bands are rendering a service in performing," wrote the *Daily Express*. "The fair sex duly appreciate their efforts to please." The martial tunes proved less popular with physicians at the hospitals, who felt that the bands were "a serious annoyance to the sick & wounded." Charles Campbell noted that eight or ten bands quartered at the Fair Grounds Hospital practiced outside the wards, interfering with the patients' rest.[32]

Many houses of worship went dark during the early summer. Congregations shrank as refugees fled, and parishioners who remained in town feared bombardments. Grace Episcopal Church, on the far fringe of the shelled zone, most often attracted the faithful during these weeks, although the majority were soldiers and officers.[33]

On Sunday July 10 Platt of St. Paul's held services at General Lee's headquarters, Violet Bank, opposite the city on the north side of the river. "The congregation . . . consisted of about a dozen ladies, Gen. Lee and some of his staff, some of Gen. Beauregard's staff and other officers and soldiers," wrote Giles Cooke. Platt selected the passage for his sermon "How Shall We Escape

If We Neglect So Great Salvation," a fitting text for the times. "It was a peaceful and picturesque scene," thought one Petersburg attendee, "while the voice of song went up mingled with the booming of distant guns." Platt held similar services at Beauregard's headquarters throughout July.[34]

Lee's soldiers pursued a variety of amusements. Although bathing rarely rose to the level of recreation, the troops appreciated washing away the dirt accumulated during weeks without rain. "We went to the city water works to rest and wash for we needed [a] bath," admitted one Virginia soldier. "We were as dirty as ground hogs." Major Cooke ran interference for the troops, arranging a schedule for men to leave the front lines and "bathe and wash their clothes in the reservoir." Lee and Beauregard created pass systems that allowed soldiers to visit Petersburg on a rotating basis. Although regulations strictly forbade the sale of alcohol, and the Petersburg Common Council leaned on the military authorities to enforce the ban, one Alabama volunteer remembered that "by paying five dollars for a common cigar, a drink of whiskey was donated by the generous proprietor." Ice cream proved almost as popular as liquor. Soldiers continued to court any eligible Petersburg female, although refugeeing had reduced the distaff population, particularly in the upper echelons of society.[35]

Soldiers and citizens alike eagerly sought the war news from both local and distant theaters. Troops from Deep South units followed the campaign in Georgia as Union armies crept closer to Atlanta. "The news of General [Joseph E.] Johnston falling back to Atlanta reached here yesterday," wrote one Georgia soldier. "Indeed I feel very sad to know that old Georgia is doomed to suffer," added an officer from Florida. A Confederate offensive in the Shenandoah Valley under Lieutenant General Jubal Early had reached the outskirts of Washington by early July, raising hopes around Petersburg that the war's focus would shift north. "If the 'large force of Rebels' under Gen. Early spoken of by the Northern papers is really in Yankee land, Gen. E ought to show them that we can shell towns too," thought one Virginia volunteer.[36]

The campaign that most interested soldiers in Petersburg, of course, was their own. Nothing encouraged the men more than the widely circulated tale of General Grant's death from shell fire on July 15. "What truth there is in the rumor I am unable to state," wrote one officer, "but only hope it is so." Dr. Claiborne also heard the story but gave it little credence. "Too good to be true I fear," he thought.[37]

Whether the Union general-in-chief was dead or alive, most Confederate soldiers interpreted the July stalemate around Petersburg as a positive sign. Charles Campbell relied on the searing summer heat to weaken Grant's armies and reduce them through disease. Other Confederates viewed the Federal attempt to encircle Petersburg and Richmond as futile. "It will be like the little man hugging the big woman, he will have to besiege one side awhile and then the other," thought one Georgia soldier. Captain Dimmock admitted that "Grant hangs on here with Bulldog tenacity, but we all think his efforts feeble & rather killing time than acting effectively to crush the rebellion. He has left-flanked it to this place & must retrograde or take Petersburg. The first would be an acknowledgment of defeat & prove disastrous in the extreme to the war dynasty, and the last Genl. Lee has not . . . seemed disposed to permit." Dr. Claiborne averred that "the people are prepared for any event except surrender. . . . And if the boys and old men could hold it against 30,000 men—surely Lee can against 100,000."[38]

In late June, Grant's forces began a bold project they hoped would end the impasse and reduce Petersburg at a single, spectacular stroke. The idea for tunneling under the Confederate line for the purpose of blowing it up originated with Brigadier General Robert B. Potter, a division commander in the Ninth Corps. On June 19 Potter noticed the vulnerability of a new Confederate fort looming barely one hundred yards from his advanced line one-half mile southeast of Petersburg. He thought that the redoubt—called by the Confederates either Pegram's Salient or Elliott's Salient—could be approached by building a trench perpendicular to the enemy works. Construction would be facilitated by a large basket work—or sap roller—filled with dirt and used to provide mobile protection for the diggers.

After consulting with one of his brigade commanders, Lieutenant Colonel Henry Pleasants, Potter altered his proposal from digging a sap to excavating a tunnel. Pleasants had experience as a mining engineer and believed that he could burrow underneath the Confederate fort, explode charges in the shaft, and open a gap in the line through which infantry could charge unimpeded. Potter presented the idea to Major General Ambrose E. Burnside, his corps commander, who passed it along to General Meade. Army headquarters expressed doubt that the concept would work. Skeptics mentioned the length required to reach the Confederate line—more than five hundred feet—and the consequent difficulty of providing without detection the necessary fresh air for the miners. Meade allowed Potter to attempt his scheme, but he made it clear that the operation would receive no particular encouragement from his headquarters.[39]

Colonel Pleasants set to work on the tunnel even before Potter informed him of its tepid endorsement by higher authorities. Relying primarily on the men of the Forty-eighth Pennsylvania Infantry, which included about one hundred former coal miners, Pleasants improvised tools, scavenged equipment, and maintained a taxing schedule that soon resulted in surprising progress. Working only in their drawers and shirts, the Pennsylvanians bustled in and out of the shaft "like so many brown gophers." Pleasants solved the ventilation problem by employing the principal that hot air rises. He ran a wooden duct from outside the tunnel entrance through an airtight door to the rear of the lengthening gallery where the miners worked. A fire at the bottom of a chimney near the entrance, but just out of sight of the Confederate fort, drew the stale air out of the shaft while fresh air from outside rushed in through the duct and to the end of the tunnel. Ubiquitous camp fires behind Union lines rendered the appearance of smoke unremarkable, while the miners took great care to conceal the excavated earth beneath brush.[40]

Despite these precautions, one Confederate officer deduced the Federal plan less than one week after it commenced. Brigadier General Edward Porter Alexander, brilliant chief of artillery in Lee's First Corps, noticed in late June that the Federals fiercely shelled a narrow corridor opposite Elliott's Salient, while adjacent areas drew much less attention. "That indicated that some operation was going on," explained Alexander, "and for several days I had expected to see zigzag approaches started on the surface of the ground." When by June 30 no saps appeared, Alexander guessed that the enemy intended to tunnel under the fort. The Georgian set off for army headquarters to explain his suspicions, but en route a sharpshooter's bullet struck him in the shoulder.

Alexander received prompt medical treatment and a furlough home to recuperate from a wound that proved disabling but not life threatening. Before leaving on the train to Richmond, Alexander stopped at General Lee's headquarters to discuss his hunch about Elliott's Salient. Lee was absent, so Alexander met with Lee's staff officer, Colonel Charles S. Venable. An English war correspondent, Francis Lawley, overheard Alexander's report and expressed skepticism about the alleged mine. The lengthiest military shaft ever constructed, explained Lawley, was only four hundred feet, and a gallery longer than that could not be properly ventilated. Alexander disagreed, pointing out that for the experienced miners in Union blue, such a run would be "child's play."[41]

When Lee learned of Alexander's speculation, he authorized countermeasures to test the theory, although Alexander thought that "Gen. Lee seems to . . . have only about one half believed my report that the enemy were mining." An engineer officer obtained enough soldier-laborers to begin the excavation of counter mines near Elliott's Salient. He sunk shafts on both sides of the fort, then extended galleries out some distance. Similar excavations commenced at two additional Confederate forts east of Petersburg. Unfortunately for the Rebels, they failed to hear Pleasants's men because their tunnels ended much higher than the twenty or more feet beneath the surface where the Union miners labored. The Confederates bored into the earth with an augur to locate a soft spot that might indicate the presence of a tunnel, but their shafts were both too shallow for the drill to reach the

Pennsylvanians' mine and too far north and south to detect it. The graycoats continued their work through July, but the longer they looked without verifying any enemy activity, the more skeptical they, and the residents of Petersburg, became.[42]

Both Dr. Claiborne and Charles Campbell credited the rumors of the Federals' subterranean strategy. "It is reported that Grant is undermining our works and I have no doubt he is trying it," Claiborne informed his wife on July 17. "But when he begins to engineer he has two of the best engineers in the world to encounter—Lee and Beauregard. He will meet a difficulty I imagine." William Corson, a Confederate soldier, punned to his fiancée on July 23 that "It is generally believed that [Grant] is mining in Lee's front trying to dig old Uncle Robert out of his trenches, but I am thinking he will find that a herculean task, too great even for the Mighty Ulysses."[43]

By July 25 the Confederates had grown so confident that the Federal mine was a myth that Walter Taylor of Lee's staff crafted a highly sarcastic description of the situation:

> Genl Grant is also reported to have undermined Petersburg; his object is to come up in rear of the town & take us in reverse. He is said to have gotten as far as Sycamore St. and is believed to be running a train of cars underneath—as smoke is constantly seen to exude through the paving stones & a rumbling noise as of a railroad train—to say nothing of an unearthly whistle—is frequently heard by gentlemen returning to camp after night, who have been entertained by kind people who treat them to ice water and *straws* [that is, alcohol]. These with the secession of Illinois & the burial of Grant are the only items of news that have reached me. . . . As Grant has been buried, I presume it is his ghost that is undermining Petersburg and this makes the matter only the more terrible.[44]

Forty-eight hours after Colonel Taylor tucked this letter in its envelope, Union soldiers two miles' distant began packing eight thousand pounds of black powder at the base of their mine, directly underneath Elliott's Salient. At 6:00 PM on July 28, Colonel Pleasants announced that he had completed his work and the mine was ready to detonate. The Union high command, initially so dubious about the practicality of the operation, now planned to make the mine explosion the centerpiece of a grand strategic operation. Grant ordered units to move north of the James River to draw a portion of Lee's army away from Petersburg. Union artillery by the score went into position to suppress fire from the Confederate trenches on either side of the mine once the powder erupted.

Meade arranged for his army to move forward, but direct responsibility for exploiting the chaos created by the mine explosion rested with Burnside's corps. Their goal was Wells (Cemetery) Hill, the high ground that Blandford

Church dominated. From there Union artillery would command Petersburg, the railroad bridge over the Appomattox River, and the rear of the Confederate defenses south and west of the city. Petersburg would surely fall if this attack succeeded. Burnside selected a division of black troops commanded by Brigadier General Edward Ferrero to make the initial assault. These African American soldiers had seen limited combat and still enjoyed high morale. They clung less instinctively to their trenches than the shell-shocked survivors of the white Ninth Corps divisions. Their charge was to begin with the detonation of the mine at 3:30 AM on July 30.[45]

Few aspects of the Federal operation went smoothly. Political concerns and military prejudice combined to deprive the black troops of their lead role in the attack. At Meade's insistence, Burnside replaced Ferrero's men at the eleventh hour with a division of poorly prepared white troops commanded by an incompetent coward, Brigadier General James Ledlie. The fuse designed to touch off the charge burned out at a splice, delaying the explosion by more than an hour. Finally, at 4:44 AM, the powder ignited and the ensuing blast killed or wounded 278 unsuspecting Confederate soldiers inside the fort.

Residents of Petersburg heard and felt the explosion, which they compared to an earthquake or the sudden eruption of a volcano. "It seemed as if the very earth would open and swallow us up," remembered Anne Banister. "Window panes were shattered and the whole air was filled with rumbling noises which terrified and deafened one. We could not hear each other speak, the din was so great." Jennie Friend recalled that the explosion shook the foundations of her house and "rattled every window." Citizens rushed out of their homes and into the streets, not fully understanding what had just occurred but appreciating that this was not simply another Union artillery barrage.[46]

Poor planning at Union headquarters and lack of leadership on the front line robbed this unique endeavor of its real potential to win the campaign for Petersburg. While General Ledlie cowered with a bottle in a bombproof, his division advanced. Instead of maneuvering around the resulting crater and charging toward Wells Hill, the confused attackers plunged into the giant hole or milled around its fringes, stunned by the effects of the blast and ignorant of their role in the assault. This delay allowed General Lee to rush across the Appomattox River and direct a counteroffensive that first limited the break in the Confederate defenses and then drove the Federals back.

The Twelfth Virginia Infantry, mostly Petersburg men, joined these counterattacks and found themselves literally fighting for their homes. One of the local soldiers, Private Henry Bird, wrote that "the knowledge of dishonor to the loved ones behind us if we failed and victory before us if we succeeded carried everything before it resistlessly." Ferrero's black troops eventually moved forward, long after any hope of Union victory that day had vanished. The sight of the African Americans in blue uniforms, many former slaves, enraged Confederate soldiers such as Bird and unleashed a ferocious, merciless, hand-to-hand fight. "The negros' charging cry of 'no quarter' was met with the stern reply of 'amen'—and without firing a single shot we closed with them," he wrote. Bird admitted that the black troops "fought like bulldogs and died like soldiers," but he boasted that "Southern bayonets dripped with blood and after a brief but bitter struggle the works were ours." By 2:30 PM the battle General Grant would call "the saddest affair I have witnessed in this war" was over.[47]

The residents of Petersburg knew few details about the fight. Union shells did land in the city, especially along Franklin Street. Late in the afternoon soldiers appearing from the front lines related to eager listeners accounts of the Confederate victory. Anne Banister's brother, a participant in the engagement, came home that evening, "his clothes . . . spattered with blood." The young soldier tried to describe the maniacal combat that took place in the horrid pit but concluded by simply expressing the hope that "never again would he be in such a battle."[48]

More graphic and disturbing reports circulated through town, particularly about the treatment that the black troops received at the hands of the infuriated Confederates. One soldier admitted that he "shot the Federals as if he were shooting rabbits," but Henry Bird revealed an even grimmer side to the affair:

> After a short rest the prisoners—of which many hundreds had broken through & gone to our rear—had to be attended to. The order was given to kill them all and rapid firing told plainly how well and willingly it was obeyed. Finally our General sickened of the slaughter and ordered it to be stayed. The figures . . . in the papers will show how we . . . suffered and what a terrible vengeance we took for the men so inhumanly butchered by the negroes in the morning.

Another Petersburger ventured out to the battlefield during a truce called on August 1 and reported that he "was literally up to the top of his shoes in blood and flesh."[49]

The Confederates' rage stemmed their belief that the use of slave-soldiers violated every social, moral, and ethical principle they held dear. Moreover, they were quick to condemn what they saw as the hypocrisy of Northern policy that advocated emancipation and equality on one hand and employed black troops as cannon fodder on the other. "I do wonder what the gentle, sympathetical, and philanthropical Aunt Harriet Beecher Stowe thinks of this sort of emancipation," wrote one Confederate artillerist, referring to the author of the famous abolitionist novel *Uncle Tom's Cabin*. "Striking off the shackle of bondage one day and the next march the dear creatures into a hole and have them shot down by the hundred. . . . But the dear old lady ought to be perfectly satisfied and gratified, for the great butchery to-day was the effect of a grand and glorious Yankee invention for transferring the Uncle Toms from slavery . . . to the blissful realms of freedom, by making angels out of them in bunches of five hundred at a time."[50]

Nearly fifteen hundred Union prisoners survived the battle and its horrible aftermath, among them approximately five hundred United States Colored Troops. The fate of these men graphically illustrated the depth of racial feelings shared by white Southerners and Northerners alike. Lieutenant General Ambrose Powell Hill, whose troops had expelled the Federals from the Crater and earned the laurels of the hard-fought victory, took command of the prisoners when they arrived in Petersburg. Hill sought to humiliate his captives by forcing them to parade through town for the amusement of the citizens — as well as to remind white residents of the potential for servile insurrection. He arranged this spectacle, unconventional during the later years of the Civil War, because of the racial mix of the Northern prisoners, directing that the white officers and soldiers be integrated with the African American prisoners. Hill understood that by doing this he would imply that white Union soldiers were no better than the former slaves who fought by their sides. Hill placed a captive Union general, William F. Bartlett, on a spavined horse at the head of this line.

The prisoners marched and countermarched through the streets of Petersburg "much after the style of a circus." Petersburgers turned out en masse, "in holiday attire [sitting] in their windows and doors and on their wide veranda[h]s, or [standing] lined up along the streets." One Union officer recalled that "we were assailed by a volley of abuse from men, women, and children that exceeded anything of the kind that I ever heard." Most of the taunts were directed as Hill intended them. "See the white and nigger equality soldiers," cried one delighted onlooker. "Yanks and niggers sleep in the same bed," screamed another. Some of the black troops were required to march with untreated wounds and could barely keep up even with the assistance of comrades.

Officers of white units suffered the greatest embarrassment. "I doubt if the white soldiers cared a straw about the matter," thought one lieutenant in the Twenty-third United States Colored Troops, "and the officers of the Fourth Division [Ferrero's black troops] who were accustomed to marching with Negro soldiers, could not be humiliated in that way, but it almost broke the hearts of very many of the officers of the white divisions, a majority of whom, I honestly believe, would have been glad to see the officers of the Fourth Division hanged or shot, if thereby they could have been relieved from the terrible humiliation of marching through Petersburg with Negro soldiers."[51]

Once the parade had ended, guards escorted the prisoners to Merchant's

Island, a tiny sliver of land in the Appomattox River just upstream from Campbell's Bridge. Various Petersburg residents, mostly men of apparent military age, stood on the riverbank and hurled scathing insults at the captives. The taunters berated the Federals for arming their slaves against them. One resident of swarthy complexion followed this line of discussion until a weary Union prisoner took exception to the man's reasoning and observed that "if there is anything in color you are only a half-breed yourself." The offended Petersburger attempted to seize a sentry's rifle to shoot the flippant Federal. The guard restrained him and suggested that if he wanted to shoot Yankees, he should enlist in the army and go to the front lines, where "you'll find plenty of white men and niggahs, too, out thar with guns that'll give you all the shootin' you want."[52]

Following current practice, most of the prisoners spent only a short time in Petersburg before moving to permanent facilities. Many officers went to Richmond's Libby Prison, while the white enlisted men traveled to Danville, Virginia, or Salisbury, North Carolina. The African American captives fared worse, most of them returning to bondage rather than being treated as prisoners of war.[53]

The wounded from the Battle of the Crater filled Petersburg with patients in gray and in blue. Most of seven hundred Confederate casualties found beds in the Confederate States or Fair Grounds Hospitals or in the reopened Virginia Hospital. Surgeons cared for others at new facilities in converted tobacco warehouses or in brigade field hospitals in Ettrick and Dinwiddie County.

The army dumped the Union wounded in Poplar Lawn at the abandoned Pavilion Hospital. Dr. Claiborne enlisted the aid of captured Union physicians to assist his overworked staff with treating the Northern casualties. Here, too, racial sentiments sometimes trumped humanity. Not only did Petersburg's "camp negroes and colored loafers of the town" refuse to aid the wounded blacks but the Federal surgeons declined to do so as well, until Claiborne compelled them to cooperate.[54]

The tragic experience of the Crater and its aftermath convinced General Grant to return to his methodical strategy of isolating Petersburg from its supply routes. The Union commander focused on the Petersburg Railroad as his first priority, seeking to sever the Cockade City and Richmond from direct communication with North Carolina and the vital blockade-running port at Wilmington. It would take several weeks to prepare the next offensive, so while Grant arranged his advance, Petersburg waited.

"Matters are quiet around Petersburg since the failure of Grant as a miner," one Southern soldier informed his sweetheart. "I presume he will continue to blast . . . at the rate of 5000 men to the mine." Petersburg remained the administrative responsibility of Beauregard's Department of

North Carolina and Southern Virginia, and General Wise continued as the commander of the First Military District—the Virginia portion of Beauregard's domain. In a practical sense, of course, General Lee directed military operations around Petersburg, although he did pay deference to Beauregard's nominal local authority. This awkward and redundant command situation simmered in the background throughout the summer, but whenever it threatened to boil over, Lee's diplomacy averted serious problems.[55]

The hot, dry summer made the days drag for the soldiers in the trenches. "The boys generally are very tired of the South-Side," confessed one Confederate. Another wrote that "I couldn't live in this country if they would give me the best farm here and I wouldn't give Culpeper or Fauquier [two Piedmont counties] for all the land from here to the Rapidan river." The engineers kept the men occupied improving existing fortifications and building new defenses. "We are flinging up Breast works all about here," verified one North Carolinian.[56]

The Confederate hospitals stayed busy. Frequent sniper fire claimed victims on the front lines, while disease ravaged the Confederate ranks. Dr. Warner Lewis Baylor, assistant surgeon at the Confederate States Hospital, tracked admissions in August. Each day new patients arrived, with the largest influx on August 20, following fierce fighting along the Petersburg Railroad three miles south of town. The Union Fifth Corps, executing Grant's strategy, had lodged itself on the tracks near Globe Tavern on August 18. Lee and Beauregard attempted unsuccessfully for the next three days to drive them away. The Federals would remain astride Lee's direct line to North Carolina for the rest of the war.[57]

Lee renewed his effort to force the Federals off the railroad on August 25 at Reams Station, eight miles south of the city. His men earned a tactical victory, soundly thrashing the proud Union Second Corps, but failed to gain Lee's objective. Some residents attributed the accelerated bombardment of Petersburg in late August to Grant's pique over the whipping he suffered at Reams Station. Union guns roared from old positions east of Petersburg and new sites to the south. "The shelling on Old St. and Sycamore is more severe than I have ever heard it," wrote Alexander Gustavus Brown, a Petersburg clergyman. "While I write I can hear the shells as they whistle through the air, falling on Old St. with terrible explosions." Thomas Claybrook Elder thought that Bollingbrook and Lombard Streets sustained the worst damage. Two citizens were killed by projectiles near the Old Market on August 27 and another lost an arm. Some shells even landed perilously close to Lee's headquarters at Violet Bank. James Albright, the Virginia gunner, thought the late August bombardment to be the worst of the campaign. "The city is catching it again to-day," Albright recorded on August 29. "Went to the front & never witnessed a heavier shelling from Mortars & guns."[58]

The David Dunlop house on the south side of Bollingbrook Street near Fifth Street suffered seventeen hits from the Federal artillery. At least four shells exploded within the home, "tearing the house to pieces" according to one Union army report made after Petersburg's capture. (Courtesy of Library of Congress)

By this time, however, artillery fusillades no longer wrought the terror they had created earlier in the summer. Women strolled about town, mindful of the projectiles but no longer paralyzed or intimidated by them. "Many people have become so used to the danger that they go about the streets as if nothing was wrong," marveled Dr. Claiborne, "and with the exception of ladies[,] sometimes Sycamore Street looks really lively." Margaret Beckwith remembered resisting the imprecations of her father to take shelter in the family's bombproof. "We had got used to the things [shells] & were not the least bit afraid." Nocturnal cannonades provided unorthodox entertainment for jaded residents. "The sight was most beautiful at night," explained

Reverend Brown. "As the shells would burst in the air the whole heavens seemed to be raining fire." Henry Bird joined his civilian friends one evening on Delectable Heights in the southern portion of town to watch "the fireworks." He thought the view "beautiful and . . . grand." Even when the shelling interrupted mealtime and "it was almost impossible to carry on conversation except by elevating the voice a good deal," citizens would gather on their porches for a cool breeze, "laughing and talking as if there was no war going on."[59]

The intermittent shelling hardly inhibited socializing by Confederate officers, either. Major Cooke spent many pleasant August evenings at various women's homes, eating ice cream and playing backgammon. Military bands, some of which strolled through town serenading private homes, provided welcome diversion for officers and civilians alike. The respite from shelling early in August revived church attendance. General Pendleton, an Episcopal clergyman before the war, sometimes delivered the sermon at St. Paul's. Many Confederates accepted the hospitality of Petersburg citizens. James Dearing, the cavalry officer, boarded in town and enjoyed the occasional watermelon provided by his hosts. One Louisiana officer sustained a minor wound in early August and recovered in a private home rather than a military hospital. "Was served with a 'Mint Julep' and a broiled chicken," he enthused. "Very nice to be wounded, I find!" as he gazed at flowers and fruit baskets that solicitous girls had sent to him.[60]

These almost bucolic reports described only one side of Petersburg life during the summer of 1864. The physical damage sustained by buildings, the dislocation of so many residents, the omnipresence of sometimes unruly soldiers and convalescents, and the disruption of every daily routine left people feeling as if they were living in terra incognita at the edge of eternity. "Everything is sadly changed here," lamented Dr. Claiborne, "nothing looks natural and nobody seems at home. I feel like a stranger and a sojourner." Reverend Brown noted the prevalence of disease in Petersburg, particularly intestinal complaints made worse by poor diets. "For fear of being sick myself I have remained in my room for a week past[,] going out only late in the evening," he admitted.[61]

During the mid-August respite from the worst of the Union bombardments, more of the early summer refugees began returning to their Petersburg homes. Some retained whatever living arrangements they had made in the counties as a safeguard against future emergencies, but for many the challenges of city life seemed less daunting than survival in the country. These challenges included the endless spiral of prices.

Examples of food costs, decried as "enormously high" by one local consumer, included watermelons for $10 to $15 each, eggs $10 per dozen, and flour $275 per barrel. As usual, some voices ascribed inflation solely to the greed of retailers. "While the speculators looked ugly at the misfortune that . . . happened to the city [the severing of the Petersburg Railroad], they inwardly rejoiced at their own good luck, and the prospects before them," sneered the *Daily Express*. "Let everyone watch carefully their maneuvers from day to day." Shortage and inflation crept into Petersburg life in sundry ways. The *Daily Register* suspended publication in August for lack of newsprint and paper stock. The common council began to screen welfare recipients to ensure that no assistance went to families of deserters. Everyone longed for fresh vegetables as home gardens shriveled under the merciless sun.[62]

The fighting near Globe Tavern and at Reams Station brought another wave of patients to Petersburg hospitals and Union prisoners to Petersburg streets. Dr. Claiborne managed to maintain decent conditions, aided by auxiliary tent hospitals in Ettrick and Dinwiddie. Federal captives from the August battles avoided the ritual humiliation inflicted after the Crater, because all these soldiers were white, and they elicited much less attention. "The sight of Yankee prisoners on the streets of Petersburg has now become such an everyday occurrence, that but few feel any interest in the matter," observed the *Daily Express*. The editor added that his readers ought to still rejoice at the presence of such captives because "prisoners taken reduce the number of our enemies, and that unless they be numerous as the sands on the seashore, this continual killing, wounding, and capturing of the invaders, must ultimately exhaust even the myrmidons of Grant."[63]

Not everyone in Petersburg ignored the prisoners. One Massachusetts soldier remembered that after he arrived in town and was placed on an island in the river, "We were counted, searched, and robbed. Everything of value was taken from us." Young boys chased after the Federals, offering to buy the buttons from their jackets for five dollars a piece. Others sought watches, offering extravagant sums in Confederate dollars. "Their . . . currency was exceedingly plentiful and correspondingly worthless," this New Englander concluded.[64]

The loss of the Petersburg Railroad required Lee to fabricate a new supply line from the south. He continued to run trains from North Carolina as far as Stony Creek, where details unloaded cargo and transferred it to wagons. These vehicles rumbled over country roads to Dinwiddie Court House and then up Boydton Plank Road into Petersburg. This latest supply system—along with the South Side Railroad, which functioned with less disruption—provided Grant his last two strategic targets. He would spend the rest of the campaign attempting to seize these routes, but after the debacle at Reams Station, it required more than one month to ready his next offensive.[65]

In the meantime, the Federals maintained their bombardment of Petersburg at levels reminiscent of June and July. An especially heavy cannonade occurred on September 4 just before midnight. Projectiles struck the homes of D'Arcy Paul, Thomas Branch, and John Claiborne, prominent residents of the city. Dr. Claiborne barely escaped death when a shell struck near the bed he had just vacated. The physician had described the shells as being "about the size of a lamp post and 22 inches long" and thought that the Union artillery could fire them "clean over the city into Dinwiddie County. The gun is so far that you can't hear the explosion at all but sitting out at night you can see the flash as of lightning—then hear the whirr—whirr of the missile for several seconds—and then the explosion or the crash into a house if it fails to explode."[66]

The intense shelling precipitated a second round of wholesale dislocation. "I think the people have pretty clearly made up their minds that they can't live here if Grant holds his present position," confessed Dr. Claiborne. Thomas Elder concluded that "the people of Petersburg have been considerably demoralized" since the shelling recommenced. "Many are removing to Richmond, N. Carolina and other places of supposed safety ... on account of the shells, and many others because it is thought it will be next to impossible for citizens to get wood and food here this winter." Alexander Brown concurred with this assessment: "It is generally agreed that all who can get away ought not to think of wintering in Petersburg. The best part of our population will go away."[67]

Union artillery blasted Petersburg throughout the month with unrelenting regularity. "Grant is a very inhuman wretch," fumed one Confederate soldier who objected to the Federal gunners targeting the churches and hospitals on Washington Street. Despite these perceptions, the record reveals no particular pattern to the shelling. Projectiles landed in residential neighborhoods, military camps on both sides of the Appomattox River, and in the city's business district. The most famous of the long-range weapons, a thirteen-inch seacoast mortar nicknamed the Dictator or the Petersburg Express (an obvious reference to the local newspaper), lobbed huge 225-pound shells toward the city and into Chesterfield County. Such projectiles could penetrate many backyard bombproof shelters. Grant's bombardments served little or no tactical purpose, but nothing disrupted citizens' lives more severely.[68]

Petersburg's chronic wartime scourges, inflation, and shortages plagued the remaining residents and city government into the autumn. The Petersburg Common Council recognized the shrinking power of the Confederate dollar at its September 1 meeting by raising municipal salaries to levels unthinkable earlier in the war. Mayor W. W. Townes now drew five hundred dollars per month and lesser officials proportionately high pay. Of course, even this compensation could not keep pace with the skyrocketing cost of living.[69]

To help facilitate the distribution of food, the common council also created a new city market out of range of Union artillery at the western end of High Street. The city's leaders authorized the purchase of one thousand cords of wood for use by the poor and families of soldiers, but by September they could no longer fund such assistance. Throughout the next few weeks the city sold its ambulance, mules, and building lots south of Fillmore Street and east of Sycamore Street, finally providing the finance committee authorization "to sell any of the assets of the City for the purpose of extinguishing [its] indebtedness." Efforts to unload city-owned Confederate bonds at par failed to find buyers. Money raised in the autumn helped purchase three thousand cords of firewood, half to be distributed free to the needy—who numbered 1,077 soldiers' wives, widows, and dependent children—with the remainder to be sold "at a profit of not to exceed one hundred per cent." The army did its part to assist Petersburg's needy by sponsoring several benefit concerts at military hospitals. A program on September 26 drew a large crowd, and at five dollars per ticket it raised considerable funds.[70]

The city's clergymen declared September 13 as a day of humiliation, fasting, and prayer. Church attendance soared, with many women dressed in mourning. Perhaps drawing some inspiration from this public display, Lee's cavalry commander, Major General Wade Hampton, set out the next day on a grand raid, returning to Petersburg on September 18 with twenty-four hundred head of purloined Union cattle. The influx of fresh beef raised morale and provided a brief improvement in the diet of Lee's army, but the "Beefsteak Raid" had no permanent impact on either the conduct of the Petersburg campaign or conditions in the city. One month after the raid a Virginia soldier noticed that "a great many ladies were on the streets & I was sorry to see that tight lacing is again becoming fashionable."[71]

Grant's campaign gradually undermined Petersburg's cotton factories, which had survived the war better than any other local industry. Many of the male employees served in militia units called to the front, and by mid-July the absence of these workers virtually ground the factories to a halt. Interruptions in the shipment of raw cotton and wool only worsened the situation, as did the occasional artillery shell. Idled women factory workers had nowhere else to turn for their livelihood. An arson fire in David Callender's cotton house in October merely added to the misery endured by this important sector of Petersburg's economy.[72]

Religious services still drew a portion of the remaining citizens, although soldiers filled most pews during September and October. Two prominent

Confederate officers, brigadier generals Walter H. Stevens and Archibald Gracie, formally entered the Episcopal faith during Petersburg's fourth wartime autumn. Stevens, chief engineer of Lee's army, was baptized at St. Paul's on September 25 at a service described as "very solemn and impressive." Lee and ten other general officers, including the corps commanders James Longstreet and Ambrose Powell Hill, witnessed the event. One week later brigade commander Gracie and fifteen soldiers received Confirmation. Some devoted officers attended as many as three services per day.[73]

A few normal aspects of municipal life persisted during the autumn of 1864. Schools opened in the southwestern precincts of the city; passenger trains from Lynchburg and Richmond maintained schedules; telegraph and mail service continued, as did operation of the library. Mechanics repaired the gas works, and the lights began to shine once again. Nevertheless, the campaign had turned the Cockade City into a citadel dominated in almost every regard by events on the battle lines. Men in uniform outnumbered civilians on the city's streets by a considerable margin.[74]

Petersburg retained its incongruous status as headquarters for the First District of the Department of North Carolina and Southern Virginia into the fall. General Beauregard nominally commanded ten thousand soldiers, including eight brigades of infantry and forty-nine pieces of artillery, until his transfer to the western theater in late September. In a practical sense, these troops had operated since mid-June as a part of an army group commanded by Robert E. Lee, whose charismatic figure unfailingly elicited notice whenever he ventured into Petersburg.[75]

Lee worshipped at either St. Paul's or Grace Episcopal Churches, and the congregation expanded in whichever building he chose. "It is quite trying to accompany the General to Church or any public place," complained the staff officer Walter Taylor. "Everybody crowds the way and stops on the pavements to have a look." Other notable officers visited Petersburg as well— such as the recuperating James Longstreet, who attended a late September dinner party in his honor at a private home.[76]

Soldiers looked for every opportunity to visit Petersburg—or run the blockade, as the men called going to town without a pass. For many, romance provided the primary motivation. "This gay social intercourse led to lovemaking and marriages, some enlisting 'for the war' only," quipped one Virginia volunteer. Most of the courtships began at parties thrown by wealthy citizens who had remained in their homes despite the bombardments. Ham Chamberlayne, a Virginia artillerist, described with great enthusiasm his visits to the Cameron mansion, although he dismissed his hosts as "nouveaux riches who press tobacco." Richmond women supplemented Petersburg belles at many such affairs, because so many of the local upperclass young ladies were refugees. One Louisiana soldier recoiled from the advances of a woman who encouraged him to linger at her home. "She is evidently fast, vain, and frivolous, romantic in the extreme, fond of admiration, and disposed to hold lightly the hymenial pledge," he shuddered. Not every romantic encounter between soldier and civilian was so casual. Chamberlayne, for one, fell deeply in love with a Petersburg girl who, for him, combined "more attractions than any other I have seen."[77]

Grant once again overawed romance when on September 29 he launched his fifth offensive against Petersburg and Richmond. By October 2 the fighting had run its course. The Federals captured portions of the Confederate line east of Richmond and extended their own fortifications westward from the Petersburg Railroad, but they failed to interdict either Boydton Plank Road or the South Side Railroad. A new batch of Union captives trudged through Petersburg en route to more permanent prisons, and soldiers and civilians breathed sighs of relief that Lee had resisted another Union push. Nevertheless, Grant's relentless campaign and incremental gains began to erode morale. "Never, in the history of our struggle, has our horizon been so darkly clouded & many have ceased to believe that behind the clouds is the sun still shining," wrote Charles Dimmock on the eve of the fighting. Henry T. Owen, a soldier in the Eighteenth Virginia Infantry, felt even less sanguine about the military situation on October 1: "I think Grant will certainly get Petersburg & Richmond in less than one month," he predicted.[78]

Some of this pessimism had spilled over into the city, where rumors of the army's impending departure circulated freely. Private Bird reported that "the evacuation of the city is growing less improbable every day," but he admitted on September 20 that he still thought it unlikely. One Virginia chaplain found the reports more believable in the midst of the September fighting, and one week later Edmund Ruffin confirmed that "the residents of Petersburg think that the town is to be evacuated."[79]

General Lee entertained no such plan. Instead, he accelerated work on the fortifications southwest of Petersburg in order to guard against another direct lunge toward Boydton Plank Road and the South Side Railroad. "They are pressing any able bodied males both black and white around Petersburg into service giving the whites muskets and the blacks spades," wrote Thomas Elder. "General Lee seems determined to give Grant a lively time." African American hospital attendants transferred to the engineer bureaus to build trenches. Of the 172 free blacks conscripted into Confederate labor service in Petersburg in 1864, 121 were assigned to the works. In neighboring Dinwiddie County, 41 out of 65 African American conscripts received similar jobs.[80]

As the Federals maintained their sporadic shelling, cooler October temperatures foretold the coming of winter. The change in the mercury and other reasons known only to entomologists prompted an infestation of grasshoppers that elicited a humorous editorial in the *Daily Express*, despite the grim military prognosis about town:

> The long-legged—we beg the ladies pardon—we mean these long-limbed insects, seem to be crowding into the city in great numbers. . . . They are to be seen flying about the streets, and make no excuse for entering one's dining room or chambers. . . . We can only account for this seeming preference for city life . . . on the ground that they are endeavoring to escape from the Yankees, who show no regard for their rights in the country whence they are driven. . . . These grass hoppers are therefore refugees who should be treated with proper consideration. We hope our citizens will not forcibly eject them from their houses, but give them free range.[81]

Petersburg's defenders found some solace in the advance of a Confederate army in Georgia in early October and the transfer of rear line troops—"bombproofs," as Henry Bird called them—to the front. Bird worried that Grant intended to hold the Petersburg lines with a thin force and send the bulk of his army to General Sherman in Georgia. In fact, Grant launched yet another offensive against Petersburg on October 27. Once again, he targeted Boydton Plank Road southwest of the city and temporarily gained a foothold there until Southern counterattacks drove him back.[82]

This would be the last significant military action at Petersburg in 1864. Union victories at Atlanta, in the Shenandoah Valley, and at Mobile Bay, Alabama, earned Abraham Lincoln a second term as president, relieving Grant of the urgency to demonstrate strategic progress at Petersburg. "I suppose we are destined to spend the winter in this part of the country and we have just moved into a house," wrote an officer on A. P. Hill's staff, acknowledging that Petersburg would remain the army's home for the foreseeable future. Little else, however, was predictable about the course of the war. A farmer near Petersburg celebrated his fifty-third birthday in October, recording the following entry in his diary: "God shall I see 54 and feel as I now do feel . . . and shall I see another 12 M[onths] of War. Oh! how cruel." The residents and defenders of Petersburg shared similar questions as they confronted what would, for most of them, be the most difficult winter of their lives.[83]

⌐ 9 ⌐

"But Darling, There Is Nothing in Petersburg"

NOVEMBER 1864–APRIL 1, 1865

O N NOVEMBER 8, 1864, civilians in the North and Federal soldiers in the field returned Abraham Lincoln to the White House for a second term—an event that doomed the Confederacy more than any battlefield defeat. Lincoln founded his reelection campaign on an uncompromising pledge to restore the Union through the successful prosecution of the war. The president's opponent, the former general-in-chief George B. McClellan, also promised a military victory, but his platform had been largely written by the peace wing of the Democratic Party. For months thoughtful men in the seceded states had embraced Lincoln's defeat, not Grant's, as the surest path to Southern independence. People in Petersburg expressed this wish with passion and conviction. "If we can only hold our own until the election at the North I think the peace party there will close the war," wrote Dr. John H. Claiborne in the late summer.[1]

Lincoln's triumph (he dominated the electoral college 212 to 21, but a shift of eighty thousand votes in key states would have thrown the contest to McClellan) crushed the hope cherished by Petersburgers and other Southerners that the Northern electorate would compel its government to stop the war. One hospital steward in Petersburg concluded resignedly, "Lincoln is elected[,] no alternative but another four years of war."[2]

Lincoln's victory and the onset of colder weather temporarily relieved Petersburg of both tactical offensives and the devastating bombardments that had wrought such physical and psychological damage on the city since the middle of June. Grant no longer needed to convince Northern voters that the armies were only one more attack away from decisive victory, and November's chill frequently caused the dirt roads around Petersburg to freeze and thaw. A weak autumn sun could not dry these rural byways—they turned to mud whenever it rained—complicating Grant's ability to move his massive army and all its wheeled vehicles. One South Carolina surgeon explained the hiatus as the product of a bargain between Lee and Grant by which the Confederates agreed to remove all government property from Petersburg in return for silencing the artillery. Of course, no such agreement existed. Rather, the Union general-in-chief simply deemed it unnecessary to torment Petersburgers with cannonades that, in any case, had never been integral to his strategy.[3]

More than four months of shelling had indeed visited havoc on Petersburg's architecture, if not altering the course of the campaign. Almost every edifice in the eastern half of the city had sustained damage. Most commercial structures in the business district, public buildings, churches, and numerous dwellings—both humble and elegant—bore scars that the Federal projectiles had inflicted. Edmund Ruffin estimated that more than twenty thousand missiles landed in Petersburg during the summer and fall— enough metal to earn Petersburg soldiers and civilians some fifty thousand dollars in government payments for scrap. Tallies vary of the surprisingly small number of lives claimed by the fusillades; Ruffin's report of four whites and eight blacks is the highest. Most of the fatalities occurred during the first three weeks of shelling, before Petersburgers learned how to protect themselves.[4]

City residents remained bitter about serving as targets for Union cannon, even after the projectiles stopped tormenting them. Most still considered the Federal shellings outside the bounds of civilized warfare, examples of "miserable cruelty and debasing malignity" on the part of the enemy. The survival of the city, despite the firing of "thousands of shells impelled by venomous disappointment and petty spite," prompted defiant citizens to predict that "none of those hireling fiends will ever enter" the corporate limits. "God, it seems to me, cannot allow such cowards to enter this place with shouts of triumph and with banners flying . . . and Lee's troops will never cease to be as a wall of stone before them," wrote one outraged resident. This optimism would be severely tested during the winter, as conditions in town grew ever more difficult.[5]

The November chill compounded the city's hardships. Food supplies continued to fluctuate according to the vagaries of markets and railroads, but they were never cheap. The *Petersburg Daily Express* reported that the city's markets contained abundant quantities of every commodity, but "it is estimated that 50 bushels of Confederate notes change hands at the New Market alone every morning, such is the high price asked for things there." Sara Rice Pryor, Roger's wife, remembered that "every particle of animal or vegetable food was consumed," leading to the disappearance of pigeons, rats, and mice that subsisted on garbage and cats who dined on the rodents. Bessie Callender, the wife of the Petersburg industrialist, remembered that her family's usual autumn dinner consisted of "a small piece of bacon . . . and a quantity of peas, some rice and stewed dried apples sweetened with sorghum."[6]

The lack of firewood caused as much suffering as the scarcity of affordable food. The army required vast quantities of fuel for heating and cooking (not to mention the wood needed to build winter huts and improve fortifications) and maintained a near monopoly on the available supply, save for whatever the Petersburg Common Council could procure for distribution to the poor. Mrs. Callender adapted by closing all her fireplaces except those in the family dining room and kitchen.[7]

New clothes were in short supply, and homespun made a comeback, along with spinning wheels and household looms. "It takes a good deal of work and planning to keep our own clothes presentable," admitted one Petersburg woman. Shoes proved even more difficult to procure. Margaret Stanly Beckwith recalled that her grandmother treasured a daily walk as about her only remaining pleasure in the fall of 1864. Margaret's aunt accompanied the old woman on these strolls. One day her aunt arrived to begin their amble when the grandmother announced that she could not venture out, explaining: "I have no shoes, a poor woman worse off than I am came to the door & I gave my shoes to her. She was bare footed." Brigadier General James Dearing summed up the situation well when explaining why he had not sent his wife a dress as she had requested: "But darling, there is nothing in Petersburg."[8]

Desperate times bred desperate acts. Thefts increased as both citizens and soldiers resorted to extralegal means to better their lots, or merely fill their stomachs. "To keep food of any kind was impossible," remembered Mrs. Pryor. "Cows, pigs, bacon, flour, everything, was stolen, and even sitting hens were taken from the nest." Lieutenant Colonel Fletcher Archer, a local officer in the Reserves, complained of the disappearance of sheep from his nearby farm, blaming soldiers and butchers in the city for the crimes. "I . . . shall endure it with as much philosophy as possible," Archer decided, the authorities being all but powerless to prevent such violations of the law.[9]

Thieves invaded Charles Collier's home in November while his wife slept in an adjacent room, and they took a trunk containing a large sum of money. The perpetrators hauled it into the yard and smashed it open with an ax, stealing gold, currency, and bonds. "I have but little doubt that some of his own servants know all about this transaction if they are not . . . parties to it," thought one neighbor, reflecting an endemic racial suspicion among white Petersburgers. Soldiers, like civilians, suffered from crime. "You can force no idea of the amount of thieving going on in & about Petersburg," wrote the engineer officer Charles H. Dimmock. The troops complained of items missing from open tents, just as Petersburg residents lamented the epidemic of domestic break-ins.[10]

Tobacco was the one precious item, albeit neither nutritious nor wearable, that Petersburg held in abundance during the last winter of the war. As much as two hundred thousand dollars' worth of the noxious weed lay withering in just one of the city's four tobacco warehouses in late November, not to mention the leaf stored in idle tobacco factories: there was simply no practical means of shipping it anywhere. Still, there was money to be made—legitimately and otherwise—for those able to serve domestic markets. Someone named Lucy absconded in November with large quantities for resale from the Oaks Warehouse. Petersburg residents wrote the governor requesting additional and more efficient tobacco inspectors, both to prevent such thefts and to obtain military exemptions for the new officials. William Nelson and his father, both Mississippians, struck up a relationship with the prominent Petersburg businessman Lemuel Peebles in a quest to exchange tobacco for sugar, both parties expecting to realize large returns by selling scarce commodities in their respective regions. Moving the goods between Mississippi and Virginia became the rub. "It would be better for you to buy a cargo of sugar and bring it on yourself," Nelson advised. "Transportation is so uncertain."[11]

The distinction between civilian and military life in Petersburg, once so apparent, had blurred considerably by late in the year. Citizens and soldiers shared many of the same challenges, diversions, and spaces. In some instances they shared even the same family connections. Fletcher Archer's local Reserve unit was stationed near Battery Thirty-five south of Petersburg. They manned their posts around the clock, spending each night on the front lines despite having families and homes just a few miles' distant. Archer maintained a faithful correspondence with his wife throughout the fall, doing his best to balance his responsibilities as an officer with his obligations as the head of his nearby household. Other men serving in units such as the Twelfth Virginia Infantry confronted the same odd experience of living in the trenches while their loved ones made do without them in a Petersburg neighborhood.[12]

Petersburg families sometimes faced the difficult task of burying their kin killed just a few miles from home. In one of the autumn engagements Corporal John Blair Banister of the Twelfth Virginia Infantry sustained a mortal wound near Burgess's Mill, a short distance southwest of Petersburg. He lingered a few days in the company of his mother, who had ventured to the field hospital to see him before he died. The family carried his body back to Petersburg and buried him in Blandford Cemetery, exploiting the suspension of the bombardments. The Banisters also interred another son at

Blandford that day who had died of disease during the summer, and been temporarily laid to rest in the family garden.[13]

Like the Banisters and other recently impoverished Petersburg citizens, the soldiers and officers in Lee's army wrestled with inflation and shortages. Troops had grown accustomed to supplementing their army rations and equipment with items procured from local markets. By the fall of 1864 Petersburg offered precious little that a hungry or threadbare Confederate could afford. One cannoneer in the Washington Artillery explained that a nice hotel meal would consume a month's wages. A haircut and a shave at a local barbershop came nearly as dear. Simply employing a seamstress to patch a pair of trousers cost twenty dollars. One Florida deserter revealed that his unit had recently received two months' extra pay and that he needed the entire sum to purchase a supper of mutton, turnips, and cabbage for himself and a comrade. Firewood for the camps proved hard to obtain—a challenge that only increased throughout the winter. These conditions stood in contrast to the mountains of supplies flowing to the Union lines through City Point and along the United States Military Railroad. Confederate soldiers could not fail to compare their diminishing resources with the abundance just across the works. More than a few Rebels at Petersburg deserted to the enemy to escape the hardships of hunger and cold.[14]

Civilian and military experiences proved inextricably linked in other ways. On December 1 the common council voted twelve thousand dollars of inflated currency to purchase either shoes or shoe leather for the Twelfth Virginia Infantry. Charity flowed in the other direction when General Lee made a symbolic two-hundred-dollar contribution to the city for the benefit of the poor, hoping to set an example for other officers. The army encouraged authorities in Petersburg to crack down on the distribution of alcohol to soldiers, and the council passed an ordinance to ban the "sale or giving away of liquor" in stores, thereby closing a loophole prohibiting merely the purchase of spirits.[15]

On a happier note, soldiers and civilians in Petersburg continued to mingle in churches and at various social affairs. The advent of brisk weather and the slackening of shelling enticed many of the upper-crust young women back to their Petersburg homes. Confederate officers reveled in the frequent gatherings held by generous Petersburg families at which eligible ladies socialized with gallant men in gray. General Longstreet's former staff officer Andrew Dunn, the mill owner Andrew Kevan, the tobacconist William Cameron, and other wealthy residents opened their parlors for sumptuous meals and rollicking parties, demonstrating that those with substantial means could still entertain in style.

Sometimes the officers acted as hosts. Mrs. Pryor assisted the romantic endeavors of Major General Cadmus M. Wilcox, who hoped to sponsor an elaborate affair—a *déjeuner à la fourchette*—to impress a Petersburg widow of whom he had grown fond. Wilcox found it impossible to supply the food necessary to produce an elegant meal, and he appealed to Sara Pryor for advice. She suggested that the menu be printed on nice cards, and when the promised repast failed to appear, explain it away as an accident of war. The stratagem worked, and the general's breakfast "was a great success."[16]

Petersburgers displayed their generosity in many ways beyond sponsoring fancy festivities for well-bred officers. The proprietor of Jarratt's Hotel extended credit to common soldiers in search of a meal. Ordinary citizens banded together to purchase a horse for Brigadier General David A. Weisiger, commander of an infantry brigade in which many Petersburg sons served. Horses had grown enormously expensive by late 1864, so this gift represented more than just a token gesture of esteem.[17]

With bombardments suspended, many churches resumed regular services. The spiritually challenging times and the limited opportunities for officers and civilians to congregate produced record attendance in the late fall and early winter. "I never saw St. Paul's more thoroughly packed . . . with females," wrote Charles Dimmock on December 4. "From the commander-in-chief to the privates in the ranks, there was a deep and sincere religious feeling in Lee's army," affirmed General John B. Gordon.[18]

The officers who attended more than one service on Sundays alternated most often between St. Paul's and Grace Episcopal Churches. St. Paul's possessed a beautiful chapel and a longer tradition of attracting affluent and influential worshippers, but the Reverend Churchill J. Gibson of Grace Church usually received better reviews as a preacher. Dimmock worshipped in both churches one day, and he thought Gibson's message "found entrance directly to the heart," while that of the Reverend William H. Platt of St. Paul's "penetrated only to the imagination, ravishing the ear but leaving no trace, making no lodgment in the heart." Another officer assessed Gibson's discourses as "plain, earnest and deeply pious," while Dimmock concluded during the winter that Platt "has become, beyond question, the most artificial man I ever saw in the pulpit."[19]

One of the best-attended services of the season had little to do with Platt's homiletics. On December 4 funeral rites were held at St. Paul's for the popular brigadier general Archibald Gracie, who had been killed while reconnoitering on the front lines. The ceremony was all the more poignant because Gracie had so recently been confirmed in the Episcopal faith at the same church.[20]

General Lee continued to alternate attendance between Grace and St. Paul's and remained the most revered figure in Petersburg, both among civilians and soldiers. On Sundays after church he often dined at the Banisters' home at the northeast corner of Washington and Jefferson Streets, encouraging observers by his dignified and confident demeanor. During the first week of November the general moved his headquarters from Violet Bank into a home on High Street. Colonel Walter Taylor selected the residence, the Beasley house, which was vacant at the time. "I took possession of a fine house—had his room nicely cleaned out and arranged, with a cheerful fire & c," wrote Taylor, but "it was entirely too pleasant for him, for he is never so uncomfortable as when comfortable." The general shifted quarters to a tent west of town for a short time before returning to the Beasley house.

Lee moved his command post again in late November, this time to the Turnbull house on the western outskirts of Petersburg, to be closer to the most active portion of the Confederate lines. Edge Hill, as the homestead was known, stood at the intersection of Cox and Long Ordinary Roads; it would serve as army headquarters until April 2, 1865. Lee enjoyed commodious quarters here—the best he had ever experienced in the field.[21]

Officers quartered in the city enjoyed relative opulence. Lee and dozens of line commanders and staff officers who resided in Petersburg homes partook of religious and social activities and received gifts of food, clothing, horses, and personal items from a grateful and generous citizenry. "We all live together eat and sleep together, have a nice house, a good cook, and plenty to eat," confirmed one satisfied staff clerk. Another lucky man admitted that "I had great reason to congratulate myself on my comfortable surroundings which were in strong contrast with the situation of the poor fellows in the ranks."[22]

The defenders on the front lines indulged in few such comforts. The common soldiers lived in crude wooden huts or canvas tents reinforced with log foundations. "The troops were suffering extremely for the want of good fires," reported Major Giles Buckner Cooke. "A good many of them without blankets, overcoats, or shoes. . . . It is incomprehensible how they can stand so much exposure." Quite understandably, Colonel Archer's Reserve troops constantly sought to escape the hardships of the trenches and spend time with their nearby families. They were not permitted to leave their positions on the front lines without a pass, and passes proved difficult to obtain.[23]

Petersburg's most prominent private soldier, Roger A. Pryor, would not be visiting home for quite some time. Pryor had resigned his commission as a brigadier general and was serving in the ranks as a courier around Petersburg. Union pickets captured him in late November while he tried to exchange newspapers across the lines. General Wilcox lived in neighboring quarters to those of Sara Pryor at Cottage Farm—a home in the western suburbs just east of the Turnbull house. Wilcox informed Mrs. Pryor of her husband's capture and attempted to secure Pryor's exchange. Grant referred the matter to Major General George G. Meade, commander of the Army of the Potomac, without recommendation. Meade declined to permit an exchange, citing the prohibition of intercourse between pickets. "Private Pryor will have to suffer the consequences of his imprudence," Meade wrote coldly. Mrs. Pryor adjusted to the absence of her husband as well as she could, buoyed by a sympathetic visit from General Lee.[24]

Spirits temporarily rebounded during the 1864 Christmas season. Soldiers, officers, and citizens collaborated to make the holiday as joyous as possible. The city's premier social event combined a tournament on December 22 with a ball and coronation party held the next day. Officers in Lieutenant General Ambrose Powell Hill's Third Corps sponsored the tournament—a series of competitions in the tradition of the English elite—at the Model Farm west of Petersburg.

Some controversy surrounded the ball. A deputation of Hill's officers approached Dr. Claiborne for permission to conduct the affair at the Virginia Hospital. Claiborne harbored serious reservations about the propriety of hosting such an ostentatious festivity "in a city—in whose every house was mourning and widowhood and orphanage—and before which brave men were every day offering up their lives in pain and sorrow." If the officers were determined to celebrate in such a fashion, they would not use a military hospital for the purpose, if the conscientious physician had anything to say about it. "I could not so far pervert the use of [a hospital] as to make it a house of revelry," he explained. The officers protested to no avail, although Claiborne did offer to refer the matter to General Lee. Having met their match, Hill's party planners used the Bollingbrook Hotel instead, and the event was reputed to be "the most magnificent ever given in the city."[25]

Impromptu and less flamboyant gatherings occurred throughout Petersburg in the days before Christmas. "The soldiers, when they left the trenches, crowded as much fun as possible into the short time allowed them, not knowing when another chance would turn up," remembered one Confederate. The liberal use of alcohol and the presence of women and dancing enlivened many of these affairs. Private Westwood A. Todd, a military clerk, remembered a spontaneous Christmas-time party held at Hope Flour Mill near Campbell's Bridge hosted by the chief miller and his wife. Spiked eggnog lubricated the guests and "an old negro fiddler, who was bald-headed, cross-eyed, and left-handed," supplied the tunes. Drinking, dancing, and various parlor games lasted until dawn, "all ending in a romp, the gentlemen, in the confusion, gathering 'favors sweet and precious.'"[26]

Charles Dimmock shared a more sedate Christmas at the Cameron mansion "with several distinguished Genl. officers & sundry others like myself of humble pretensions." The evening featured a spectacular and improbable meal of "imported soup, oyster pie, salmon salad, fried oysters, turkey, roast beef, tongue, corned beef, cheese & a whole shoate." Wines of numerous varieties, eggnog, and hot whiskey punch helped wash down "cakes of all sorts—imported and homemade" and plum pudding. The feast took six hours to consume.[27]

General Lee took his Christmas dinner at the Banister home. Although Lee ate much of the meal, he only picked at his serving of turkey. Mrs. Banister was about to inquire if her guest would prefer dark meat when the general explained that he intended to save his portion for one of his staff officers, Lieutenant Colonel Charles Marshall, who was ill back at the Turnbull house. "He has had nothing to eat but corn bread and sweet potato coffee," explained Lee. "I hope you will allow me to take this to him, as I am sure he will be greatly helped by such a delicious meal." Mrs. Banister readily agreed to prepare something for Marshall, but insisted that General Lee eat his allotment as well. The Confederate commander left the Banister home with a linen napkin filled with turkey and potatoes for the ailing colonel, which Marshall later told Mrs. Banister saved his life.[28]

Petersburg's churches did their best to celebrate the holiday. Members at St. Paul's went to considerable lengths to decorate their sanctuary. Wreaths appeared on the church walls and evergreen and cedar festoons flowed from the chandeliers to the galleries and around the pulpit. Reverend Platt, apparently at his oratorical best, delivered a memorable sermon, enhanced by excellent music. The entire service proved, for one officer, "one of the most impressive scenes I ever witnessed."[29]

In private homes on Christmas Eve all around Petersburg, children hung stockings by their fireplaces as in years past. Parents, however, understood that the little ones were liable to be "disappointed with Santa Claus" in 1864. Colonel Archer, using military allusions, wrote his wife from Battery Thirty-five that he was

> sorry that the Yankees have blockaded Old Santa Claus so effectually as to cut off his usual supplies. . . . The poor old fellow must feel pretty blue as he thinks of his trip over the house tops . . . with his lean . . . and empty chariot, stopping only here and there to dispense . . . apples to some fortunate ones while the great many of little sleeping innocents . . . he was compelled to neglect altogether. I presume he wishes most heartily the Yankees were a better people and would go home, mind their own business and let his southern homes alone.[30]

The rank and file of the Army of Northern Virginia faced as bleak a Christmas as did the local children, although citizens in Richmond and Petersburg tried valiantly to improve the holiday for the men in gray. The idea to prepare a great Christmas dinner for Virginia troops originated in late November. Soon the concept expanded to include all the soldiers in Lee's army. Committees in both cities organized fund-raising events and marshaled their limited resources to prepare as much food as possible to treat the sufferers in the trenches. When it became clear that all the arrangements could not be completed before December 25, the organizers moved the target date to New Year's Day.

The *Daily Express* promoted contributions for the great dinner, and a fund-raising tableaux at Miss Nora Davidson's school helped underwrite the effort. Expectations ran high among the hungry men huddled in their winter quarters. Sadly, the great dinner turned out to be a great disappointment for most of the soldiers. "We each received a few mouthfuls—a teaspoonful of apple butter to a man," grumbled one North Carolinian. A Georgia soldier remembered that "I got a little piece of turkey and two small pieces of meat and about four good mouthfuls of light bread." Colonel Archer expressed less dissatisfaction with the portion delivered to his unit south of town: "Of course, after so much handling and humbug . . . it does not look as [plentiful] as when first cooked, but it seems to be good and substantial consisting of mutton, shoats, turkey, chicken, potatoes & c." Archer sent four potatoes home to his wife so that she could share a little in the bounty.[31]

The soldiers' dinner fiasco began 1865 on a dispiriting note. "This is the last of the holidays," wrote Mrs. Eleanor Platt in a New Year's Eve letter, "for which I am thankful." The season ultimately did more to remind Petersburgers of their sad plight than to provide them reason for joy. More and more, residents and defenders looked inward, as much as to Lee's army, for the spiritual strength to face a fourth year of war. "If we as a people deserve our independence and freedom, it will merely be granted to us by the God of battles," thought one Confederate. Charles Dimmock captured the mood of many on New Year's Day when he told his wife that "the present is to me as a terrible dream & the occasional smile is made soon to give place to an expression consonant with the gloom of the present."[32]

Life in Petersburg at the start of the new year unraveled at an alarming pace. "Perhaps it is well that you are not here to meet the contaminating influences which seem to reach even the most staid & sober," wrote one man to his absent wife. "When society is so utterly shaken from its propriety all must feel in some measure the shock." Property crimes driven by poverty and desperation, such as the burglary in mid-January at Venable's Flour Mill in which thieves stole a large amount of meal, continued to make news. "The soldiers around Petersburg have been breaking open and robbing mills to get something to eat," admitted one Virginia volunteer. Similarly, tobacco and flour stored at various Petersburg warehouses disappeared on a regular basis, abetted by inadequate security at these once thriving facilities.[33]

Jail populations swelled while army regiments shrank, depleted by disease and desertion. Governor William Smith tried to address both problems by signing pardons for some petty Petersburg thieves in return for their military service. Such dubious recruits now constituted acceptable reinforcements for the dwindling Army of Northern Virginia. The Florida soldier who came to Mrs. Callender's door epitomized the woeful condition prevailing in many units of Lee's army and explained why some men stooped to crime. "His worn cotton clothes were hardly sufficient . . . to conceal his nakedness," she wrote. "When I handed him food his hands were filthy, his nails long like claws, and between his fingers were sores, which he said were itch. I handed him some food on a plate, but he began at once to eat like a wild animal."[34]

One of the more notorious crimes of the season occurred in late January. Although it did not involve a soldier, the victim was a military wife. Mrs. Sarah Goodman had boarded a Petersburg-bound South Side Railroad train to visit her husband, who served under General Lee. The tracks a few miles west of Petersburg were under repair for a short distance, creating a break in the line that required shuttles to meet eastbound trains stopped at the gap. These cars carried passengers and freight for the remainder of the journey into town. Two gentlemen assisted Mrs. Goodman with her luggage at the transfer point, helped her board the shuttle train, and introduced her to a slave named Gilley, who, they said, would drive her to accommodations once she arrived. Mrs. Goodman and Gilley reached the city without incident. Gilley then loaded Mrs. Goodman and her baggage onto a wagon and began to drive, ostensibly, to a Mr. Smithsalls, where she expected to spend the night.

Gilley steered the vehicle into a rough field under the pretense of following a shortcut and then assaulted his passenger. Money apparently motivated the attack, as Gilley reached into Mrs. Goodman's bosom, where he had seen her hide some currency, in the process choking his victim, striking her in the head, and knocking her to the ground. The woman lost consciousness for some time. When she revived she stumbled to a nearby house, "nearly frozen," encountering a Mrs. Moncus, who considered her "the greatest object of pity I ever seen. Her clothes were torn, face beaten, bonnet off, she was very bloody and could hardly walk." Mrs. Moncus removed the victim's garments and found bruises covering her body. "Her clothes smelt horribly, just like a negro does in summer."

Mrs. Goodman provided a description of her assailant to a Petersburg policeman, who discussed the crime with his colleagues. One of the officers knew a black man answering Mrs. Goodman's description who lived in the West Ward. The police quickly apprehended Gilley and placed him in jail. A search of the suspect's residence revealed some of Mrs. Goodman's belongings. Gilley protested his innocence of the worst of the charges, explaining that Mrs. Goodman had fallen on her own, and only then did he decide to take some of her property and run.

The Petersburg Hustings Court heard the case less than three weeks later.

City Councilman Alexander Donnan served as Gilley's court-appointed attorney, but the outcome of the trial was all but certain given Mrs. Goodman's explicit testimony, the physical evidence, and the racial circumstances of the case. The court found the defendant guilty of "making an assault with intent to ravish and carnally know," the kind of crime committed by an African American against a white that drew only one penalty in the South.

The court specified that Gilley be hanged on March 24 at the Poor House grounds. Executions normally took place in the yard of the city jail, but the court assumed that the jail yard would be too small to accommodate the crowd that would gather to witness this kind of justice. The court, consistent with Virginia law, compensated Gilley's owner four thousand dollars for the loss of his property. When the superintendent of the Poor House objected to hosting the execution, arguing that the spectacle promised to disrupt the quiet required at the nearby Fair Grounds Hospital, the justices agreed to move the venue back to the city jail yard.[35]

Although crimes of Gilley's magnitude were rare in wartime Petersburg, the social disruption of the times undermined the delicate foundation on which urban slavery relied. Thoughtful men foresaw slavery's demise, regardless of the outcome of the war. "The peculiar institution I apprehend has its days numbered," wrote Captain Dimmock, "& its end will grow out of gradual emancipation." Dr. Claiborne agreed, citing the burden that slavery imposed on him as reason enough to abandon the system. "As an investment . . . [slaves] are unprofitable and exceedingly troublesome—and I have often wished I was happily rid of them all." Such opinions would have been unthinkable four years earlier, indicating how much pressure the turmoil of the war had exerted on Petersburg's most fundamental social and economic institution.[36]

Aside from criminal activity and the weakening of slavery, there were more subtle signs of social disintegration. "Society here, as elsewhere, is upturned & the conduct of St. Paul's congregation as it leaves the church is utterly discreditable," wrote one parishioner. "Tonight the church was in a hum with voices & many did not hesitate to laugh quite loudly." Goods and services had reached prices beyond the fantastic, and an astronomical inflation rate staggered the imagination. Flour sold for an outrageous $600 per barrel on January 7, only to soar to $1,000 per barrel just three weeks later. An apple cost $2 and a pair of boots $250. Many Confederate officers had not been paid for months, so in an ironic sense, unthinkable prices proved irrelevant to those with no money. "I do feel so poor when I think my savings are worth just about two barrels of flour," wrote Captain Dimmock.[37]

The winter of 1865 brought cold temperatures but mercifully little snow—a small blessing because "our people are poorly prepared for [a deep snow]," observed Colonel Archer. Firewood competed with food as the most coveted necessity of life. Mrs. Pryor resorted to felling ornamental trees to keep warm. Others sent wagons deep into the countryside to gather enough fuel to cook and heat their homes.[38]

Welfare expenses had by 1865 overwhelmed the city's ability to meet them. On February 1 the Petersburg Common Council appropriated ten thousand dollars to the Poor House, but the members admitted they did not know how to raise the money. The council began to consider rescinding the prohibition against selling alcohol in town as a means of generating more revenue.

City leaders sought to balance support of the national war effort with the welfare of their constituents. The Nitre and Mining Bureau suggested exchanging the lead weights in the city clock at the courthouse for iron counterbalances. Requisitions for funds to purchase shoes for Petersburg soldiers in the field forced councilmen to make difficult choices for spending the city's limited means. Petersburg's economy, like that in the rest of the Confederacy, teetered on the brink of collapse. The removal of machinery in the city's cotton mills for fear of its capture should Petersburg fall signaled the total demise of one of the city's strongest industries.[39]

Petersburg's military hospitals functioned through the winter, grim places as they were. Lieutenant George William Beale, a wounded Virginian remanded to the Confederate States Hospital, described the typical experience that most patients endured at these facilities. Each of the hospital's three floors housed one ward for two hundred patients. In February, with every bed full, the patients illustrated every degree of health—from those who had essentially recovered to those drawing their final breaths.

A bell called ambulatory patients to a common dining hall. "A few feeble candles lit up the gathering darkness of the long room, cast a pale and sickly light on the group, and made me feel much as though I had entered some dim Plutonian chamber and was breaking bread (that was all there was to break) with pallid shades of the dead," wrote a horrified Beale. Four black hospital stewards made daily rounds, removing the deceased on stretchers—a dispiriting spectacle for surviving patients. At other times these versatile stewards turned troubadours and comforted their patients by singing hymns. Physicians placed yellow cards above the cots of patients deemed critical or terminal. When Beale noticed that such a card had appeared above his head, he knew that his life depended on leaving the hospital. Beale's brother obtained a pass from General Lee, discharging the critically ill lieutenant to convalesce with friends in the country. "I . . . saw the door close behind me on the Confederate Hospital, its gloom and horrors," remembered the grateful Beale.[40]

The winter of 1865 did not pass without its small enjoyments. Church attendance in Petersburg remained popular, particularly when clerical celebrities such as Robert Lewis Dabney, Stonewall Jackson's former chief of staff, came to preach in the Tabb Street Presbyterian Church and the First Baptist Church on Washington Street. Dabney's favorite sermon during his visit addressed the theme of the bondage of sin.[41]

Quiet along the front lines and the cessation of shelling allowed many of the officers' wives to journey to Petersburg for prolonged visits with their husbands. Those without wives, such as Major General Bushrod R. Johnson, joined the social whirl. Johnson courted a widow named Panill, "a woman of noble and generous character." "Old Bush gave a party at his quarters the other evening," reported Charles Dimmock, "& he danced every quadrille." Dimmock predicted, however, that the widowed lady would retire from active society "when those pretty sisters come back from N.C." Local bachelors, who began to blacken their mustaches to masquerade their advancing years, also sought female companionship. Such social maneuvering was not for everyone. One older Petersburg lady briefly agreed to venture back into the world of eligible women, but exposure to the rituals of courtship convinced her to shun social life in order to avoid "the absurdities" associated with the customs of the time.[42]

Petersburg society also began organizing what it called starvation parties. These foodless fêtes featured music and dancing enjoyed by Confederate officers and Petersburg belles who indulged in imaginary delicacies. Not all of the social occasions in 1865 Petersburg lacked refreshments, however. The Camerons bested every other Petersburg family in procuring edible delicacies that they served to large numbers of guests at elaborate soirees. William Cameron honored one general with an early February event that included a shameless menu of meat, game, oysters, cakes, ice cream, oranges, figs, raisins, almonds, and copious amounts of whiskey, wine, and eggnog. "The supper was really elegant," beamed an unashamed Charles Dimmock, "& we all did credit to [it]." Couples twirled through the Camerons' large rooms until dawn. Walter Taylor of Lee's staff, who lived at Edge Hill with the general, admitted that he had to decide either to avoid Petersburg altogether or plan on visiting almost every day. "The people are very hospitable & if you mingle with them, invitations to dinner, supper & c. come thick & fast."[43]

General Lee—"a smashing looking man," thought one admirer—frequently rode the two miles east from the Turnbull house into town to attend church or share a meal with a Petersburg family. After services Lee was fond of flirting with Petersburg's young socialites, such as Mary Tabb Bolling and Mollie Banister. "The old genl. goes smooching around among all the pretty girls," chuckled Captain Dimmock, "& joked them as if he were a boy of 18." Lee also entertained city residents at his headquarters. "General Lee is himself a great ladies man," observed one member of his staff; he "visits a good deal himself and [is] very fond of having the girls visit him." Anne Banister remembered riding to Edge Hill in an ambulance in order to romp outdoors under the admiring gaze of the Confederate commander. The Banister girls never forgot Lee's desire to exchange photographs with them or his admonitions against whipping the mules that drew their wagon between Edge Hill and home.[44]

By January 1865 Lincoln's reelection, the desperate military situation, and the hardships endemic to life in Petersburg prompted expressions of defeatism. "Met Dr. Lassiter tonight," recorded Giles Cooke, "he boldly proclaimed that he advocates a reconstruction of the Union. . . . He has many who sympathize with him." A few weeks later Walter Taylor questioned the endurance of patriotism in the city: "The Petersburg folks are becoming somewhat calmer; they have demonstrated . . . however, that they are more interested in their pockets than in their country."[45]

New hope for Confederate independence returned on January 29 when a distinguished delegation of Confederate officials arrived in Petersburg. Vice President Alexander Stephens, Virginia Senator Robert M. T. Hunter, and Assistant Secretary of War John A. Campbell had come from Richmond on their way to meet with President Lincoln and other federal officials to explore a possible adjustment of the war. Lincoln had signaled a willingness to discuss peace terms "to the people of our one common country"—a sticking point of enormous consequence. Jefferson Davis wanted no part of a process that would deny Confederate nationhood, but he agreed to send this prestigious trio to represent his government nonetheless. Davis knew the negotiations would fail—his instructions to the Confederate commissioners virtually ensured it. But the president hoped that a collapse of these talks would convince Southerners that the Lincoln administration was uncompromising, place the burden of refusing to consider peace on the shoulders of the North, and thus reinvigorate his citizens' flagging commitment to prosecuting the war.[46]

Stephens, Hunter, and Campbell received Grant's permission to cross the lines into City Point on January 31, and they went by boat to Hampton Roads shortly thereafter. They met with Lincoln onboard the Union steamer *River Queen* on February 3. The conference achieved nothing, as Davis intended all along, except to allow the Confederate president to call for renewed dedication to independence earned on the battlefields.[47]

On February 5 General Grant added an ironic postscript to the failed peace conference. Committing one cavalry division and two infantry corps, he aimed at cutting one of Petersburg's principal supply arteries, Boydton Plank Road, near Dinwiddie Court House. The midwinter expedition surprised Lee and the rest of his army. "There was quite an excitement in the city . . . owing to the advance of the enemy on our right," confessed Captain

Dimmock. "Many officers & men left the churches," including General Lee, to respond to the emergency. The engagement, called the battle of Hatcher's Run, extended over three days and entailed bitter, costly fighting. The armies finally returned to their lines in an ice and snow storm on February 7, accomplishing little except to extend the defense lines a few miles and to leave more than twenty-five hundred casualties on the frozen ground.[48]

Major General John Pegram, a division commander in Gordon's Second Corps, was the battle's most lamented victim. Pegram was born in Petersburg in 1832, and he had crafted a military career of distinction for a man so young. Captured while commanding a small army in western Virginia early in the war, Pegram served after his exchange as a staff officer under Generals P. G. T. Beauregard and Braxton Bragg in the western theater. He transferred to Virginia in 1864, rising to command of Robert Rodes's old division in the fall.

Pegram's January 19, 1865, marriage to the renowned Baltimore belle Hetty Cary—"the universally acknowledged queen of society"—provided the social highlight of Richmond's winter season. The attractive young couple honeymooned near Pegram's headquarters outside of Petersburg. At Hatcher's Run the general's division found itself in the thick of the fighting on February 6 when a bullet struck Pegram in the chest, killing him almost instantly. Mrs. Pegram, a bride of less than three weeks, accompanied her husband's body to Richmond shortly after his death, a sobering and disheartening spectacle that some in the capital and in Petersburg saw as an ill omen. Lee expressed his sympathy to Pegram's widow, commenting that "we are left to grieve at his departure, cherish his memory & prepare to follow."[49]

Grant's offensive at Hatcher's Run seemed so pointless that the editor of the *Daily Express* characterized the operation as a struggle to control a woodlot. Two weeks later, however, when citizens became aware of the development of contingency plans for the emergency removal or destruction of the city's tobacco and cotton inventory, the belief again spread that the army intended to evacuate. "People are leaving Petersburg rapidly," wrote Lieutenant William Clopton of the Fayette (Virginia) Artillery, "and everything certainly looks badly for the 'little cockade city.'"[50]

The city's authorities avoided hysteria and worked calmly with the army to designate safe places for the mass burning of stored commodities to minimize the likelihood of a general conflagration. After a few days of near panic and confusion, the citizens also began to understand that General Lee was not on the brink of abandoning them to the enemy. "You ought not to have inferred the evacuation of Petersburg from my letters," General Henry A. Wise scolded his wife. "There is no intention of evacuating this place if it can be held." Fletcher Archer conveyed the same message to his spouse: "The idea of a speedy evacuation of Petersburg seems at last to have shared the fate of all such reasoning and been consigned to the oblivion it so richly deserves."[51]

Had General Wise and Colonel Archer been included in the highest councils of the Army of Northern Virginia, they would not have been so sanguine. Robert E. Lee, recently named general-in-chief of all Confederate forces, had recommended to President Davis in February that Petersburg and Richmond be forsaken should his newly appointed lieutenant in the Carolinas, General Joseph E. Johnston, prove unable to stop the junction of two Union armies there. Lee wished to avoid trapping his forces between numerically superior enemies. Ironically, as the fears of evacuation evaporated in Petersburg, Lee met with General John Gordon to determine how best to deal with the increasingly desperate military situation in central Virginia. The battle of Hatcher's Run reminded Confederate strategists that Grant's noose must inevitably tighten around Petersburg and Richmond. Once the Federals severed Petersburg's supply lines, Lee's army would have to escape under severe pressure or starve within the city's defenses.

Lee and Gordon ultimately developed a plan to attack the Federals east of Petersburg. Such an assault might compel the Northerners to constrict their lines to the west and allow Lee to detach troops to reinforce Johnston in North Carolina, while defending a shortened front at Petersburg. Alternately, Lee's offensive might at least create a diversion that would allow him to withdraw his troops entirely and effect a general rendezvous with Johnston's men, somewhere southwest in Virginia or North Carolina. Such a battle plan would take time to arrange, as would any large-scale movement away from Petersburg, so local citizens would enjoy at least another few weeks of the military status quo until events on the battlefield determined their fate.[52]

Life in Petersburg during these weeks grew increasingly chaotic. Two consecutive council meetings adjourned for lack of a quorum. When enough members finally appeared, their agenda included the resignation of one council member, the unfunded appropriation of thirty thousand dollars per month for the support of the Poor House (when the entire city budget had been thirty-five hundred dollars for the fiscal year commencing in July 1861), and the surprising repeal of the prohibition against alcohol sales in the city. Workers could no longer remove the carcasses of mules and horses in a timely manner, and their decaying bodies sent a foul odor through the portions of town adjacent to Brickhouse Run. Citizens ran out of coal in early March, when cold temperatures still required home heating. Later in the month, Petersburg's state senator Robert R. Collier resigned his seat in Richmond, stacking another small governmental problem atop the heap of Petersburg's woes.[53]

No issue better illustrated the turmoil engulfing the Confederacy, and Petersburg along with it, than proposals to arm the slaves. Although discussion of making soldiers out of slaves began as early as the summer of 1863, not until the last winter of the war did this radical concept receive serious consideration. General Lee championed such a measure after the first of the year, reasoning that the defections of fugitives in areas occupied by Union armies reduced the question to whether slaves would fight with the Confederacy or against it. By late February, Jefferson Davis reluctantly embraced the idea as well. The Virginia General Assembly passed the first laws authorizing the enlistment of slaves on March 4 and 5. The Confederate Congress followed suit one week later.

An Alabama soldier at Petersburg wrote home sarcastically that "I suppose we will have a force of 300,000 negro troops in the field & it will take all the whites for officers (ha ha ha). I expect to be a brigadier General yet, but anything rather than subjugation." Confederate deserters fabricated stories that multiple regiments of blacks were drilling near Petersburg, a figure reported by one journalist to be twenty thousand men in twenty-two regiments. In reality, no organized black Confederate units appeared in the Cockade City, although the governor did renew his call on March 4 for slaves and free blacks to report as laborers. The city's quota in March for this more traditional black military service numbered 87 out of nearly 1,150 male free blacks and slaves residing in Petersburg.[54]

The hardships and disruptions of everyday life failed to distract Petersburgers from the impending—and inevitable—military confrontation. "We are all expecting a fight very soon around here," wrote one resident on March 20. Dr. Claiborne explained to his wife that the city had not been evacuated—nor would it be, "unless the R.R. connection . . . be severed to the extent that supplies cannot be brought in. When that happens, the Army will fall back without notice to anybody in my opinion and it may happen at any time."[55]

Instead of the Union attack against the city's supply lines that Petersburgers expected, General Lee initiated the first major military action of the spring: a desperate offensive that he hoped would alter the gloomy military equation at Petersburg. John Gordon led the assault on March 25 against a Federal strongpoint called Fort Stedman, near Prince George Court House Road, one mile north of the Crater and about the same distance east of Blandford Church. The night before the attack, General Gordon had met with a number of officers at his temporary headquarters, the J. Pinckney Williamson home on South Market Street, and sent two men into the business district in search of white cotton cloth. The advance troops, charged with overwhelming the Union pickets outside Fort Stedman before dawn, would use the material as identifying armbands. Mr. Williamson personally guaranteed the purchase that, after Mrs. Gordon and others tore the fabric into strips, arrived at the front for distribution.

The operation against Fort Stedman began well enough. Confederate infantry overpowered the fort's defenders and rolled up the enemy works for several hundred yards both north and south. Hope that the attack would open the escape route to the west burned brightly, but in short order the Federals limited the margins of Gordon's penetration and then marshaled fresh troops to counterattack. Waves of bluecoats drove Gordon's men into the captured fort or across the no-man's-land between the lines, where converging Union fire felled them in windrows. When the fighting ended at 9:00 AM, Gordon had lost between twenty-seven hundred and four thousand men. Lee's so-called last grand offensive had fizzled, the Army of Northern Virginia remained in its Petersburg defenses, and the strategic initiative passed to the Federals. Grant would never relinquish it.[56]

General Meade had been at City Point when Gordon started his attack, but he soon returned to the Petersburg lines. Communications from the far Union left southwest of Petersburg suggested that strong probes toward the Confederate positions in their front might reveal vulnerable defenses. Meade's Second and Sixth Corps advanced in the morning and early afternoon, eventually seizing a large segment of the Confederate picket line. Withstanding concerted Confederate counterattacks, the Federals refaced the captured picket lines and dispatched their own sentries several hundred yards north to the newly won positions. Few in Petersburg appreciated the significance of this Federal victory, an engagement that some called the battle of Jones Farm. "There has been some pressing on our right but not a great deal," reported Colonel Archer on the night of the twenty-fifth. Dr. Claiborne dismissed "the affair on the right" as "not important." Charles Dimmock told his wife on March 27 that "we have a little stir on the lines within the last few days but nothing valuable has been accomplished." In truth, the capture of the Confederate picket line would prove to be a decisive factor in the collapse of the Petersburg defenses one week later.[57]

The genesis of the collapse occurred in the Shenandoah Valley, in eastern North Carolina, and at Grant's headquarters' cabin in City Point, as well as in the trenches southwest of Petersburg. Major General Philip "Little Phil" Sheridan, Grant's favorite lieutenant and a cavalry commander of relentless aggressiveness and massive ego, vanquished the remnant of the Confederate army in the Valley on March 2. He then led more than ten thousand of his seasoned troopers southeast, destroying Confederate facilities en route and arriving near Richmond just as Meade's forces secured the Confederate picket lines southwest of Petersburg. In North Carolina, William Sherman's army defeated Johnston's outmanned divisions at Bentonville, southeast of Raleigh, from March 19 to 21. Rather than pursuing Johnston, Sherman opted to unite with other Federal armies moving inland from the Carolina coast to consolidate his position and prepare for a joint offensive with Grant that he hoped would end the war.

While his troops refitted at Goldsboro, North Carolina, Sherman journeyed north by steamer to Hampton Roads, then up the James River to City Point. He met with Sheridan and Grant on the night of March 27 at the commanding general's modest cabin. The Union's three most renowned soldiers laid plans to reduce the Army of Northern Virginia and capture Petersburg and Richmond in the process. Sherman would commence a march northward from Goldsboro in early April and either seize Burkeville Junction at the intersection of the South Side and Richmond & Danville Railroads or march directly against Lee at Petersburg, depending on events. Grant assigned Sheridan's cavalry responsibility for cutting Boydton Plank Road and the South Side Railroad west of Petersburg. Sheridan would then operate independently as circumstances dictated, perhaps joining Sherman in North Carolina. Sheridan protested such a role, preferring to deliver the hammer blows around Petersburg that he believed would destroy Lee before Sherman could reach Virginia.

Grant acceded to his subordinate's wishes. He modified his strategy to give Sheridan the lead in the impending offensive around Petersburg. Little Phil's troops would range far to the southwest and target Petersburg's remaining two supply lines, supported on his right by Major General Gouverneur K. Warren's Fifth Corps and Major General Andrew A. Humphreys's Second Corps. Troops from the Army of the James would shift secretly from northeast of Richmond to fill the gaps in the lines created by Humphreys southwest of Petersburg. The campaign would begin on March 29.[58]

General Lee learned about Sheridan's shift to the Richmond-Petersburg front, if not the details of the Federal scheme, and assumed that the Union cavalry would renew Grant's efforts to sever the South Side Railroad. The Confederate commander realized full well the need to reinforce his right to resist such a thrust, but he had few options for doing so. Three small cavalry divisions under Major General Fitzhugh Lee and George Pickett's Division of five thousand Virginia infantry represented the army's entire reserve force not deployed along Lee's thirty-seven-mile defensive perimeter. On March 28 Lee prepared to concentrate Pickett and the cavalry around an obscure Dinwiddie County crossroads called Five Forks. This intersection controlled the shortest route to the South Side Railroad beyond the Confederate trenches, presenting Grant with his most likely intermediate objective.[59]

Early the next morning Sheridan's cavalry advanced toward Dinwiddie Court House, which they occupied without serious opposition. To the northeast, two divisions of Warren's corps clashed with Bushrod Johnson's Division near the Lewis farm on Quaker Road. After a sharp fight Johnson's troops retired to their lines along White Oak Road, ceding Boydton Plank Road to the Federals. General Lee responded to this dreaded, if anticipated, offensive by immediately dispatching Pickett and Fitz Lee to Five Forks and redeploying a few brigades from elsewhere along his lines to reinforce Johnson.

Following a day of rain, on March 31 three Confederate brigades struck Warren's Federal infantry south of White Oak Road, driving two blue-clad divisions from the field. Warren, however, used his superior numbers to counterattack in the afternoon and regained the lost ground. North of Dinwiddie Court House another Confederate assault led by Pickett and Fitz Lee drove Sheridan back onto his reserves, nearly routing the Union horsemen. With Warren's men on their flank and in their rear, however, Pickett and Fitz Lee had no choice but to sacrifice the fruits of their victory over Sheridan and retire to Five Forks. Here they assumed a blocking position guarding the South Side Railroad, establishing a defense line of more than one-and-one-half miles around the crossroads.

Fully recovered from the shock of the previous day, on April 1 Sheridan now planned to overwhelm the Confederate defenders in his front and capture the railroad, an accomplishment he deemed tantamount to ending the campaign for Petersburg. He relied on his infantry under Warren to execute a turning movement against the Confederate left flank at Five Forks, isolated by several miles from the end of the permanent Confederate line east along White Oak Road. Warren required more time to position his troops than Sheridan anticipated, and when he began his attack, Warren missed his target due to Sheridan's faulty intelligence. Eventually the Federals did find their prey and routed Pickett and Fitz Lee—wounding, capturing, or killing three thousand of the Confederate defenders. Sheridan's victory at Five Forks would set the stage for the campaign's final and decisive day.[60]

Although civilians and soldiers in Petersburg knew few details about the unfolding drama southwest of the city or its ominous portents, some sensed trouble brewing. Colonel Samuel H. Walkup of the Forty-eighth North Carolina Infantry thought on March 27 that Petersburg "had a gloomy, desolate, deserted, haunted appearance like some plague had depopulated it [and] spread its deadly wings still over its environs." The former lieutenant colonel of the Fifty-second Virginia Infantry, John D. Ross, was in Petersburg and noticed cotton and tobacco piled in the streets ready to be burned. Ross assumed that the forlorn-looking city was about to be abandoned.[61]

Readers of the local newspaper, however, would have discerned few hints that life in Petersburg was any different during the last week in March than it had been all winter. The *Daily Express* noted the dearth of crime from the mayor's court, concluding that "the morals of the city have evidently become much improved of late. . . . All is quiet in the city." On March 31 a faulty stovepipe set the Norfolk & Petersburg Railroad depot ablaze, but the fire department responded to the alarm in competent fashion and extinguished the flames. The Petersburg Common Council met on April 1 (as Sheridan prepared to scatter the defenders at Five Forks), conducted routine business, and adjourned with no special mention of any impending emergency. An auction house sold one slave in the business district; citizens bid on condemned army horses and mules; commerce at various city stores transpired as usual. A cheery *Daily Express* article even noticed that spring weather had elicited delightful fresh blooms, save for the apricot blossoms killed by a recent frost.[62]

Visiting town in late March, Acting Adjutant James E. Hall of the Thirty-first Virginia Infantry considered Petersburg to be "one of the nicest cities I ever saw." He thought that the citizens seemed "as if they are of a caste of mind . . . unassailable by ruin and misfortune, for the same light-hearted gayety seems to exist now as that which characterized the 'Cockade City' before the war." Even Major Cooke, who had been witness to a part of the fighting on April 1, returned to his quarters after sharing supper with relatives in Petersburg, making no special mention in his diary of imminent doom. Only those with hindsight would have noted the irony of the recent presentation by Major John Tyler at Mechanics Hall entitled "Our National Crisis," for on the night of April 1 the Confederate flag had fewer than thirty-six hours to fly over the Cockade City.[63]

⌐ 10 ⌐

"Tis Midnight Yet With Us"

APRIL 2–AUGUST 1865

ON APRIL 1, 1865, an anxious, expectant group gathered around Fanny Gordon in the Market Street home of J. Pinckney Williamson. Mrs. Gordon, wife of the Confederate corps commander, delivered the couple's third son that day to the relief and delight of her attendants. Such an important family event under any other circumstance would have drawn General John B. Gordon to his wife's bedside. The child's arrival, however, occurred on the eve of the most important day in Petersburg's history. In the wake of the battle of Five Forks, the fate of the Cockade City, the Army of Northern Virginia, and the Confederate States of America rested on the leadership of Robert Lee and Ulysses Grant, and the performance of their respective armies.[1]

While Mrs. Gordon welcomed her son into the world, ten miles southwest of Petersburg General Grant looked up from the light of his headquarters' campfire and recognized an approaching staff officer, Colonel Horace Porter. Grant had assigned Porter as his liaison with Major General Philip Sheridan on April 1, authorizing Porter to represent his views and report regularly via courier on the conduct of the day's events. Porter brought word of the victory at Five Forks, news that unleashed a spirited celebration at Grant's command post. "For some minutes there was a bewildering state of excitement, and officers fell to grasping hands, shouting, and hugging each other like school-boys," remembered Porter. Everyone in Grant's camp believed that Sheridan's triumph cleared access to the South Side Railroad and that Little Phil could be astride Petersburg's last remaining supply line in the morning. Grant, however, did not participate in the rejoicing. He understood the distinction between opportunity and achievement, realizing full well the unfinished nature of the day's events.[2]

General Lee also grasped the import of the situation created by the debacle on April 1. The loss of the South Side Railroad would force him to abandon Petersburg, and with it the capital at Richmond, or face the strangling entrapment of his army. He must do something to redeem the situation, but what? The last of his reserve troops around Petersburg had been stampeded at Five Forks. Lee turned to Lieutenant General James Longstreet, his "old war horse," whose troops guarded the fortifications northeast of Richmond. He ordered Longstreet to move units from the far side of the James River to Petersburg to bolster the beleaguered divisions around the Cockade City. Whatever chance Lee had of orchestrating an organized withdrawal from Richmond and Petersburg and saving the Army of Northern Virginia would depend on the timely arrival of Longstreet's reinforcements.

Grant appreciated his opponent's shortage of both fighting men and strategic options, but he maintained respect for Lee's aggressive generalship. Since June the Confederate commander had invariably mounted a counterattack whenever losing a portion of his line to one of Grant's offensives—he had done so with some success as recently as March 31 at White Oak Road and Dinwiddie Court House. Anticipating a similar response following the battle at Five Forks, Grant sent one of his infantry corps to reinforce Sheridan. Then he took a step he had avoided since the disaster at the Crater in July: he ordered a massive frontal attack to begin at dawn.

Direct advances against strong fortifications such as those ringing Petersburg almost never worked. The risk of crossing hundreds of yards of open ground in the face of small arms and artillery fire mercilessly delivered from behind formidable works normally outweighed any possible gains. This time Grant banked on Lee's need to weaken his lines in order to assemble the anticipated counteroffensive at Five Forks. The Union commander sought to strike simultaneously along the entire Petersburg front, hoping to achieve a breakthrough somewhere while repulsing any attack at Five Forks.[3]

The rank and file of the Federal army also understood the danger of charging across the shelterless ground in front of the Confederate works. While they wrote letters home on the night of April 1 (which many believed would be their last), Grant ordered his artillery to blanket the Petersburg lines with an overwhelming display of firepower. Perhaps this would persuade Lee to abandon his works, or at the least knock out some of the ordnance that would contest the infantry attack. Around 10:00 PM on April 1, nearly 150 cannon opened from positions east, south, and southwest of the city. The Confederate general Cadmus M. Wilcox considered the barrage "at times equal in brilliancy to a vivid meteoric display." One Pennsylvania soldier remembered that "the whole night was hideous with screaming shells and bombs tracing networks of livid fire over the peaceful heavens." After three hours the firing slackened, and relative quiet settled over the expectant troops.[4]

Few people slept in Petersburg that night. The intensity of the bombardment and the strategic context in which it took place distinguished it from earlier cannonades. No one on the battle lines rested either. Union soldiers crept to their jump-off positions following the artillery barrage and waited for signal guns that would launch their attack in the predawn gloom. Resolute Confederates rechecked cartridge boxes and tried to ignore their thin ranks behind the parapets. About 4:40 AM on April 2 Grant's climactic offensive commenced. East of the city the Union Ninth Corps demonstrated, while their comrades south of town charged toward Gordon's lines guarding Jerusalem Plank Road. The Confederates lost ground, but Gordon's men fought with ferocious determination and could not be driven entirely from their maze of trenches, traverses, and ramparts.

Southwest of the city the Union Sixth Corps gained more success. Striking a portion of Lieutenant General Ambrose Powell Hill's Third Corps line on the Banks, Boisseau, and Hart farms, the Federals reached the Confederate earthworks. A pitiless hand-to-hand fight ensued between fourteen thousand Federals and ten game but grossly outnumbered regiments of Georgians and North Carolinians. By 5:15 AM the bluecoats completed the decisive breakthrough that had eluded them since June, cleaving Lee's army in two.[5]

Reaction to the breakthrough came swiftly at Confederate headquarters. General A. P. Hill had left his residence at the Venable cottage in Petersburg's western suburbs early that morning and ridden to Edge Hill to consult with Lee and the newly arrived Longstreet regarding operations for the day. Suddenly a staff officer burst in to announce the presence of Yankees in the fields just southwest of Lee's command post. Hill and several aides dashed off to investigate. The general's escort had dwindled to a lone sergeant when the pair encountered two Sixth Corps soldiers in a patch of woods one-half mile behind the captured Confederate line. These Pennsylvanians were among the hundreds of undisciplined troops who had participated in the breakthrough and were now roaming through the countryside in small groups, seeking trophies and adventure. Hill boldly demanded that the two stray Northerners surrender. The Federals responded with rifle fire, striking the Confederate corps commander in the chest and killing him instantly.[6]

Sixth Corps officers eventually reorganized their victorious troops and pointed them southwest toward Hatcher's Run, four miles' distant. Three Confederate brigades blocked their way. The Federals began their advance about 6:30 AM, and within two and a half hours they had overwhelmed the Southern defenders, who fought valiantly until their lines became untenable. Adding fresh troops from the Twenty-fourth Corps to their ranks, the weary Sixth Corps soldiers reversed direction and plodded northeast on Boydton Plank Road, aiming for Petersburg's inner defenses.

Gordon maintained his grip on the city's southern bulwarks and the Federals made no serious attempts to assault east of town, but the juggernaut moving toward Lee's headquarters and the interior fortifications just west of Petersburg threatened not only the city but the very existence of Lee's army. All the surviving Confederate units west of the breakthrough were either in retreat or deployed in forlorn rearguard actions near the South Side Railroad. A crisis had arisen unprecedented in the history of the Army of Northern Virginia.[7]

By midmorning Lee had formulated a reasonably accurate picture of his army's desperate situation. The best he could hope to achieve would be to hold Grant at bay until nightfall, when darkness could shield his withdrawal from Petersburg and Richmond. His goal then would be to unite the disparate elements of his army scattered northeast of Richmond, in Chesterfield County, around Petersburg, and west of the breakthrough. Their rendezvous point would be along the Richmond & Danville Railroad west of Petersburg. This rail line might sustain the reunited divisions as they moved southwest to join Joseph E. Johnston's army in North Carolina to continue the war.

Lee dictated a message to Lieutenant Colonel Walter Taylor of his staff for transmission to Secretary of War John C. Breckinridge, explaining the situation at Petersburg in clear, unvarnished language. This telegram arrived in Richmond at 10:40 AM:

> I see no prospect of doing more than holding our position here till night. I am not certain that I can do that. If I can I shall withdraw to-night north of the Appomattox, and, if possible, it will be better to withdraw the whole line to-night from James River. The brigades on Hatcher's Run are cut off from us; enemy have broken through our lines and intercepted between us and them. . . . I advise that all preparation be made for leaving Richmond to-night.

President Davis learned of Lee's message while on his way to Sunday worship. He left the services at St. Paul's Episcopal Church before they had concluded, beginning what would be a frantic and tragic sixteen hours in the doomed Confederate capital.[8]

In Petersburg the gravity of the military situation revealed itself with less clarity but no less drama. About breakfast time military authorities implemented emergency measures to torch the caches of tobacco stored in the city's warehouses. Petersburg "was full of great clouds of . . . acrid, stinging smoke," remembered one resident. Many citizens interpreted the fires as proof that the long-dreaded evacuation was imminent, although others "laughed scornfully at the idea, remarking that the thing was not only incredible but an absolute impossibility and . . . nothing more than Dame Rumour *April Fooling* us." "The excitement is high & numbers are leaving the city," reported a Virginia soldier who noticed quite a few blacks joining the white refugees, a phenomenon rarely seen during previous civilian flights. Union shells plunged into the city, adding to the confusion. "Every kind of rumor in circulation; people are flying in every direction," recalled one Petersburg woman. "We all try and keep composed." A wounded Confederate gunner fresh from the front lines recounted that "at least half the people [were] standing on the streets or in their doorways and many and eagerly were the questions asked regarding the state of affairs."[9]

More wounded Confederates poured into the chaotic city, arriving in ambulances and on stretchers throughout the morning, "the moans mingling with the cries of women, the shrieking and bursting of shell, and the hoarse orders of men in authority." Only the Confederate and the Fair Grounds Hospitals remained open. Dr. John H. Claiborne, head of medical administration in Petersburg, learned of the peril west of the city from an officer who thundered past his Washington Street office. The confusion made it impossible for Claiborne to formulate any definite plans.[10]

The Petersburg Common Council also sought clarification of the military situation and its potential impact on the city. Sixteen of twenty council members met in emergency session that morning and emerged a short time later with a resolution drafted by D'Arcy Paul acknowledging that the unthinkable might actually occur before day's end: "A Committee consisting of the Mayor and two members be appointed to wait on Genl Lee and request that he inform said committee at such time as he may deem it necessary, whether he contemplates evacuating this city, and that if an evacuation is contemplated said committee be instructed to surrender the City to the commander of the Federal Army and request protection for the persons of the citizens and their property."[11]

Lee's failure to apprise city authorities of their impending fate must be understood in the context of the desperate tactical situation west of Petersburg. Lee had no time to parley with civilian delegations as thousands of Union soldiers threatened his last lines of defense. Just north of Boydton Plank Road and one-half mile west of the nearly empty Dimmock Line, two small forts, Gregg and Whitworth, guarded an approach to the city. The first reinforcements, four small Mississippi regiments under Brigadier General Nathaniel Harris, arrived in time to occupy the forts. Shortly after noon no fewer than seven thousand Northern troops commenced a series of assaults against the Mississippians, a handful of artillerists, and survivors of the breakthrough.

Fort Gregg "raged like the crater of a volcano, emitting flashes of deadly battle-fires enveloped in flame and cloud, wreathing our flag ... in the smoke of death," remembered Harris. The forlorn defenders traded their lives for time as the first of Longstreet's fresh brigades poured across the

Appomattox and into the old ramparts of the Dimmock Line. When the Federals finally captured Forts Gregg and Whitworth about 3:00 PM, 714 of their comrades lay on the fields in front of the bloody bastions, a greater number than the garrisons of the two Confederate positions combined. At least half of the troops in the two forts were killed, wounded, or captured.[12]

While the contest swirled at Fort Gregg, one mile to the north General Lee found himself directly in the line of fire at the Turnbull house. Lee had committed all his available infantry to meet other emergencies, so when the bulk of the Union Sixth Corps arrived opposite Edge Hill, he had only a handful of artillery batteries and his headquarters' personnel to block its path. Shells crashed through army headquarters as the Southern gunners frantically pulled lanyards and sponged red-hot barrels, loading rounds of canister and spherical case as fast as they could. The cannoneers held out for some time, repulsing one Federal charge and inflicting considerable losses. Major General Horatio Wright's frustrated Northern brigades realigned to gain the flanks of the ragged artillery formation and began picking off battery horses, moving faster than the gunners could reposition their pieces.

The artillery commander Lieutenant Colonel William Poague realized that his battalion was "in imminent danger of being bagged," and he ordered the guns to withdraw. Lee remained at his headquarters directing affairs until the last possible moment, then he joined his staff and the cannoneers in a hasty departure as minie balls whizzed overhead. Most of Poague's ordnance escaped and unlimbered behind reserve fortifications along high ground on the eastern side of Rohoic Creek. The Sixth Corps troops overran Edge Hill and approached the new Confederate position, but by then the Northerners had finally exhausted their energy. Only a few of the most determined Union soldiers ventured across the stream to test the last Confederate line before withdrawing to safety.[13]

Gordon's powder-stained men continued to fight musket butt to bayonet in the warren of trenches south of town, refusing to allow the Ninth Corps to punch through. With Longstreet's brigades in place between Boydton Plank Road and the river, the tactical situation around Petersburg stabilized. It had been a near thing. Lee's army—battered, bloodied, and beaten—had barely avoided annihilation on April 2.

The Confederate commander halted less than one mile west of Edge Hill at Cottage Farm, a little south of Cox Road and about halfway to Petersburg. Following his release from prison, Roger A. Pryor had shared Cottage Farm with his wife, Sara, until the morning's excitement prompted the Pryors to move into a vacant house in Petersburg. Joined by Generals Longstreet, Wilcox, Henry Heth, and others, Lee finalized his plan for evacuating Petersburg and Richmond and reuniting his scattered army at Amelia Court House. The small county seat lay forty miles west of Petersburg and was the closest point on the Richmond & Danville Railroad convenient to all elements of Lee's fractured command. The withdrawal from the Cockade City would commence at 8:00 PM. Lee circulated detailed orders to his subordinates to guide the dangerous operation in the immediate presence of the enemy.[14]

Following preparation of these instructions, Lee departed to inspect his lines. During his absence the delegation representing the Petersburg Common Council—Mayor W. W. Townes and councilmen James Boisseau and Charles F. Collier—arrived at Cottage Farm. The general returned after a brief time and promptly received the worried officials. The trio spoke plainly about their desire to know Lee's plans. Collier remembered that "the General was apparently calm and collected, but very reticent, only replying to the committee that he would communicate with us at the residence of Mr. [D'Arcy] Paul at 10 o'clock." Lee's desire to avoid exacerbating the unrest that already infected Petersburg by confirming his intention to abandon the city explained his lack of candor. The less confusion on the streets as his soldiers crossed the river that night, the more expeditious would be his perilous withdrawal. The gentlemen retired, pessimistic but uncertain of Petersburg's fate, and agreed to reconvene at Mr. Paul's Union Street home that evening to await Lee's report.[15]

In the meantime Dr. Claiborne received authorization to evacuate the city "with . . . as many surgeons, hospital attaches, servants & c., as could be spared from hospital service, and to cross the river at Campbell's Bridge." Claiborne decided to leave all but four doctors, four assistants, one medical wagon and driver, and a handful of slaves in town to provide for the bedridden. While Claiborne prepared to depart, Lee telegraphed the secretary of war that "it is absolutely necessary that we should abandon our position tonight, or run the risk of being cut off in the morning. I have given all the orders to officers on both sides of the river, and have taken every precaution that I can to make the movement successful. It will be a difficult operation, but I hope not impracticable. Please give all the orders that you find necessary in and about Richmond."[16]

The hours passed slowly for the anxious people in Petersburg as afternoon at last gave way to evening. "The sadness and solemnity of that Sabbath day can never be forgotten," remembered one resident. A worship service at Grace Episcopal Church drew few attendees. General Wilcox sent a staff officer to inform a local woman, whom he had befriended, of the army's upcoming departure. Similarly, Major Giles Buckner Cooke of Lee's staff visited Mrs. David Callender and a few others to advise them of the impending evacuation and warned them to stay indoors should street fighting erupt. Most residents realized their worst fears only when Lee's men began to pull silently out of their lines and march through town toward the Appomattox River bridges. "Soon after nightfall the dull roll of muffled artillery could be heard in the streets," wrote a chaplain on Gordon's staff. "Citizens began to retire into their houses—blinds were closed, tears were wept; hearts ached & heads wondered."[17]

Longstreet's troops and what remained of A. P. Hill's corps used the Battersea pontoon bridge upstream from Petersburg to effect their escape. Gordon's men filed through town heading for the Pocahontas Bridge. These troops saw weeping women on the curbs "as in the agony of despair, that the . . . once lovely 'Cockade City' was being abandoned to the ruthless invader." Other citizens evinced a more pragmatic attitude. Gordon's chaplain noticed one man "more provident or enterprising than others rolling a wheel barrow on which was a barrel of flour"—loot from Petersburg buildings now unprotected or in flames. "Great fires were raging in the city, for the authorities were burning the big warehouses filled with all kinds of army stores, and the flames were leaping skyward, illuminating the city and surrounding country," observed one Confederate soldier.[18]

Major Henry Kyd Douglas spent part of the evening saying good-bye to friends in town while his unit waited to begin its retreat. "There was no sleeping in Petersburg that night," Douglas later wrote, "no night except for the darkness. It was all commotion and bustle." The last person Douglas saw before beginning his withdrawal was Miss Mary Tabb Bolling, the popular Petersburg socialite who would marry a Confederate general after the war. "She uttered not a word of fear or complaint," recalled Douglas, but "the infinite sadness of her silence was pathetic beyond words." The soldiers "spoke with bated breath if they broke silence at all," lost in their own contemplations of an uncertain future. Once the organized troops had cleared the streets, a dark blanket of quiet covered Petersburg in dreadful anticipation. One woman recalled that "the silence, the dead stillness of the last night of that army in Petersburg, the darkness and the hush, wrapped us in a pall. . . . With every light extinguished Petersburg was indeed 'The City of Awful Night.'"[19]

Although the army moved toward the bridges with commendable discipline considering the desperate circumstances of that fateful night, not every soldier performed his duty. Some, surrendering to their baser instincts, joined the looting that also tempted a number of residents. One Petersburg man was "trotting along and shoving a pushcart loaded with groceries from the burning warehouses," when his vehicle struck an obstacle in the street "and dumped his load on the ground." A soldier witnessed this accident, broke ranks, and filled his haversack with flour that spilled from a barrel broken by the fall. He then grabbed a ham and scooped a canteen-full of syrup from the stolen supplies before regaining his place in line. Other men discovered caches of liquor and had become drunk. Such troops, as well as

soldiers who simply gave up and rested alongside the streets too exhausted
or dispirited to remain with their units, would be left behind by the retreat-
ing army.[20]

Most of the men, however, controlled their despair and kept pace with
their comrades. "I am almost demoralized, cannot see what will become of
us," thought one Virginian. "I feel as if I had just as well to die as live." Some
Petersburg citizens, such as the old secessionist Edmund Ruffin, shared
such gloomy sentiments. "I am without any resource left, either of property
or escape," he wrote. "I have no conveyance for flight, no place of refuge, &
even if having both, I would have no means for support. . . . I cannot consent
to live a pauper on the charity of strangers abroad."[21]

General Lee displayed characteristic self-control during this difficult
night. He dispatched Major Cooke to report to the Petersburg councilmen
as he had promised and somehow remembered to return a borrowed chair
to the Reverend Theodorick Pryor. At 10:00 PM Cooke arrived at the Paul
home, where he had been a frequent visitor on happier evenings, and confirmed for the waiting officials what by then had become obvious to everyone: the army would be completely out of Petersburg by midnight, leaving
the city in charge of its civilian authorities. After the councilmen digested this
crushing news, they decided to reconvene at Mr. Paul's home at 4:00 AM.
There they would divide into small groups, each responsible for a different
route into the city, and attempt to find a Union officer who would agree to
accept Petersburg's surrender and guarantee the safety of its citizens and
their property.

Mayor Townes and Councilman Collier left after the meeting and wandered the streets, brooding about the grave duty that faced them in the
morning. They stopped at the house on Washington Street occupied earlier
that day by Roger and Sara Pryor, refugees from Cottage Farm. Mrs. Pryor
answered the door and listened as the mayor requested that her husband
accompany him and Collier on their portentous mission. "Oh, he cannot—
he cannot," Mrs. Pryor protested. "How can you ask him to surrender his old
home? Besides, he is worn out, and is now sleeping heavily." Townes understood. Meanwhile Major Cooke continued to bid farewell to friends, relations, and the young Betty Page of whom he had grown fond during his stay
in town. "The feelings of that night will ever be remembered," wrote Cooke.
"Parting . . . was truly heartrending."[22]

Most of the soldiers marched across either the Battersea pontoon bridge
above the city or the Pocahontas Bridge in town, because the railroad bridge
had an open floor and could not easily accommodate pedestrians. Colonel
Asbury Coward of the Fifth South Carolina Infantry oversaw the movement
across the Battersea bridge, while other officers superintended the crossing
in the city. Lee ordered the spans burned to deny their use to the Federals

once all organized units had reached the north bank. Some soldiers prepared the bridges for ignition while the rest of the troops, joined by a few citizens and runaway slaves, stumbled across in the darkness.

The torrent of Confederate troops moving from Petersburg into Chesterfield County became a trickle by midnight. Although scores of stragglers remained in town along with some deserters and those too exhausted to continue, it would have been reckless to wait until every willing Confederate gained the left bank. The survival of Lee's army depended on reaching fresh supplies and reorganizing at Amelia before the Federals could attack. About 2:00 AM on April 3 officers at the bridges received orders to set them ablaze.[23]

Captain Oscar Hinrichs, an engineer, lit the flames at the Pocahontas Bridge. "We heard a big explosion, and, looking back, we saw the timbers of the bridge rising skyward and changing ends like arrows," recounted one Confederate soldier. Seeing the flames to the east, Colonel Coward ordered the Battersea bridge destroyed as well. Lee's weary warriors, who had suffered and sacrificed beyond calculation in the defense of Petersburg for so many months, turned to look one final time at the forlorn metropolis. "The lurid glare of the burning city lighted our steps, and cast its spectral shadows on the dark waters beneath," wrote one Virginian.[24]

Dr. Claiborne crossed on Campbell's Bridge. When he reached the heights at Ettrick, he paused to gaze at his hometown — "the city for a hundred years of happy homes, of brave men, and of fair women." Every observer realized that by morning Petersburg would be under Union control. "O, how sad I felt to think so noble a little city should so soon be in Yankee hands!" a Virginia soldier despaired. Major Cooke lingered on the north side of the Appomattox longer than almost any other officer, tending to the destruction of the bridges. "My heart ached in contemplations of what might be done," thought Cooke, who, just before dawn, believed he heard the enemy "coming into the city shouting and shrieking like so many Serbs."[25]

Cooke had, indeed, detected the presence of Union troops during the predawn hours of April 3, although on the previous evening the Federal high command had no certain knowledge that Lee would cede Petersburg without further resistance. General Grant had considered the fighting on April 2 to be "one of the greatest victories of the war," and made plans that night to exploit his gains. He sent orders to the corps commanders Wright and Major General John G. Parke of the Ninth Corps to "place all your artillery in position and open with your guns upon the enemy at 5 a.m. to-morrow. In case you should discover . . . any intention to evacuate his position, or any evidence of weakness, you will follow this bombardment by an assault on his lines." Grant also suggested that President Lincoln meet with him in the morning at a point to be determined, depending on the military circumstances then prevailing.[26]

As the night of April 2 wore on, evidence mounted within Union lines that Petersburg might fall without another fight. Federal soldiers watched as flames from the city's buildings illuminated the night sky. Petersburg "had been burning during the day," wrote one Northern newspaper correspondent, "but its appearance now was heightened by its vivid contrast with the darkness of night, and was sublime beyond expression." Confederate deserters drifted into Federal picket posts and confirmed the increasing suspicion that Lee was in the process of evacuating Petersburg. Private Thomas Troy of the Fifty-first Pennsylvania Infantry crept into town during the night and returned to his superiors with an eyewitness confirmation of the Confederate withdrawal.

Between 1:30 AM and 3:20 AM Union units from east, south, and west of Petersburg received orders to prepare a cautious advance toward the Confederate earthworks. The first to venture toward Petersburg were the First Michigan Sharpshooters and the Second Michigan Infantry. They began their move west toward Petersburg at 3:10 AM. About the same time members of the Petersburg Common Council gathered at D'Arcy Paul's home, divided into small groups, and moved out on the roads leading into town to intercept advancing Federals and surrender the city.[27]

The Michigan troops under Colonel Ralph Ely discovered the main Confederate fortifications abandoned and, after permitting themselves "three hearty cheers," pressed carefully into Petersburg, reaching the city shortly after 4:00 AM. Twenty-five minutes later the bluecoats approached the short street leading to the courthouse, the city's most prominent landmark. Major Clement A. Lounsberry, an officer on Ely's staff, encountered three of the councilmen bearing a flag of truce. "But the gallant major could listen to no proposition until the 'old flag' was floating from the highest point of the courthouse steeple," wrote Ely.

At precisely 4:28 AM, according to Ely, men from the First Michigan Sharpshooters hoisted their regimental banner above the courthouse. Moments later the Second Michigan boys raised their colors above the Customs House a block away. Color Sergeant William T. Wixcey remembered flying the flag from the courthouse, the first Union colors to wave over Petersburg in almost four years: "It was yet dark when we made our way into the courthouse and up the winding stairs into the clock tower. For want of a better place to display our colors we opened the door of the clock face and thrust them out through it, and there . . . floated the dear old flag. . . . Our hearts were too full for utterance, so we clasped hands and shed tears of joy, for we knew that the beginning of the end had come."

In short order Major Lounsberry accepted a surrender document from the local officials. The message, addressed to Grant "or the Major-General commanding U.S. Forces in Front of Petersburg," read: "General: The city of

Petersburg having been evacuated by the Confederate troops, we, a committee authorized by the common council, do hereby surrender the city to the U.S. forces, with a request for the protection of the persons and property of its inhabitants." It was signed by Townes, Collier, and Paul.[28]

Unaware of events at the courthouse, the mayor and Charles Collier were at that moment at the Model Farm hoping to relinquish the city to some responsible Federal officer. Proceeding cautiously on foot and carrying a white handkerchief attached to a stick, the two gentlemen reached the abandoned Confederate works overlooking Rohoic Creek near Cottage Farm. They had not seen a single bluecoat and fancied themselves undetected as well.

Suddenly a signal gun sounded to the southwest and "instantaneously, there sprang forth, as from the bowels of the earth . . . a mighty host of Federal soldiers, and then . . . such a shout of victory as seemed to shake the very ground on which we stood," recalled Collier. The two civilians found themselves in the midst of the Union advance authorized the night before. Collier and Townes attempted to stop some ranking officer to explain their intentions, but none wished to be diverted from a triumphant dash into Petersburg. Some of the officers did hurriedly invite the city officials to join them as they ran east toward town, "promising to protect us and . . . our people."[29]

Thousands of Northern soldiers now poured into the streets from the east, south, and west, although the vast majority of Grant's forces remained in their fortifications and did not participate in the occupation. Some units, assisted by local African Americans, served as makeshift firefighters, extinguishing the flames consuming the Pocahontas Bridge but failing to save Campbell's Bridge and a number of other structures. Observant soldiers captured Confederate stragglers before they could escape across the Appomattox River in small boats.[30]

Among the captives was Corporal Joseph S. Kimbrough of the Fourteenth Georgia Infantry. Kimbrough had fallen asleep and spent the night in Petersburg with a number of his enervated comrades. About an hour after daylight the "hoarse huzzas" of the Federals awoke these slumbering stragglers, who snatched up their rifles and made for the bridges. Seeing the railroad span in ruins and the Pocahontas Bridge in flames filled Kimbrough with dread: "No language can describe my feelings as I gazed across that muddy, swollen stream and realized that there was no chance to cross nor time to escape." Kimbrough tossed his rifle into the swirling waters of the Appomattox before the Federals arrived and demanded his surrender.[31]

The 121st New York Infantry placed flags on the public buildings throughout Petersburg, explaining Councilman Collier's observation that the courthouse had been "festooned" with Union banners. Other Federals indulged in less patriotic activities. "We secured a lot of Confederate currency and postage stamps, and routed out a lot of stragglers and sneaks, hid about the city," wrote one New Yorker. "At the Commissary we secured some nice hams and some apple jack that was quite smooth, and under its softening influence we forgave a good many of our foes."[32]

A number of house servants delighted in revealing the whereabouts of Confederate soldiers hiding in private homes. When the Federals entered one of these dwellings to collect prisoners, one woman provided the intruders "a startling exhibition of their ability to blackguard us." Other Petersburg females displayed more restraint as they implored the Northern troops to share rations. "Ladies begging me to give them something to eat," wrote Lieutenant Philip R. Woodcock of the 121st New York Infantry. "Had an entertaining time with them. Ladies fainted away which required my help."[33]

Union soldiers earned mixed reviews from Petersburg homeowners. One woman remembered that as a small child on April 3 her attention was drawn by the sound of the regimental bands—what she believed was a festive parade. Against her mother's instructions she began to sing along with the music, choosing the only songs in her repertoire, Southern patriotic tunes. Years later she recalled: "An intoxicated Union soldier stepped up to me and said 'Sing, you little curly headed rebel.' I looked at mother and she told me to go ahead and sing. The soldier gave me a dime."

This same lady described an incident involving a Federal officer searching door-to-door for concealed firearms. When the Northerner approached her house, the little girl stood next to a loyal female slave who denied that any men were home. The girl's father heard the exchange and appeared at the window admonishing his servant for lying and directing that the Northerner be shown in. When asked about the presence of weapons, the man produced the family shotgun and invited the soldier to search the building if he wished. "There's no need sir," responded the respectful visitor, "I know when I'm talking to a gentleman."[34]

A similar episode transpired at the Callender home on Jefferson Street near Poplar Lawn. The young Tom Callender ignored his father's advice to stay indoors and ventured out to the gateposts with a slave boy to watch the excitement. Soon a Union soldier asked whether there were any men in the house, and Tom cheerfully revealed that his father was home, resulting in an order that Mr. Callender appear at the courthouse soon after breakfast to register with the authorities.

After Callender departed, a Federal officer from Minnesota appeared at the gate and beckoned Mrs. Callender to the front yard. He told her that he had posted a provost guard at the corner of Jefferson and Marshall Streets and that should she encounter any problem she should summon the detail to her assistance. An hour later three Union soldiers approached the house looking for whiskey. When Mrs. Callender coldly explained that she had given most of her liquor to Confederate soldiers the previous night and poured out the rest, the disappointed Federals grew belligerent. Identifying her inquisitor as an Irishman, Bessie Callender remarked that "you have enough wrong to redress in your own country; what did you come here for?" The immigrant replied that he "did not care which side whipped, I just wanted the money," which prompted Mrs. Callender to unleash a torrent of verbal abuse toward someone she considered an unprincipled mercenary. "I hope you will suffer all through eternity for your taking part in a wicked war, in what did not concern you," she scolded. She then threatened to call the provost guard if the intruders did not disperse, which caused them to "put their hands on the fence and [go] over like monkeys."[35]

Roger Pryor proved to be the biggest catch netted during the morning occupation. Around 7:30 AM General Wright learned that one of his brigade commanders had interviewed Pryor, who confirmed the Confederate evacuation, adding ominously that General Lee was "very bitter and disposed to fight it out to the last." Captain James Deane of the Second Connecticut Heavy Artillery also claimed to have interrogated Pryor both for military intelligence and about where to place guards to prevent destruction of public property. A third Union officer reported seeing Pryor at Councilman William R. Mallory's home on High Street that morning, Pryor expressing relief that the war was almost over. Eventually three "German soldiers" barged into the Pryors' residence and marched the ubiquitous former general off for destinations unknown, a prisoner for the second time in four months.[36]

Petersburg's African Americans provided a far more enthusiastic reception for the Union troops than did their white neighbors. "By the time we were fairly in the city streets, the colored brother (and sister) had caught on that something was up," wrote Captain Deane. "And what praise they did bestow on us — even my big awkward horse came in for a share of admiration." Another Connecticut soldier recalled that "as we entered the street there was a line of shanties inhabited by darkies who were on top of their houses and fences waving their hats shouting, 'The Lord bless the Yankees. . . .'" According to the New Englander Michael Kelly, "the colored portion of the people were wild with singing, praysing [sic] God for sending the Yankee hosts to free them, clap[p]ing hands . . . singing hymns, shaking hands, pushing one another with joy."[37]

Petersburg's blacks reserved their warmest welcome for the United States Colored Troops of Brigadier General William Birney's Twenty-fifth Corps division. Elements of three brigades marched into the city around 6:00 AM. "We were among the first troops to enter Petersburg," wrote Sergeant Major William McCoslin of the Twenty-ninth United States Colored Troops, "and the orderly, well-behaved disposition of our command elicited the praise of our officers, and the universal commendations of the people, sobriety and decorum being the order of the day." McCoslin's claim notwithstanding, one Confederate chaplain stationed at the Fair Grounds Hospital testified that the black troops stole chickens from residences in the neighborhood. The chaplain of the 127th United States Colored Troops remembered that African Americans thronged the streets and sang spirituals, celebrating their liberation with biblical analogy.[38]

The Georgia prisoner Corporal Kimbrough offered a quite different description of the Federal army's first hours in Petersburg:

> We were taken through the streets . . . where everything was in terrible commotion. Irish women, negro women, men, and boys were running hither and thither, some of them with slabs of bacon on their heads and others with sacks and bundles of various sorts and sizes. We were marched by and in front of a regiment or brigade of negro troops, who cursed and abused us to their hearts' content without any protest from either our captors or the white officers who commanded them.[39]

Colonel James Hubbard of the Second Connecticut Heavy Artillery temporarily assumed the duties of provost marshal in Petersburg and immediately took steps to secure the streets. Councilman Collier credited the bluecoats with establishing a reasonable degree of order under circumstances that could easily have degenerated into anarchy. "Every effort was made by the Federal officers and troops to protect the persons and property of our citizens," wrote Collier. "Safeguards were sent to every house for which they were asked. . . . Everything was at once systematized by the military, and comparative order and quiet reigned under martial law." One Connecticut soldier confessed that "a little pillaging was done," but soon enough guards protected the stores and extinguished the smoldering fires.[40]

Other Federal troops occupied Petersburg on the morning of April 3. Colonel Oliver Edwards assigned the Thirty-seventh Massachusetts Infantry, armed with repeating weapons, as sentries while additional soldiers from west of Petersburg drifted into the city fulfilling less formal functions. Lieutenant Robert Pratt of the Fifth Vermont Infantry noted that the town's businesses were all deserted. "There was nothing strange about the appearance of this city," remembered another Vermonter, "except its remarkable silence. Stores, shops, and all public buildings were closed; nearly all the male inhabitants had fled with the army, save old men and negroes."[41]

General Parke began garrisoning Petersburg about 10:00 AM. Brigadier General Orlando B. Willcox's division, assisted by some cavalry, established firm control of the city. They also conducted a reconnaissance across the river to verify the direction of Lee's retreat, and in the course of the next twenty-four hours snared more than 1,000 prisoners, 830 small arms, and seven battle flags. "In two hours," boasted Willcox, "Petersburg . . . was as quiet, and property and persons as safe as in Washington, an instance of discipline and good conduct on the part of the troops unsurpassed in military history." Some Petersburg residents concurred, expressing "surprise to find the utmost decorum prevailing which ever way [we] turned."⁴²

Curious Northerners ranged across the entire city. "Marks of bombardment were plentiful on all sides," recalled one New Yorker, "chimneys down, holes through brick walls and little drifts of debris, mortar and brick, in yard and street." Despite this damage, a Connecticut captain liked what he saw of the conquered town. "This is a beautiful city, splendid . . . buildings composed of banks, halls, churches, court house, [and] many factories," he wrote. A New York reporter concurred, thinking that Petersburg had "a very clean and respectable appearance and . . . many residences here that would do no discredit to Fifth Avenue."⁴³

One Ohio soldier was less impressed, thinking that Petersburg revealed a "lack of energy & enterprise" with its "old-fashioned houses [and] narrow streets." Colonel Theodore Lyman of Meade's staff agreed. "The main part of the town resembles Salem [Massachusetts], very much, *plus* the southern shiftlessness and *minus* the Yankee thrift," he judged. Lyman did admit that the houses on South Market Street were "all very well kept and with nice trees." The New Englander went next to Blandford Cemetery and then to the Crater. He grew reflective about the empty fortifications whose defenders had once visited mayhem on the Union army, the scarred earth now bearing mute testimony to the end of a long, sad chapter in a long, sad war. "Upon these parapets, whence the rifle-men have shot at each other, for nine long months, in heat and cold, by day and by night, you might now stand with impunity and overlook miles of deserted breastworks and covered ways!" mused Lyman. "It was a sight only to be appreciated by those who have known the depression of waiting through summer, autumn and winter for so goodly an event!"⁴⁴

Another poignant incident unfolded on the other side of town. During the overnight evacuation cannoneers from the Washington Artillery of Louisiana placed the body of Private Frank E. Coyle, killed in the fighting that day, against the wall of the Second Presbyterian Church on West Washington Street. A note laid on Coyle's chest requested that "some kind friend will please bury this man." The Petersburg businessman William E. Morrison spotted this pathetic figure and determined to carry out the wishes of the deceased soldier's comrades.

Morrison secured the assistance of his neighbor William H. Tappey, a slave named Jack Hill, and the Reverend Churchill J. Gibson of Grace Church to dig a grave. It took them some time to complete the task. By the time they finished, Federal units had begun marching past them on Washington Street. Mrs. Morrison remembered: "Just as Mr. Gibson with his sweet sonorous voice uttered those impressive words of the Episcopal burial service . . . and he lifted the body wrapped in its blanket . . . a Yankee soldier, either a sutler or camp follower, evidently a German from his accent, lounged up to the fence with a short pipe in his mouth and a red cap on his head and asked in drawling contemptuous tones 'Putting Jonnie in the ice-house, eh?'"

Reverend Gibson ignored the irreverent witness and continued with the service. At that moment a Union officer of some rank appeared, dismissed the sardonic German with a flourish of his sword, and said respectfully, "A brave soldier, no doubt whom you are giving a soldier's funeral." According to Mrs. Morrison, another Union officer ordered his passing men to honor Private Coyle by coming to "present arms" as the burial party committed Coyle to the ground.[45]

Abraham Lincoln was the most notable Northern visitor to Petersburg on April 3. The president had eagerly accepted Grant's invitation of the previous day to meet with the general-in-chief in anticipation of momentous news from Petersburg and Richmond. Lincoln left City Point by rail at 9:00 AM, aware that Petersburg was in Union hands. Accompanied by his son Tad, Admiral David Dixon Porter, the naval captain John S. Barnes, and William Crook, his bodyguard, Lincoln arrived at Hancock Station on the United States Military Railroad, just west of Jerusalem Plank Road, about 10:00 AM. Captain Robert Lincoln, the president's other surviving son, now serving on Grant's staff, greeted his father on behalf of the commanding general. Grant had arranged a small cavalry escort and Lincoln mounted the general's horse, Cincinnati.

The entourage moved north along Jerusalem Plank Road, encountering a brigade of Union troops marching out of town to gather their knapsacks and rejoin their division. "We met President Lincoln, and Admiral Porter . . . and we cheered them," recorded one Connecticut sergeant. Lincoln enjoyed the attention from his soldiers much more than a quick tour of the abandoned earthworks south of town, still littered with unburied corpses from the previous day's combat. The bodyguard, Crook, noticed that Lincoln's face again "settled into its old lines of sadness" while viewing the carnage, and one of the cavalry escort thought he saw tears in the president's eyes.[46]

Lincoln arrived at Thomas Wallace's house on South Market Street sometime around 11:00 AM. Moments earlier Grant and members of his staff watched with some amusement as a crowd of excited blacks besieged General Meade, attempting to sell him Confederate bank notes. Seeing the president, Grant and his staff left their seats on the front porch and descended the steps. Lincoln "dismounted in the street, and came in through the front gate with long and rapid strides, his face beaming with delight," remembered one witness. "He seized General Grant's hand as the general

Thomas Wallace, a Petersburg lawyer, lived in this house on South Market Street. On the morning of April 3, 1865, Lieutenant General Ulysses S. Grant and President Abraham Lincoln met on the front porch to discuss Grant's capture of Petersburg, the presumed occupation of Richmond, and the impending end of the war. (Courtesy of the Petersburg Museums)

stepped forward to greet him, and stood shaking it for some time, and pouring out his thanks and congratulations with all the fervor of a heart which seemed overflowing with . . . joy. I doubt whether Mr. Lincoln ever experienced a happier moment in his life." The general responded warmly but with his usual reserve. "He didn't appear exultant, and he was as quiet as he had ever been," recalled Crook.[47]

Lincoln congratulated Grant on his great victory and said with a twinkle in his eye, "Do you know, general, I have had a sort of sneaking idea all along that you intended to do something like this." The chief executive then mentioned that he had guessed that General Sherman's army in North Carolina would have played a role in the conquest of Petersburg. Grant replied that he had been anxious to arrange events so that the Army of the Potomac would earn the sole honor of defeating Lee: "I said to him that if the Western armies should be even upon the field, operating against Richmond and Lee, the credit would be given to them for the capture, by politicians and non-combatants from the section of country which those troops hailed from." Grant feared that intersectional bickering would result if the eastern army did not win its own major campaign. Lincoln admitted that he had never considered the question in that light, being so fully occupied with the desire for victory he had not cared where or with whom it originated.

The president spent the next half an hour discussing his views on Reconstruction and his commitment to a lenient policy toward the vanquished South. While Major General George H. Sharpe, the army's chief of military information, tamed a restless and hungry Tad with sandwiches, the two dignitaries remained in conversation, hoping to receive word that Richmond had fallen. During this historic meeting Thomas Wallace appeared and invited his guests inside. Wallace had known the president years earlier when both were Whig politicians, and according to a reporter, "was suddenly transformed into a Union man by the magic influence of triumphant bayonets." Grant declined the gesture because he was smoking one of his omnipresent cigars, so the famous pair conducted their ninety-minute meeting out of doors on what had developed into a beautiful spring day. "When our conversation was at an end Mr. Lincoln mounted his horse and started on his return to City Point, while I and my staff started to join the army, now a good many miles in advance," wrote Grant. The president returned to the railroad, pausing occasionally to speak with some of Petersburg's liberated slaves.[48]

The army had gained complete control of Petersburg by then, despite the presence of some apple jack whiskey that tempted bibulous Federal soldiers. Confederate medical personnel stationed in the city's two hospitals received paroles extending to the city limits even as they continued working with patients. Stores and markets remained shuttered, so the needy of both races wandered across the battle lines into abandoned Federal camps looking for something to eat. Representatives of the United States Christian Commission quickly established a relief station for African Americans on Tabb Street. As the afternoon progressed, more white Petersburgers emerged from their homes, some wearing an article of white clothing to indicate their pacific intent.[49]

Two Federal infantry officers, Major Robert C. Eden of the Thirty-seventh Wisconsin and Captain Charles McCreery of the Eighth Michigan, entered the deserted offices of the *Petersburg Daily Express* that afternoon to commence a unique endeavor. They began printing their own publication, *Grant's Petersburg Progress*, a newspaper aimed at the Northern soldiers. The editors defined their journalistic tone in the inaugural edition: "In starting a paper, making love and many other pursuits and amusements of life a necessary preliminary step is a declaration of intentions," they explained. Commenting on conditions in the city with humor and sarcasm, the editors noted that "a five cent piece and a copper penny . . . found in the Petersburg Court House this morning" were believed to be the only specie in town. Eden and McCreery predicted that the stores would reopen soon and that the hugely inflated prices prevailing prior to the Union occupation were sure to drop. In point of fact, Federal sutlers with their goods soon appeared in town adopting vacant storefronts for their operations.[50]

The realization that the city was under Northern occupation exacted an emotional toll on some Petersburgers. "When the truth came to me, we are in the Federal lines, I could not keep my tears back, my heart was so sick," admitted Mrs. Callender. Like her husband, all white citizens had to report their presence to the provost marshal and take an oath of allegiance to the United States in order to travel outside the town—which, under General Willcox's oversight, remained remarkably peaceful. Mayor Townes and others hoped to retain his efficient leadership in the city. "It is more quiet & more safe here for everybody to-night than it is in Detroit," the Michigan general wrote his wife on April 4. Still, Willcox looked forward to leaving garrison duty and resuming command in the field.[51]

On April 3 General Meade appointed Gouverneur K. Warren, whom Sheridan had summarily relieved at Five Forks, to take command at Petersburg, City Point, and Bermuda Hundred. Warren assumed his duties on April 4, sharing an office with General Willcox at the corner of Washington and Adams Streets before Willcox departed to rejoin his division. The next day Major General George L. Hartsuff arrived with orders to take charge of Petersburg. Some confusion resulted between Warren and Hartsuff as to which general held the legitimate authority, but Grant soon confirmed Hartsuff's supremacy. Petersburg's new military leader was a native of New York, but as a lad he had moved with his family to Michigan and entered West Point from that state. Described as "fair and burly, with a boyish face," this career soldier possessed a reputation as a stern disciplinarian. He had held a variety of wartime assignments while suffering the effects of wounds received in the old army and at the 1862 battle of Cedar Mountain.[52]

In announcing his appointment in orders published on April 5, Hartsuff assigned the division of Brigadier General Edward Ferrero to garrison the city. Major Seneca R. Cowles of the Tenth New York Artillery took over as provost marshal. Colonel George C. Kibbe of the Sixth New York Heavy Artillery became post commandant of Petersburg. Hartsuff directed Cowles to "institute such measures and appoint such guards and patrols as will ensure quiet and good order. Gen. Ferrero will make a permanent detail of 500 men to report to him as guards." Hartsuff appropriated Centre Hill, the Bolling mansion, as his headquarters, and authorized his staff to select vacant buildings for their own offices.

Hartsuff permitted civilian authorities to exercise many of their normal

George Lucas Hartsuff (1830–74). Major General Hartsuff commanded Petersburg for more than four months following the city's Union occupation. He proved to be surprisingly popular with Petersburg citizens who valued his "high sense of justice and . . . appreciation of our interests and feelings." (Courtesy of Library of Congress)

duties and responsibilities, and encouraged citizens to pursue their daily activities as long as they obeyed all laws and regulations. He declared the city markets open and urged farmers and merchants to resume commercial transactions once they had registered with the provost office. Hartsuff allowed army sutlers to conduct business in town, realizing that these quasi-military retailers had better access to inventory than did the cash-strapped local businessmen. He reinstituted the prohibition against the sale of alcohol under penalty of confiscation and further punishment. "Quiet and good order are alike creditable and necessary and must be enforced at all hazards," explained the general. "It is, therefore, earnestly enjoined upon officers and soldiers and requested of citizens to aid the proper authorities, civil and military, in its preservation."[53]

Hartsuff limited Union military presence in Petersburg to the provost guard and soldiers on official leave to minimize potential conflicts with citizens. Federal troops returned private property seized from its owners, although the garrison confiscated everything belonging to the Confederate government. He also instituted humanitarian relief for residents. Women, children, the elderly, and the disabled could draw army rations. "Many who, no doubt, were blatant rebels . . . are eating the bread of loyalty with a relish of satisfaction, if not with thanks," one reporter commented wryly. The provost guard enforced a curfew for both visiting soldiers and civilians and displayed disproportionate vigilance toward African Americans. These measures resulted in the maintenance of laudable calm in the city, just a few days after Lee's evacuation. "There is nothing to disturb the almost universal quiet except the whistle of the locomotives on Grant's RR and the steamers as they pass up the Appomattox to Petersburg within sight of our camp," wrote a relaxed Vermont soldier on April 5. "I went down to the river and went swimming."[54]

Petersburg accommodated a few visitors during the first week of April, including a group of Englishmen who traveled by private yacht from New York with the unlikely purpose of touring the Virginia battlefields. Navigating their craft through the blockade at Hampton Roads, they cruised up the James, disembarked at City Point, and boarded the Military Railroad, making their way into Petersburg on April 5. They thought the Cockade City "presented a most desolate appearance," due to the heavy shell damage. They saw a fair number of African Americans on the streets but comparatively few whites. "The few inhabitants spoken to were loud in their praise of the way the Federal troops had behaved," wrote one of the British sightseers. "Beyond looting some tobacco, there was no pillaging or violence of any kind."[55]

President Lincoln returned to Petersburg during the week. On April 6 his wife had joined him at City Point, eager to act on her husband's promise to allow her to see Richmond and Petersburg. Mary Todd Lincoln brought a small retinue with her from Washington, including Massachusetts Senator Charles Sumner, the young marquis de Chambrun of France, Senator and Mrs. James Harlan of Iowa, and Attorney General James Speed. Elizabeth Keckley, a former Petersburg slave, also accompanied the first lady. Keckley officially served as Mrs. Lincoln's dressmaker, but their close association had made her a trusted confidant.

The presidential party decided to visit Petersburg on Saturday April 8. The group boarded a special train on the newly repaired City Point Railroad, passing the deserted Union and Confederate fortifications en route. Lincoln, characteristically, permitted black waiters from his steamship, the *River Queen*, to ride along. When the cars reached Petersburg, the visitors began to explore the city. "Crowds of darkies were in the streets greeting and cheering loudly the author of their independence," recalled the marquis de Chambrun. "Every now and then a white man could be seen hastening to take refuge in some house, in order to escape the sight of his conqueror" (a phenomenon that helped persuade Senator Sumner of the importance of the African American vote to the administration's future). Lincoln greeted sol-

The Bolling mansion, Centre Hill, has stood in the middle of the city since 1823. General Beauregard used it in June 1864 as his headquarters, as did General Hartsuff after Petersburg's capture, as suggested by the flag and musicians in this image. (Courtesy of the Petersburg Museums)

diers and officers and visited Hartsuff's headquarters at Centre Hill, while Elizabeth Keckley wandered about once familiar streetscapes that brought back "painful memories" of her years in bondage. Eventually the group reboarded its train and rolled slowly back to City Point, the president taking time to admire a particularly beautiful tree and rescue a turtle from the tracks.[56]

Direct telegraph links to Washington provided Lincoln with the news that Secretary of State William Seward had been badly injured in a carriage accident, prompting the president's return to the capital. Late on April 9, back in Washington, Lincoln learned of Lee's surrender at Appomattox Court House, ninety-six miles west of Petersburg. Army bands in Petersburg played celebratory tunes when they heard the good news, and the Christian Commission treated General Hartsuff to a serenade at Centre Hill.[57]

The demise of the Army of Northern Virginia ended the war in the Old Dominion. Although at first some Petersburg citizens refused to believe such dire news, Confederate wounded, prisoners taken during Lee's retreat, and parolees surrendered at Appomattox soon passed through the city. Among the latter, General Gordon returned to escort his wife and newborn son home to Georgia. Gordon complained that none of the recently emancipated slaves in Petersburg could be persuaded to join his family as a nurse, resenting the intransigence of blacks who no longer felt obliged to obey the orders of every white man. In fact, countless freedman poured into Petersburg from rural areas to the west, seeking subsistence or simply exercising the novel exercise of free movement.[58]

The news of President Lincoln's assassination reached Petersburg by April 16 and was made public the next day. Roger Pryor, Judge William T. Joynes, John Lyon, and other prominent citizens organized a mass meeting that adopted resolutions condemning the crime and expressing "indignation and sympathy." One Northern observer detected less grief than such pronouncements suggested. "The people seemed to take little notice of the catastrophe," he wrote. "Two bells out of six upon the places of worship made out to toll, while the others remained silent. Still the Government is feeding thousands of these broken-down rebels, who are cursing it with the same breath which its charity has infused into them."[59]

Most white Petersburgers displayed overt sympathy for the Confederate cause in the weeks following the city's surrender. Former Confederate officers moved about town wearing side arms and emblems of rank. Northerners found this behavior inappropriate and offensive. Paroled soldiers attended church, visited friends, and spent pleasant days in leisure. Most considered the white Union garrison polite, but they bitterly resented any contact with African American troops. Petersburg's upper-class women maintained their dignity and pride despite the humiliation of having to apply to the Federal military for food. "If one were to judge by their dress, very few of them would be regarded as objects of charity," thought one Northerner. "Many of them come in silks, and are otherwise respectably attired." Some pragmatic ladies were not above bringing small gifts to the Yankee commissary officers, hoping in return to receive a larger than normal share of supplies.[60]

Enough rehabilitation and cleanup had occurred by the third week of April to lend the city a "business appearance." Stores opened, ship traffic returned to the Appomattox River, and shell-damaged structures came under initial repair. Andrew F. Crutchfield began republishing the *Daily Express*, this time with a distinctly pro-Union editorial orientation in contrast to the paper's wartime bent. Edmund Ruffin, the area's most unrepentant citizen, considered Crutchfield "a Yankee slave & tool," and the black journalist Thomas Morris Chester of the *Philadelphia Press* resented Crutchfield's ability to profit through what he considered transparent insincerity. "Mercy to this class is a weakness," he thought. Ruffin preferred the reincarnation of the *Petersburg News* that appeared in May under the editorship of the ex-Confederate soldier and politician Anthony M. Keiley. "I fear that his slight approach toward independence & patriotism will cause himself or his paper to be sacrificed," predicted Ruffin. This proved prophetic, for the authorities shut down Keiley's disloyal journal in short order.[61]

Union soldiers returning from victories over Lee and Johnston (who surrendered near Durham, North Carolina, in late April) passed through Petersburg in April and early May. The African American soldiers of the Twenty-fifth Corps paraded through town on May 3 and 4, eliciting the full gamut of responses. "There is no remedy so effectual in chilling the warm blood of the South as to put arms in the hands of the negroes," thought one black Northern journalist. "The influence of this element upon the F. F. V.'s—*Fleet-Footed Virginians*—has ever been of a demoralizing tendency upon the relics which may in part explain why it is they are kept so far from these large towns."[62]

General Philip Sheridan established temporary headquarters in an elegant Petersburg mansion and dislocated Mrs. Pryor in the process. He encamped his cavalrymen on the outskirts of town. On May 3 the Fifth Corps arrived. Its commanding officer, Major General Charles Griffin, sent word to General Warren that the corps wished to salute him as it passed through on its way to Washington. Warren and his wife watched emotionally from the balcony of the Bollingbrook Hotel as his admiring former troops marched past, with bands playing, caps raised, and voices shouting affection for the deposed New Yorker.[63]

Petersburg's garrison became a subdivision of the Department of Virginia on April 19, which in turn formed a part of the Military Division of the James. Another reorganization in May gave General Hartsuff responsibility for the District of the Nottoway, a component of the Department of Virginia. Hartsuff maintained District headquarters at Centre Hill and from there presided over three subdistricts and the Post of Petersburg, of which Colonel Edward Martindale of the Eighty-first United States Colored Troops assumed command. Martindale had his own regiment, the Tenth New York Artillery, one battalion of the Forty-first New York Infantry, and the Thirty-third New York Battery to occupy the city.[64]

By this time Hartsuff had a substantial military administration in Petersburg, utilizing more than sixty buildings for the various functions of his district. Tobacco factories became barracks or temporary housing for transient freedmen. Private homes and commercial buildings served as offices,

This view of the David Dunlop house is one of a number of images taken along the eastern end of Bollingbrook Street shortly after the Union occupation. Within a few weeks, citizens made progress cleaning up the city and restoring their homes and their lives. (Courtesy of Library of Congress)

and Library Hall provided the venue for courts-martial. Hartsuff continued to operate the two former Confederate hospitals, treating the wounded and sick from both armies. African Americans and destitute white civilians received care at a separate facility that dispensed medicines to those who could not afford them. As Petersburg refugees returned to their homes, they discovered an efficient and relatively clean city in the first stages of rebuilding. Rowdy Union soldiers occasionally disturbed the peace, but Hartsuff took swift steps to punish offenders and restore discipline.[65]

Beneath the surface, however, the city seethed with resentment born of four years of bitter war and two centuries of racial division. "Oh, why are we . . . left so desolate and in the power of a foe we utterly loathe," lamented one former Confederate chaplain. Henry Dearborn Bird, superintendent of the shattered South Side Railroad, advised resignation and acceptance in a letter to his son, a Confederate prisoner of war about to be released from a Maryland camp. "The state is quieting down and people are going to work, and the war will soon be a thing of the past" he wrote. "I [have] been to see Genl Lee and he told me that all the soldiers who desired to return to their native places and intended to remain, should take the oath of allegiance to the U. States and become good citizens. When that great & good man says they ought to do so, I am sure I need not add any thing to satisfy you of the propriety of taking the oath."[66]

The young Henry Bird, formerly of the Twelfth Virginia Infantry, re-turned to Petersburg in June. He followed his father's advice and swore alle-giance to the United States, but he felt the need to apologize to his fiancée for apparently violating his fealty to the Confederacy. Bird justified his oath by explaining that doing so was a requirement for a marriage license. More-over, any former soldier who refused to declare his loyalty was subject to the damning testimony of unscrupulous people seeking to ingratiate themselves with the occupying authorities. Bird noted that many were only too eager to incriminate former Confederates and would even "swear that the Chesa-peake Bay is a pine thicket" for a few dollars.

Bird explained that signing the oath and obeying the regulations of the military administration were not synonymous with accepting Petersburg's postwar social order. "It is both sad and laughable to see the smoked Yankees parading the streets in all their Sunday finery and then to think of the change that will come over the spirit of their dream in less than six months," Bird wrote, referring to the African American garrison troops and his hope that in short order the prewar racial hierarchies would reemerge. "My dar-ling, we are all strangers in the land now. . . . All day and every day our mas-ters and their equals parade the streets . . . a Yankee is almost as good as a 'nigger' and if the latter don't object, we ought not to. Some of the white-livered ex-masters allow their wives to be insulted in the grossest manner by their former slaves. . . . The *ladies* of the town will not speak to the Yanks."[67]

No issue proved more difficult in the weeks following Union occupation than the relationship between Petersburg's whites, on the one hand, and freedmen and black soldiers, on the other. Responsibility for trouble ran in both directions. General Hartsuff complained that some of his black troops destroyed private property and excited "the colored people to acts of outrage against the persons and property of white citizens. . . . Colored soldiers are represented as having straggled about, advising Negroes not to work on the farms, where they are employed, and been told by the soldiers that if they had not arms to use against their former masters, that 'the Soldiers' would

The Federal army occupied Petersburg from April 3 through August 3, 1865, when General Hartsuff removed his men to the western outskirts of town. Local citizens tolerated white Union soldiers, but they despised the African American troops who helped garrison the city. (Courtesy of Library of Congress)

This image of Bollingbrook Street taken in the early spring of 1865 suggests Petersburg's once and future elegance, despite shell damage visible on the dwelling in the foreground. Petersburg would eventually regain its economic prosperity, but never again did it reach the international prominence it experienced from 1861 to 1865. (Courtesy of Library of Congress)

furnish them." (At the same time, some white Federal soldiers abused local blacks, especially after imbibing illicit alcohol.) White Petersburgers complained when their former slaves refused to work, and they bitterly resented any display of authority by black troops, which they interpreted as unconscionable disrespect.[68]

Interaction between white residents and white Northern officers and their spouses remained frosty, but less volatile. In postwar Petersburg the racial divide proved harder to bridge than the sectional one. The opinionated black correspondent Thomas Chester delighted in what he called the "indifference to the existence of the chivalry" that Union officers' wives displayed. He thought their demeanor would convince "this deluded people that there are some persons from the North who are unwilling to be patronized by disloyalists." Accepting domination by blue-clad soldiers and the unthinkable submission to armed African Americans left many white Petersburgers spiritually devastated. "Tis midnight yet with us," wrote one gentleman. "Earth's face is one wide dazzling waste, and buries the works of men."[69]

Despite these deep-seated social tensions, General Hartsuff continued to institute municipal improvements. Still, most Petersburgers struggled with severe economic hardships beyond Hartsuff's ability to rectify. The general managed the affairs of blacks in the city until the arrival of the Freedmen's Bureau in June. He assisted former slaves to find employment on the farms and plantations in his district but advised unemployed African Americans not to come to Petersburg looking for work. Many still did, but few opportunities awaited them.[70]

Hartsuff opened a military hospital, conducted a city census, and improved public health by reinterring the corpses that rain had exposed in their shallow battlefield graves. Soldiers cleaned the streets and collected garbage. In mid-June the general formed a "Court for the Settlement of Claims and Adjustments," assigning three prominent Petersburgers—William T. Joynes, Andrew Kevan, and James M. Venable—as magistrates. This court heard cases involving civil matters and represented a significant first step toward restoring the local judiciary, although the army still provided police services in town. A 10:00 PM curfew, strictly enforced except for those with passes issued by the provost marshal, served to limit violence and crime.[71]

Locals, as early as September 1864, had predicted that the city would attract tourists curious to see the sights associated with the war. These predictions began to come true in late May 1865. "The influx of northern visitors, both male & female continues without abatement," testified one resident. "Already, strangers are flocking hither from distant quarters to view the various spots now rendered so famous by the deadly conflicts," confirmed another. Partly to satisfy the demands of visitors, but mostly to make their own lives more comfortable, the army and its military merchants "provided the city with every conceivable thing to cater to that appetite," including ladies clothing, sweets, teas and coffee, beef, chicken, and vegetables. Most Petersburgers could not afford such indulgences. "Our kindred people are congregating slowly and with determination to return to their desolated homes, provisionless, many pennyless [sic] unless ... Providence looks down with pity on the feeble toil of mortals almost lost to hope," wrote one dispirited citizen.[72]

On August 3 Hartsuff allowed civilian officials to resume full municipal authority. He removed the garrison to the western outskirts of town, although the provost marshal still provided law enforcement, turning miscreants over to local authorities for prosecution. Three weeks later General Hartsuff left his position as commander of the District of the Nottoway, ending the first chapter in Petersburg's long road back from its experience in the crucible of war. Hartsuff believed that the people of Petersburg were law abiding, "respectable and loyally conservative." Many residents returned Hartsuff's warm sentiments and regretted his departure, acknowledging his "high sense of justice and ... appreciation of our interests and feelings."[73]

The Reconstruction era would continue in Petersburg for another nine years, until local elections restored a white, conservative administration to power. But the return of the antebellum political leadership by no means extinguished the impact of the Civil War on the Cockade City. This legacy endured in shell-pocked buildings; haunting, grass-grown fortifications; vast cemeteries; and the enigmatic struggle between black and white Petersburgers for political, economic, and social power.

As the years muted the suffering, sacrifice, and complexity of Petersburg's Civil War heritage, a new civic memory, laden with heroic myths, emerged in its place, the echoes of which can still be heard in some Petersburg neighborhoods. "The beleaguered town, girdled with steel and fire, bore herself with proud and lofty port," read a typical postwar simplification. Lost Cause romanticism notwithstanding, it is this real spirit that imbues Petersburg with its unique identity—the past's silent gift, or curse, to present and future generations.[74]

NOTES

Abbreviations

CCD	Charles Campbell, Diary, Charles Campbell Papers, W&M
CCM	Common Council Minutes
CHDP	Charles Henry Dimmock Papers, VHS
Duke	Perkins Library, Duke University, Durham, North Carolina
EPJL	Executive Papers of John Letcher, LOV
EPWS	Executive Papers of William Smith, LOV
FAL	Fletcher Archer Letter, City of Petersburg
LOV	Library of Virginia, Richmond
MOC	Eleanor Brockenbrough Library, Museum of the Confederacy, Richmond
NARA	National Archives and Records Administration
NCDAH	North Carolina Department of Archives and History, Raleigh
PCW	William D. Henderson, *Petersburg in the Civil War*
OR	*The War of the Rebellion: A Compilation of the Official Records of the Union and Confederate Armies*
PNB	Petersburg National Battlefield, Petersburg
TBD	Thomas Bragg, Diary, Thomas Bragg Papers, UNC
UNC	Southern Historical Collection, Wilson Library, University of North Carolina, Chapel Hill
UVA	Alderman Library, University of Virginia, Charlottesville
VHS	Virginia Historical Society, Richmond
W&M	Earl Gregg Swem Library, College of William & Mary, Williamsburg, Va.

1. "Helping to Inaugurate Revolution"

1. Trowbridge qtd. in Gordon Carroll, *Desolate South, 1865–1866*, 113–14. For information on Trowbridge's tour and book, see Buck, *Road to Reunion*, 17–19. Trowbridge's original publication appeared under the title *The South: A Tour of its Battle-fields and Ruined Cities* (Hartford, 1866).

2. "Report of Houses in Petersburg, Virginia Struck by Shells during the Siege from June 15, 1864, to April 3, 1865," Record Group 94, NARA. The inventory is reprinted in Calkins, *Auto Tour of Civil War Petersburg, 1861–1865*, 54–74.

3. J. G. Scott and Wyatt, *Petersburg's Story*, 1–164. This is the best of several comprehensive histories of Petersburg.

4. J. G. Scott and Wyatt, *Petersburg's Story*, 57–58; Miss Evelyn Taylor to Mrs. Watson Stott, March 28, 1841, and Misses Mendell and Hosmer, in *Notes of Travel and Life*, both qtd. in Wyatt, "Rise of Industry in Ante-Bellum Petersburg," 3, 6; *Richmond Dispatch*, December 4, 1856.

5. Henderson, *Petersburg in the Civil War* (hereafter cited Henderson, *PCW*), 1; J. G. Scott and Wyatt, *Petersburg's Story*, 94–96. Petersburg traded primarily with Northern ports, which served as intermediate stops between Virginia and Europe. The James River did occasionally freeze solid, closing the shipping lanes for short periods. See Scarborough, *Diary of Edmund Ruffin* 1:26.

6. J. G. Scott and Wyatt, *Petersburg's Story*, 94–95; R. L. Jones, *Dinwiddie County*, 132–33; H. D. Dozier, *History of the Atlantic Coast Line Railroad*, 22–30; Sutherland, *Seasons of War*, 11. The Petersburg Railroad would be known informally as the Weldon Railroad, the Petersburg & Weldon Railroad, or the Southern Road. Most Civil War histories call this line the Weldon Railroad.

7. J. G. Scott and Wyatt, *Petersburg's Story*, 97; H. D. Dozier, *History of the Atlantic Coast Line Railroad*, 35–83; R. L. Jones, *Dinwiddie County*, 111. The Richmond & Petersburg Railroad was controlled by Richmond for the benefit of the capital city, not Petersburg. This line's spur from Port Walthall Junction to Port Walthall on the Appomattox, for example, competed with City Point and Petersburg for James River commerce. Norfolk, Richmond, and Petersburg engaged in spirited economic competition during the antebellum years. Rice, in "Internal Improvements in Virginia, 1775–1860," surveys these rivalries. Pocahontas is in 2006 connected to the south bank of the Appomattox River thanks to the post–Civil War creation of a new river channel adjacent to the city of Colonial Heights.

8. Henderson, *PCW*, 4; J. G. Scott and Wyatt, *Petersburg's Story*, 94–96; Writer's Program: Dinwiddie County, *Countrey of the Apamatica*, 111–12; Parramore, *Norfolk*, 187.

9. Qtd. in J. G. Scott and Wyatt, *Petersburg's Story*, 93. Petersburg's 2006 primary road network echoes its antebellum highway system, except for Halifax Road, which is replicated by a series of secondary roads.

10. Henderson, *PCW*, 1; Henderson, "Evolution of Petersburg's Economy, 1860–1900," 23; Goldfield, *Urban Growth in the Age of Sectionalism, Virginia, 1847–1861*, 198.

11. Henderson, *PCW*, 9–10; Furgurson, *Ashes of Glory*, 4; Goldfield, *Urban Growth in the Age of Sectionalism, Virginia, 1847–1861*, 190; Jackson, *Free Negro Labor and Property Holding in Virginia, 1830–1860*, 52, 64–65.

12. Henderson, *Unredeemed City*, iii; Wyatt, "Rise of Industry in Ante-Bellum Petersburg," 19–24; Henderson, *PCW*, 3–8. Writers often compared Petersburg's weather to that of Atlanta, Georgia.

13. Henderson, *PCW*, 8–9.

14. Henderson, "Evolution of Petersburg's Economy, 1860–1900," 25; Henderson, *PCW*, 5–7; Reuben Ragland to John Letcher, January 12, 1861, Executive Papers of John Letcher (hereafter cited EPJL), Series 1, Box 7, Folder 1, LOV. All future references are to Series 1. Governors appointed bank directors and their correspondence is full of endorsements for and petitions from candidates for these positions.

15. U.S. Bureau of the Census, *Agriculture of the United States in 1860*. Soil exhaustion from decades of tobacco production and accelerating competition from railroad cities such as Lynchburg and Danville posed threats to Petersburg's economic preeminence in the late antebellum years.

16. U.S. Bureau of the Census, *Population Schedule of the Eighth Census, 1860,* LOV; Crofts, *Reluctant Confederates,* 39; J. W. Smith, "Role of Blacks in Petersburg's Carrying Trade and Service-Oriented Industry, 1800–1865," 47; Hartzell, "Explanation of Freedom in Black Petersburg, Virginia, 1865–1902," 134. The breakdown of the 18,266 total 1860 population included white males, 4,657; white females, 4,685; total whites, 9,342; free black males, 1,429; free black females, 1,815; total free blacks, 3,244; slave males, 2,845; slave females, 2,835; total slaves, 5,680; total blacks, 8,924.

17. Jackson, *Free Negro Labor and Property Holding in Virginia,* 91–92; U.S. Bureau of the Census, *Population Schedule of the Seventh Census, 1850,* LOV. For a vivid summary of the precarious position that free blacks occupied in antebellum Virginia, see Edmund Ruffin, "The Free Negro Nuisance and How to Abate It," in Scarborough, *Diary of Edmund Ruffin* 1:621–26.

18. Lebsock, *Free Women of Petersburg,* 90; Jackson, *Free Negro Labor and Property Holding in Virginia,* 93–99. Jackson provides a table of occupations for all free African Americans.

19. Henderson, *PCW,* 5; Schweninger, *Black Property Owners in the South, 1790–1915,* 77; Jackson, *Free Negro Labor and Property Holding in Virginia,* 138, 156–58, 167, 212, 220–22; Lebsock, *Free Women of Petersburg,* 103, 116.

20. Lebsock, *Free Women of Petersburg,* 154; Henderson, *PCW,* 7; Jackson, *Free Negro Labor and Property Holding in Virginia,* 176. For a general discussion of industrial slavery, see Starobin, *Industrial Slavery in the Old South.*

21. Jackson, *Free Negro Labor and Property Holding in Virginia,* 159–63; Lebsock, *Free Women of Petersburg,* 11; E. L. Jordan, *Black Confederates and Afro-Yankees in Civil War Virginia,* 9. For more information on Gillfield Baptist Church, see Jackson, *Short History of the Gillfield Baptist Church of Petersburg, Virginia.*

22. Henderson, *PCW,* 1, 7; J. G. Scott and Wyatt, *Petersburg's Story,* 100–107. Petersburg's well-to-do Scotch-Irish followed the Presbyterian faith. The old English residents attended St. Paul's Episcopal Church, while the increasingly numerous and prosperous Baptists and Methodists built new churches in the late antebellum period.

23. Henderson, *PCW,* 14–15; J. G. Scott and Wyatt, *Petersburg's Story,* 117–20.

24. Henderson, *PCW,* 5; J. G. Scott and Wyatt, *Petersburg's Story,* 109, 122, 144–50, 154–55. A smaller theater existed in the Benevolent Mechanics Hall. Among the antebellum Petersburg newspapers that did not continue publishing during the Civil War were the *Petersburg True Democrat,* the *Daily South-Side Democrat,* the *Daily Press,* and the *Virginia Index.*

25. For excellent summaries of Petersburg's urban landscape in the 1850s, see Henderson, *PCW,* 4–5 and J. G. Scott and Wyatt, *Petersburg's Story,* 156–64.

26. Henderson, *PCW,* 158; J. G. Scott and Wyatt, *Petersburg's Story,* 130–32.

27. Henderson, *PCW,* 18, 158; J. G. Scott and Wyatt, *Petersburg's Story,* 130; Wallace, *Guide to Virginia Military Organizations, 1861–1865,* 234; Henderson, *Twelfth Virginia Infantry,* 1.

28. Wallace, *Guide to Virginia Military Organizations, 1861–1865,* 234, 242; Henderson, *Twelfth Virginia Infantry,* 1; Henderson, *PCW,* 158, 160.

29. Henderson, *PCW,* 13–14. Competitive politics survived in Petersburg despite the collapse of the formal Whig Party. Petersburg residents, like other urban Virginians, faced a relatively heavy tax burden imposed by Virginia's rural-dominated legislature.

30. One of the best accounts of the election of 1860 is Potter, *Impending Crisis, 1848–1861,* 405–47. For Douglas's appearance in Petersburg, see Lutz, *Prince George-Hopewell Story,* 155–56.

31. Shanks, *Secession Movement in Virginia, 1847–1861*, 245, passim; U.S. Office of the Adjutant General, Case Files of Applications from Former Confederates for Presidential Pardons, Charles F. Collier's petition of June 29, 1865, M1003, Roll 58, Record Group 94, NARA; Henderson, *PCW*, 18–19.

32. Shanks, *Secession Movement in Virginia, 1847–1861*, 112, 118; Henderson, *PCW*, 18–19. Pate had suffered the indignity of being captured by John Brown at gunpoint on June 2, 1856.

33. Diary of Richard Eppes, October 21, 1860, Eppes Family Muniments, VHS; Henderson, *PCW*, 18–19; Abstract Vote, City of Petersburg, Item 279, RG 13, LOV; R. L. Jones, *Dinwiddie County*, 134; Lutz, *Prince George–Hopewell Story*, 155–56. The vote counts were as follows: Petersburg: Bell 970, Douglas 613, Breckinridge 223; Dinwiddie County: Bell 389, Breckinridge 254, Douglas 183; Prince George County: Bell 342, Breckinridge 191, Douglas 126. Lincoln received no recorded votes in any of the jurisdictions. Whig sentiments survived in Virginia under both the American Party standard, better known as the Know-Nothings, and as the Opposition Party in the 1859 gubernatorial election.

34. *New York Herald* and *Petersburg Bulletin* qtd. in Shanks, *Secession Movement in Virginia, 1847–1861*, 121; Cornelia Beckwith, letter, December 24, 1860, Julie Beckwith Grossmann Collection; A. K. Davis, *Three Centuries of an Old Virginia Town*, 12; J. G. Scott and Wyatt, *Petersburg's Story*, 169. The editor of the *Bulletin* contacted Virginia's leading secessionist, Edmund Ruffin, on November 19 requesting a number of secession pamphlets for distribution in town. Ruffin sent him three hundred. See Scarborough, *Diary of Edmund Ruffin* 1:499.

35. *Petersburg Intelligencer* qtd. in Shanks, *Secession Movement in Virginia, 1847–1861*, 120. For Virginia's moderate position in the sectional crisis following Lincoln's election, see Shanks, *Secession Movement in Virginia, 1847–1861*, 121–41.

36. Boney, *John Letcher of Virginia*, 102–3.

37. Shanks, *Secession Movement in Virginia, 1847–1861*, 122, 128, 132; Boney, *John Letcher of Virginia*, 79; Roger A. Pryor to John Letcher, EPJL, Box 7, Folder 1. Biographical background on Roger A. Pryor is available in the memoirs of his wife, Sara, Mrs. Roger A. Pryor, *My Day* and *Reminiscences of Peace and War;* and Waugh, *Surviving the Confederacy.* Ruffin was an outspoken critic of Wise and had his share of disagreements with Mr. Pryor.

38. Common Council Minutes (hereafter cited CCM), January 1, 1861; *Petersburg Daily Express*, January 8, 1861; Parramore, *Norfolk*, 199.

39. *Petersburg Daily Express*, January 12, 1861; Shanks, *Secession Movement in Virginia, 1847–1861*, 147. For background information on Meade's activities in Charleston, see Detzer, *Allegiance*, 63, 133–35.

40. *Petersburg Daily Express*, January 14, 1861. The numbers of Petersburg free blacks making this discounted trip on the Baltimore & Ohio Railroad is unknown.

41. Giles Buckner Cooke to Colonel F. H. Smith, January 21, 1861, Giles Buckner Cooke Papers, VHS; CCM, January 22 and February 1, 1861. Zouave units would be established in both the Union and Confederate armies and were modeled on elite French colonial troops in Algeria.

42. Shanks, *Secession Movement in Virginia, 1847–1861*, 149–50; Boney, *John Letcher of Virginia*, 104–5.

43. *Petersburg Daily Express*, March 11, 1861; Henderson, *PCW*, 19; Reese, *Proceedings of the Virginia State Convention of 1861* 1:795. Petersburg's vote for reference was 1,134 in favor and 317 opposed. Another candidate, John Lyon, who was a Petersburg attorney, attracted little support. See *Petersburg Daily Express*, January 14, 1861. Edmund

Ruffin stated that there was a "stronger Douglas & Union support . . . & more prevalence of blind unionism" in Petersburg and Prince George County than "in any other county of the lower country" (Scarborough, *Diary of Edmund Ruffin* 1:535).

44. Shanks, *Secession Movement in Virginia, 1847–1861*, 158–60.

45. Reese, *Proceedings of the Virginia State Convention of 1861* 1:113–15; Potter, *Impending Crisis, 1848–1861*, 531–32. The so-called Crittenden Compromise, already rejected by Congress, consisted of ten points, the most important providing assurances for Southern slaveholders in the territories.

46. Reese, *Proceedings of the Virginia State Convention of 1861* 1:116–17.

47. Ibid., 1:166–71.

48. Nichols, *Disruption of American Democracy*, 457, 474–75; Boney, *John Letcher of Virginia*, 104.

49. Potter, *Impending Crisis, 1848–1861*, 550–51; Nichols, *Disruption of American Democracy*, 484–85; Shanks, *Secession Movement in Virginia, 1847–1861*, 170–72.

50. R. L. Jones, *Dinwiddie County*, 135; Reese, *Proceedings of the Virginia State Convention of 1861* 1:276–77; *Petersburg Daily Express* qtd. in Shanks, *Secession Movement in Virginia, 1847–1861*, 173, original emphasis.

51. Potter, *Impending Crisis, 1848–1861*, 560–68; *Petersburg Daily Express*, March 5, 1861; Shanks, *Secession Movement in Virginia, 1847–1861*, 176. For the mixed reaction of Southern moderates to Lincoln's speech, see McPherson, *Battle Cry of Freedom*, 262–63, and Crofts, *Reluctant Confederates*, 260. "Sucker" was a term applied to residents of Illinois, not an individual aspersion against Lincoln.

52. Shanks, *Secession Movement in Virginia, 1847–1861*, 176–78; Reese, *Proceedings of the Virginia State Convention of 1861* 1:404–7.

53. Mrs. T. G. Keen to "My dear daughter," March 7, 1861, Keen Family Letters, MOC; George S. Bernard to "My Dear Father," March 9, 1861, George S. Bernard Papers, UVA; CCM, February 19 and March 1, 15, 1861.

54. *Petersburg Daily Express*, March 11, 1861.

55. Reese, *Proceedings of the Virginia State Convention of 1861* 2:37–39, original emphasis.

56. Ibid., 2:39.

57. Ibid., 2:40; Shanks, *Secession Movement in Virginia, 1847–1861*, 187. The vote was 879 in favor of Collier's resolutions and 762 opposed.

58. Crofts, *Reluctant Confederates*, 277; Shanks, *Secession Movement in Virginia, 1847–1861*, 187; Reese, *Proceedings of the Virginia State Convention of 1861* 2:206–7, original emphasis.

59. Mrs. T. G. Keen to "My Dear Daughter," March 14, 1861, Keen Family Letters, MOC; CCM, March 16, 1861; Telegram from William T. Joynes to John Letcher, March 17, 1861, EPJL, Box 8, Folder 3; Rable, *Civil Wars*, 47.

60. Shanks, *Secession Movement in Virginia, 1847–1861*, 179–83.

61. Reese, *Proceedings of the Virginia State Convention of 1861* 2:541–44; Shanks, *Secession Movement in Virginia, 1847–1861*, 183–90.

62. CCM, April 1, 1861; G[eorge]. C. Davis to John Letcher, April 8, 1861, EPJL, Box 8, Folder 6; George S. Bernard to "My dear Father," April 12, 1861, original emphasis, George S. Bernard Papers, UVA.

63. Shanks, *Secession Movement in Virginia, 1847–1861*, 191–98. Ruffin reached Charleston on March 3, choosing to leave Virginia prior to Lincoln's inauguration to "avoid being, as a Virginian, under his government for even an hour." Pryor resigned his seat in Congress prior to the inauguration, and he arrived in South Carolina about April 10

after a brief stop in Petersburg. See Scarborough, *Diary of Edmund Ruffin* 1:557, and Mrs. R. A. Pryor, *My Day*, 158–59.

64. Shanks, *Secession Movement in Virginia, 1847–1861*, 198–201; Scarborough, *Diary of Edmund Ruffin* 1:602.

65. George S. Bernard to "My dear Father," April 12, 1861, George S. Bernard Papers, UVA; Telegram from Charles F. Collier to John Letcher, April 16, 1861, EPJL, Box 8, Folder 7; CCM, April 15, 1861. Bernard named Hamilton Stone, David Ewing, and Stephen Bratton as the young men leaving for Charleston. Edmund Ruffin reported seeing in Charleston on April 15 "several late comers from Petersburg & the neighboring country, & among them Roger A. Pryor, who came lately & has taken service as Aid to the Governor [of South Carolina]" (Scarborough, *Diary of Edmund Ruffin* 1:601).

66. Shanks, *Secession Movement in Virginia, 1847–1861*, 203–4; Reese *Proceedings of the Virginia State Convention of 1861* 4:144–45, 164–65.

67. Ibid., 4:111–13, J. G. Scott and Wyatt, *Petersburg's Story*, 129. The Rives farm would be the setting for the battle on June 9, 1864 (see chapter 7). For commentary on the contest between Rives and Ruffin, see Scarborough, *Diary of Edmund Ruffin* 1:534–38, 542–44.

2. "War Had Come Indeed"

1. Mrs. T. G. Keen to "My dear Daughter," April 18, 1861, Keen Family Letters, MOC; *Richmond Daily Dispatch*, April 20, 1861.

2. David A. Weisiger to W[illiam]. H. Richardson, April 18, 1861, EPJL, Box 8, Folder 8.

3. Henderson, *PCW*, 21; Henderson, *Twelfth Virginia Infantry*, 1–2; M. S. Beckwith, "Reminiscences, 1844–1865," 3, VHS. Edmund Ruffin was none too fond of his son-in-law, whom he called "the greatest curse & trouble of my life," and "a spendthrift & worthless husband." Scarborough, *Diary of Edmund Ruffin* 1:xxvii, 6, 44. The infantry companies would all become part of the Twelfth Virginia Infantry, a regiment dominated by Petersburg troops.

4. George S. Bernard to "My Dear Father," April 20, 1861, George S. Bernard Papers, UVA.

5. M. S. Beckwith, "Reminiscences," 3, VHS; *Richmond Daily Dispatch*, April 23, 1861; J. G. Scott and Wyatt, *Petersburg's Story*, 170.

6. *Richmond Daily Dispatch*, April 23, 1861; John A. Weddell, letter, April 28, 1861, Julie Beckwith Grossmann Collection.

7. Telegram from Thomas Wallace to John Letcher, April 20, 1861, and telegram from Thomas P. Branch to John Letcher, April 20, 1861, EPJL, Box 9, Folder 2. George W. Munford, secretary of the commonwealth, responded to Branch: "Virginia wants all her sons. Patriotism should induce the Petersburg Light Dragoons to wait for orders. Troops must be kept in reserve in case of necessity" (Telegram from George W. Munford to Thomas P. Branch, April 20,, 1861, EPJL, Box 9, Folder 2).

8. *Richmond Daily Dispatch*, April 21, 23, 1861; Henderson, *PCW*, 22; Henderson, *Twelfth Virginia Infantry*, 2; Bernard, *War Talks of Confederate Veterans*, xvii; Wallace, *Third Virginia Infantry*, 14; Henderson, *Forty-first Virginia Infantry*, 4. For information on Walter Gwynn, see Allardice, *More Generals in Gray*, 110.

9. Telegram from James R. Branch to Thomas Branch, April 22, 1861, and letter from A. Overton to John Letcher, April 23, 1861, EPJL, Box 9, Folders 5, 6.

10. Telegrams from David G. Potts and T[homas]. H. Campbell to John Letcher,

April 20, 22, 1861, EPJL, Box 9, Folders 2, 5; Anna Birdsall Campbell, Diary, April 25, 1861, Charles Campbell Papers, W&M; Jackson, "Free Negroes of Petersburg, Virginia," 387; *Richmond Daily Dispatch*, April 29, 1861; Henderson, *PCW,* 23.

11. *Richmond Daily Dispatch*, April 25, 1861; C.M. Hubbard to John Letcher, April 26, 1861, *War of the Rebellion: A Compilation of the Official Records of the Union and Confederate Armies* (hereafter cited *OR*), Series 1, 51: pt. 2, 47. All references are to Series 1 unless otherwise noted.

12. CCM, April 22, 23, 1861.

13. Henderson, *PCW,* 21; *Richmond Daily Dispatch*, April 29, 1861.

14. Mrs. R. A. Pryor, *Reminiscences of Peace and War,* 131–34.

15. *Richmond Daily Dispatch*, April 23, 1861; Anna Birdsall Campbell, Diary, April 22, 23, 24, 1861, Charles Campbell Papers, W&M; William E. Morrison, letter, April 28, 1861, Julie Beckwith Grossmann Collection; J. F. Stephenson, "My Father and His Household, Before, During, and After the War," 22, Blanton Family Papers, VHS; Mrs. B. Callender, "Personal Recollections of the Civil War," 1–2, PNB; Henderson, *PCW,* 24.

16. Telegram from E[dgar]. L. Brockett to John Letcher, April 19, 1861, EPJL, Box 8, Folder 9; *Richmond Daily Dispatch*, April 20, 21, 1861. Ford's brother ran a popular book and stationery store on Sycamore Street.

17. Telegram from T[homas]. H. Campbell to John Letcher, April 23, 1861; S. Bassett French to John Letcher, April 23, 1861; Thomas T. Cropper to John Letcher, April 21, 1861, EPJL, Box 9, Folders 7, 6, 3; *Richmond Daily Dispatch*, May 2, 1861.

18. *Richmond Daily Dispatch*, April 20, 26, 1861. Voluminous correspondence to Governor Letcher between April 18 and 23 involving the seizure of ships along the Appomattox River can be found in the EPJL. The *Jamestown* would be converted into a wooden gunboat and serve as a part of the James River Squadron participating in the battle of Hampton Roads, March 8–9, 1862.

19. Anonymous correspondent to John Letcher, April 19, 1861, and Thomas Whitworth to John Letcher, April 22, 1861, EPJL, Box 8, Folder 9 and Box 11, Folder 2. For a crisp summary of the Federal evacuation of the Gosport Naval Yard, see Quarstein, *CSS Virginia,* 6–18.

20. Quarstein, *CSS* Virginia, 12, 15; telegram from Major General Walter Gwynn to Letcher, April 21, 1861, EPJL, Box 9, Folder 3.

21. Telegram from John M. Davenport to Governor Letcher, April 21, 1861, EPJL, Box 9, Folder 3. See Bill, *Beleaguered City,* 42–43, for *Pawnee* Sunday in Richmond.

22. J. F. Stephenson, "My Father and His Household, Before, During, and After the War," 18–19, Blanton Family Papers, VHS; Mrs. B. Callender, "Personal Recollections of the Civil War," 1, PNB.

23. Robert R. Collier and J[ohn]. H. Claiborne to Governor Letcher, April 17, 18, 1861, EPJL, Box 8, Folders 7, 8. Regular Confederate forces relieved Gwynn of command on May 23, prompting Collier to write his deposed commander a complimentary letter defending Gwynn's performance from unnamed critics. See Collier and others to Gwynn, May 23, 1861, EPJL, Box 21, Folder 1.

24. The following 1861 correspondence to the governor is in the EPJL: William A. Dudley, April 19, Box 8, Folder 9; Thomas Branch, April 20, 23, Box 9, Folders 1, 6; Richard H. Baptist, April 27, Box 10, Folder 2; James Lafsey, April 27, Box 10, Folder 2; Robert C. Donnan, April 28, Box 10, Folder 3; James Boisseau, April 29, Box 10, Folder 4; B. G. Black, April 29, Box 10, Folder 4; William B. Michie, April 27, Box 11, Folder 4.

25. *Richmond Daily Dispatch*, April 29, 23, 1861. These reports were posted two days

prior to their publication by the Petersburg correspondent to the *Daily Dispatch*, "Mon Coeur," who reported on April 20 that "everything like business has been completely suspended."

26. Wallace, *Third Virginia Infantry*, 9–10, 14; Henderson, *Twelfth Virginia Infantry*, 2; *Richmond Daily Dispatch*, May 4, 1861; appointment of Thomas Branch as quartermaster and commissary of troops, May 4, 1861, EPJL, Box 11, Folder 1. The Cockade Rifles would eventually join the Third Virginia Infantry, while the Archer Rifles became part of the Twelfth Virginia Infantry. Information on Wilson can be found in R. K. Krick, *Lee's Colonels*, 373–74. Fort Powhatan occupied a site on the south side of the James thirty miles down river from Richmond, commanding the first narrow channel coming upriver from Hampton Roads. Colonel Andrew Talcott of the engineers selected the site of old Fort Powhatan in response to a request that Robert E. Lee made in late April to prepare fortifications along the James River.

27. Wallace, *Guide to Virginia Military Organizations, 1861–1865*, 122–23; *Richmond Daily Dispatch*, April 26, 1861; Henderson, *Forty-first Virginia Infantry*, 7–8; Henderson, *PCW*, 22; William Caskie Kerr to John E. Meade, June 4, 1861, Ruffin-Meade Family Papers, UNC. The McRae Rifle Guards, Ragland Guards, and Cockade Cadets would all join the Forty-first Virginia Infantry.

28. Driver, *Fifth Virginia Cavalry*, 23–24; W. H. Coffin to Governor Letcher, June 13, 1861, EPJL, Box 15, Folder 1. This unit would become a part of the Fifth Virginia Cavalry.

29. Driver, *Fifth Virginia Cavalry*, 1; Balfour, *Thirteenth Virginia Cavalry*, 5; *Richmond Daily Dispatch*, May 17, 20, 1861; Henderson, *PCW*, 22. The Petersburg Cavalry would also join the Fifth Virginia Cavalry.

30. Wallace, *Guide to Virginia Military Organizations, 1861–1865*, 7, 96; Henderson, *PCW*, 23, 160–61; Weaver, *Branch, Harrington and Staunton Hill Artillery*, 5; James R. Branch to Governor Letcher, May 19, 1861, EPJL, Box 13, Folder 2, LOV; Chernault and Weaver, *Eighteenth and Twentieth Battalions of Heavy Artillery*, 7. Lee's Life Guard first served in the Twelfth Virginia Infantry. Rambaut's Artillery was a part of the Eighteenth Battalion of Virginia Heavy Artillery. The 1860 census lists approximately 2,240 white men aged 18 to 45 residing in Petersburg. Fewer than 1,000 of them registered under mandatory state law in the spring of 1862. See chapter 3.

31. Anna Birdsall Campbell, Diary, April 22, 1861, Charles Campbell Papers, W&M; *Richmond Daily Dispatch*, April 29, 1861; David G. Potts to William Richardson, April 26, 1861, EPJL, Box 11, Folder 4; Wallace, *Guide to Virginia Military Organizations, 1861–1865*, 203, 205; Henderson, *PCW*, 22. Potts's home guard unit remained independent.

32. *Richmond Daily Dispatch*, April 29, May 2, 13, 15, 1861; Henderson, *PCW*, 163; Wallace, *Guide to Virginia Military Organizations, 1861–1865*, 205. The *Richmond Daily Dispatch* mentioned the Young Men's Reserve Guard twice, identifying a "Rev. Pratt" as the commander, not Platt. Neither Wallace nor Henderson lists this organization among Petersburg's home guard contingents.

33. *Richmond Daily Dispatch*, April 26, 1861; Anna Birdsall Campbell, Diary, April 24, 1861, Charles Campbell Papers, W&M; Littleton L. Lee to Governor Letcher, EPJL, Box 11, Folder 3.

34. *Richmond Daily Dispatch*, April 29, May 2, 1861; Wyckoff, *History of the Second South Carolina Infantry: 1861–65*, x–xiii.

35. Anna Birdsall Campbell, Diary, April 29, 1861, Charles Campbell Papers, W&M; *Richmond Daily Dispatch*, May 15, 20, 1861; "Sketch of 12 Months Service in the Mobile Rifle Co.," 154. For reports of more Confederate troop arrivals in April and May, see *Rich-*

NOTES TO PAGES 46–50

mond Daily Dispatch, May 4, 6, 24, 1861; telegram from Captain W. C. Musgrove to John Letcher, May 4, 1861, EPJL, Box 11, Folder 3; and Barefoot, *General Robert F. Hoke*, 24–25.

36. *Richmond Daily Dispatch*, May 4, 13, 20, 1861.

37. Mrs. T. G. Keen to "Dear Daughter," May 5, 1861, Keen Family Letters, MOC; *Richmond Daily Dispatch*, May 6, 1861.

38. *Richmond Daily Dispatch*, May 4, 1861; W. W. Townes to Governor Letcher, May 9, 1861, EPJL, Box 12, Folder 1; CCM, May 22, 1861. On May 10, 1861, these men were certified as elected to the common council: East Ward: J. A. Johnston, Samuel Lecture, H[armon]. W. Siggins, J. T[homas]. Young, C[harles]. F. Collier, T[homas]. D. Watson. South Ward: B. J. Butterworth, R[obert]. A. Martin, Wesley Grigg, B[enjamin]. B. Vaughan, Alex[ander] Donnan, John W. Booth. Center Ward: D'Arcy Paul, Charles Corling, Lewis Lumsford, Lemuel Peebles, William L. Watkins, John P. May. West Ward: W. L. Lancaster, David May, D[avid]. G. Potts, J[ohn]. A. Hair, James R. Branch and Arch[ibald]. Gray. Townes was reelected as mayor. See CCM, May 10, 1861.

39. The EPJL are full of requests for military and civilian appointments from Petersburg residents. See, for example, Col. E[dgar]. L. Brockett to Letcher, May 1, 1861, Box 10, Folder 7; Thomas Branch to Letcher, May 6, 1861, Box 11, Folder 3; Alexander W. Weddle to Letcher, May 11, 1861, Box 12, Folder 3; C[harles]. O. Sanford to General Walter Gwynn, May 13, 1861, Box 12, Folder 4; H. L. Hopkins to Letcher, May 14, 1861, Box 12, Folder 5; and Charles F. Collier to Letcher, May 17, 1861, Box 12, Folder 8.

40. *Petersburg Daily Express*, May 4, 1861. For background on the relocation of the Confederate capital, see W. C. Davis, *Government of Our Own*, 388–91.

41. Anna Birdsall Campbell, Diary, May 2, 1861, Charles Campbell Papers, W&M; Mrs. T. G. Keen to "Dear Daughter," May 5, 1861, Keen Family Letters, MOC; *Richmond Daily Dispatch*, May 4, 1861.

42. J. R. Dowell to John Letcher, April 19, 22, 1861, Box 8, Folder 9 and Box 9, Folder 5; W. C. Bass to John Letcher, May 11, 17, 1861, Box 13, Folder 1, 7; Charles Ellis to John Letcher, April 26 and June 25, 1861, Box 10, Folder 2 and Box 15, Folder 4; W[illiam]. T. Joynes to John Letcher, May 13, 1861, Box 12, Folder 4, all in EPJL; Charles Campbell, Diary (hereafter cited CCD), July 2, 1861, Charles Campbell Papers, W&M.

43. Anna Birdsall Campbell, Diary, May 4, 1861, Charles Campbell Papers, W&M; *Richmond Daily Dispatch*, April 26, 1861. The woman abused for her Northern heritage was the wife of the grocer Benjamin Stewart, whose business suffered because of his wife's nativity. See Henderson, *PCW*, 27.

44. *Richmond Daily Dispatch*, May 25, 1861.

45. Telegram from C[harles]. O. Sanford to T. H. Wynne, May 12, 1861, and telegram from D. G. Duncan to John Letcher, May 28, 1861, Box 12, Folder 4 and Box 13, Folder 9, EPJL; Boney, *John Letcher of Virginia*, 131; W. C. Kerr to "Dear Meade" (John E. Meade), June 4, 1861, Ruffin-Meade Family Papers, UNC; Cooper, *Jefferson Davis, American*, 343; W. C. Davis, *Union That Shaped the Confederacy*, 131; Henderson, *PCW*, 27.

46. W. C. Kerr to "Dear Meade" [John E. Meade], June 4, 1861, Ruffin-Meade Family Papers, UNC; T. H. Williams, *P. G. T. Beauregard*, 66.

47. Mrs. R. W. Meade to "My beloved son" [John E. Meade], June 4, 1861, Ruffin-Meade Family Papers, UNC; Thomas Branch to John Letcher, June 4, 1861, EPJL, Box 14, Folder 4.

48. Henderson, *PCW*, 25–26; Anna Birdsall Campbell, Diary, April 27, 1861, Charles Campbell Papers, W&M; CCM, May 1, 1861. The *Richmond Daily Dispatch* published a letter written on April 26 by Lieutenant Colonel Henry Heth of the quartermaster service

to Quartermaster Benjamin Franklin Ficklen observing that "it is necessary and important that the railroads in Richmond and Petersburg should be connected . . . for the transmission of troops and supplies." Governor Letcher endorsed the letter: "This arrangement must be carried out" (Manarin, *Richmond at War,* 33).

49. *OR,* Series 4, 1:394, 485–86; Convention Records of 1861, Series 2, Box 3, Folder 7, no. 59, LOV. The same ordinance called for a connection in Richmond between the Richmond, Fredericksburg & Potomac Railroad and the Richmond & Petersburg line. For commentary on the lack of progress in connecting the railroads, see CCD, July 9, 11, 12, 15, 19, 1861.

50. CCD, June 30 and July 5, 11, 15, 18, 20, 1861.

51. CCM, July 17, 1861; CCD, July 20, 1861; Henderson, *PCW,* 29.

52. Thomas Claybrook Elder to "My dear Wife," July 25, 1861, Thomas Claybrook Elder Papers, VHS; CCD, July 20, 1861.

53. CCM, June 1, 12, and July 1, 1861. Total expenditures for the fiscal year were $144, 711.04.

54. CCM, June 20 and July 1, 5, 1861, July 1, 1861, CCD, July 6, 1861.

55. CCM, June 12 and July 1, 1861; *Richmond Daily Dispatch,* July 2, 1861.

56. A[nthony]. M. Keiley to John Letcher, June 16, 1861, EPJL, Box 15, Folder 3. The Petersburg Riflemen were Company E, Twelfth Virginia Infantry. Examples of other Petersburg-based solicitations to the governor can be found in Box 14, Folders 4, 6, 7, and Box 15, Folder 2, EPJL.

57. Alexander Falconer to Governor Letcher, June 18, 1861, EPJL, Box 15, Folder 2.

58. Bessie Meade Callender to "My dear Brother" [John E. Meade], May 21, 1861, Ruffin-Meade Family Papers, UNC; *Richmond Daily Dispatch,* June 10, 1861; Minutes of the Ladies Club of Washington Street Church, July 23, 1861, Charles Campbell Papers, W&M; CCD, July 6, 1861.

59. Bessie Meade Callender to "My dear John" [John E. Meade], June 17, 1861, Ruffin-Meade Family Papers, UNC; *Petersburg Daily Express,* qtd. in Lutz, *Prince George-Hopewell Story,* 160. The battle of Big Bethel on June 10, 1861, occurred outside of Hampton. This small Confederate victory, the first armed conflict of the war in eastern Virginia, assumed a popular importance well beyond its strategic significance.

60. Anonymous correspondent to Governor Letcher, June 20, 1861, EPJL, Box 15, Folder 3; CCD, July 6, 10, 1861; *Petersburg Daily Express,* qtd. in Lutz, *Prince George-Hopewell Story,* 160.

61. *Richmond Daily Dispatch,* May 20, 27 and June 3, 1861; *Petersburg Daily Express,* July 17, 1861; George Lyon to Governor Letcher, July 19, 1861, telegram from W[illiam]. T. Joynes to Governor Letcher, June 8, 1861, and Samuel V. Watkins to Governor Letcher, July 15, 1861, EPJL, Box 16, Folder 4; Box 14, Folder 6; and Box 16, Folder 2. The Second Presbyterian Church was erected in 1861–62 at a cost of thirty thousand dollars. See *History of the Second Presbyterian Church,* 13. For information on David Todd, see Baker, *Mary Todd Lincoln,* 223.

62. Telegram from Mayor Townes to Governor Letcher, June 6, 1861; Mayor Townes to Governor Letcher, June 20, 1861; William E. Short to Governor Letcher, June 24, 1861, EPJL, Box 14, Folder 5; Box 15; Folder 3; and Box 15, Folder 4; *Petersburg Daily Express,* July 17, 1861.

63. Mrs. John E. Meade, Sr. to "My dear son" [John E. Meade Jr.], July 27, 1861, Ruffin-Meade Family Papers, UNC.

64. Mrs. John E. Meade, Sr. to "My Dear Son" [John E. Meade Jr.], July 16, 1861, Ruffin-Meade Family Papers, UNC. The battle in Missouri was probably the one at Carthage on July 5.

65. CCD, July 20, 21, 1861; Henderson, *PCW*, 29. Stephens was en route to preside over the third session of the Provisional Confederate Congress. See Schott, *Alexander H. Stephens of Georgia*, 343. Hennessy, *First Battle of Manassas* is helpful on First Manassas.

66. CCD, July 24, 1861; Bessie Meade Callender to John E. Meade Jr., July 25, 1861, Ruffin-Meade Family Papers, UNC; George S. Bernard to "My dear Father," July 25, 1861, George S. Bernard Papers, UVA.

3. "The World Is Turned Upside Down and Topsy Turvey"

1. CCD, July 26, 1861; Henderson, *PCW*, 29; M. S. Beckwith, "Reminiscences," 4, VHS.

2. CCD, July 31, 1861; M. S. Beckwith, "Reminiscences," 4, 9, VHS; *Petersburg Daily Express*, July 22, 1861.

3. CCD, July 23, August 12, 1861; Heslop, *Pastors, Pulpits, and Petersburg*, 32; *Richmond Daily Dispatch*, July 23, 1861. For information on the Evangelical Tract Society, see Rev. W. Cuttino Smith, "Personal Reminiscences of the Confederate War," in L. T. Mills, *South Carolina Family*, 92. In May 1862 the Evangelical Tract Society maintained its offices at 38 Bollingbrook Street, a former insurance office. See *Petersburg Daily Express*, May 1, 1862.

4. *Petersburg Daily Express*, July 22, 1861; CCD, August 8, 1861; Henderson, *PCW*, 35.

5. CCD, July 20, August 14, and October 8, 1861.

6. CCD, July 26, 27, 29, 30 and August 8, 10, 14, 1861. One Petersburg correspondent reported that the connection was finished on August 12. See *Richmond Daily Dispatch*, August 15, 1861. For reports of derailments, see CCD, August 28 and September 2, 1861.

7. *Petersburg Daily Express*, July 24, 1861; CCD, July 26, 29, 30, 1861; Henderson, *PCW*, 31–32. A Richmond newspaper reported that on August 13 only forty patients occupied three hospitals in Petersburg, a surprisingly low number. See *Richmond Daily Dispatch*, August 15, 1861. East Hill was located east of North Jefferson Street between Franklin and Henry Streets.

8. *Petersburg Daily Express*, September 11, 1861; R. G. Scott, *Forgotten Valor*, 309.

9. CCD, September 20, 1861; *Petersburg Daily Express*, September 23, 1861.

10. CCD, October 31 and November 23, 1861; *Petersburg Daily Express*, November 23, 1861.

11. CCD, November 24, 1861; *Petersburg Daily Express*, November 25 and December 23, 1861.

12. Correspondence, January 25, 30, 1862, EPJL, Box 20, Folder 3.

13. CCD, July 4 and August 16, 28 and September 20, 1861; *Petersburg Daily Express*, November 23, 1861; *Richmond Daily Dispatch*, October 1, 1861; CCM, December 2, 1861; Henderson, *Forty-first Virginia Infantry*, 7; Henderson, *PCW*, 33; Wallace, *Guide to Virginia Military Organizations, 1861–1865*, 122–23. The company, eventually renamed the Confederate Cadets, became part of the Forty-first Virginia Infantry.

14. *Petersburg Daily Express*, September 7, 26, 1861; Wallace, *Third Virginia Infantry*, 18; William T. Joynes to [illegible], August 20, 1861, EPJL, Box 17, Folder 2.

15. Lemuel Peebles, January 7, 1862; John E. Wills, November 23, 1861; and Thomas C. Elder, January 31, 1862, all to Governor Letcher, EPJL, Box 20, Folder 1; Box 18, Folder 8; and Box 20, Folder 5. The governor denied Wills's request.

16. A careful reading of Charles Campbell's diaries provides a good record of Petersburg inflation. For the summer of 1861, see entries of July 10 and August 20, 28, 31; also see *Petersburg Daily Express*, July 17 and August 2, 29, 1861. Poor transportation contributed to shortages. In November, Campbell noticed juice streaming from a "good many

barrels of oranges" shipped to the Richmond depot from New Orleans, indicating spoilage (CCD, November 20, 1861).

17. *Petersburg Daily Express,* August 3, 29, 1861. William Henderson called my attention to the anti-business bias exhibited in such comments and attributed that bias to "a heritage of Jacksonian Democrat thinking & before that Jeffersonian agrarianism." He pointed out that "a weak economy unable to fight a war & supply the civilian sector simultaneously" was just as likely to blame for shortages as was greed (Henderson to the author, letter, December 26, 2003).

18. *Petersburg Daily Express,* September 20, November 23 and December 3, 1861; CCD, October 15 and November 12, 1861.

19. CCD, July 25, August 13 and October 11, 28, 31, 1861; Henderson, *PCW,* 36–37. The Petersburg Common Council increased its issue of paper money from fifty thousand dollars to sixty-five thousand on August 1, fueling inflation.

20. CCD, December 21, 1861; J. F. Stephenson, "My Father and His Household, Before, During, and After the War," 22, Blanton Family Papers, VHS; *Petersburg Daily Express,* December 3, 19, 27, 1861.

21. *Petersburg Daily Express,* September 21, November 5 and December 3, 19, 1861; CCM, November 1, 8, 1861; Bessie Meade Callender to "My Dear John" [John E. Meade], October 17, 1861, Ruffin-Meade Family Papers, UNC. The Women's Relief Association was also known as the Women's Relief Society.

22. *Petersburg Daily Express,* September 20, 1861; CCD, September 26, 1861; CCM, August 7 and September 2, 1861.

23. *Petersburg Daily Express,* November 5, 20 and December 23, 27, 1861; J. G. Scott and Wyatt, *Petersburg's Story,* 120; *Petersburg Daily Progress,* December 19, 1861.

24. CCD, December 26, 1861. Campbell stated that seven thousand dollars was raised for the purchase of arms for a Missouri unit.

25. *Petersburg Daily Express,* December 23, 1861, and January 1, 1862.

26. CCD, September 25, 1861; *Richmond Dispatch,* July 10, 1861. Brigadier General E. Kirby Smith had been wounded at Manassas and while recovering in Lynchburg, married Miss Selden. Ellis died on July 7 while seeking to restore his health in Western Virginia.

27. Bessie Meade Callender to "My dear John" [John E. Meade], October 17, 1861, Ruffin-Meade Papers, UNC.

28. W. T. Joynes to John Letcher, July 30, 1861, EPJL, Box 16, Folder 7.

29. CCM, October 1, 1861; *Petersburg Daily Express,* October 24, 1861; CCD, November 18, 20, 1861. The Petersburg Common Council did appropriate funds to purchase clothing for the city's free blacks sent to the Peninsula to build fortifications. See Brewer, *Confederate Negro,* 192n7.

30. *Petersburg Daily Express,* September 7, 1861, and January 21, February 6, and March 3, 1862.

31. *Petersburg Daily Express,* July 24, September 20, November 5, 20 and December 3, 23, 27, 1861; Mrs. John E. Meade to "My beloved son" [John E. Meade], August 22, 1861, Ruffin-Meade Family Papers, UNC.

32. *Arkansas True Democrat,* December 12, 1861; *Petersburg Daily Express,* December 27, 1861, and January 1, 1862; Henderson, *PCW,* 29.

33. *Richmond Daily Dispatch,* July 2, 1861; CCD, July 25, August 10 and December 16, 26, 1861; *Petersburg Daily Express,* September 17, 1861, and January 1, 1862; Henderson, *PCW,* 35–37.

34. CCD, October 7, 13 and December 21, 1861; *Petersburg Daily Express,* Septem-

ber 20 and December 23, 1861. In addition to the unsold tobacco stored at factories, the city's four tobacco warehouses had a capacity of 6,400 hogsheads. See John W. P. Pool to John Letcher, October 7, 1861, EPJL, Box 18, Folder 4. Two prominent Petersburg renters at this time were A. B. Dickerson of the Confederate post office, formerly minister to Nicaragua, and Thomas Bragg, former governor and United States Senator from North Carolina, and the Confederacy's attorney general. See CCD, December 7, 1861; Thomas Bragg, Diary (hereafter cited TBD), Thomas Bragg Papers, UNC. Bragg also maintained a Richmond residence.

35. For a cogent summary of the impact of the war on business in Petersburg during 1861, see Henderson, *PCW*, 38–39.

36. The intriguing case of John G. Guthrey's arrests in New York City in August and December 1861 can be followed in *OR*, Series 2, 2:509–30. The 1860 census spelled his name Guthrie.

37. *Petersburg Daily Express*, January 1, 21, February 4, 27, and March 3, 1862; CCD, January 17, March 6, 8, and April 2, 1862; *Macon Daily Telegraph*, November 28, 1861, qtd. in Iobst, *Civil War Macon*, 91. Blind Tom performed a similar act in Richmond in late January and early February. See Scarborough, *Diary of Edmund Ruffin* 2:226–29, for a description of Ruffin's encounter with the musician. Wiggins moved to a farm near Warrenton, Virginia, after the Civil War and performed for decades. He died in 1908.

38. *Petersburg Daily Express*, February 3, 7, 1862; CCD, January 23 and February 24, 1862; TBD, January 31, 1862; M. S. Beckwith, "Reminiscences," 4, VHS. In addition to violations of the law, the growing coarseness of society was reflected by rude behavior in church. See *Petersburg Daily Express*, February 8, 1862.

39. CCD, January 22, 1862; *Petersburg Daily Express*, February 3, 1862.

40. CCD, January 21, February 13, and March 26, 1862; *Petersburg Daily Express*, January 21, 1862; TBD, January 27, 1862.

41. CCD, February 28, 1862; *Petersburg Daily Express*, March 3 and May 16, 1862. The saga of Corcoran's imprisonment and the efforts to gain his release can be followed in *OR*, Series 2, 2:1, 113; 3:131–32, 182–83, 191–92, 197, 202, 204, 209, 217, 242, 265, 324–25, 401, 403, 429, 460–61, 467, 475, 535, 539, 561, 568, 578, 595, 601, 604, 618–19, 654, 739, 785, 887; 4:14, 21, 25, 36, 148, 350, 394–95, 400, 437. Corcoran was at last exchanged August 14, 1862, for Colonel Roger W. Hanson, a Kentuckian and future commander of the famous Orphan Brigade.

42. *Petersburg Daily Express*, February 27 and March 3, 1862; CCD, March 1, 1862.

43. E. M. Thomas, *Confederate Nation*, 150–51; CCD, March 3, 1862; Henderson, *PCW*, 42–43.

44. *Petersburg Daily Express*, March 6, 1862; CCD, March 6, 7, 11, 1862. General Orders Number 11 is printed in *OR* 51: pt 2, 493. Davis did exempt certain legal matters such as the probate of wills and the qualification of guardians from his proclamation. Cities outside of Virginia, such as Mobile, Alabama, also sought the establishment of martial law. See Bergeron, *Confederate Mobile*, 23.

45. Henderson, *PCW*, 43; CCD, March 8, 18, 1862; Wallace, *Guide to Virginia Military Organizations, 1861–1865*, 242.

46. Printed copies of the February 8, 1862, act, Letcher's proclamations of February 13, and the General Orders of February 13 issued to enforce the act can be found in EPJL, Box 21, Folder 4. For the political background of Letcher's actions, see Boney, *John Letcher of Virginia*, 156–57, and Wallace, *Guide to Virginia Military Organizations, 1861–1865*, 235–36. For a discussion of Confederate conscription, see McPherson, *Battle Cry of Freedom*, 428–33.

47. CCD, February 11 and March 6, 1862; John Prince to John Letcher, February 19, 1862, EPJL, Box 20, Folder 6; *Petersburg Daily Express* qtd. in the *Charleston Mercury*, March 21, 1862; *Petersburg Daily Express*, February 27 and March 3, 6, 1862; Balfour, *Thirteenth Virginia Cavalry*, 6. The act regarding exemptions and Letcher's proclamation establishing local exemption boards are in EPJL, Box 21, Folder 4. For information on Confederate substitution, see A. B. Moore, *Conscription and Conflict in the Confederacy*, 27–51. The Cockade Cavalry served in the Thirteenth Virginia Cavalry.

48. Wallace, *Guide to Virginia Military Organizations, 1861–1865*, 236; Boney, *Governor Letcher of Virginia*, 159; *OR* 51: pt. 2, 495; A Proclamation by the Governor of Virginia, March 10, 1862, EPJL, Box 21, Folder 4.

49. CCD, March 12, 13, 1862; Telegram from John Davenport to Governor Letcher, March 13, 1862, and Letcher's March 11 proclamation, EPJL, Box 21, Folders 2, 4.

50. CCM, March 13, 1862; CCD, March 13, 1862; Henderson, *PCW*, 43.

51. *Petersburg Daily Express*, February 8, 1862; CCD, February 13, 14, 18, 28, 1862; TBD, February 22, 1862.

52. CCD, March 1, 2, 1862; TBD, March 10, 1862. Information on the voyage of the CSS *Nashville* can be found in Musicant, *Divided Waters*, 331–32.

53. CCD, March 14, 31, 1862; *Petersburg Daily Express*, April 7, 1862.

54. CCD, April 2, 1862; *Petersburg Daily Express*, April 17, 1862; TBD, April 17, 1862; CCM, April 9, 1862; J.E. Christian to John Letcher, April 28, 1862, EPJL, Box 21, Folder 5.

55. CCM, May 1, 1862; *Petersburg Daily Express*, May 2, 1862. Lemuel Peebles, D'Arcy Paul, and Harmon W. Siggins formed the committee sent to Richmond.

56. TBD, May 4, 1862. An excellent account of McClellan's Peninsula campaign is Sears, *To the Gates of Richmond*. For the destruction of the *Virginia*, see Quarstein, *CSS Virginia*, 148–63.

57. TBD, May 5, 6, 1862; The tobacco inspectors Vaughan, Garland, Wyatt, and Blick to John Letcher, May 12, 1862, EPJL, Box 21, Folder 7; CCM, May 9, 1862.

58. TBD, May 5, 9, 13, 1862; *Petersburg Daily Express*, May 14, 1862.

59. TBD, May 9, 13, 15, 1862; Agnes Beckwith to "Dear Bro Julian" [Julian Ruffin], May 13, 1862, Ruffin-Meade Family Papers, UNC. Incongruously, Petersburgers packed Phoenix Hall for a minstrel show and patronized a fund-raising *tableaux* on the night following the battle of Drewry's Bluff. See *Petersburg Daily Express*, May 14, 16, 1862.

60. "An Act To Authorize the Governor of Virginia to Co-operate with the Confederate Government in and about the Defences of Richmond and Petersburg," EPJL, Box 21, Folder 7; M. S. Beckwith, "Reminiscences," 5–7, VHS; Henderson, *Twelfth Virginia Infantry*, 18; TBD, June 2, 1862. See chapter 4 for the strategic context of the May 15 battle of Drewry's Bluff and for details regarding Petersburg casualties at Seven Pines.

61. TBD, June 26, 27, 28 and July 2, 1862; CCD, June 23, 1862; M. S. Beckwith, "Reminiscences," 5, VHS.

62. *Petersburg Daily Express*, April 15, 17, 1862; Election Certification dated May 9, 1862, EPJL, Box 21, Folder 7. Travis Eppes was the fourth candidate for Pryor's seat. The Fourth Congressional District included Petersburg and the counties of Prince George, Chesterfield, Powhatan, Amelia, Dinwiddie, Nottoway, Cumberland, and Goochland. For commentary on Pryor's dual service as an officer and a member of Congress, see Scarborough, *Diary of Edmund Ruffin* 2:157.

63. *Petersburg Daily Express*, April 7 and May 1, 2, 1862; CCM, May 9, 1862. The May 2 edition of the *Daily Express* includes a list of the candidates for more than fifteen elected city offices.

64. The EPJL, Boxes 17–24, contain numerous letters to the governor written between

September 1861 and December 1862 by or on behalf of Petersburgers. The endorsement of Collier can be found under the date September 20, 1861, Box 17, Folder 8; Wallace's solicitation on behalf of Keiley and a similar appeal from Timothy Rives are in Box 18, Folder 7 and Box 17, Folder 8.

65. CCD, January 27, 1862; *Petersburg Daily Express*, February 6, 7, 8, 1862.

66. TBD, July 14, 1862; J. F. Stephenson, "My Father and His Household, Before, During, and After the War," 23, Blanton Family Papers, VHS; Scarborough, *Diary of Edmund Ruffin* 2:276; *Petersburg Daily Express*, February 3, 1862; CCD, March 26 and April 2, 1862.

67. *Petersburg Daily Express*, April 7 and May 14, 1862; TBD, April 25 and May 1, 1862.

68. *Petersburg Daily Express*, April 7 and May 1, 1862; CCD, June 16, 1862.

69. CCD, June 17, 22, 1862; George W. Wills to "My dear Sister," July 7, 1862, William Henry Wills Papers, UNC.

70. TBD, September 4, 1862; French, *Two Wars*, 155–56; James [King] Wilkerson to "Dear father & Mother & Brothers & sisters," November 24, 1862, James King Wilkerson Papers, Duke.

71. Scarborough, *Diary of Edmund Ruffin* 2:409; *Richmond Christian Observer*, December 4, 1862; CCM, December 1, 1862.

72. Governor Letcher's correspondence fully documents the state's efforts to regulate salt distribution. See Thomas Wallace to Governor Letcher, October 10, 1862, Box 23, Folder 1; George W. Munford to Thomas Wallace, October 11, 1862, Box 23, Folder 1; Thomas P. Devereaux to Governor Letcher, October 11, 1862, Box 23, Folder 2; G. A. Wueffer to Governor Letcher, October 11, 1862, Box 23, Folder 2; William T. Joynes to Governor Letcher, November 1, 1862, Box 23, Folder 4; document describing the distribution of salt throughout the state, November 11, 1862, Box 23, Folder 4; George W. Munford to Thomas Campbell, December 10, 1862, Box 23, Folder 7; Lewis Lunsford to G. W. Munford, December 24, 1862, Box 24, Folder 2; and William T. Joynes to Governor Letcher, December 19, 1862, Box 24, Folder 1, EPJL; Scarborough, *Diary of Edmund Ruffin* 2:458, 485, 488. Ruffin pegged the price of salt at 50 cents per pound on October 4 and as much as 64.5 cents a month later.

73. *Petersburg Daily Express*, January 18, 1862.

74. CCM, January 1, February 1, April 1, June 6, 19, July 1, August 1, September 1 and October 11, 1862; *Petersburg Daily Express*, March 3, May 2, 1862.

75. CCD, March 20, 1862.

76. CCM, March 18, November 1, 3, 10, 22, and December 23, 1862.

77. *Petersburg Daily Express*, April 7, 17 and May 1, 2, 14, 1862; TBD, April 11 and May 4, 1862; J. B. Jones, *Rebel War Clerk's Diary*, 1:210; E. L. Jordan, *Black Confederates and Afro-Yankees in Civil War Virginia*, 170, 208.

78. E. L. Jordan, "Different Drummers," 64; E. L. Jordan, *Black Confederates and Afro-Yankees in Civil War Virginia*, 210; Brewer, *Confederate Negro*, 83–84, 90–91; M. S. Beckwith, "Reminiscences," 10, VHS.

79. J. F. Stephenson, "My Father and His Household, Before, During, and After the War," 24, VHS; Scarborough, *Diary of Edmund Ruffin* 2:350–53.

80. Waugh, *Surviving the Confederacy*, 209.

81. Thomas W. Gaither to "Brother Burges," November 3, 1862, Gaither Family Papers, UNC.

82. Joseph J. Cowand to "Dear Cosin" [Winifred A. Cowand], December 29, 1862, Winifred A. Cowand Papers, Duke.

83. Thomas W. Gaither to "Dear Friends," December 26, 1862, Gaither Family Papers, UNC; Joseph J. Cowand to "Dear Cosin" [Winifred A. Cowand], December 29, 1862, Winifred A. Cowand Papers, Duke.

84. Corsan, *Two Months in the Confederate States*, 147–51.

4. "We Are Entirely Defenseless Here"

1. Hill qtd. in Bridges, *Lee's Maverick General*, 181.

2. Charles Campbell documented the arrival of many of the Confederate regiments that passed through town. See CCD, July 28 and 29, August 9, 10, 28, 31, September 6, 9, 25, and October 17, 18, 25, 1861; G. H. Mills, *History of the Sixteenth North Carolina Regiment in the Civil War*, 1; *Petersburg Daily Express*, September 21, 1861.

3. A good summary of North Carolina's coastal geography and military significance and the action at Fort Hatteras is provided in Barrett, *Civil War in North Carolina*, 31–46.

4. R[obert]. R[uffin]. Collier to John Letcher, August 31, 1861, EPJL, Box 17, Folder 4. Other amateur strategists viewed the loss of Fort Hatteras with more alarm. See Scarborough, *Diary of Edmund Ruffin* 2:116, for example.

5. Barrett, *Civil War in North Carolina*, 62–64. *OR* 4:715 contains Special Orders Number 272 assigning Wise to the military district comprised of "that part of North Carolina east of the Chowan River, together with the counties of Washington and Tyrrell" as a part of Huger's Department of Norfolk.

6. Trotter, *Ironclads and Columbiads*, 63–66; *OR* 9:123; CCD, December 10, 14, 1861, and January 15, 1862; G. L. Sherwood and Weaver, *Fifty-ninth Virginia Infantry*, 30.

7. William J. Clarke Papers, UNC; CCD, November 26 and December 17, 31, 1861; Clark, *Histories of the Several Regiments and Battalions from North Carolina* 2:271; *Petersburg Daily Express*, February 8, 1862. See chapter 3 for the kind treatment the citizens of Petersburg afforded the Twenty-fourth North Carolina Infantry. A series of Confederate defeats in western Virginia in 1861 prompted the War Department in Richmond to shift troops out of this theater.

8. CCD, February 12, 14, 1862. A good account of the fighting at Roanoke Island can be found in Barrett, *Civil War in North Carolina*, 66–91. Edmund Ruffin considered the outcome "the worst disaster of the war!" (Scarborough, *Diary of Edmund Ruffin* 2:231).

9. Henderson, *PCW*, 32; Dr. Thomas Withers to "My dear John" [John Grammar Brodnax], August 28, 1861, John Grammar Brodnax Papers, UNC; CCD, August 29 and September 2, 1861; *Petersburg Daily Express*, September 20, 1861.

10. *Petersburg Daily Express*, September 20, 1861; CCD, October 26, 1861; Thomas W. Gaither to "My Dear Friends," November 6, 1862, Gaither Family Papers, UNC.

11. *Petersburg Daily Express*, September 20, 1861; Kate De Rosset Kennedy to her sister, November 1, 1861, De Rosset Family Papers, UNC; CCD, October 29, 1861.

12. Henderson, *PCW*, 38–39, 44; *Petersburg Daily Express*, November 5, 1861; Mrs. Kate De Rosset Kennedy to her sister, November 1, 1861, De Rosset Family Papers, UNC; Saval, "Montage of a City under Siege," 111–13; Davi[d]son, "Confederate Hospitals at Petersburg, Va.," 338–39. Claiborne submitted his resignation from the state senate on Christmas Day 1861. See Claiborne to John Letcher, December 25, 1861, EPJL, Box 19, Folder 2.

13. *Petersburg Daily Express*, April 17 and May 1, 1862; Cunningham, *Doctors in Gray*, 156–57.

14. CCD, October 26, 1861, February 6 and April 5, 1862; *Petersburg Daily Express*, December 23, 1861; Scarborough, *Diary of Edmund Ruffin* 2:259; Beers, *Confederacy*, 375; Brewer, *Confederate Negro*, 34; Henderson, *PCW*, 36.

15. CCD, January 15, 1862; R. L. Jones, *Dinwiddie County*, 140; Henderson, *PCW*, 56; Vandiver, *Civil War Diary of General Josiah Gorgas*, 90; Beers, *Confederacy*, 244; Brewer, *Confederate Negro*, 41.

16. Henderson, *PCW*, 56–57; Beers, *Confederacy*, 382–83; CCD, December 22, 1862; Brewer, *Confederate Negro*, 34.

17. *OR* 11: pt. 3, 403. Winder's expanded jurisdiction around Petersburg replicated the territory placed under martial law earlier in the month. See chapter 3.

18. More detailed information on the evacuation of the Yorktown lines and Norfolk is available in Sears, *To the Gates of Richmond*, 59–92, and Newton, *Joseph E. Johnston and the Defense of Richmond*, 130–56.

19. *OR* 11: pt. 3, 493–98. For Pannill's relationship to Moore's Tobacco Warehouse, see William Pannill and John T. Robertson to Governor Letcher, September 16, 1863, EPJL, Box 27, Folder 6.

20. *OR* 11: pt. 3, 499, 504, 512; 9:472. Branch's Company of Virginia Light Artillery had been first assigned to the Twelfth Virginia Infantry, then transferred as Company K, Sixteenth Virginia Infantry. On March 18, 1862, Branch's company became an artillery battery. See Wallace, *Guide to Virginia Military Organizations, 1861-1865*, 29, 96, 99.

21. *OR* 11: pt. 3, 508–9; TBD, May 8, 1862. By May 8 McClellan's attempt to block Johnston's retreat up the Peninsula had failed and the Army of the Potomac continued its slow progress toward Richmond.

22. *Petersburg Daily Express*, May 14, 16, 1862.

23. Henderson, *Twelfth Virginia Infantry*, 15; Robert C. Mabry to "My Dear Wife," May 12, 1862, Robert C. Mabry Papers, NCDAH; James Eldred Phillips, Memoir, May 11, 1862, James Eldred Phillips Papers, VHS; K. Wiley, *Norfolk Blues*, 19–20; Crew and Trask, *Grimes' Battery, Grandy's Battery, and Huger's Battery Virginia Artillery*, 25; W. A. Todd, "Reminiscences," 11, UNC; Edmund J. Williams to "Dear Ma," May 16, 1862, Edmund Jones Williams Papers, UNC. Among the other units documented to be in Petersburg between May 14 and 16 are Moorman's (Virginia) Battery, the Atlantic (Virginia) Artillery, Grimes's (Virginia) Battery, Huger's (Virginia) Battery, the Richmond (Virginia) Howitzers, the United (Virginia) Artillery, the Ninth Virginia Infantry, and the Thirty-first North Carolina Infantry.

24. "A Sketch of 12 Months Service," 186–87; Henderson, *Twelfth Virginia Infantry*, 15. For a description of the fighting at Drewry's Bluff, see E. Bearss, *River of Lost Opportunities*, 15–67.

25. K. Wiley, *Norfolk Blues*, 20–21; Driver, *Fifth Virginia Cavalry*, 19; Isaac Walters to "My dear Wife," May 31, 1862, Lucy S. Costen Papers, UNC; Henderson, *PCW*, 46–47; *OR* 11: pt. 3, 553, 559, 565, 568; Tribble, *Benjamin Cason Rawlings*, 38, 43; Trask, *Sixty-first Virginia Infantry*, 4–5. Armistead's Brigade included the Ninth Virginia Infantry, Fourteenth Virginia Infantry, Fifty-third Virginia Infantry, Fifth Virginia Battalion and Turner's (Virginia) Battery. Walker's Brigade consisted of the Third Arkansas Infantry, Twenty-seventh North Carolina Infantry, Forty-sixth North Carolina Infantry, Forty-eighth North Carolina Infantry, Thirtieth Virginia Infantry, Second Georgia Battalion, and Fourteenth Virginia Cavalry Battalion.

26. *OR* 11: pt. 3, 556, 628–29; J. W. H. Porter, *Record of Events in Norfolk County, Virginia*, 304–5; Brown, *Signal Corps, U.S.A., in the War of the Rebellion*, 219; Tidwell, *Come Retribution*, 84–86; R. E. L. Krick, *Staff Officers in Gray*, 221; Henderson, *PCW*, 47, 49. I am indebted to Thomas DiGiuseppe of West Newbury, Massachusetts, for sharing his extensive information on Captain Milligan.

27. Henderson, *PCW*, 47–49; TBD, June 6, 1862. Beckwith told his family during a

visit home on May 25 that he believed he would die during his first battle. It would not be until October 18 that the Beckwiths, using a map provided by a Confederate soldier, recovered Julian's body, identified by a book and a shirt button. In his diary Edmund Ruffin expressed emotion on learning of the death of his grandson. Scarborough, *Diary of Edmund Ruffin* 2:330–32.

28. K. Wiley, *Norfolk Blues,* 22. Edmund Ruffin considered Colonel Lomax a valuable officer and man. Scarborough, *Diary of Edmund Ruffin* 2:328.

29. Samuel H. Walkup, Diary, June 2, 17, 1862, Samuel H. Walkup Papers, UNC; B. W. Jones, *Under the Stars and Bars,* 35; TBD, June 16, 1862.

30. Samuel H. Walkup to "My ever Charming Minnie," June 13, 1862, Samuel H. Walkup Papers, UNC; Joseph J. Cowand to "Dear Cosin" [Winifred A. Cowand], June 16, 1862, Winifred A. Cowand Papers, Duke. For more on Corporal Cowand's romantic techniques, see chapter 3.

31. Albert N. Johnson to "Miss Adline," June 18, 1862, Albert M. White Papers, UNC; Isaac Walters to "My Darling Wife," June 18, 1862, Lucy S. Costen Papers, UNC.

32. TBD, June 12, 13, 1862; *OR* 11: pt. 3, 598.

33. *OR* 11: pt. 3, 607, 610–11. Although Burnside had discussed with McClellan the possibility of organizing an offensive south of the James in cooperation with the Army of the Potomac, nothing had been done by June 18 to implement such a strategy.

34. *OR* 11: pt. 3, 613; CCD, June 23, 1862; Samuel H. Walkup, Diary, June 24, 1862, Samuel H. Walkup Papers, UNC; TBD, June 26, 1862.

35. TBD, June 27, 1862. For information on the aborted naval expedition up the Appomattox, see *Official Records of the Union and Confederate Navies in the War of the Rebellion* 7:502–3, 523–24; E. Bearss, *River of Lost Opportunities,* 84–88; Johnson, *Rear Admiral John Rodgers, 1812–1882,* 208–15; Henderson, *PCW,* 50.

36. Henderson, *PCW,* 50–52; CCD, July 13, 1862; TBD, July 2, 1862; Gallagher, *Fighting for the Confederacy,* 118–19.

37. TBD, July 3, 1862; Henderson, *PCW,* 53.

38. TBD, July 7, 11, 1862; *OR* 9:476; Isaac Walters to "My dear wife," July 4, 1862, Lucy S. Costen Papers, UNC; Samuel H. Walkup, Diary, July 6, 1862, Samuel H. Walkup Papers, UNC; Wagstaff, *James A. Graham Papers, 1861–1884,* 126–27; Scarborough, *Diary of Edmund Ruffin* 2:369, 373; Henderson, *PCW,* 53. Daniel's Brigade included the Forty-third, Forty-fifth, and Fiftieth North Carolina infantry regiments. The Forty-fourth North Carolina Infantry was among Martin's reinforcements.

39. CCD, July 14, 1862; Leon, *Diary of a Tar Heel Confederate Soldier,* 8–9; Soldier in Second Georgia Battalion to "Dear Mother," July 17, 1862, Anna Blue McLaurin Papers, UNC.

40. CCD, July 12, 1862; *OR* 9:476. For a biographical sketch of Theophilus Hunter Holmes, see Castel, "Theophilus Holmes," 10–17.

41. *OR* 11: pt. 3, 646. Bridges, *Lee's Maverick General,* remains the best analysis of Daniel Harvey Hill's personality and Civil War career.

42. *OR* 11: pt. 2, 939, 19: pt. 1, 1018; CCM, March 5 and May 6, 1862; Brewer, *Confederate Negro,* 155; Henderson, *PCW,* 47.

43. Samuel H. Walkup, Diary, July 26, 28, 1862, Samuel H. Walkup Papers, UNC; TBD, August 2, 1862; *OR* 11: pt. 3, 663, 667–68, pt. 2, 939; Charles H. Dimmock to Robert E. Lee, February 1, 1866, Charles Henry Dimmock Papers (hereafter cited CHDP), VHS.

44. Henderson, *PCW,* 55; George W. Wills to "My Dear Sister," August 4, 1862, William Henry Wills Papers, UNC; Bridges, *Lee's Maverick General,* 88; Schiller, *Captain's War,* 9; Thomas Rowland to "My dear Mother," August 16, 1862, Thomas Rowland Papers, MOC; Brewer, *Confederate Negro,* 155; *OR* 11: pt. 2, 939, 19: pt. 1, 1018.

45. *OR* 11: pt. 2, 936, 940; pt. 3, 643. Brigadier General Gabriel J. Rains conducted extensive evaluations of the riverbank and recommended Fort Powhatan as an advantageous spot to place batteries against Union naval traffic. See Scarborough, *Diary of Edmund Ruffin* 2:374–76, 381–82. A good summary of Lee's strategic thinking at this time is in Freeman, *R. E. Lee* 2:264–68.

46. *OR* 11: pt. 2, 936–37, 943.

47. *OR* 19: pt. 1, 1019; 11: pt. 2, 937, 939. Coggin's Point had also been known as Merchant's Hope Point.

48. *OR* 11: pt. 2, 936–7, 939. French gained his experience at Evansport, a Confederate battery position at a narrow point along the right bank of the Potomac in what is, in 2006, Quantico, Virginia.

49. *OR* 11: pt. 2, 939–43; Lane, *Dear Mother*, 173; French, *Two Wars*, 148. Hill's chief of artillery, Major Scipio Francis Pierson, had conducted a cursory examination of Coggin's Point on July 29 under the direction of Edmund Ruffin. See Scarborough, *Diary of Edmund Ruffin* 2:391.

50. *OR* 11: pt. 2, 940, 944; Lane, *Dear Mother*, 174; French, *Two Wars*, 148; Scarborough, *Diary of Edmund Ruffin* 2:391–93. Beechwood at this time belonged to Ruffin's son, Edmund Jr., who had acquired it from his father before the war.

51. *OR* 11, pt. 2, 942–43; Scarborough, *Diary of Edmund Ruffin* 2:397.

52. *OR* 11: pt. 2, 940, 944–45; French, *Two Wars*, 148; Lane, *Dear Mother*, 175; Scarborough, *Diary of Edmund Ruffin* 2:393–94.

53. *OR* 11: pt. 2, 941–42, 946; Lane, *Dear Mother*, 175–77; French, *Two Wars*, 149; Scarborough, *Diary of Edmund Ruffin* 2:394–96; Joseph J. Cowand to "Dear Cosin" [Winifred A. Cowand], August 4, 1862, Winifred A. Cowand Papers, Duke.

54. *OR* 11: pt. 2, 942, 946, 934–35; Lane, *Dear Mother*, 176; French, *Two Wars*, 149; Sears, *For Country, Cause and Leader*, 269; W. C. Sherwood and Nicholas, *Amherst Artillery, Albemarle Artillery, and Sturdivant's Battery*, 117–19.

55. *OR* 11: pt. 2, 938–39.

56. *OR* 11, pt. 2, 935; Scarborough, *Diary of Edmund Ruffin* 2:399–400. McClellan thought Maycox was Ruffin's house and considered its destruction "a rather hard case . . . but it could not be avoided" (Sears, *Civil War Papers of George B. McClellan*, 382). Douglas Southall Freeman argues that the barren results of the Coggin's Point operation undermined Lee's confidence in Hill as a department commander and contributed to his decision to reassign Hill later that month. Freeman, *Lee's Lieutenants* 2:54–55.

57. *OR* 11: pt. 2, 935; Sears, *To the Gates of Richmond*, 351–52.

58. Lane, *Dear Mother*, 177–78; J[ulius]. S. Joyner to "Dear Bro," August 23, 1862, Joyner Family Papers, UNC.

59. Scarborough, *Diary of Edmund Ruffin* 2:400–410; *OR* 11: pt. 1, 76; W. C. Sherwood and Nicholas, *Amherst Artillery, Albemarle Artillery, and Sturdivant's Battery*, 119; G. L. Sherwood, *Mathews Light Artillery, Penick's Pittsylvania Artillery, Young's Halifax Artillery, and Johnson's Jackson Flying Artillery*, 51–52; Samuel H. Walkup, Diary, August 16, 1862, Samuel H. Walkup Papers, UNC; Howard McCutchan to "Miss Anna," August 18, 1862, Anna Blue McLaurin Papers, UNC. In addition to Beechwood, the Ruffin family owned Ruthven Plantation situated a few miles away.

60. Schiller, *Captain's War*, 11; Crew and Trask, *Grimes' Battery, Grandy's Battery, and Huger's Battery Virginia Artillery*, 26–27; Sloan, *Reminiscences of the Guilford Grays, Co. B. Twenty-seventh N.C. Regiment*, 38; Leon, *Diary of a Tar Heel Confederate Soldier*, 9–13; *OR* 51: pt. 2, 1075, 19: pt. 1, 1019; Freeman, *Lee's Lieutenants* 2:54–55. Hill's biographer speculates that Lee's doubts about Hill stemmed also from the Carolinian's poor health and "queer temperament." See Bridges, *Lee's Maverick General*, 148–49.

McClellan's departure became common knowledge in Petersburg by August 16. See Scarborough, *Diary of Edmund Ruffin* 2:415.

61. Freeman, *Lee's Lieutenants* 1:243, 262; *OR* 11: pt. 3, 671.

62. *OR:* 12, pt. 3, 930–31, 18:742, 748; Freeman, *Lee's Lieutenants* 2:53–54, 145. The Department of North Carolina was occasionally called the Department South of James River. Gustavus Smith's still delicate health probably influenced Lee's decision to remove him from an active field assignment.

63. Both French and Smith wrote about their wartime experiences. See French, *Two Wars,* and G. W. Smith, *Confederate War Papers.* Brief sketches are available in Freeman, *Lee's Lieutenants* 1:163, 2:472. See also Hudson, *Odyssey of a Southerner.*

64. *OR* 18:750–51, 759; Clark, *Histories of the Several Regiments and Battalions from North Carolina* 2:336; Henderson, *PCW,* 57–58. Pettigrew had been wounded and captured at Seven Pines. He was exchanged in August and assumed command of a new brigade composed of the Eleventh, Twenty-sixth, Forty-fourth, Forty-seventh, and Fifty-second North Carolina infantry regiments. The conduct of the operations involving French's department in the autumn of 1862 lies outside the scope of this study. For information on these actions, see *OR* 18:741–895 and Barrett, *Civil War in North Carolina,* 131–48.

65. TBD, September 19 and November 7, 1862; W. C. Sherwood and Nicholas, *Amherst Artillery, Albemarle Artillery, and Sturdivant's Battery,* 120–21; *OR, Supplement,* pt. 3, 2:634–35; *OR* 18:759, 764, 773, 793–94, 19: pt. 2, 694–95, 697–99, 710, 715. Gustavus Smith served as acting Confederate secretary of war between November 17 and 21 in addition to commanding his military department.

66. James King Wilkerson to "Dear Father," October 13, 31, 1862, James King Wilkerson Papers, Duke; Wright, *Memoirs of Alfred Horatio Belo,* 13; *OR* 18:788; French, *Two Wars,* 157.

67. James King Wilkerson to "Dear Father," October 31, 1862, and to "Dear Parents," November 15, 1862, James King Wilkerson Papers, Duke.

68. French, *Two Wars,* 157; Radley, *Rebel Watchdog,* 60. Smallpox also plagued Petersburg's soldiers during the fall and winter of 1862.

69. James King Wilkerson to "Dear Parents," November 15, 1862, James King Wilkerson Papers, Duke; French, *Two Wars,* 157–58; Henry Thweatt Owen Papers, November 24, 1862, LOV; Isaac McIntosh to "Dear Brother," December 22, 1862, Hattie McIntosh Papers, UNC. The best summary of early war prisoner administration and the effects of the cartel of July 1862 is in Hesseltine, *Civil War Prisons,* 1–113.

70. James King Wilkerson to "Dear Parents," December 16, 1862, James King Wilkerson Papers, Duke. The Confederates executed deserters by firing squad.

71. *OR* 18:742; Charles H. Dimmock to R[obert]. E. Lee, February 1, 1866, CHDP; French, *Two Wars,* 147.

72. Henderson, *PCW,* 55–56; *OR* 18:762; James King Wilkerson to "Dear Father," October 13, 1862, James King Wilkerson Papers, Duke. The lawmakers in Richmond authorized their measure in October.

73. Letters of Samuel G. French and Charles H. Dimmock to Common Council, CCM, December 12, 1862.

74. CCM, December 12, 13, 1862; Brewer, *Confederate Negro,* 155–56; Weaver, *Fifty-fourth Virginia Infantry,* 58.

75. Barrett, *Civil War in North Carolina,* 139–48; French, *Two Wars,* 152. French turned Foster back at Goldsboro on December 17. On November 30 one of Burnside's subordinates, Brigadier General John Gibbon, had suggested that Burnside avoid a

frontal attack at Fredericksburg by using a combined operation to seize Petersburg. Such an operation would isolate Richmond and compel its capture, argued Gibbon. Nothing came of Gibbon's prescient suggestion. See *OR* 21:812–13 and M. H. Jordan, "Gibbon's Plan for Taking Petersburg in '62," 17.

76. James King Wilkerson to "Dear Parents," December 16, 1862, James King Wilkerson Papers, Duke; *OR* 18:811–12, 816.

77. *OR* 18:807, 811–12; Weaver, *Sixty-third Virginia Infantry*, 24; Weaver, *Fifty-fourth Virginia Infantry*, 57–59, 66; Chapla, *Fiftieth Virginia Infantry*, 61–62; Alderman, *Twenty-ninth Virginia Infantry*, 21–23. The returns of December 20, 1862, reported 4,186 men present and absent in Colston's command, 2,244 present, and 2,054 effective for duty.

5. "We Are on the Eve of Great Events"

1. CCD, June 30 and August 10, 1863; Thomas W. Gaither to "Dear Father," January 15, 1863, Gaither Family Papers, UNC; Mary Harper to "Dear Sone," January 12, 1863, John Lane Stuart Papers, Duke; Alderman, *Twenty-ninth Virginia Infantry*, 31; CCM, January 24, 1863, and March 4, 1864; J. B. Wilson to "Dear Father," January 14, 1863, Heartt-Wilson Papers, UNC.

2. *Petersburg Daily Register,* April 27, 1864.

3. CCD, August 27 1863, and January 27, 1864; Joseph D. Stapp to "Dear Mother," January 29, 1864, Joseph D. Stapp Letters, VHS; Heartsill, *Fourteen Hundred and Ninety-one Days in the Confederate Army,* 124.

4. John G. Brodnax to William A. Carrington, February 9, 1863, John Grammar Brodnax Papers, Duke. The record is unclear as to the fate of Hospital Steward A. G. Bradley.

5. Prescription Records of the Second North Carolina Hospital, Petersburg, Virginia, UNC; John Grammar Brodnax Papers, February 12, 1863, Duke.

6. CCD, July 1 and September 1, 1863; Mills, *A South Carolina Family,* 92–93; Warner Lewis Baylor to Mary Anne Chappell, March 16, 1863, Baylor Family Papers, VHS; Letters of February 6, March 14, and April 26, 1863, Whitefield Family Papers, NCDAH. Whitefield's family eventually recovered his body from Petersburg in 1867.

7. Wilson, *Confederate Industry,* 104, 124, 133; CCD, August 27, 1863.

8. William Smith to the presidents and directors or owners and operators of cotton factories in the commonwealth, March 25, 1864; Lynch and Callender to Col. Munford, April 1, 1864, and John B. Dunn to Col. Munford, April 5, 1864, all in Executive Papers of William Smith (hereafter cited EPWS), Box 2, Folders 2, 5, LOV.

9. Wilson, *Confederate Industry,* 139, 194–95, 332–33n53; Beers, *Confederacy,* 382–83; Henderson, *PCW,* 57. Jackson had supervised the powder works in Petersburg in 1862.

10. John B. Wilson to "Dear Father," January 14, 1863, Heartt-Wilson Papers, UNC.

11. Wise, *Lifeline of the Confederacy,* 236–40, 245; Henderson, *PCW,* 74–75; CCD, December 7, 1863. The *City of Petersburg* ran the blockade in May 1864, delivering 178 cases containing 7,476 pairs of shoes. Wilson, *Confederate Industry,* 177.

12. Henderson, *PCW,* 62; CCD, June 30, 1863; Charles Ellis to Col. G[eorge]. W. Munford, February 18, 1863, and William T. Joynes to John Letcher, July 1, 1863, EPJL, Box 25, Folder 5; Box 27, Folder 1. The City Point Railroad had merged with the South Side Railroad in 1854 and officially became the Eastern Branch of the South Side Railroad.

13. CCM, May 3, 1864; CCD, August 10, 1863; List of the tobacco stored in Petersburg warehouses, February 29, 1864, EPWS, Box 1, Folder 6; Henderson, *PCW,* 101. Some tobacco manufacturing continued during the war for the Southern domestic market.

14. CCD, January 22, 1864. Particularly helpful with the evolution of Confederate conscription and mandatory labor and its impact on the war effort are Rable, *Confederate Republic* and Wilson, *Confederate Industry.*

15. C[harles]. O. Sanford and Lemuel Peebles to Governor [William] Smith, and reply, February 6, 9, 1864, EPWS, Box 1, Folder 5. Governor Smith's response reflected his antebellum record of Jacksonian Democracy in its more radical antibusiness form.

16. Thomas Wallace to Governor [William] Smith, January 18, 1864, EPWS, Box 1, Folder 2. The bank teller described in the text was Edward A. Goodwyn, a former cavalry officer who had resigned due to poor health.

17. There are many applications for exemption on behalf of white collar workers. See James E. Cuthbert to John Letcher, August 7, 1863, EPJL, Box 27, Folder 3; Directors of the Bank of Petersburg, January 19, 1864; Daniel Dodson, January 21, 1864, and John Kevan, January 21, 1864, all to Governor [William] Smith, EPWS, Box 4, Folder 3, Box 1, Folder 2, and Box 1, Folder 2; CCM, March 18, 1864.

18. Message of the Governor, February 25, 1864, EPWS, Box 1, Folder 6.

19. J[ohn]. B. Wilson to "Dear Father," April 13, 1864, Heartt-Wilson Papers, UNC; Wise, *Lifeline of the Confederacy*, 145–48.

20. Scarborough, *Diary of Edmund Ruffin* 2:590, 624.

21. Charles Dimmock to Elizabeth Lewis Selden, March 29, 1863, CHDP.

22. Henderson, *PCW*, 60; CCD, November 9, 1863; M. E. Massey, *Ersatz in the Confederacy*, 29.

23. A variety of sources mention prices and inflation. See, for example, Scarborough, *Diary of Edmund Ruffin* 2:574, 3:396; *Petersburg Daily Express*, April 27, 1864; John H. Claiborne to "My Dear Wife," April 17, 1864, John H. Claiborne Papers, UVA; CCD July 29, September 2, October 12, 17, 26, November 5, 7, 10, 23, 26, 29, 1863, and January 13 and April 27, 1864. The Confederate soldier earned just eleven dollars per month, increased to eighteen dollars in June 1864. Wages through the second year of the war increased in civilian pursuits an average of 55 percent, providing graphic evidence of the impact of inflation on buying power. See McPherson, *Battle Cry of Freedom*, 440, and B. I. Wiley, *Life of Johnny Reb*, 136.

24. Waugh, *Surviving the Confederacy*, 207–8; CCD, October 7, 1863; Lutz, *Prince George–Hopewell Story*, 162.

25. *Petersburg Daily Register*, January 11, 1864.

26. CCD, October 31, 1863; Scarborough, *Diary of Edmund Ruffin* 2:613; Eaton, *History of the Southern Confederacy*, 234; Henderson, *PCW*, 60.

27. Mrs. B. Callender, "Personal Recollections of the Civil War," 3, PNB; Julian Ruffin to "My dear Lottie," December 28, 1863, Ruffin-Meade Family Papers, UNC; *Petersburg Daily Express*, January 2, 1864.

28. CCM, February 2, June 3 and October 1, 1863, and February 1, March 1, 22, and April 1, 1864.

29. CCM, August 1 and October 17, 21, 1863; CCD, October 22, 31 and December 9, 1863.

30. Henderson, *PCW*, 78–79; CCD, October 31, November 13, 18 and December 4, 1863, and February 14, 15, 1864; *Petersburg Daily Express*, March 19, 1864.

31. *Petersburg Daily Register*, March 15, 1864; *Petersburg Daily Express*, March 15, 1864.

32. Henderson, *PCW*, 78; Lewis Lunsford (state agent for salt distribution in Petersburg) to John Letcher, February 5, 17, 1863, EPJL, Box 25, Folders 4, 5; CCM, October 21, 1863.

33. CCM, February 1, 9, 22 and March 1, 1864.

34. *OR*, Series 4, 2:842–45; CCD, October 3, 1863, and February 24, and March 12, 1864; Scarborough, *Diary of Edmund Ruffin* 3:352; E. M. Thomas, *Confederate Nation*, 264–65; R. C. Todd, *Confederate Finance*, 112–14, 148–52.

35. Pardon issued by Governor Letcher to Thomas Kershaw convicted of manslaughter and Mayor W. W. Townes to John Letcher, May 9, 1863, EPJL, Box 25, Folder 2 and Box 26, Folder 4; *Petersburg Daily Express*, April 14 and August 1, 1863; *Greensboro Patriot*, April 16, 1863, John Grammar Brodnax Papers, Duke; Henderson, *PCW*, 60–61. Fortunately, the hospital had been emptied for cleaning and renovation, so no patients were injured.

36. *Petersburg Daily Express*, August 1, 1863; *Petersburg Daily Register*, April 27, 1864.

37. CCD, December 25, 1863; *Petersburg Daily Register*, April 16, 1864.

38. CCM, January 5, 1863; William Joynes to Col. George W. Munford, January 8, 1864, EPWS, Box 1, Folder 1. Joynes won election to the court in the summer of 1863.

39. Scarborough, *Diary of Edmund Ruffin* 2:624–25.

40. *Petersburg Daily Register*, January 26 and April 16, 23, 1864; *Petersburg Daily Express*, April 20, 25, 1864; Henderson, *PCW*, 61.

41. Brewer, *Confederate Negro*, 88–89, 46–47.

42. John Lane Stuart to "Dear Mother," July 22, 1863, John Lane Stuart Papers, Duke.

43. CCD, September 16, 1863.

44. The legislation guiding the impressment of slaves and free blacks can be found in the EPWS, Box 1, Folder 2, along with documents outlining the specific quotas required of Virginia jurisdictions. Other relevant documents pertaining to Petersburg's quotas are in the EPJL, Box 25, Folders 1, 2, 4, 8, and the EPWS, Box 1, Folder 6. For the March 1863 request for free black labor, see J. F. Gilmer to R.E. Lee, March 9, 1863, *OR* 51: pt. 2, 682–83. The city's contribution to slaveholders is addressed in CCM, March 1, 7 and April 1, 1863.

45. *Petersburg Daily Register*, March 5, 1864. Ironically, this edition described a lecture that Rev. M. M. Henkle gave at Library Hall, explaining the "superb happiness, social and moral, of the slave over the free negro—North and South."

46. *Petersburg Daily Express*, March 21, 1863; Charles Dimmock to Elizabeth L[ewis]. Selden, August 15, 1863, CHDP; Morrill, *My Confederate Girlhood*, 52–53; Jensen, *Thirty-second Virginia Infantry*, 110.

47. *Petersburg Daily Express*, August 15, 1863; CCD, December 26, 1863, and January 11, 25, 1864; F. S. M. to Governor William Smith, February 29, 1864, Box 1, Folder 6, EPWS.

48. CCD, July 19, September 29, October 2, and December 9, 1863; Corsan, *Two Months in the Confederate States*, 250–52.

49. CCD, October 16, November 18, 1863, February 2, and April 12, 1864; *Petersburg Daily Register*, March 15, 1864.

50. Avary, *Dixie after the War*, 109.

51. Charles Dimmock to "My dear Lissie" [Elizabeth Lewis Selden], January 11, 1863, Charles Dimmock to "Dear Lissie" [Elizabeth Lewis Selden], January 21, March 15, 29, and August 15, 1863, CHDP.

52. Thomas Claybrook Elder to "My Dear Wife," March 26, 1863, Thomas Claybrook Elder Papers, VHS; CCD, December 26, 1863.

53. *Petersburg Daily Register*, January 26, 1864.

54. CCD, November 24, December 3, 1863; *Petersburg Daily Express*, June 13, 1863, and March 3, 1864; *Petersburg Daily Register*, March 3, 1864.

55. CCD, October 11, 1863, and January 15, 22, 1864; *Petersburg Daily Register,* March 3, 4, 1864; Henderson, *PCW,* 81.

56. *Petersburg Daily Express,* June 8, 1863; CCD, February 2 and April 8, 1864.

57. CCD, October 6, 14 and November 7, 1863, and January 11, 1864. President Davis returned to Richmond from the western theater in early November, passing through Petersburg on November 7. General Breckinridge was en route to Richmond from Dalton, Georgia.

58. CCD, November 18, 1863, and January 3, 1864; A. J. Leavenworth to John Letcher, December 15, 1863, EPJL, Box 28, Folder 7.

59. Results of the 1863 and 1864 municipal elections are in CCM, May 4, 1863, and May 6, 1864: East Ward: Samuel Lecture; J. T[homas]. Young; James Boisseau; Charles F. Collier; Harmon W. Siggins, and George Davison, 1863. Lecture; Young; Boisseau; Collier; Siggins and William R. Mallory, 1864. Center Ward: D'Arcy Paul; Robert P. Stainback; Charles Corling; Thomas Withers; Lemuel Peebles, and Joseph Finley McIlwaine, 1863. Paul; Stainback; Corling; J. Pinckney Williamson; Flavius Eugene Davis, and William Lafayette Watkins, 1864. South Ward: B. J. Butterworth; Alexander Donnan; Wesley Grigg; Thomas W. Rowlett; Robert A. Martin, and Benjamin Boisseau Vaughan, 1863 and 1864. West Ward: W. L. Lancaster; William R. Johnson; David F. May; William A. Dudley; David G. Potts, and Robert Leslie, 1863. Lancaster; Johnson; William E. Hinton; Robert A. Young; F. D. Williamson, and Z. D. Mitchell, 1864.

60. CCM, May 4, 1863, May 6 and June 1, 1864.

61. Governor's Proclamation announcing the resignation of Thomas S. Gholson as Judge of the Second Circuit, May 26, 1863, and Governor's Proclamation declaring Joynes elected Judge of Second Judicial Court, July 18, 1863, EPJL, Box 26, Folder 4, and Box 27, Folder 1.

62. The correspondence from the Colliers to the governor can be found in EPJL, Box 26, Folders 4, 7. For background on the Colliers, the Gholsons, and the election, see Current, *Encyclopedia of the Confederacy* 1:367–68, 2:684. Rable, *Confederate Republic,* discusses the development of pro- and anti-Davis political factions in the Confederacy.

63. Rable, *Confederate Republic,* 218–19. George Wythe Munford was William Smith's primary rival.

64. For applications regarding bank directorships in 1863 and 1864, see EPJL, Box 25, Folder 1, 2, and EPWS, Box 1, Folder 1, 2. Examples of appeals for appointments as inspector of tobacco can be found in EPJL, Box 25, Folder 1, Box 27, Folder 6, Box 28, Folder 7. Petersburgers also contacted John Letcher and William Smith seeking commissions as notaries public. See EPJL, Box 26, Folder 2 and EPWS, Box 2, Folder 6.

65. CCD, August 6, July 11, June 28, 1863; James Seddon to John Letcher, August 3, 1863, and Governor's Proclamation of June 13, 1863, EPJL, Box 27, Folder 3, and Box 26, Folder 7.

66. The statistics regarding the draft in the Fourth Congressional District are in *Petersburg Daily Express,* June 8, 1863. Some of the men who had provided substitutes and were now liable for military service challenged the legality of the measure. Judge Joynes heard one such case shortly after he assumed the bench. See CCD, August 14, 1863.

67. *Army and Navy Messenger* qtd. in Silver, *Confederate Morale and Church Propaganda,* 52–53.

68. Rev. W[illiam]. H[enry]. Wheelwright to Governor William Smith, April 16, 1864, EPWS, Box 2, Folder 6.

69. CCD, July 7, September 5, 24, 26, and November 28, 1863; Henderson, *PCW,* 63–66.

70. John H. Claiborne to "My Dear Wife," April 25 and May 3, 1864, John H. Claiborne Papers, UVA; CCD, April 29, 1864. For discussions of Confederate morale on the eve of the 1864 campaigns, see McPherson, *Battle Cry of Freedom*, 718–19 and Power, *Lee's Miserables*, 1–13.

6. "I Must Confess That I Am More Concerned for Petersburg Than for Richmond"

1. *OR* 18:823–24, 865. French's manpower present for duty numbered less than twenty-seven thousand. In early January Major General John G. Foster, Union commander in New Bern, commanded a total of twenty-four thousand soldiers, much fewer than French believed, leaving the two sides, counting the Federals at Suffolk, about evenly matched. See Barrett, *Civil War in North Carolina*, 150–52.

2. *OR* 51: pt. 2, 667. Colston approved Pryor's disposition of troops along the Blackwater River line before returning to Petersburg.

3. January 8, 9, 10, 1863, EPJL, Box 25, Folder 1; *OR* 18:834–36; Scarborough, *Diary of Edmund Ruffin* 2:537. The counties subject to the call included Greensville, Dinwiddie, Brunswick, Lunenburg, Mecklenburg, Halifax, Charlotte, Pittsylvania, Henry, Patrick, Franklin, Nottoway, Prince Edward, and Campbell.

4. Henderson, *PCW*, 59; Charles Collier to James Seddon, March 12, 1863, *OR* 51: pt. 2, 684–85; Special Orders Number 76, *OR* 51: pt. 2, 690.

5. Colonel Jeremy F. Gilmer to Governor Letcher, January 12, 1863, and to Secretary of War James Seddon, January 13, 1863, EPJL, Box 25, Folders 1, 2. See chapter 5 for details on the laws accelerating the impressment of black labor. For slave owner resistance to impressment, see Rable, *Confederate Republic*, 193.

6. Special Orders of January 15, 25, 1863, Henry Thweatt Owen Papers, LOV; G. L. Sherwood, *Mathews Light Artillery, Penick's Pittsylvania Artillery, Young's Halifax Artillery, and Johnson's Jackson Flying Artillery*, 57.

7. Wills, *War Hits Home*, 86–94. Pryor's engagement was called the battle of Kelly's Store or Deserted House.

8. Hill qtd. in Bridges, *Lee's Maverick General*, 162–63. The disgruntled Hill had privately expressed his intent to resign as early as November 1862. He suffered equally from chronic spinal problems and perceived slights from the press for his performance in the Maryland campaign.

9. Bridges, *Lee's Maverick General*, 163–64; Freeman, *Lee's Lieutenants* 2:421–22; James Seddon to Zebulon Vance, January 17, 1863, Daniel Harvey Hill Papers, NCDAH.

10. Bridges, *Lee's Maverick General*, 164–65; Freeman, *Lee's Lieutenants* 2:422–24; *OR* 18:861. Brigadier General Robert Ransom communicated with Lee.

11. Bridges, *Lee's Maverick General*, 164–66; Freeman, *Lee's Lieutenants* 2:424–27; *OR* 18:872; French, *Two Wars*, 154–55. Hill respected Gustavus Smith and regretted being removed from his command. Smith served in Charleston as a volunteer aide to General Beauregard, an officer always glad to welcome any enemy of Jefferson Davis.

12. *OR* 18:883–84, 889, 895–96. Complete summaries of the strategic context prompting Longstreet's move to Petersburg can be found in Freeman, *Lee's Lieutenants* 2:467–69; Wert, *General James Longstreet*, 228–29; and Sanger and Hay, *James Longstreet*, 118–20. Inexplicably, Longstreet's new department omitted the word "Southern" in referring to the Virginia portion of his military jurisdiction. Although two of Longstreet's biographers see in this evidence of Longstreet's ambition to supersede Lee in command of all the Old Dominion, the name change was probably more superficial than sinister. See Eckenrode and Conrad, *James Longstreet*, 160.

13. Wills, *War Hits Home*, 108–10; Sanger and Hay, *James Longstreet*, 120–24; Wert, *General James Longstreet*, 229–31; *OR* 18:953. General Orders Number 34 stated that Elzey's command headquartered in Richmond was responsible for Richmond's defense north of the James River, French's Department of Southern Virginia with headquarters "at some central point near Blackwater [River]" controlled "all that portion of Virginia south of the James River and east of the county of Powhatan," and Hill's Department of North Carolina headquartered in Goldsboro retained jurisdiction over the Tarheel State. The location of Longstreet's headquarters was left to the commander's discretion.

14. *OR* 18:900, 915–17; Special Orders dated March 6, 7, 25, 1863, Henry Thweatt Owen Papers, LOV.

15. Wallace, *Seventeenth Virginia Infantry*, 44–45; Wallace, *First Virginia Infantry*, 39. Richard B. Garnett's and James L. Kemper's Brigades would be detached from Pickett's Division to participate in an offensive in North Carolina. See L. J. Gordon, *General George E. Pickett in Life and Legend*, 102.

16. Records of the Military Court, Longstreet's Corps, Docket of the Military Court of the Department of Virginia and North Carolina, Confederate States of America Collection, MOC.

17. *Savannah* (Ga.) *Republican*, April 8, 1863; Thomas J. Goree to "My dearest Mother" [Sarah Williams Kittrell Goree], March 13, 1863, in Goree, *Thomas Jewett Goree Letters*, 179.

18. Charles Dimmock to Elizabeth Lewis Selden, March 8, 1863, CHDP. Dimmock proposed marriage in this letter.

19. The complex strategic thinking driving Longstreet's offensives are beyond the scope of this narrative. Interested readers should consult Freeman, *Lee's Lieutenants* 2:473–82; Wills, *War Hits Home*, 111–30; Wert, *General James Longstreet*, 231–34; and Barrett, *Civil War in North Carolina*, 149–56, from which I developed this paragraph. Jenkins arrived on the Blackwater Line on March 9 and took command. Pryor petulantly resigned his commission on being superseded first by Colston and then by Jenkins. Colston's brigade returned to southwestern Virginia and its commander transferred to the Army of Northern Virginia, assuming command of a division in Jackson's corps.

20. Account qtd. in Wert, *General James Longstreet*, 234. For Longstreet's departure, see *OR* 18:975. French's frame of mind and Hill's activities at New Bern and Washington, North Carolina, are addressed in Freeman, *Lee's Lieutenants* 2:482, 474–79. Longstreet did not explain his decision to leave French out of the Suffolk operation, but Freeman infers that Longstreet favored Jenkins over French, which is the explanation that French offered. See Freeman, *Lee's Lieutenants* 2:481, and French, *Two Wars*, 160.

21. For a complete history of the Suffolk campaign, see, Cormier, *Siege of Suffolk*. Briefer summaries are available in Wills, *War Hits Home*, 131–84, Wert, *General James Longstreet*, 234–41, and Freeman, *Lee's Lieutenants* 2:482–94. Longstreet and his staff returned to Petersburg on the night of May 4 and left for Richmond by train at 7:00 PM May 5. See Osmun Latrobe, Diary, May 5, 1863, VHS.

22. *OR* 18:978, 51: pt. 2, 723; Jensen, *Thirty-second Virginia Infantry*, 109; Tidwell, *Come Retribution*, 100.

23. *Petersburg Daily Express*, April 8, 1863. The Hargrave Blues are misidentified as the Hargrove Blues in the *Official Records*. Along with the Confederate Guard, they became a part of the Ninth Virginia Infantry in November 1863. See Wallace, *Guide to Virginia Military Organizations, 1861–1865*, 92, 96.

24. Heartsill, *Fourteen Hundred and Ninty-one Days in the Confederate Army*, 122–25.

25. There are many sources documenting Longstreet's transit through Petersburg in early May. See in particular Divine, *Eighth Virginia Infantry*, 19, from which I took the quotation; Wallace, *Third Virginia Infantry*, 35; Stocker, *From Huntsville to Appomattox*, 94; Manarin, *Fifteenth Virginia Infantry*, 43; and *OR* 51: pt. 2, 701, 703.

26. *OR* 51: pt. 2, 705, 718, 1056, 1067.

27. *OR* 18:1057, 1066; James W. Albright, Diary, May 24, 1863, VHS.

28. *OR* 18:1077; 51: pt. 2, 716; 25: pt. 2, 827; Freeman, *Lee's Lieutenants* 2:699. Ransom's division included the brigades of Micah Jenkins and Joseph R. Davis, numbering between them nearly six thousand men. Robert Ransom received promotion to major general effective May 26, 1863. See *OR* 18:1067. French's transfer to Mississippi had been contemplated as early as March 1. See French, *Two Wars*, 159.

29. Charles Dimmock to Elizabeth Lewis Selden, June 1, 1863, CHDP.

30. *OR* 18: 1076–77, 1086; D. H. Hill to "My Dear Wife," June 23, 1863, Daniel Harvey Hill Papers, NCDAH; Bridges, *Lee's Maverick General*, 181–88; Freeman, *Lee's Lieutenants* 2:700. Daniel's Brigade went to Lee in exchange for a brigade of Georgians under Brigadier General Alfred H. Colquitt. Cooke's Brigade went to Richmond in early June.

31. *OR* 27: pt. 3, 911; Bridges, *Lee's Maverick General*, 189–90.

32. *OR* 27: pt. 3, 917, 936, 941. Other correspondence relating to the deployment of Hill's forces can be found in *OR* 27: pt. 3, 933–40.

33. D. H. Hill to "My Dear Wife," June 23, 1863, Daniel Harvey Hill Papers, NCDAH; Pearce, *Diary of Captain Henry A. Chambers*, 117; James W. Albright, Diary, June 12, 1863, VHS; Henry Brantingham and W. H. S. Burgwyn, Diary, June 7, 1863, NCDAH.

34. D. H. Hill to "My dear precious old wife," June 25, 1863, Daniel Harvey Hill Papers, NCDAH; *OR* 27: pt. 3, 964–65, 968, 980, 412, 945; Special Orders Number 156, July 12, 1863, D. H. Hill Papers, LOV; Bridges, *Lee's Maverick General*, 192–93. The command situation in Richmond became complicated because Elzey did not leave to join the Army of Northern Virginia. Hill directed the mobile troops defending Richmond while Elzey retained control of the city's garrison.

35. *OR* 51: pt. 2, 724, 27: pt. 3, 972, 990, 1003; Special Orders Number 165, D. H. Hill Papers, LOV; Bridges, *Lee's Maverick General*, 193–94.

36. For a brief sketch of Ransom's career, see Current, *Encyclopedia of the Confederacy* 3:1307–8; *OR* 27: pt. 3, 1001, 1005, 1006. Ransom would report through Elzey, who had resumed command of the Department of Richmond, as long as he was physically in the Richmond area.

37. *OR* 27: pt. 3, 1000–1001; Holland, *Twenty-fourth Virginia Cavalry*, 47; Jensen, *Thirty-second Virginia Infantry*, 110–11.

38. CCD, July 12–14, 1863; CCM, July 14, 1863; James W. Albright, Diary, July 12, 1863, VHS; *OR* 27: pt. 3, 1065.

39. *OR* 27: pt. 3, 1065; CCD, July 19, 1863; Edward Phifer to "My Dear Mother," July 14, 21, 1863, Phifer Family Papers, UNC.

40. *OR* 27: pt. 3, 1004; Charles Dimmock to Elizabeth Lewis Selden, July 26, 1863, CHDP; Henderson, *PCW*, 62–63.

41. *OR* 27: pt. 3, 1044; CCD, July 27, 28, 1863; *OR, Supplement* pt. III, 3:247, pt. II, 64:623; Coker, *History of Company G, Ninth S.S. Regiment*, 126.

42. *OR* 27: pt. 3, 1053–54, 51: pt. 2, 745; CCD, August 1, 1863; Marlow, *Matt W. Ransom*, 80–83. Ransom's engagement that saved the bridge at Weldon was styled the battle of Boone's Mill.

43. D. H. Hill to Samuel Cooper, August 13, 1863, George Henry Venable Papers, VHS; Haskell, "Reminiscences of the Confederate War, 1861–1865," 89, John Cheeves

Haskell Papers, UNC; Samuel H. Walkup, Diary, July 1, 1863, Samuel H. Walkup Papers, UNC. For examples of the praise bestowed on Jenkins by superior officers, see Current, *Encyclopedia of the Confederacy* 2:844. Jenkins's Brigade consisted of the First South Carolina Volunteers, Second South Carolina Rifles, Fifth South Carolina Infantry, Sixth South Carolina Infantry, Hampton Legion, and Palmetto Sharpshooters.

44. James A. Seddon to John Letcher, August 3, 1863, EPJL, Box 27, Folder 3; Warner Lewis Baylor to "My dearest Mary," August 5, 1863, Baylor Family Papers, VHS.

45. CCD, August 7, 8, 17, 1863; *OR* 29: pt. 2, 649; Henderson, *PCW,* 69.

46. William E. Hardy to "Dear Father," August 7, 1863, William E. Hardy Papers, Duke; CCD, August 4, 1863; Thomas Rowland to "My Dear Lizzie," August 6, 1863, Thomas Rowland Papers, MOC.

47. CCD, August 20, 1863; *OR* 29: pt. 2, 669; Micah Jenkins to "My dear Friend" [Thomas J. Goree], August 10, 1863, Goree, *Thomas Jewett Goree Letters,* 191. Jefferson Davis requested on August 22 that 5,340 slaves be impressed to finish the fortifications around Richmond and Petersburg. See Davis to John Letcher, EPJL, Box 27, Folder 3.

48. *OR* 29: pt. 2, 706. For additional information on the transfer of Longstreet's corps to the West, see Freeman, *Lee's Lieutenants* 3:217–28. Ransom's Brigade remained in North Carolina.

49. CCD, September 10, 1863; Silver, *Life for the Confederacy as Recorded in the Pocket Diaries of Pvt. Robert A. Moore,* 166; Freeman, *Lee's Lieutenants* 3:227–28; Henderson, *PCW,* 70.

50. CCD, September 10, 12, 14, 1863; Henry A. Wise to "My dear Wife," September 15, 1863, Wise Family Papers, VHS.

51. Collins, *Forty-sixth Virginia Infantry,* 45.

52. CCD, September 13, 1863; *OR* 29: pt. 2, 713; Petersburg newspaper qtd. in Jensen, *Thirty-second Virginia Infantry,* 112. Wise's Brigade did not go to Georgia with Longstreet but to Charleston, South Carolina, instead.

53. L. J. Gordon, *General George E. Pickett in Life and Legend,* 123, passim; CCD, September 15, 1863; Charles Dimmock to Elizabeth Lewis Selden, September 20, 1863, CHDP; Henderson, *PCW,* 70–71. More details regarding the wedding are provided in Pickett, *Pickett and His Men,* 320–21, but Mrs. Pickett's postwar accounts are fraught with fabrications and too unreliable to use without caution and corroboration. Another questionable source, Inman, *Soldier of the South,* 82, offers the detail that the Petersburg businessman Reuben Ragland arranged the special train that carried the Picketts to Richmond.

54. *OR* 51: pt. 2, 769, 29: pt. 2, 746; Henderson, *PCW,* 71; J. G. Scott and Wyatt, *Petersburg's Story,* 173; Pickett, *Pickett and His Men,* 343–44; Robert Taylor Scott to "My Darling Fan," September 30, 1863, Keith Family Papers, VHS. Whiting assumed command of the defenses of Wilmington.

55. CCD, September 21, 1863; *OR* 29: pt. 2, 765, 30: pt. 2, 741; Henderson, *PCW,* 71.

56. CCD, September 19, 25, 1863; Henry Thweatt Owen to "My dear Wife," September 27, 1863, Henry Thweatt Papers, LOV; W. C. Sherwood and Nicholas, *Amherst Artillery, Albemarle Artillery, and Sturdivant's Battery,* 190; James W. Albright, Diary, September 16, 1863, VHS. Brigadier General Montgomery Corse's Brigade, once a part of Pickett's Division but detached for the protection of Richmond and not present at Gettysburg, marched to Petersburg on September 13 but departed the next day by rail for southwest Virginia and was not present when Pickett assumed command of the city.

57. Robert Taylor Scott to "My dearest Fan," October 7, 1863, Keith Family Papers, VHS; *OR* 51: pt. 2, 771.

58. Gregory, *Thirty-eighth Virginia Infantry*, 45; Sublett, *Fifty-seventh Virginia Infantry*, 33; Gregory, *Fifty-third Virginia Infantry and Fifth Battalion Virginia Infantry*, 66–67; Trask, *Ninth Virginia Infantry*, 28–29; Manarin, *Fifteenth Virginia Infantry*, 50; Alderman, *Twenty-ninth Virginia Infantry*, 35.

59. James W. Albright, Diary, October 2, 1863, VHS. Albright would marry Mattie on October 19, as she was about to return to her home in Isle of Wight County. CCD, September 18 and October 15, 20, 23, 1863; Sanders, *Dear Hattie*, 78.

60. CCD, September 27, 1863; Wallace, *Guide to Virginia Military Organizations, 1861–1865*, 125; James F. Milligan to George Pickett, October 10, 1863, James Milligan's Compiled Service Record, copy provided by Thomas M. DiGiuseppe; Henderson, *PCW*, 71–73. Batte's battalion included Company A under Captain William E. Hinton, organized September 9, 1863; Company B under Captain Thomas W. Branch, organized September 11, 1863; and Company C under Captain A. B. Morrison, organized October 13, 1863.

61. Relevant correspondence among Pickett, his subordinates, and the War Department during November can be found in *OR* 29: pt. 2, 827–30, 834, 847.

62. *OR* 29: pt. 2, 847–48, 850–51, 853.

63. For an account of Pickett's carriage accident, see CCD, November 14, 1863.

64. CCD, December 11, 14, 15, 1863. Pickett's departmental returns for December 31, 1863, are in *OR* 29: pt. 2, 906–7. The record is unclear as to why Clingman came to Petersburg in December rather than Ransom, as Ransom's men were engaged in repelling minor raids in eastern North Carolina at the time. Pickett probably thought it best not to disturb Ransom's veterans, familiar as they were with the region, and simply brought Clingman north instead.

65. Pickett to Seddon, December 18, 1863, William J. Clarke Papers, UNC; *OR* 29: pt. 2, 897; Clark, *Histories of the Several Regiments and Battalions from North Carolina* 1:395–96.

66. David W. Pipes, Memoir, Historic New Orleans Collection; Sanders, *Dear Hattie*, 78, 83; Owen, *In Camp and Battle with the Washington Artillery*, 308–9.

67. James Thomas Perry, Diary, January 16, 25–28 and February 7, 1864, James Thomas Perry Papers, VHS; CCD, January 22 and February 15, 1864; Brewer, *Confederate Negro*, 21; Henderson, *PCW*, 80.

68. *OR* 33:1067–68, 1070–74; CCD, January 9, 1864; Gunn, *Twenty-fourth Virginia Infantry*, 49; Wallace, *Third Virginia Infantry*, 42. Kemper had been captured on July 3 at Gettysburg.

69. *OR* 33:1090–91; Thrush H. Massey to "Dear Brother and Sister," January 16, 1864, Fatima Massey Williams Papers, UNC.

70. Lee to Jefferson Davis, January 2, 1864, Dowdey and Manarin, *Wartime Papers of R. E. Lee*, 646–47; *OR* 33:1102–1104; CCD, January 30, 1864; Barrett, *Civil War in North Carolina*, 202–3; J. I. Robertson, *Eighteenth Virginia Infantry*, 25–26; Wallace, *Seventeenth Virginia Infantry*, 56; R. K. Krick, *Thirtieth Virginia Infantry*, 45; Manarin, *Fifteenth Virginia Infantry*, 52–53; Barefoot, *General Robert F. Hoke*, 108–10; Schiller, *Captain's War*, 118. New Bern was often spelled "New Berne."

71. Barrett, *Civil War in North Carolina*, 202–12; L. J. Gordon, *General George E. Pickett in Life and Legend*, 129, 135; *OR* 33:1151.

72. Schiller, *Captain's War*, 121–24; Pearce, *Diary of Captain Henry A. Chambers*, 176; Robert Taylor Scott to "My Dear Fan," February 26, 1864, Keith Family Papers, VHS.

73. *OR* 33:100, 1201–2, 51: pt. 2, 849–50; Schiller, *Captain's War*, 123. Milligan received promotion to major effective July 17, 1863.

74. *OR* 33:1206–10; CCD, March 5, 1864; Joseph D. Stapp to "Dear Mother," March 6, 1864, Joseph D. Stapp Letters, VHS; Henderson, *PCW*, 82. On February 17, 1864, the Confederate Congress passed an act that extended the age of conscription to include all white men between the ages of seventeen and fifty. Those seventeen and eighteen and older than forty-five were to constitute the Reserves. See Wallace, *Guide to Virginia Military Organizations, 1861–1865,* 218.

75. Schiller, *Captain's War,* 128, 132; *OR* 33:1231–32; CCD, March 28, 1864. President Davis had removed the unpopular Bragg from command of the Army of Tennessee in December 1863 following Bragg's disastrous defeat at Chattanooga in November.

76. *OR* 51: pt. 2, 857; L. J. Gordon, *General George E. Pickett in Life and Legend,* 135.

77. *OR* 33:1274, 51: pt. 2, 864–65. The texts of the scouting reports can be reviewed in *OR* 51: pt. 2, 857–63. Summaries of the situation are in L. J. Gordon, *General George E. Pickett in Life and Legend,* 136, and W. G. Robertson, *Back Door to Richmond,* 44–46.

78. CCD, April 9, 1964; *OR* 33:1292, 1307–1308; L. J. Gordon, *General George E. Pickett in Life and Legend,* 136–37.

79. L. J. Gordon, *General George E. Pickett in Life and Legend,* 137; *OR* 36: pt. 2, 950.

7. "The Hurly Burly Produced by the Descent of the Yankees"

1. Schiller, *Captain's War,* 136; John H. Claiborne to "My dear Wife," April 24, 1864, John H. Claiborne Papers, UVA.

2. CCD, April 25, 1864; W. G. Robertson, *Back Door to Richmond,* 32–33; *OR* 33:957–58.

3. *Petersburg Daily Register,* April 27, 1864; A. H. Massey to "Dear Sister," April 28, 1864, Fatima Massey Williams Papers, UNC; *Richmond Daily Enquirer,* May 3, 1864. The hospitals operating in Petersburg at this time included the Wayside Hospital, Surgeon M. P. Scott in charge; the South Carolina Hospital, which served soldiers from South Carolina, Alabama, Mississippi, and Louisiana, Surgeon Francis P. Porcher in charge; the Virginia Hospital, Surgeon J. H. Pottenger in charge; the Confederate Hospital, which served soldiers from Georgia and Texas, Surgeon Smith in charge; the Poplar Lawn Hospital, which served North Carolina soldiers, Surgeon R. P. Page in charge; the North Carolina Hospital, Surgeon John G. Brodnax in charge; and the General or Fair Grounds Hospital, used primarily for paroled Confederate prisoners of war, Surgeon John B. Strachan in charge.

4. *Petersburg Daily Express,* May 4, 1864; Thomas Branch to William Smith, May 31, 1864, EPWS, Box 3, Folder 3.

5. CCD, May 2, 5, 1864; *Petersburg Daily Express,* May 4, 1864. Approximately four hundred militiamen mustered at Anderson Seminary on May 4 in response to this requirement.

6. The best background to the Bermuda Hundred campaign is in W. G. Robertson, *Back Door to Richmond,* 13–54. One historian of this phase of the war described Benjamin Butler as "the only senior officer in the Virginia theater more star-crossed and self-destructive than George Pickett" (Richard Selcer to the author via e-mail, July 5, 2004).

7. *OR* 36: pt. 2, 955–58; W. G. Robertson, *Back Door to Richmond,* 58–62, 65–66; Henderson, *PCW,* 103; L. J. Gordon, "Generalship of George E. Pickett after the Battle of Gettysburg," 170–71.

8. CCD, May 5, 1864; Charles Campbell, Diary, May 5, 1864, Charles Campbell Papers, Duke; Owen, *In Camp and Battle with the Washington Artillery,* 310; Weaver, *Virginia Home Guards,* 190–92; *OR* 36: pt. 2, 957; W. G. Robertson, *Back Door to Richmond,* 66–67. Campbell attached himself to Company B of the Second Class Militia and received

an assignment to guard Confederate prisoners confined in a filthy store on Market Street near the river, rather than marching east to the front lines.

9. W. G. Robertson, *Back Door to Richmond*, 67–68; *OR* 51: pt. 2, 891, 36: pt. 2, 960; Bridges, *Lee's Maverick General*, 262. Beauregard officially divided his Department of North Carolina and Southern Virginia into three districts on May 5, naming Petersburg as headquarters for the First Military District. He did not specify a commander for the First District in these General Orders Number 3, although he did name Robert Hoke and Chase Whiting commanders of the Second and Third Districts, respectively. Pickett was under orders to report to his division at Hanover Junction and remained in Petersburg only because of the current military emergency. See *OR* 51: pt. 2, 891–92.

10. W. G. Robertson, *Back Door to Richmond*, 69–70; Schiller, *Captain's War*, 139; Henderson, *PCW*, 103.

11. W. G. Robertson, *Back Door to Richmond*, 76–78; James Thomas Perry, Diary, May 6, 1864, James Thomas Perry Papers, VHS.

12. CCM, May 6, 1864; W. G. Robertson, *Back Door to Richmond*, 78. The vote was eleven to two in favor, with one abstention. Mrs. Pickett did her part in the emergency by opening her Petersburg home to frightened townspeople.

13. *Petersburg Daily Express*, May 7, 1864, original emphasis; W. G. Robertson, *Back Door to Richmond*, 79–83.

14. For a detailed description of these military events, see W. G. Robertson, *Back Door to Richmond*, 83–91, 95–107, and Schiller, *Bermuda Hundred Campaign*, 85–98, 105–15. August V. Kautz's account of his raid is in "Operations South of the James," 534.

15. Pickett, *Pickett and His Men*, 344; W. G. Robertson, *Back Door to Richmond*, 90, 109; *OR* 51: pt. 2, 903; Schiller, *Captain's War*, 141. Beauregard's biographer, T. Harry Williams, wondered if the general's desire to "avoid command responsibility" explained his tardy departure for Petersburg. Steven E. Woodworth considered Beauregard's absence "vintage" behavior, typical of that officer's pattern of citing illness to avoid crucial situations. Williams, *Napoleon in Gray*, 211; Woodworth, "General P. G. T. Beauregard and the Bermuda Hundred Campaign," 206.

16. CCD, May 8, 1864; Fletcher Archer to "My Dear Wife," May 8, 1864, Fletcher Archer Letters (hereafter cited FAL), City of Petersburg.

17. Hagood, *Memoirs of the War of Secession*, 228–30. For detailed descriptions of the fighting on May 9, see W. G. Robertson, *Back Door to Richmond*, 111–16; Schiller, *Bermuda Hundred Campaign*, 117–50; and Longacre, *Army of Amateurs*, 81–84.

18. *OR* 36: pt. 2, 587, 593–94; W. G. Robertson, *Back Door to Richmond*, 119–20; Longacre, *Army of Amateurs*, 81–82.

19. *OR* 51: pt. 2, 906, 915; John H. Claiborne to "My Dear Wife," May 14, 1864, John H. Claiborne Papers, UVA; Elliott qtd. in Barefoot, *General Robert F. Hoke*, 172; Benjamin Jones to "My Dear Friend," May 12, 1864, B. W. Jones, *Under the Stars and Bars*, 176; Fletcher Archer to "My Dearest Wife," May 10, 1864, FAL; W. G. Robertson, *Back Door to Richmond*, 122. Kautz's men destroyed three sections of the Petersburg Railroad: at Stony Creek, the Nottoway River bridge, and near Jarratt's depot. Work crews began to repair the damage as soon as the blue-clad cavalry departed. The initial Confederate reinforcements left their heavy baggage at Jarratt's, crossed the streams on the ruins of the bridges or by fording, and met trains sent from Petersburg to Stony Creek. See W. G. Robertson, *Back Door to Richmond*, 104.

20. *OR* 36: pt. 2, 986; Henry Alexander Carrington to "My Beloved Wife," May 12, 1864, Carrington Family Papers, VHS; Woodworth, "General P. G. T. Beauregard and the Bermuda Hundred Campaign," 210–11; L. J. Gordon, *General George E. Pickett in Life*

and Legend, 139; W. G. Robertson, *Back Door to Richmond,* 128; Schiller, *Bermuda Hundred Campaign,* 161.

21. *Petersburg Daily Register,* May 13, 1864; *Petersburg Daily Express,* May 13, 1864; John H. Claiborne to "My Dear Wife," May 14, 1864, John H. Claiborne Papers, UVA.

22. Special Orders Number 5, May 10, 1864, *OR 36:* pt. 2, 987; Henry Wise to "My dear Wife," May 11, 1864, Wise Family Papers, VHS.

23. *OR 51:* pt. 2, 921; W. G. Robertson, *Back Door to Richmond,* 139–40; Freeman, *Lee's Lieutenants* 3:474. The two infantry brigades belonged to Brigadier Generals Alfred Colquitt and James G. Martin. Robert Ransom had returned to Virginia in late April from duty in West Virginia and eastern Tennessee and served as the commander of the Department of Richmond.

24. This condensed account of the complicated strategic events between May 11 and 15 is drawn from W. G. Robertson, *Back Door to Richmond,* 139–53; Woodworth, "General P. G. T. Beauregard and the Bermuda Hundred Campaign," 210–19, and Freeman, *Lee's Lieutenants* 3:478–85. Beauregard's plans in his own words can be found in *OR 36:* pt. 2, 200–201.

25. John H. Claiborne to "My dear Wife," May 16, 1864, John H. Claiborne Papers, UVA. Information on the fighting at Drewry's Bluff and Whiting's misadventures on May 16 are in W. G. Robertson, *Back Door to Richmond,* 153–215, Woodworth, "General P. G. T. Beauregard and the Bermuda Hundred Campaign," 221–28; Williams, *Napoleon in Gray,* 218–20; Schiller, *Bermuda Hundred Campaign,* 228–92; and Freeman, *Lee's Lieutenants* 3:486–92. For Whiting's assessment of the situation and his belief that Petersburg was the Federals' true strategic objective, see *OR 36:* pt. 2, 1005–6.

26. John H. Claiborne to "My Dear Wife," May 18, 1864, John H. Claiborne Papers, UVA; *OR 51:* pt. 2, 939, 36: pt. 3, 811; D. H. Hill to "My Dear Wife," May 22, 1864, Daniel Harvey Hill Papers, NCDAH; W. G. Robertson, *Back Door to Richmond,* 216–25; Freeman, *Lee's Lieutenants* 3:492–95. Generals Wise and James Martin were the officers who refused to serve under Whiting. Whiting had acknowledged their dissatisfaction by turning command over to Hill on the morning of May 17, "deeming that harmony of action was to be preferred at that time to any personal consideration, and feeling . . . physically unfit for action" (Whiting's report in *OR 36:* pt. 2, 258–59).

27. *Petersburg Daily Register,* May 18, 1864; Henry A. Wise to "My beloved wife," May 27, 1864, Wise Family Papers, VHS. The Confederates had repaired damage to the Petersburg Railroad by May 17.

28. Henderson, *PCW,* 107–8; M. S. Beckwith, "Reminiscences," 12, VHS; Scarborough, *Diary of Edmund Ruffin* 3:435.

29. *Petersburg Daily Express,* May 20, 21, 1864.

30. Schiller, *Captain's War,* 145; Giles Buckner Cooke, Diary, June 5, 8, 1864, Giles Buckner Cooke Papers, VHS; James W. Albright, Diary, June 7, 1864, VHS; *Petersburg Daily Express,* May 26, 1864; *Petersburg Daily Register,* June 6, 1864.

31. David J. Logan to "My Dear Wife," June 8, 1864, qtd. in S. N. Thomas and Silverman, *"Rising Star of Promise",* 164–65; *Petersburg Daily Express,* May 31, 1864; *Petersburg Daily Register,* June 1, 1864; CCM, June 8, 1864. The arrest statistics were 211 white males, 12 white females, 189 male slaves, 63 female slaves, 70 free black men, and 55 free black women. Petersburg maintained a police force of fifteen officers led by Captain Robert C. Donnan.

32. *OR 36:* pt. 3, 818–19, 821, 833, 835, 865; Bridges, *Lee's Maverick General,* 264; Cummings, *Yankee Quaker Confederate General,* 286–88; Henderson, *PCW,* 108. Wise's

biographer wrote of the general's elevation to district commander that "the command sounded imposing, although the intention may again have been to remove him from the field." Simpson, *Good Southerner*, 278.

33. *OR* 36: pt. 2, 971–72, 1012; Wallace, *Guide to Virginia Military Organizations, 1861–1865*, 218, 221, 226; Henderson, *PCW*, 108–9.

34. Anthony M. Keiley to William Smith, June 1, 1864, EPWS, Box 3, Folder 3.

35. *OR* 36, pt. 3, 286. For more detail on Butler's plans, Beauregard's responses, and the shifting of troops north of the James, see W. G. Robertson, *Back Door to Richmond*, 230–35 and Schiller, *Bermuda Hundred Campaign*, 317–22. For Butler's political aspirations, see Longacre, *Army of Amateurs*, 126. As evidence of the need for Confederate manpower at this time, Dr. Claiborne wrote one of his Petersburg surgeons on June 1, "I have been instructed to have all convalescents and slightly wounded men in Hospitals at this post examined without delay and to return to their commands all able to bear arms" (Claiborne to John G. Brodnax, June 1, 1864, John Grammar Brodnax Papers, Duke).

36. *Petersburg Daily Register*, June 2, 1864.

37. See W. G. Robertson, *Back Door to Richmond*, 237–39, W. G. Robertson, *Battle of Old Men and Young Boys*, 17–24, and Longacre, *Army of Amateurs*, 125–30 for details regarding Butler's plans.

38. *OR* 36: pt. 2, 277. The best tactical account of the fighting on June 9 is W. G. Robertson, *Battle of Old Men and Young Boys*. See 19–24 for a summary of Butler's preparations for the attack. Another good overview is Longacre, *Army of Amateurs*, 125–39.

39. Confederate deployments are summarized in W. G. Robertson, *Battle of Old Men and Young Boys*, 15–16. General R. E. Colston wrote that the Dimmock Line had so deteriorated from a lack of maintenance that "a horseman could ride over [it] without the least difficulty almost everywhere" ("Repelling the First Assault on Petersburg," 535). Colston wrote that Wise assigned him to "the provisional command of the post of Petersburg" but Robertson says that Colston "had no responsibility for defending anything . . . and had not yet received orders" for a new assignment. It is probable that Colston's authority in Petersburg was unofficial and conveyed to him casually by Wise. See Colston, "Repelling the First Assault on Petersburg," 535, and W. G. Robertson, *Battle of Old Men and Young Boys*, 35.

40. W. G. Robertson, *Battle of Old Men and Young Boys*, 19–33.

41. Keiley, *Prisoner of War*, 6–7; A. B. Pryor, "Child's Recollections of War," 54; W. A. Todd, "Reminiscences," 224, UNC; W. G. Robertson, *Battle of Old Men and Young Boys*, 34–37; Claiborne, *Seventy-five Years in Old Virginia*, 217; Waugh, *Surviving the Confederacy*, 213–14.

42. *OR* 36: pt. 2, 317, pt. 3, 719; W. G. Robertson, *Battle of Old Men and Young Boys*, 40–48.

43. *OR* 36: pt. 2, 308, pt. 3, 719; Archer, "Defense of Petersburg," 118; W. G. Robertson, *Battle of Old Men and Young Boys*, 13–16, 55, 59.

44. Keiley, *Prisoner of War*, 7; Archer, "Defense of Petersburg," Robert A. Martin, and Mrs. David Callender, all in Bernard, *War Talks of Confederate Veterans*, 116, 139, 142; *OR* 36: pt. 2, 317; W. G. Robertson, *Battle of Old Men and Young Boys*, 34–35, 57. Archer described the specific deployment of his various companies in "Defense of Petersburg," 117–18.

45. Archer, "Defense of Petersburg"; W. G. Robertson, *Battle of Old Men and Young Boys*, 60–64; Colston, "Repelling the First Assault on Petersburg," 536; *OR* 36: pt. 2, 311, 313, 318.

46. Colston, "Repelling the First Assault on Petersburg," 536–37; Archer, "Defense of Petersburg," 119, 132; W. G. Robertson, *Battle of Old Men and Young Boys*, 40–41, 72–73. Robertson identified Dearing's camps as at Dunn's farm, while John Trusheim, a member of Graham's Battery, referred to their bivouac as the Ruffin farm.

47. Hinton, "Eye Witness," John Trusheim, and Lossie Hill, all in Bernard, *War Talks of Confederate Veterans*, 130–34; W. G. Robertson, *Battle of Old Men and Young Boys*, 73–74; M. S. Beckwith, "Reminiscences," 18–19, VHS; Waugh, *Surviving the Confederacy*, 217; Henderson, *PCW*, 110.

48. Good accounts of the fighting on the Rives farm are in W. G. Robertson, *Battle of Old Men and Young Boys*, 63–67; Colston, "Repelling the First Assault on Petersburg," 537; Charles F. Collier and Robert A. Martin, both in Bernard, *War Talks of Confederate Veterans*, 137–38, 141; *OR* 36: pt. 2, 318; Keiley, *Prisoner of War*, 11.

49. J. William Young, in Bernard, *War Talks of Confederate Veterans*, 133; W. G. Robertson, *Battle of Old Men and Young Boys*, 68–76; *OR* 36: pt. 2, 313.

50. *OR* 36: pt. 2, 309; Hinton, "Eye Witness," William Cameron, and Mrs. David Callender, all in Bernard, *War Talks of Confederate Veterans*, 132, 136–37, 142–43; W. G. Robertson, *Battle of Old Men and Young Boys*, 76–78; Longacre, *Army of Amateurs*, 135.

51. M. S. Beckwith, "Reminiscences," 15–16, VHS; Colston, "Repelling the First Assault on Petersburg," 537; W. G. Robertson, *Battle of Old Men and Young Boys*, 88. For a roster of the casualties of June 9 based in part on Archer's narrative, see "Defense of Petersburg," Bernard, *War Talks of Confederate Veterans*, 121–22, and W. G. Robertson, *Battle of Old Men and Young Boys*, 107–8. Total losses for the day were seventy-eight Confederates and thirty-six Federals, including four killed. For detailed information on the Union casualties, see *OR* 36: pt. 2, 309.

52. A. B. Pryor, "Child's Recollections of War," 54; MacRae, *Americans at Home*, 158.

53. Mrs. B. Callender, "Personal Recollections of the Civil War," 7, PNB; CCM, June 10, 1864; Wise to "My dear wife," June 12, 1864, Wise Family Papers, VHS; Wise qtd. in Archer, "Defense of Petersburg," 122; Henderson, *PCW*, 110–11. For a day or two after June 9, Butler considered renewing the attack on Petersburg using Hincks and Kautz, but the presence of Beauregard's reinforcements and the absence of the element of surprise persuaded him to defer. See Longacre, *Army of Amateurs*, 135–39, for additional reactions in the Army of the James to the failure of June 9.

54. Emblematic of Petersburg's postwar reverence for the heroism of its citizens on June 9 is this verse printed in M. C. Harrison, *Home to the Cockade City!* 81–82:

> Dare we forget the aged sire
> And beardless boy who braved the fire
> Of foes in fierce bravado thrown
> To topple roof and altar stone
> And make of Petersburg a pyre?
> Or Graham's guns, in righteous ire
> Bold-voiced, exulting victor choir
> Re-echoing down the years their tone
> Dare we forget?
> Let other days cease to inspire
> But raise the Stars and Bars still higher
> Above old Blandford's graves bloom-strown
> The Ninth of June's our very own!
> Our ideals blacken in the mire
> If we forget!

55. *OR* 36: pt. 3, 896.

56. John H. Claiborne to "My dear wife," June 12, 1864, John H. Claiborne Papers, UVA; *Petersburg Daily Register,* June 14, 15, 1864; *OR* 40: pt. 2, 652–53.

57. *OR* 40: pt. 2, 655–56. Beauregard's defenders at Petersburg included the Twenty-sixth, Thirty-fourth, and Forty-sixth Virginia Infantry regiments, one company of the Sixty-fourth Georgia Infantry, the Twenty-third South Carolina Infantry, Archer's Reserve Battalion, Batte's Reserve Battalion, Hood's Reserve Battalion, and Sturdivant's (Virginia) and Slaten's (Georgia) artillery batteries. See Howe, *Wasted Valor, June 15–18, 1864,* 167n25.

58. Unidentified North Carolina soldier to "Dear Father," June 15, 1864, Lucy Tunstall Alston Williams Papers, UNC; *Petersburg Daily Register,* June 16, 1864; CCD, June 15, 1864; Giles Buckner Cooke, Diary, June 15, 1864, Giles Buckner Cooke Papers, VHS; Longacre, *Army of Amateurs,* 148–54; Henderson, *PCW,* 112. Casualty figures and a detailed account of the fighting on June 15 are in Howe, *Wasted Valor, June 15–18, 1864,* 27–37. Beauregard's description of the fighting is in "Four Days of Battle at Petersburg," 540–41.

59. Robert Allen, Diary, June 16, 1864, Allen Family Papers, VHS; CCD, June 16, 1864; Giles Buckner Cooke, Diary, June 16, 1864, Giles Buckner Cooke Papers, VHS. For details about the tactical situation on June 16, see Howe, *Wasted Valor, June 15–18, 1864,* 37–58.

60. *OR* 51: pt. 2, 1078–79; M. S. Beckwith, "Reminiscences," 25, VHS; *Petersburg Daily Register,* June 17, 1864; Freeman, *Lee's Lieutenants* 3:534. A description of the complex and sanguinary fighting on June 17 is in Howe, *Wasted Valor, June 15–18, 1864,* 58–101.

61. *Petersburg Daily Register,* June 18, 1864; CCD, June 17, 1864; M. S. Beckwith, "Reminiscences, 23–24, VHS; Mrs. B. Callender, "Personal Recollections of the Civil War," 7, PNB; MacRae, *Americans at Home,* 158–59.

62. M. S. Beckwith, "Reminiscences," 23–24, VHS; Mrs. B. Callender, "Personal Recollections of the Civil War," 7, PNB.

63. Beauregard, "Four Days of Battle," 543. More details on the establishment of Beauregard's final defense line and the release of Confederate reinforcements from the Army of Northern Virginia can be found in Howe, *Wasted Valor, June 15–18, 1864,* 107–9 and Freeman, *Lee's Lieutenants* 3:530–38. Kershaw's Division of Longstreet's corps followed by Field's Division were the first two units from Lee's army to arrive in Petersburg.

64. Morrill, *My Confederate Girlhood,* 60–61; Elmore, *Diary of J. E. Whitehorne 1st Sgt Co. F Twelfth Va Infantry A. P. Hill's Third Corps A. N. Va.,* 50–51; MacRae, *Americans at Home,* 159; Henderson, *Forty-first Virginia Infantry,* 65; Henderson, *Twelfth Virginia Infantry,* 79.

65. CCD, June 18, 1864; Charles S. Venable to "My Dear Sir," date illegible, Charles Scott Venable Papers, VHS; Beauregard, "Four Days of Battle," 544. The bulk of the information in this paragraph is taken from Howe, *Wasted Valor, June 15–18, 1864,* 117–34.

66. Howe, *Wasted Valor, June 15–18, 1864,* 136; Grant, *Personal Memoirs,* 2:298; James Thomas Perry, Diary, June 18, 1864, James Thomas Perry Papers, VHS.

8. "Enough to Move the Heart of Any Man"

1. Claiborne, *Seventy-five Years in Old Virginia,* 204; Mrs. R. A. Pryor, *My Day,* 199; Unknown North Carolina soldier to his mother, June 19, 1864, Joyner Family Papers, UNC; James W. Albright, Diary, June 20, 1864, James W. Albright Papers, UNC; John Turner to no salutation, June 26, 1864, John R. Turner Papers, Duke. Mrs. Roger Pryor described the reaction to the Union shelling as "terror and demoralization" (Mrs. R. A.

Pryor, *My Day*, 200). The Virginia Central Railroad continued to serve Richmond from the west on an irregular basis.

2. Henderson, *PCW*, 117, 120; Claiborne, *Seventy-five Years in Old Virginia*, 206; A. L. Wiatt, *Twenty-sixth Virginia Infantry*, 181–82.

3. Giles Buckner Cooke, Diary, June 20, 1864, Giles Buckner Cooke Papers, VHS; CCM, June 20, 1864; CCD, June 20, 1864; Henderson, *PCW*, 118–19.

4. Mrs. R. A. Pryor, *My Day*, 200; Giles Buckner Cooke, Diary, June 25, 1864, Giles Buckner Cooke Papers, VHS; Scarborough, *Diary of Edmund Ruffin* 3:471; Nevins, *Diary of Battle*, 429; Charles Dimmock to "My dearest Lissie" [Elizabeth Lewis Selden], June 30, 1864, CHDP; William D. Alexander, Diary, June 20, 1864, William D. Alexander Papers, UNC; *Petersburg Daily Register*, June 22, 1864; R. H. Moore, *Richmond Fayette, Hampden, Thomas, and Blount's Lynchburg Artillery*, 117; William Clopton to "My dear Mother & Sisters," June 22, 1864, Clopton Family Papers, Duke.

5. Mrs. B. Callender, "Personal Recollections of the Civil War," 11, PNB; CCD, June 21, 25, 26, 30, 1864; Owen, *In Camp and Battle with the Washington Artillery*, 331; Unidentified letter, June 25, 1864, Ruffin-Meade Family Papers, UNC; M. S. Beckwith, "Reminiscences," 20–21, VHS; David Washington Pipes, Memoir, 50, VHS; James W. Albright, Diary, June 25, 27, 1864, VHS; Charles Dimmock to "My dear Mother," June 26, 1864, CHDP; William D. Alexander, Diary, June 27, 30, 1864, William D. Alexander Papers, UNC; Mrs. R. A. Pryor, *My Day*, 199; *Petersburg Daily Register*, June 24, 1864; Saval, "Montage of a City under Siege," 71. Saval says that the Commissary Office moved four times and finally wound up at the terminal office of the Upper Appomattox Canal. General Wise moved district headquarters to the Dunlop House near Campbell's Bridge. On June 26 Charles Campbell reported the temperature at "105 in the shade. The whole town is enveloped in dust" (CCD, June 26, July 3, 1864). Simpson, *Good Southerner*, 280–81.

6. Henry A. Wise to "My beloved wife," June 27, 1864, Wise Family Papers, VHS; CCD, June 23, 28, 1864; *Petersburg Daily Register*, June 28, 29, 1864.

7. For a general account of the late June offensives, see the two best tactical overviews of the Petersburg campaign: Trudeau, *Last Citadel*, 56–87, and Horn, *Petersburg Campaign*, 75–95. An account of the Wilson-Kautz cavalry operation is Eanes, *"Destroy the Junction."* During the cavalry raid, the Reverend Theodorick Pryor (Roger Pryor's father and a chaplain in the Confederate army) was captured on Boydton Plank Road near Dinwiddie Court House but later made his escape. See Eanes, *"Destroy the Junction,"* 11–14, and CCD, June 24, 27, 1864.

8. CCD, June 22, 23, 1864; Julia A. Patterson to "My dear Madam," June 24, 1864, Phifer Family Papers, UNC; Henderson, *PCW*, 122–23. Echoing a familiar theme, the *Petersburg Daily Express* in its June 29 edition ridiculed one foreign-born prisoner and by extension the immigrant portion of the Union army: "We would give his name for the benefit of the community, but for the life of us, we cannot spell it, and nobody could pronounce it, if it were in print. Judging by his own pronunciation his name is fully six inches long and pure German."

9. W. A. Todd, "Reminiscences," 229, UNC.

10. *Petersburg Daily Register*, June 24, 1864. Syme's reference is to Butler's reputation for stealing silverware and other valuables from homes in New Orleans when he acted as the military administrator of the city in 1862.

11. Trudeau, *Last Citadel*, 92; J. G. Scott and Wyatt, *Petersburg's Story*, 221; CCD, June 29, 1864. In regard to the unusually warm summer, Dr. Claiborne thought that the season brought "heat not often equaled at this latitude—dust such as has never been sur-

passed anywhere" (John H. Claiborne to "My dear Wife," July 11, 1864, John H. Claiborne Papers, UVA). See also Neese, *Three Years in the Confederate Horse Artillery*, 302–3.

12. CCD, June 29, 1864; William Clopton to "My dear Sister Joyce," June 29, 1864, Clopton Family Papers, Duke.

13. Henderson, *PCW*, 127; Mrs. R. A. Pryor, *My Day*, 202; M. S. Beckwith, "Reminiscences," 22, VHS; Charles Dimmock to "My dearest Lissie" [Elizabeth Lewis Selden], June 30, 1864, CHDP.

14. Julia A. Patterson to "My dear Mrs. [John] Phifer," June 30, 1864, Phifer Family Papers, UNC; Charles Dimmock to "My dearest Lissie" [Elizabeth Lewis Selden], June 30, 1864, CHDP; Owen, *In Camp and Battle with the Washington Artillery*, 331–32; David Washington Pipes, Memoir, 50–51, VHS; Mrs. R. A. Pryor, *My Day*, 201; M. S. Beckwith, "Reminiscences," 21, VHS; CCD, July 2, 3, 1864; Claiborne, *Seventy-five Years in Old Virginia*, 206; Henderson, *PCW*, 126.

15. Henry Wise to "My beloved wife," July 1, 1864, Wise Family Papers, VHS; Neese, *Three Years in the Confederate Horse Artillery*, 303; C. G. Chamberlayne, *Ham Chamberlayne*, 242; Tower, *Lee's Adjutant*, 171; "Rebel," memoir, Lowry Shuford Collection, NCDAH. The author was probably Fannie E. Waddell, then living in Rocky Mount, N.C., who wrote under the name of "Rebel."

16. James W. Albright, Diary, July 2, 1864, VHS; CCD, July 2, 3, 1864; Owen, *In Camp and Battle with the Washington Artillery*, 335; J. F. Stephenson, "My Father and His Household, Before, During, and After the War," 33, Blanton Family Papers, VHS; Robert Taylor Scott to Fanny Scott, July 4, 1864, Keith Family Papers, VHS; Edward Bagby to "My dear Sue," July 9, 1864, Clarke Family Papers, VHS; Thomas Claybrook Elder to "My Dear Wife," July 11, 1864, Thomas Claybrook Elder Papers, VHS.

17. CCD, July 5, 8, 1864; John H. Claiborne to "My dear wife," July 11, 1864, John H. Claiborne Papers, UVA; Edward Bagby to "My dear Sue," July 24, 1864, Clarke Family Papers, VHS; Giles Buckner Cooke, Diary, July 7, 1864, Giles Buckner Cooke Papers, VHS; Davie Hampton to "Dear Uncle," July 21, 1864, Caleb Hampton Papers, Duke; Robert Phifer to "My dear Aunt," July 12, 1864, Phifer Family Papers, UNC. The literary reference is to the poem "The Deserted Village," published in 1770 by the Irish writer Oliver Goldsmith.

18. M. S. Beckwith, "Reminiscences," 22, VHS; John R. Turner to "My Dear Mother," July 18, 1864, John R. Turner Papers, Duke; John H. Claiborne to "My dear Wife," July 14, 1864, John H. Claiborne Papers, UVA; M. E. Massey, *Refugee Life in the Confederacy*, 75–76, 105.

19. Corson, *My Dear Jennie*, 122; Charles Dimmock to Mrs. Elizabeth S. Dimmock, July 8, 1864, CHDP; Morrill, *My Confederate Girlhood*, 61–62; R. H. Moseley, *Stilwell Letters*, 272–73. The Georgia soldier thought it shameful that so many ladies carried looking glasses rather than Bibles.

20. Thomas Claybrook Elder to "My dear Wife," July 27, 1864, Thomas Claybrook Elder Papers, VHS; CCD, July 16, 1864; Henderson, *PCW*, 128.

21. M. S. Beckwith, "Reminiscences," 20, VHS; Unidentified author, "Early Reminiscences of the War Between The States During the Siege of Petersburg," Bird Family Papers, VHS; Mrs. B. Callender, "Personal Recollections of the Civil War," 8, PNB; CCD, June 30, 1864.

22. Mrs. B. Callender, "Personal Recollections of the Civil War," 11, PNB; Owen, *In Camp and Battle with the Washington Artillery*, 339–40, 349–51; Giles Buckner Cooke, Diary, July 8, 1864, Giles Buckner Cooke Papers, VHS; E. B. Williams, *Rebel Brothers*, 101–2.

23. Mrs. R. A. Pryor, *My Day*, 201–2, and *Reminiscences of Peace and War*, 280 and A. B. Pryor, "Child's Recollections of War," 54; *Petersburg Daily Express*, July 7, 1864; J. G. Scott and Wyatt, *Petersburg's Story*, 221.

24. CCD, July 2, 3, 5, 8, 11, 15, 16, 1864; James W. Albright, Diary, July 2, 1863, VHS; Claiborne, *Seventy-five Years in Old Virginia*, 206; Crew and Trask, *Grimes' Battery, Grandy's Battery, and Huger's Battery Virginia Artillery*, 45; K. Wiley, *Norfolk Blues*, 132–33; CCM, July 13, 15, 1864. Inexplicably, Colonel David Lang of Florida wrote on July 18 that "very few fires have resulted from their shelling" (Groene, "Civil War Letters of Colonel David Lang," 364–65).

25. Charles Dimmock to Mrs. Elizabeth S. Dimmock, July 8, 1864, CHDP; Thomas Claybrook Elder to "My dear wife," July 27, 1864, Thomas Claybrook Elder Papers, VHS; Owen, *In Camp and Battle with the Washington Artillery*, 332; David Washington Pipes, Memoir, 50–51; VHS; Mrs. B. Callender, "Personal Recollections of the Civil War," 14, PNB; S. W. Benson, *Berry Benson's Civil War Book*, 175–76; Henderson, *PCW*, 121, 128; Saval, "Montage of a City under Siege," 47; John H. Claiborne to "My dear Wife," July 17, 1864, John H. Claiborne Papers, UVA; J. G. Scott and Wyatt, *Petersburg's Story*, 219. The new post office was in a chapel. "Two slats taken out of a window shutter admit letters which drop into a mail bag" (CCD, July 11, 1864). Grace Episcopal Church had not been completed in the summer of 1864, so the Reverend Churchill Gibson held services in the basement.

26. John H. Claiborne to "My dear Wife," July 14, 21, 1864, John H. Claiborne Papers, UVA; CCM, July 1, 1864; Saval, "Montage of a City under Siege," 80. The Petersburg police force had to replace its chief, Robert C. Donnan, who had been dismissed for drunkenness and misconduct and the desertion of one of its officers to the Federals. William T. Patison became the new captain of the night watch. CCM, September 17, 1864; CCD, July 6, 1864.

27. John H. Claiborne to "My dear Wife," July 25, 27, 1864, John H. Claiborne Papers, UVA.

28. CCD, June 21, 24 and July 2, 8, 11, 1864; *Petersburg Daily Register*, June 30, 1864.

29. J. W. Jones, *Christ in the Camp*, 258; CCD, June 27, 1864.

30. *Petersburg Daily Register*, June 27, 1864; Edward Bagby to "My dear Sue," July 24, 1864, Clarke Family Papers, VHS; Elliott Lemuel Story, Diary, July 13, 1864, VHS; John H. Claiborne to "My dear wife," July 19, 1864, John H. Claiborne Papers, UVA; CCD, July 6, 1864; Charles Dimmock to Mrs. Elizabeth S. Dimmock, July 8, 1864, CHDP. The first significant rain in months fell on July 19.

31. CCD, June 12, 24 and July 12, 13, 15, 18, 19, 21, 22, 1864; R. H. Moseley, *Stilwell Letters*, 272–73; Wright, *Confederate Letters of Benjamin H. Freeman*, 46–47; John H. Claiborne to "My dear Wife," July 21, 1864, John H. Claiborne Papers, UVA; Charles Dimmock to Mrs. Elizabeth S. Dimmock, July 8, 1864, CHDP; James King Wilkerson to "Dear Mother," July 17, 1864, James King Wilkerson Papers, Duke; Mrs. R. A. Pryor, *My Day*, 204.

32. Henry A. Wise to "My Dear Wife," June 25, 1864, Wise Family Papers, VHS; Carmichael, *William R. J. Pegram*, 142; CCD, July 14, 15, 22, 1864; *Petersburg Daily Express*, June 29, 1864.

33. William Nelson to his mother, July 5, 1864, William C. Nelson Papers, University of Mississippi; Giles Buckner Cooke, Diary, July 2, 3, 1864, Giles Buckner Cooke Papers, VHS; CCD, July 10, 1864.

34. Giles Buckner Cooke, Diary, July 10, 1864, Giles Buckner Cooke Papers, VHS; James W. Albright, Diary, July 10, 1864, VHS; Tower, *Lee's Adjutant*, 173–74; George

Henry Venable to "Dear Mother," July 24, 1864, George Henry Venable Papers, VHS; Charles Dimmock to Mrs. Elizabeth S. Dimmock, July 24, 1864, CHDP. Platt's text came from Hebrews 2:3.

35. William Russell, Diary, July 15, 1864, William Russell Papers, Duke; Giles Buckner Cooke, Diary, June 30 and July 9, 1864, Giles Buckner Cooke Papers, VHS; CCM, July 13, 1864; Stocker, *From Huntsville to Appomattox*, 182; Tower, *Lee's Adjutant*, 174; R. H. Moseley, *Stilwell Letters*, 274.

36. R. H. Moseley, *Stilwell Letters*, 274; Groene, "Civil War Letters of Colonel David Lang," 364; Edward Bagby to "My dear Sue," July 9, 1864, Clarke Family Papers, VHS.

37. Robert Taylor Scott to "My Dear Fan," July 16, 1864, Keith Family Papers, VHS; John H. Claiborne to "My dear Wife," July 19, 21, 25, 1864, John H. Claiborne Papers, UVA; CCD, July 22, 1864; Charles Dimmock to Mrs. Elizabeth S. Dimmock, July 24, 1864, CHDP; George Henry Venable to "Dear Mother," July 24, 1864, George Henry Venable Papers, VHS. On July 25 Claiborne admitted that "Grant not dead, I think."

38. John R. Turner to "My Dear Mother," July 18, 1864, John R. Turner Papers, Duke; John H. Claiborne to "My dear Wife," July 17, John H. Claiborne Papers, UVA; CCD, July 5, 6, 22, 1864; Robert Taylor Scott to "My Dear Fan," July 4, 1864, Keith Family Papers, VHS; R. H. Moseley, *Stilwell Letters*, 274; Charles Dimmock to Mrs. Elizabeth S. Dimmock, July 8, 1864, CHDP. On July 1 John Syme of the *Petersburg Daily Register* complained bitterly that the War Department had requested that he print no news about military affairs at Petersburg until the department had cleared it. By then, Syme fumed, the story had appeared in the Richmond papers.

39. *OR* 40: pt. 2, 220, 396–97; Cavanaugh and Marvel, *Battle of the Crater*, 4–5. Captain Richard Pegram commanded the battery at the fort and Brigadier General Stephen Elliott provided infantry support from his South Carolina brigade.

40. Cavanaugh and Marvel, *Battle of the Crater*, 5–8; Trudeau, *Last Citadel*, 102.

41. Gallagher, *Fighting for the Confederacy*, 444–46; E. P. Alexander, *Military Memoirs of a Confederate*, 563–65.

42. E. P. Alexander, *Military Memoirs of a Confederate*, 565; Gallagher, *Fighting for the Confederacy*, 449–50; Cavanaugh and Marvel, *Battle of the Crater*, 11.

43. John H. Claiborne to "My dear Wife," July 17, 1864, John H. Claiborne Papers, UVA; CCD, July 22, 1864; Corson, *My Dear Jennie*, 121–22.

44. Tower, *Lee's Adjutant*, 176–77, original emphasis.

45. Background on the completion of the mine and the Union attack plans can be found in Cavanaugh and Marvel, *Battle of the Crater*, 11–36 and Trudeau, *Last Citadel*, 105–8. The Federals devoted eighty-one pieces of heavy artillery to support the infantry exploiting the mine. See *OR* 40: pt. 1, 658–59.

46. A. B. Pryor, "Child's Recollections of War," 55; J. F. Stephenson, "My Father and His Household, Before, During, and After the War," 33, Blanton Family Papers, VHS; Mrs. R. A. Pryor, *Reminiscences of Peace and War*, 289–90; MacRae, *Americans at Home*, 161. Details about the explosion of the mine and the debate over the use of the African American troops are in Cavanaugh and Marvel, *Battle of the Crater*, 20–41.

47. Henry Bird to Margaret Randolph, August 5, 1864, Bird Family Papers, VHS; Ulysses S. Grant to "Maj. Gen. Halleck, Washington," August 1, 1864, Simon, *Papers of Ulysses S. Grant* 11:361; Trudeau, *Last Citadel*, 112. The best description of the Battle of the Crater is Cavanaugh and Marvel, *Battle of the Crater*, 41–102. As early as June 27, General Henry A. Wise promised brutal fighting should Confederate troops encounter African American soldiers: "The negro soldiers are no doubt incited to give no quarter from the fury with which they are excited by the enemy's account of Fort Pillow. We will

certainly show them and their white officers no quarter" (Henry A. Wise to "My beloved wife," June 27, 1864, Wise Family Papers, VHS). The battle at Fort Pillow occurred near Memphis in April 1864. Confederate troops there allegedly killed a number of African American soldiers after they had surrendered, generating wide publicity in the North.

48. John H. Claiborne to "My dear Wife," July 30 1864, John H. Claiborne Papers, UVA; A. B. Pryor, "Child's Recollections of War," 55.

49. Henry Bird to Margaret Randolph, August 5, 1864, and "Memoir of the Crater" by unidentified author, Bird Family Papers, VHS. The August visitor was William Weddell.

50. Neese, *Three Years in the Confederate Horse Artillery,* 307.

51. Trudeau, *Like Men of War,* 247–48; Stevens, *As if It Were Glory,* 192–93. A. P. Hill might also have wished to impress Petersburg's blacks with the cruel fate that awaited slaves who ran away to join the Union army.

52. Stevens, *As if It Were Glory,* 193.

53. Henderson, *PCW,* 130; Cavanaugh and Marvel, *Battle of the Crater,* 106.

54. Henderson, *PCW,* 129–30; Haskell, "Reminiscences of the Confederate War, 1861–1865," 105–6, John Cheeves Haskell Papers, UNC.

55. Corson, *My Dear Jennie,* 125; Simpson, *Good Southerner,* 280–81; Freeman, *Lee's Lieutenants* 3:554–55.

56. Corson, *My Dear Jennie,* 125; John R. Turner, no salutation, June 26, 1864, John R. Turner Papers, Duke; Charles Dimmock to Mrs. Elizabeth S. Dimmock, July 8 and August 8, 1864, CHDP; John Lane Stuart to "Dear Mother," August 12, 14, 1864, John Lane Stuart Papers, Duke; C. G. Chamberlayne, *Ham Chamberlayne,* 255–56.

57. Records of Warner Lewis Baylor, Baylor Family Papers, VHS; Giles Buckner Cooke, Diary, August 21, 1864, Giles Buckner Cooke Papers, VHS. A detailed account of the battle of the Weldon Railroad is in Horn, *Destruction of the Weldon Railroad,* 54–113.

58. Scarborough, *Diary of Edmund Ruffin* 3:526–27; Henry Bird to Margaret Randolph, August 28, 1864, Bird Family Papers, VHS; Alexander Brown to "My Dear Fannie," August 29, 1864, Alexander Gustavus Brown Papers, VHS; Thomas Claybrook Elder to "My Dear Wife," August 29, 1864, Thomas Claybrook Elder Papers, VHS; John H. Claiborne to "My dear Wife," August 28, 1864, John H. Claiborne Papers, UVA; Tower, *Lee's Adjutant,* 186–87; James W. Albright, Diary, August 29, 1864, VHS. The serious shelling recommenced on August 24, so revenge for Reams Station was not Grant's motive for renewing his bombardments.

59. Minor, "Some Glimpses at the Siege of Petersburg," United Daughters of the Confederacy Collection, MOC; Gallagher, *Fighting for the Confederacy,* 474; John H. Claiborne to "My dear Wife," August 28, 1864, John H. Claiborne Papers, UVA; M. S. Beckwith, "Reminiscences," 21, VHS; Alexander Brown to "My Dear Fannie," August 31, 1864, Alexander Gustavus Brown Papers, VHS; Henry Bird to Margaret Randolph, August 29, 1864, Bird Family Papers, VHS; A. B. Pryor, "Child's Recollections of War," 56; MacRae, *Americans at Home,* 161.

60. Giles Buckner Cooke, Diary, June 19, August 3, 7, 9, 25 and September 3, 1864, Giles Buckner Cooke Papers, VHS; CCD, June 26, 1864; William D. Alexander, Diary, August 28 and September 5, 1864, William D. Alexander Papers, UNC; Pearce, *Diary of Captain Henry A. Chambers,* 212; James Dearing to "My precious wife," August 18, 1864, Dearing Family Papers, VHS; Owen, *In Camp and Battle with the Washington Artillery,* 348.

61. John H. Claiborne to "My dear Wife," August 7, 1864, John H. Claiborne Papers, UVA; Alexander Brown to "My Dear Fannie," August 9, 1864, Alexander Gustavus Brown

Papers, VHS. Charles Dimmock believed that his diet of bacon and bread "are all else than good for diarrhea" (Charles Dimmock to Mrs. Elizabeth S. Dimmock, July 8, 1864, CHDP).

62. Alexander Brown to "My Dear Fannie," August 12, 1864, Alexander Gustavus Brown Papers, VHS; John H. Claiborne to "My Dear Wife," August 14, 1864, John H. Claiborne Papers, UVA; George William Beale to "Mother," August 20, 1864, George S. Bernard Papers, UVA; Joseph Stapp to "Dear Mother," August 17, 1864, Joseph D. Stapp Letters, VHS; *Petersburg Daily Express*, August 22, 1864; Saval, "Montage of a City under Siege," 76; CCM, August 16, 1864; W. A. Todd, "Reminiscences," 262, UNC.

63. Cunningham, *Doctors in Gray*, 65–66, 74–75, 159; Saval, "Montage of a City under Siege," 115, 117; *Petersburg Daily Express*, August 22, 1864.

64. Billings, *History of the Tenth Massachusetts Battery of Light Artillery in the War of the Rebellion*, 451–52.

65. The definitive examination of Grant's September offensives is Sommers, *Richmond Redeemed*. Disruptions in the Petersburg Railroad that Charles Campbell mentioned in early July resulted from operations conducted by the Union Sixth Corps between June 23 and July 2 that took about one week to repair. See CCD, July 2, 6, 11, 1864; Rosenblatt and Rosenblatt, *Anti-Rebel*, 232–33; Corson, *My Dear Jennie*, 119–20, and Scarborough, *Diary of Edmund Ruffin* 3:491.

66. J. W. Jones, *Christ in the Camp*, 258; John H. Claiborne to "My dear Wife," September 4, 1864, John H. Claiborne Papers, UVA; Giles Buckner Cooke, Diary, September 4, 1864, Giles Buckner Cooke Papers, VHS; Scarborough, *Diary of Edmund Ruffin* 3:555. The large shells reminded one Petersburg resident of "an ice cream freezer" ("Early Reminiscences," Bird Family Papers, VHS).

67. John H. Claiborne to "My dear Wife," September 4, 1864, John H. Claiborne Papers, UVA; Thomas Claybrook Elder to "My dear Wife," September 11, 1864, Thomas Claybrook Elder Papers, VHS; Alexander Brown to "My dear Fannie," September 6, 1864, Alexander Gustavus Brown Papers, VHS.

68. Joe Joyner to "My dear Mother," September 15, 1864, Joyner Family Papers, UNC; Scarborough, *Diary of Edmund Ruffin* 3:566; Driver and Ruffner, *First Battalion Virginia Infantry, Thirty-ninth Battalion Virginia Cavalry, Twenty-fourth Battalion Virginia Partisan Rangers*, 75; Osborne, *Private Osborne, Massachusetts Twenty-third Volunteers*, 226–27; Henry Bird to Margaret Randolph, September 28, 1864, Bird Family Papers, VHS; R. K. Krick, *Fredericksburg Artillery*, 81.

69. CCM, September 1, 1864. Other monthly salaries included $250 for the keeper of Blandford Cemetery, $300 for the captain of the Night Watch and bailiffs, and $200 for the keeper of the powder magazine. In late July the city councilman David G. Potts, treasurer of the Petersburg Railroad, sought to double the freight rate that had been raised less than five months earlier. The cost of operating the Richmond & Petersburg Railroad almost quadrupled during the 1863–64 fiscal year. See Potts to Thomas DeWitt, July 30, 1864, and report, May 26, 1864, Richmond & Petersburg Railroad Company, both in Board of Public Works Papers, LOV.

70. CCM, September 1, 5, October 4, 13, 22 and November 1, 1864; List of Soldiers and Sailors Families—Residents of Petersburg, September 1864, MOC; Pearce, *Diary of Captain Henry A. Chambers*, 220, 223. The sale of the building lots generated $70,276.25 less auction charges.

71. Giles Buckner Cooke, Diary, September 13, 1864, Giles Buckner Cooke Papers, VHS; William D. Alexander, Diary, September 13, 1864, William D. Alexander Papers,

UNC; Journal of Charles Norborne Berkeley Minor, 9–10, Roller Family Papers, VHS; John H. Claiborne to "My dear Wife," September 18, 1864, John H. Claiborne Papers, UVA; Daniel Sifford to "Dear Nease," September 23, 1864, Harriet McIntosh Papers, UNC; James W. Albright, Diary, October 20, 1864, VHS; Henderson, *PCW,* 131; Trudeau, *Last Citadel,* 192–201.

72. Wilson, *Confederate Industry,* 219–20; Fletcher Archer to "My Dear Wife," October 22, 1864, FAL.

73. Pearce, *Diary of Captain Henry A. Chambers,* 217, 219–20; Minor, "Some Glimpses at the Siege of Petersburg," MOC; Journal of Charles Norborne Berkeley Minor, September 25 and October 4, 1864, Roller Family Papers, VHS; Giles Buckner Cooke, Diary, October 3, 1864, Giles Buckner Cooke Papers, VHS. Beauregard attended St. Joseph's Catholic Church in Petersburg. See Bailey, *Century of Catholicism in Historic Petersburg,* 18.

74. Henderson, *PCW,* 131–32.

75. *OR* 42: pt. 2, 1231–32; Williams, *Napoleon in Gray,* 236–42.

76. Charles Dimmock to Mrs. Elizabeth S. Dimmock, September 25, 1864, CHDP; Tower, *Lee's Adjutant,* 190–91; Mrs. B. Callender, "Personal Recollections of the Civil War," 11, PNB; Owen, *In Camp and Battle with the Washington Artillery,* 355. Lee occupied pew 44 at St. Paul's. Dimmock wrote that after church at Grace Episcopal on September 11, Lee approached him and shook his hand. "This he did to no one else. Such a manifestation of approbation from Genl. Lee is prized more than any or all promotion" (Charles Dimmock to Mrs. Elizabeth S. Dimmock, September 11, 1864, CHDP). For Longstreet's presence, see Journal of Charles Norborne Berkeley Minor, September 27, 1864, Roller Family Papers, VHS. Longstreet had been wounded on May 6 and would not return to duty until October.

77. W. A. Todd, "Reminiscences," 262, UNC; C. G. Chamberlayne, *Ham Chamberlayne,* 276, 284, 295–96; Haskell, "Reminiscences of the Confederate War, 1861–1865," 106–7, John Cheeves Haskell Papers, UNC; Rosen, *Jewish Confederates,* 190. The offended soldier was Private Eugene Levy of the Donaldsonville Artillery.

78. Pearce, *Diary of Captain Henry A. Chambers,* 221; Charles Dimmock to Mrs. Elizabeth S. Dimmock, September 25, 1864, CHDP; Henry T. Owen to "Dear Wife," October 1, 1864, Henry Thweatt Owen Papers, LOV.

79. Henry Bird to "My dear Maggie" [Margaret Rudolph], September 20, 1864, Bird Family Papers, VHS; A. L. Wiatt, *Confederate Chaplain William Edward Wiatt,* 205; Scarborough, *Diary of Edmund Ruffin* 3:599.

80. Thomas Claybrook Elder to "My dear Wife," October 13, 1864, Thomas Claybrook Elder Papers, VHS; Brewer, *Confederate Negro,* 126; Ingram, *In View of the Great Want of Labor: A Legislative History of African American Conscription in the Confederacy.* As early as September 11, large numbers of African American workers were improving Confederate fortifications southwest of Petersburg. See James A. Bryan, Diary, September 11, 1864, Bryan Family Papers, UNC.

81. W. H. Guy to "Cousin Elizabeth," October 13, 1864, Elizabeth Shenton Papers, VHS; Henry Vaughan McCrea, *Red Dirt and Isinglass: A Wartime Biography of a Confederate Soldier,* 521; John H. Claiborne to "My dear Wife," October 15, 17, 1864, John H. Claiborne Papers, UVA; *Petersburg Daily Express,* October 16, 1864.

82. Journal of Charles Norborne Berkeley Minor, October 9, 1864, VHS; Henry Bird to "Maggie Darling" [Margaret Rudolph], October 15, 1864, Bird Family Papers, VHS. The fighting that culminated Grant's sixth offensive at Petersburg is known by various names, most often the battle of Burgess's Mill.

83. John R. Turner to "Dear Sallie," October 4, 1864, John R. Turner Papers, Duke; Crofts, *Cobb's Ordeal*, 268.

9. "But Darling, There Is Nothing in Petersburg"

1. John H. Claiborne to "My dear Wife," July 30 and August 26, 1864, John H. Claiborne Papers, UVA. The local Reserves commander Fletcher Archer thought the election would "have untold influence upon the affairs of our Confederacy" (Fletcher Archer to "My Dear Wife," November 8, 1864, FAL). For the election of 1864, see Waugh, *Reelecting Lincoln*, esp. 148–58.

2. Waugh, *Reelecting Lincoln*, 354. For typical reactions to Lincoln's election, see Trudeau, *Last Citadel*, 253.

3. William D. Alexander, Diary, November 17, 1864, William D. Alexander Papers, UNC; Charles Dimmock to his wife, November 1, 1864, CHDP; J. I. Robertson, *Civil War Letters of General Robert McAllister*, 548; Scarborough, *Diary of Edmund Ruffin* 3:654–55; Welch, *Confederate Surgeon's Letters to His Wife*, 116.

4. Scarborough, *Diary of Edmund Ruffin* 3:654–55; J. G. Scott and Wyatt, *Petersburg's Story*, 220; Saval, "Montage of a City under Siege," 49–51. I have been able to document nine deaths from shelling, all but two of them occurring in late June or early July.

5. John Keen to "My dear mother," December 6, 1864, Keen Family Letters, MOC.

6. *Petersburg Daily Express*, November 30, 1864; Mrs. R. A. Pryor, *Reminiscences of Peace and War*, 267, and *My Day*, 208; Mrs. B. Callender, "Personal Recollections of the Civil War," 11, PNB.

7. Mrs. B. Callender, "Personal Recollections of the Civil War," 9–10, PNB; Fletcher Archer to "My Dear Wife," November 18 and December 27, 1864, FAL; Trudeau, *Last Citadel*, 258.

8. Letter from unknown author to "My dear Sister," date unknown, Historical Stories File, PNB; M. S. Beckwith, "Reminiscences," 14–15, VHS; James Dearing to "My own Darling," December 5, 1864, Dearing Family Papers, VHS.

9. Mrs. R. A. Pryor, *Reminiscences of Peace and War*, 267, and *My Day*, 208; Fletcher Archer to "My Dear Wife," November 8, 10, 1864, FAL.

10. Fletcher Archer to "My Dear Wife," November 8, 1864, FAL; Charles Dimmock to Mrs. Elizabeth S. Dimmock, November 20, 1864, CHDP; Giles Buckner Cooke, Diary, December 13, 1864, Giles Buckner Cooke Papers, VHS; Trudeau, *Last Citadel*, 257.

11. Pearce, *Diary of Captain Henry A. Chambers*, 231; B[enjamin]. B. Vaughan to Governor William Smith, November 30, 1864, and William F. Bowden to Smith, November 3, 1864, EPWS, Box 4, Folders 8, 5; William Nelson to his father, December 30, 1864, William C. Nelson Papers, University of Mississippi.

12. Fletcher Archer to "My Dear Wife," October 3, 14, 17, 19, 21, 25, November 2, 9, 16, and December 18, 21, 1864, FAL.

13. A. B. Pryor, "Child's Recollections of War," 56–57.

14. David Washington Pipes, Memoir, 59, VHS; Nevins, *Diary of Battle*, 483; Giles Buckner Cooke, Diary, November 23, 1864, Giles Buckner Cooke Papers, VHS; Charles A. Jordan to "Dear Friend Lucy" [Lucy Stacy], December 10, 1864, Stacy Family Papers, VHS; Power, *Lee's Miserables*, 237.

15. CCM, November 1 and December 1, 1864; Saval, "Montage of a City under Siege," 92.

16. William C. Nelson to his brother, November 17, 1864, William C. Nelson Papers, University of Mississippi; Owen, *In Camp and Battle with the Washington Artillery*, 332–33, 354; Henderson, *PCW*, 132; Mrs. R. A. Pryor, *Reminiscences of Peace and War*, 324–

26. How men such as William Cameron obtained the luxuries with which he entertained his guests remains a mystery.

17. Saval, "Montage of a City under Siege," 73; David A. Weisiger to "Gentlemen," December 17, 1864, David Addison Weisiger Papers, VHS.

18. Charles Dimmock to Mrs. Elizabeth S. Dimmock, December 4, 1864, CHDP; J. B. Gordon, *Reminiscences of the Civil War,* 416.

19. Pearce, *Diary of Captain Henry A. Chambers,* 230–32, 240; Journal of Charles Norborne Berkeley Minor, December 4, 1864, Roller Family Papers, VHS; Charles Dimmock to Mrs. Elizabeth S. Dimmock, January 1, 1865, CHDP; Giles Buckner Cooke, Diary, November 12, 27, 1864, Giles Buckner Cooke Papers, VHS. Gibson subscribed to the Evangelical Episcopal persuasion, a form of the religion that stressed the need to avoid the pitfalls of life such as drinking, gambling, and pursuits of the flesh. This "low church" style of passionate preaching appealed to some of the worshippers quoted in the text, compared to the more ritualistic "high church" approach that the Reverend William Platt took. See Henderson, *PCW,* 17 and Henderson to the author, November 23, 2004.

20. Giles Buckner Cooke, Diary, December 2, 1864, Giles Buckner Cooke Papers, VHS; Mrs. B. Callender, "Personal Recollections of the Civil War," 12, PNB; Charles Dimmock to Mrs. Elizabeth S. Dimmock, December 4, 1864, CHDP. See chapter 8 for Gracie's Confirmation.

21. A. B. Pryor, "Child's Recollections of War," 56; Charles Dimmock to Mrs. Elizabeth S. Dimmock, November 6 and December 18, 1864, CHDP; Fletcher Archer to "My Dear Wife," November 3, 1864, FAL; Tower, *Lee's Adjutant,* 202–3, 206; Mrs. R. A. Pryor, *Reminiscences of Peace and War,* 300, and *My Day,* 210–11; Freeman, *R. E. Lee* 3:525–26. Captain Dimmock wrote that Lee "seems to give Grace the preference & goes there much oftener than to St. Paul's" (Charles Dimmock to Mrs. Elizabeth S. Dimmock, December 25, 1864, CHDP).

22. John Godwin to "My Darling sweet wife," November 8 and December 1, 1864, Godwin Family Papers, VHS; Journal of Charles Norborne Berkeley Minor, November 24, 1864, Roller Family Papers, VHS; Patterson, *From Blue to Gray,* 84–85.

23. Giles Buckner Cooke, Diary, November 22, and December 12, 1864, and January 2, 1865, Giles Buckner Cooke Papers, VHS; W. A. Todd, "Reminiscences," 263–65, UNC; Fletcher Archer to "My Dear Wife," December 16, 1864, FAL.

24. Patterson, *From Blue to Gray,* 84; Mrs. R. A. Pryor, *My Day,* 216–224; Simon, *Papers of Ulysses S. Grant* 13:41–42.

25. William D. Alexander, Diary, December 22, 1864, William D. Alexander Papers, UNC; John H. Claiborne to "My dear Wife," December 21, 1864, John H. Claiborne Papers, UVA; William Clopton to "My Dear Sisters," December 25, 1864, Clopton Family Papers, Duke.

26. William J. Pegram to "My Dear Mother," December 22, 1864, Confederate Military Leaders Collection, MOC; Bessie Meade Callender to "My dear Mother," December 25, 1864, Ruffin-Meade Family Papers, UNC; W. A. Todd, "Reminiscences," 270–80, UNC.

27. Charles Dimmock to Mrs. Elizabeth S. Dimmock, December 25, 1864, CHDP.

28. A. B. Pryor, "Child's Recollections of War," 56.

29. Pearce, *Diary of Captain Henry A. Chambers,* 235–36; William D. Alexander, Diary, December 25, 1864, William D. Alexander Papers, UNC.

30. Bessie Meade Callender to "My dear Mother," December 25, 1864, Ruffin-Meade Family Papers, UNC; Fletcher Archer to "My dear Wife," December 21, 1864, FAL.

31. *Petersburg Daily Express,* December 29, 1864; Power, *Lee's Miserables,* 229–33;

Greene, *Breaking the Backbone of the Rebellion,* 109; Fletcher Archer to "My Dear Wife," January 4, 1865, FAL.

32. Eleanor Beverley (Meade) Platt to "My dear Mother," December 31, 1864, VHS; Giles Buckner Cooke, Diary, December 25, 1864, Giles Buckner Cooke Papers, VHS; Charles Dimmock to "My dearest Lissie" [Mrs. Elizabeth S. Dimmock], January 1, 1865, CHDP.

33. Charles Dimmock to Elizabeth S. Dimmock, January 15, 1865, CHDP; Murphy, *Tenth Virginia Infantry,* 114; Fletcher Archer to "My Dear Wife," January 16, 1865, FAL; Dinwiddie Grigg to Governor William Smith, February 7, 1865, EPWS, Box 5, Folder 7.

34. "Governor's Communication on the Subject of Pardons, Reprieves, Etc.," EPWS, Box 5, Folder 5; Mrs. B. Callender, "Personal Recollections of the Civil War," 13, PNB.

35. A series of documents pertaining to Gilley's trial are in EPWS, Box 5, Folder 5. Gilley hanged on March 24, but the rope broke on the first attempt and he had to be dropped a second time. The evidence does not allow the identification of Mrs. Goodman's husband. Dozens of men named Goodman served with the Army of Northern Virginia late in the war.

36. Charles Dimmock to Mrs. Elizabeth S. Dimmock, January 22, 1865, CHDP; John H. Claiborne to "My dear Wife," December 21, 1864, John H. Claiborne Papers, UVA.

37. Charles Dimmock to Mrs. Elizabeth S. Dimmock, January 15, 22, 1865, CHDP; Fletcher Archer to "My dear Wife," January 7, 1865, FAL; John Godwin to "My Darling Wife," January 25, 1865, Godwin Family Papers, VHS; Owen, *In Camp and Battle with the Washington Artillery,* 363.

38. Charles Dimmock to Mrs. Elizabeth S. Dimmock, January 8, 1865, CHDP; Fletcher Archer to "My dear Wife," January 3, 18, 1865, FAL; Waugh, *Surviving the Confederacy,* 244–45.

39. CCM, January 2 and February 1, 1865; Wilson, *Confederate Industry,* 220.

40. Beale, *Lieutenant of Cavalry in Lee's Army,* 202–5.

41. Pearce, *Diary of Captain Henry A. Chambers,* 241–42, 248–49. Dabney's sermon was entitled "The Bondage of Sin: A Sermon on Acts VIII." Dabney Papers, Union Theological Seminary. My thanks to George C. Rable of the University of Alabama for calling this topic to my attention. Dabney spoke in Petersburg in mid-January and early March.

42. Charles Dimmock to Mrs. Elizabeth S. Dimmock, January 8, 15 and February 12, 1865, CHDP; Giles Buckner Cooke, Diary, February 28, 1865, Giles Buckner Cooke Papers, VHS.

43. Waugh, *Surviving the Confederacy,* 258–59; Briscoe Gerard Baldwin to "My dear Gussey," February 12, 1865, Stuart Family Papers, VHS; Charles Dimmock to Mrs. Elizabeth S. Dimmock, February 12, 1865, CHDP; Tower, *Lee's Adjutant,* 221.

44. Welch, *Confederate Surgeon's Letters to His Wife,* 122–24; Charles Dimmock to Mrs. Elizabeth S. Dimmock, January 22 and February 10, 1865, CHDP; Briscoe Gerard Baldwin to "My dear Gussey," February 12, 1865, Stuart Family Papers, VHS; A. B. Pryor, "Child's Recollections of War," 56–57.

45. Giles Buckner Cooke, Diary, January 9, 1865, Giles Buckner Cooke Papers, VHS; Tower, *Lee's Adjutant,* 228.

46. Some in Petersburg understood the origin of the peace conference to be a suggestion to mount a combined Union-Confederate attack against the puppet French government in Mexico. See, for example, Charles Dimmock to Mrs. Elizabeth S. Dimmock, January 29, 1865, CHDP.

47. For a brief summary of the background and conduct of the Hampton Roads Peace

Conference, see McPherson, *Battle Cry of Freedom*, 821–25; Schott, *Alexander H. Stephens of Georgia*, 439–48; and Cooper, *Jefferson Davis, American*, 509–13.

48. Charles Dimmock to "My dearest Lissie" [Mrs. Elizabeth S. Dimmock], February 5, 1865, CHDP. Accounts of the battle of Hatcher's Run are in Trudeau, *Last Citadel*, 312–22 and Greene, *Breaking the Backbone of the Rebellion*, 143–49.

49. Letter from unknown author to "My dear Sister," date unknown, Historical Stories File, PNB; Giles Buckner Cooke, Diary, February 6, 1865, Giles Buckner Cooke Papers, VHS; Charles Dimmock to Mrs. Elizabeth S. Dimmock, February 12, 1865, CHDP; Mrs. B. Callender, "Personal Recollections of the Civil War," 14, PNB; Robert E. Lee to Hetty Cary Pegram, February 11, 1865, Robert Edward Lee Papers, VHS; Putnam, *Richmond during the War*, 342–43; Furgurson, *Ashes of Glory*, 297–98; V. Dabney, *Richmond, the Story of a City*, 187–88. There is no biography of John Pegram.

50. *Petersburg Daily Express*, February 10, 1865; Nathaniel Riddick to his son, John, and Mills Riddick to "Dear Sister," February 25, 28, 1865, respectively, Riddick Family Papers, courtesy of Brian S. Wills; William Clopton to "My Dear Mother & Sisters," February 24, 1865, Clopton Family Papers, Duke; William D. Alexander, Diary, February 25, 1865, William D. Alexander Papers, UNC.

51. Driver and Ruffner, *The First Battalion Virginia Infantry*, 43; CCM, March 1, 1865; Henry Wise to "My beloved wife," February 26, 1865, Wise Family Papers, VHS; Fletcher Archer to "My dear Wife," March 8, 1865, FAL.

52. For a more detailed explanation of Lee's strategy at this stage of the Petersburg campaign, see Greene, *Breaking the Backbone of the Rebellion*, 149–52.

53. CCM, February 14, 20, 21, 1865; James W. Albright, Diary, February 23, 1865, VHS; Fletcher Archer to "My Sweet Wife," March 2, 1865, FAL; Robert R. Collier to Governor William Smith, March 24, 1865, EPWS, Box 5, Folder 8.

54. Joseph D. Stapp to "Dear Mother," March 4, 1865, Joseph D. Stapp Letters, VHS; *OR* 46: pt. 2, 991; E. L. Jordan, *Black Confederates and Afro-Yankees in Civil War Virginia*, 236–37; EPWS, Box 5, Folder 7 and Box 7, Folder 1. A notice appeared in the April 1, 1865, edition of the *Petersburg Daily Express* encouraging slaves to enlist for military service. For a brief review of the effort to enlist African Americans in the Confederate army at Petersburg, see Greene, *Breaking the Backbone of the Rebellion*, 114–15, and for Lee's support of the concept, Freeman, *R. E. Lee* 3:544.

55. Mills Riddick to "Dear Sister," March 20, 1865, Riddick Family Papers, courtesy of Brian S. Wills; John Claiborne to "My Dear Wife," March 9, 1865, John H. Claiborne Papers, UVA.

56. Calkins, *Auto Tour*, 27; Eckert, *John Brown Gordon*, 110; J. B. Gordon, *Reminiscences of the Civil War*, 406. For a thorough treatment of the battle of Fort Stedman, see Trudeau, *Last Citadel*, 329–54.

57. Fletcher Archer to "My Dear Wife," March 25, 1865, FAL; John Claiborne to "My dear Wife," March 26, 1865, John H. Claiborne Papers, UVA; Charles Dimmock to "My dearest Lissie" [Mrs. Elizabeth S. Dimmock], March 27, 1865, CHDP. For a detailed description of the fighting southwest of Petersburg on March 25, see Greene, *Breaking the Backbone of the Rebellion*, 160–85.

58. For more detailed discussions of the Union plans, see Greene, *Breaking the Backbone of the Rebellion*, 205–11; Bradley, *This Astounding Close*, 40–46; Grant, *Personal Memoirs*, 436–39.

59. Greene, *Breaking the Backbone of the Rebellion*, 210–11, 246–47n20.

60. Information on the conduct of this phase of the Petersburg campaign is in E.

Bearss and Calkins, *Battle of Five Forks,* and Greene, *Breaking the Backbone of the Rebellion,* 218–42.

61. Samuel H. Walkup, Diary, March 27, 1865, Samuel H. Walkup Papers, UNC; Oram, "Harper's Ferry to the Fall of Richmond: Letters of Colonel John De Hart Ross, C.S.A., 1861–1865," 174.

62. *Petersburg Daily Express,* March 30, 31, 1865; CCM, April 1, 1865; Henderson, *PCW,* 134–35.

63. Ashcraft, *Thirty-first Virginia Infantry,* 86; *Petersburg Daily Express,* March 30, 1865; Giles Buckner Cooke, Diary, April 1, 1865, Giles Buckner Cooke Papers, VHS. The speaker might have been John Tyler of Richmond, a former enrolling and staff officer in the Army of Northern Virginia.

10. "Tis Midnight Yet With Us"

1. Eckert, *John Brown Gordon,* 10, 115. The boy, named John Brown Gordon Jr., would die at age nineteen of typhoid fever.

2. H. Porter, *Campaigning with Grant,* 434, 441–43.

3. For details behind the strategic thinking on the night of April 1, see Greene, *Breaking the Backbone of the Rebellion,* 257–70.

4. Cadmus M. Wilcox, "Defense of Batteries Gregg and Whitworth, and the Evacuation of Petersburg," *Southern Historical Society Papers* 4:25; Thomas F. McCoy, Memoir, Frank R. McCoy Papers, Library of Congress; Greene, *Breaking the Backbone of the Rebellion,* 270–71.

5. Wilcox, "Defense of Batteries Gregg and Whitworth," 25; Mrs. R. A. Pryor, *My Day,* 252. For information on the Ninth Corps attack on April 2 and a detailed tactical description of the Sixth Corps breakthrough, see Greene, *Breaking the Backbone of the Rebellion,* 442–50, 293–338.

6. A summary of the circumstances surrounding A. P. Hill's death is in Greene, *Breaking the Backbone of the Rebellion,* 343–52. The Union soldiers who confronted Hill were Corporal John Mauk and Private Daniel Wolford, both of the 138th Pennsylvania Infantry.

7. For the Sixth Corps movement to Hatcher's Run and the fighting along the railroad at Sutherland Station, see Greene, *Breaking the Backbone of the Rebellion,* 352–63, 430–42.

8. Freeman, *R. E. Lee* 4:49; *OR* 46: pt. 3, 1378; Furgurson, *Ashes of Glory,* 319–21. A comprehensive look at Richmond on April 2, 1865, is Lankford, *Richmond Burning,* 60–112. While some accounts state that Davis learned of Lee's message while in church, it is clear that Postmaster General John H. Reagan informed the president of its contents while the chief executive was en route to St. Paul's.

9. A. B. Pryor, "Child's Recollections of War," 57; James W. Albright, Diary, April 2, 1865, VHS; Charles F. Collier, "War Recollections. Story of the Evacuation of Petersburg, by an Eye-Witness," *Southern Historical Society Papers* 22:69–70; Elizabeth Vass Wilkerson, transcriber, "Diary, Marriage Records, Etc. of Rev. L. C. Vass," Rev. L. C. Vass, Diary and Papers, ts., MOC; William Simpson to "My dearest Annie," May 20, 1865, original emphasis, William Skinner Simpson Papers, LOV; Driver and Ruffner, *The First Battalion Virginia Infantry,* 44; Wilcox, "The Defense of Batteries Gregg and Whitworth," 25; K. Wiley, *Norfolk Blues,* 217.

10. Claiborne, "Last Days of Lee and His Paladins," 238–40.

11. CCM, April 2, 1865; Collier, "War Recollections," 70.

12. Nathaniel Harris to William Mahone, August 2, 1866, Personal Papers Collection, William Mahone Papers, 1866–1895, LOV. Harris had been stationed in Chesterfield County. For a detailed tactical account of the battles for Forts Gregg and Whitworth, see Greene, *Breaking the Backbone of the Rebellion*, 379–418.

13. Cockrell, *Gunner with Stonewall*, 111–12; Giles Buckner Cooke, Diary, April 2, 1865, Giles Buckner Cooke Papers, VHS. The details of the fight for Lee's headquarters are in Greene, *Breaking the Backbone of the Rebellion*, 419–30.

14. Freeman, *Lee's Lieutenants* 3:683 and *R. E. Lee* 4:53–54; Wilcox, "Defense of Batteries Gregg and Whitworth," 32–33; Mrs. R. A. Pryor, *Reminiscences of Peace and War*, 347, and *My Day*, 253–56. Roger Pryor gained his release from Fort Lafayette in February through the influence of both Horace Greeley and Abraham Lincoln. Cottage Farm was also known as the McIlwaine House, which Wilcox mistakenly called Captain McQuaine's house.

15. Freeman, *R. E. Lee* 4:55; Collier, "War Recollections," 70.

16. Claiborne, "Last Days of Lee and His Paladins," 239; *OR* 46: pt. 3, 1379, pt. 1, 1265.

17. Collier, "War Recollections," 70; Patterson, *From Blue to Gray*, 90; Abner Crump Hopkins, Memoir, VHS; Mrs. B. Callender, "Personal Recollections of the Civil War," 14–15, PNB.

18. The North Carolina soldier H. C. Wall quoted in Trudeau, *Last Citadel*, 401; Abner Crump Hopkins, Memoir, VHS; Bradwell, "Last Days of the Confederacy," 57.

19. Douglas, *I Rode with Stonewall*, 330; Abner Crump Hopkins, Memoir, VHS; Mary E. Morrison, Memoir, VHS. Mary Tabb Bolling would marry W. H. F. "Rooney" Lee, General Robert Lee's son, at St. Paul's Episcopal Church on November 28, 1867.

20. Bradwell, "Last Days of the Confederacy," 57.

21. J. E. Whitehorne, Diary, April 2, 1865, UNC; Scarborough, *Diary of Edmund Ruffin* 3:830.

22. A. B. Pryor, "Child's Recollections of War," 57; Collier, "War Recollections," 71; Mrs. R. A. Pryor, *Reminiscences of Peace and War*, 350; Giles Buckner Cooke, Diary, April 2, 1865, Giles Buckner Cooke Papers, VHS.

23. Kimbrough, "From Petersburg to Hart's Island Prison," 499; Bradwell, "Last Days of the Confederacy," 57; Abner Crump Hopkins, Memoir, VHS; James W. Albright, Diary, April 2, 1865, VHS; Bond and Coward, *South Carolinians*, 170–71.

24. Marvel, *Lee's Last Retreat*, 32; Bradwell, "Last Days of the Confederacy," 57; Bond and Coward, *South Carolinians*, 171; Thomas P. Devereaux, "From Petersburg to Appomattox," 7, Thomas Pollack Devereaux Papers, UNC; Dayton, *Diary of a Confederate Soldier*, 133.

25. Claiborne, *Seventy-five Years in Old Virginia*, 262; James W. Albright, Diary, April 2, 1865, VHS; Giles Buckner Cooke, Diary, April 2, 1865, Giles Buckner Cooke Papers, VHS. For other summaries of the evacuation of Petersburg, see Henderson, *Petersburg in the Civil War*, 135; Trudeau, *Last Citadel*, 401–2; and Greene, *Breaking the Backbone of the Rebellion*, 461–66.

26. Simon, *Papers of Ulysses S. Grant* 14:327, 330; *OR* 46: pt. 3, 449–50, 480–82.

27. *New York Times* correspondent J. R. Hamilton, qtd. in Trudeau, *Last Citadel*, 402. Much of this portion of the narrative is adapted from Greene, *Breaking the Backbone of the Rebellion*, 469–79, see esp. 470.

28. *OR* 46: pt. 1, 1047–48; Wixcey, "First Flag in Petersburg." No one identified the three councilmen who surrendered Petersburg. Private William R. Fox of the Ninety-fifth Pennsylvania Infantry received a Medal of Honor for capturing the Confederate flag from the Customs House. How he achieved this rather than someone from the Second

Michigan Infantry is unclear. See Letters Received Enlisted Branch, Entry 409, File B-15442, 1878, Record Group 94, NARA.

29. Collier, "War Recollections," 71–72. There were several versions of this story in addition to the one quoted in the text. See Greene, *Breaking the Backbone of the Rebellion*, 471–74.

30. Trudeau, *Last Citadel*, 406–7; Charles Wolcott of the Sixty-first Massachusetts Infantry quoted in Calkins, *Auto Tour*, 13. According to the Northern newspaper correspondent Thomas Morris Chester, the structures that the Confederates burned on April 2 included the Central Tobacco Warehouse; the West Hill Tobacco Warehouse; the Norfolk & Petersburg depot; Rowlett's lumber yard; the Pocahontas, Campbell, and Battersea Bridges; and the bridge leading from the South Side Railroad depot to the repair shops across the Appomattox. See Blackett, *Thomas Morris Chester*, 313–14.

31. Kimbrough, "From Petersburg to Hart's Island Prison," 499–500.

32. Best, *History of the 121st New York State Infantry*, 212–13; Collier, "War Recollections," 72.

33. Best, *History of the 121st New York State Infantry*, 213; Statement of First Lieutenant Philip Rufus Woodcock, GAR Record Book, C. J. Powers Post 391, and Philip R. Woodcock, Diary, April 3, 1865, David Ward Collection.

34. Mrs. J. H. Slater, Memoir, Bird Family Papers, VHS.

35. Mrs. B. Callender, "Personal Recollections of the Civil War," 14–15, PNB. In citing these accounts I am mindful of the embellishment inherent in many such memoirs.

36. *OR* 46: pt. 3, 521; Deane, "Following the Flag," Connecticut Historical Society; Butterfield, "Personal Reminiscences With the Sixth Corps, 1864–5," 89; "The Sixth Corps," *New York Herald*, April 7, 1865; Mrs. R. A. Pryor, *My Day*, 257.

37. Deane, "Following the Flag"; E. S. Roberts, "War Reminiscences"; Michael Kelly, Diary, April 3, 1865, Connecticut Historical Society. Kelly served in the Second Connecticut Heavy Artillery.

38. Trudeau, *Like Men of War*, 428–29; Rev. L. C. Vass, Diary and Papers, MOC. Although the African American correspondent Thomas M. Chester credited the black troops with being the first to enter Petersburg, there can be no question that they followed the white units, as described in the text. See Blackett, *Thomas Morris Chester*, 313.

39. Kimbrough, "From Petersburg to Hart's Island Prison," 500.

40. E. S. Roberts, "War Reminiscences"; Collier, "War Recollections," 72.

41. Bowen, *History of the Thirty-Seventh Regiment Massachusetts Volunteers*, 412; Journal of Lieutenant Robert Pratt, April 3, 1865, Lieutenant Robert Pratt Papers, Vermont Historical Society; Haynes, *History of the Tenth Regiment Vermont Volunteers*, 147.

42. *OR* 46: pt. 1, 932, 1019, 1040; William Simpson to "My dearest Annie," May 20, 1865, William Skinner Simpson Papers, LOV.

43. Kilmer, "Petersburg"; Michael Kelly, Diary, April 3, 1865, Connecticut Historical Society; *New York Tribune*, April 6, 7, 1865.

44. Horace N. Snow, Eighth Ohio Infantry, Snow Family Papers, Duke; Agassiz, *Meade's Headquarters, 1863–1865*, 340–41, original emphasis.

45. Mary E. Morrison, Memoir, VHS; *History of the Second Presbyterian Church*, 26; Owen, *In Camp and Battle with the Washington Artillery*, 450. Although this anecdote is corroborated in multiple sources, its postwar romanticism must be accepted cautiously.

46. Edward S. Roberts, Diary, April 3, 1865, Connecticut Historical Society. An excellent account of Lincoln's visit to Petersburg is in Trudeau, *Last Citadel*, 410–12, from which Crook's observation is quoted.

47. Agassiz, *Meade's Headquarters, 1863–1865*, 341; Henderson, *PCW*, 137; Grant,

Personal Memoirs, 2:459; H. Porter, *Campaigning with Grant,* 450; Crook qtd. in Trudeau, *Last Citadel,* 411; *OR* 46: pt. 3, 520–21, 524.

48. Trudeau, *Last Citadel,* 411–12; H. Porter, *Campaigning with Grant,* 450–52; Grant, *Personal Memoirs,* 2:459–61; Blackett, *Thomas Morris Chester,* 314; Henderson, *PCW,* 137. One version of the Lincoln-Grant conference has Lincoln requesting permission from Wallace's son to enter the house. "You are not going to let that man come into the house!" cried the youngster. "I think it would not do to try to stop a man from coming in who has fifty thousand men at his back," replied the elder Wallace, who then joined the two dignitaries on the porch. See McFeely, *Grant,* 213–14, 540n38, for his source. Sharpe's title was deputy provost marshal general and he held the brevet rank of major general. See Fishel, *Secret War for the Union,* 287, 647n57.

49. Henderson, *PCW,* 137–38; *New York Tribune,* April 6, 7, 1865; W. D. Baylor to "Dear Brother," April 10, 1865, Baylor Family Papers, VHS.

50. *Grant's Petersburg Progress,* April 3, 1865; Henderson, *Unredeemed City,* 9; Collier, "War Recollections," 72; Henderson, *PCW,* 137–38.

51. Mrs. B. Callender, "Personal Recollections of the Civil War," 16, PNB; Collier, "War Recollections," 72; R. G. Scott, *Forgotten Valor,* 642; Blackett, *Thomas Morris Chester,* 315. Edmund Ruffin resented the requirement that citizens swear that their oaths of allegiance were given freely. Ruffin believed that such enforced hypocrisy by the Federals was typical of "these vilest of wretches & tyrants" (Scarborough, *Diary of Edmund Ruffin* 3:877).

52. D. M. Jordan, *"Happiness Is Not My Companion,"* 237; *OR* 46: pt. 3, 462, 514, 536; *Grant's Petersburg Progress,* April 5, 1865; Townsend, *Rustics in Rebellion,* 242; Henderson, *Unredeemed City,* 10–13. Hartsuff's command was officially called United States Forces, Petersburg. See Welcher, *Union Army, 1861–1865,* 1:141.

53. General Orders Number 1 appears in *OR* 46: pt. 3, 613–14, April 6, 1865. A copy of the original order is in the Baylor Family Papers, April 5, VHS. The text varies slightly. See also Henderson, *PCW,* 139.

54. Henderson, *PCW,* 140; William Rolfe to his father, April 5, 1865, Eugene L. Rolfe Collection; Blackett, *Thomas Morris Chester,* 315.

55. Letter, April 8, 1865, Edward Moseley Letters, VHS; J. I. Robertson, "English Views of the Civil War," 207–8. Congressman Elihu Washburne of Illinois and Senator Henry Wilson of Massachusetts visited Petersburg during the week as well. See Mrs. R. A. Pryor, *My Day,* 257.

56. Keckley, *Behind the Scenes,* 163–70; de Pineton, "Personal Recollections of Mr. Lincoln," 28–29; de Pineton, *Impressions of Lincoln and the Civil War,* 77–81; Donald, *Lincoln,* 579–80; Charles Sumner to Salmon P. Chase, April 10, 1865, B. W. Palmer, *Selected Letters of Charles Sumner,* 282; Baker, *Mary Todd Lincoln,* 230, 241.

57. Donald, *Lincoln,* 580–81; Taylor, *Gouverneur Kemble Warren,* 230; Henderson, *Unredeemed City,* 12–13.

58. Henderson, *PCW,* 142–43; Rev. L. C. Vass, Diary and Papers, MOC; J. B. Gordon, *Reminiscences of the Civil War,* 454–55.

59. Waugh, *Surviving the Confederacy,* 296–97; Mrs. R. A. Pryor, *My Day,* 258; Blackett, *Thomas Morris Chester,* 318; *Richmond Whig,* April 17, 1865; Lankford, *Richmond Burning,* 224. Both Churchill Gibson and William Platt had to be ordered to stop leading a prayer for the president of the Confederate States many weeks after Lee had surrendered. Church Records, Christ and Grace Episcopal Church, LOV.

60. Blackett, *Thomas Morris Chester,* 312, 316; Pearce, *Diary of Captain Henry A. Chambers,* 265; A. L. Wiatt, *Confederate Chaplain William Edward Wiatt,* 240. A former

Confederate chaplain serving in one of the military hospitals in Petersburg reported that Hartsuff issued orders on May 9 that "all insignia of rank, military buttons, etc." were to be removed from Confederate uniforms worn in town by May 15. "We are under lords many now," observed the minister (Rev. L. C. Vass, Diary, May 10, 1865, Rev. L. C. Vass, Diary and Papers, MOC).

61. Blackett, *Thomas Morris Chester*, 319; Scarborough, *Diary of Edmund Ruffin* 3:877, 908–9; Henderson, *PCW*, 140–41.

62. Blackett, *Thomas Morris Chester*, 319, 332, original emphasis.

63. Henderson, *PCW* 143; Mrs. R. A. Pryor, *My Day*, 259; D. M. Jordan, *"Happiness Is Not My Companion,"* 238–39; W. H. Roberts, *Drums and Guns around Petersburg*, 71–72; Rev. L. C. Vass, Diary, May 3, 1865, Rev. L. C. Vass, Diary and Papers, MOC; *OR, Supplement*, 30: pt. 2, 400; Jesse Bean, Diary, May 9, 1865, Jesse S. Bean Papers, UNC. The Reverend Vass reported that no local residents, black or white, cheered as either Meade's or Sherman's armies passed through Petersburg in May on their way to Washington. See Rev. L. C. Vass, Diary, May 11, 1865, Rev. L. C. Vass, Diary and Papers, MOC.

64. Henderson, *Unredeemed City*, 13–16; *OR* 46: pt. 1, 2, pt. 3, 1198; Welcher, *Union Army, 1861-1865*, 1:143. Petersburg's place in the United States Army organization after the Union occupation changed often. The United States Forces, Petersburg, Virginia, under General Hartsuff was established as a part of the Department of Virginia on April 6. On April 19 the Military Division of the James was created under the command of Major General Henry Halleck, of which the Department of Virginia, headquartered in Richmond and commanded by Major General E. O. C. Ord, was a part. On June 14 Major General Alfred Terry relieved Ord and thus became Hartsuff's direct superior. On June 27 the Department of Virginia joined the Military Division of the Atlantic, replacing the defunct Military Division of the James. The May 22 order establishing the District of the Nottoway created three subdistricts in the counties south, west, and southeast of Petersburg. These subdistricts—the Roanoke, the Appomattox, and the Blackwater—were commanded, respectively, by Edward Ferrero, Charles H. Smith, and Gilbert H. McKibben, all, along with Colonel Martindale, reporting to Hartsuff in Petersburg as district commander. See Welcher, *Union Army, 1861-1865*, 1:139–43.

65. Henderson, *PCW*, 141; Henderson, *Unredeemed City*, 21. William Simpson hired carpenters in late May to repair damage to his High Street home caused by a Union provost captain and his men, who had used the dwelling early in the occupation. Simpson to "My dearest Annie," May 20, 1865, William Skinner Simpson Papers, LOV.

66. Rev. L. C. Vass, Diary, May 3, 1865, Rev. L. C. Vass, Diary and Papers, MOC; Henry D. Bird to "My dear son," May 27, 1865, Bird Family Papers, VHS. For the desolate condition of the South Side Railroad, see Henry D. Bird to Charles Palmer, June 20, 1865, Flournoy, *Calendar of Virginia State Papers and Other Manuscripts*, 442–43.

67. Henry Bird to Margaret Randolph, June (date unspecified) 1865, original emphasis, Bird Family Papers, VHS. Rev. Vass reported that one Petersburg lady was mortified to tears when two Union officers volunteered to escort her to church against her wishes. Rev. L. C. Vass, Diary, June 1, 1865, Rev. L. C. Vass, Diary and Papers, MOC.

68. Berlin, *Freedom*, 737; Rev. L. C. Vass, Diary, May 3, 1865, Rev. L. C. Vass, Diary and Papers, MOC; Henderson, *Unredeemed City*, 20–21; Blackett, *Thomas Morris Chester*, 333. William Simpson believed that the future of blacks was the most interesting aspect of the transition in Petersburg from war to peace. See Simpson to "My dear Annie," May [date unspecified] 1865, William Skinner Simpson Papers, LOV.

69. Blackett, *Thomas Morris Chester*, 333; John S. Epes to "My dear Sister," June 1, 1865, Rosalia E. Taylor Papers, Duke.

70. Henderson, *Unredeemed City,* 16–18; *OR* 46: pt. 3, 1159–60.

71. Henderson, *Unredeemed City,* 19–20, 23–24; *Petersburg Daily Express,* June 19, 1865; Blackett, *Thomas Morris Chester,* 334; William Simpson to "My dearest Annie," May 20, 1865, William Skinner Simpson Papers, LOV.

72. Henry Bird to "Dearest Maggie," September 24, 1864, Bird Family Papers, VHS; John S. Epes to "My dear Sister," June 1, 1865, Rosalia E. Taylor Papers, Duke; William Simpson to "My dearest Annie," May 20, 1865, William Skinner Simpson Papers, LOV. Battlefield tourism became such big business in Petersburg that Jarratt's Hotel published an illustrated tour guide for visitors. See *A Guide to the Fortifications and Battlefields around Petersburg.*

73. Henderson, *Unredeemed City,* 25–27. One local newspaper declared that "there is no portion of the South in which the [military] Administration has so general a support as this" (*Petersburg Daily Index,* August 22, 1865).

74. A. C. Gordon, *Memories and Memorials of William Gordon McCabe,* 181. A comprehensive and highly recommended study of the postwar period in Petersburg through 1874 is Henderson, *Unredeemed City.*

BIBLIOGRAPHY

The sources are organized into those in manuscript form and those that have been published. The published sources are divided into government records, newspapers, memoirs and personal papers, reference documents, unit histories of regiments and other military organizations written by members of the units and modern historians, articles and essays, and secondary sources. An author's works may appear in multiple sections depending on the nature of the publication.

Primary Sources

MANUSCRIPTS

Centre Hill Mansion, City of Petersburg
  Fletcher Archer Letters

Office of the Clerk of City Council, City of Petersburg
  Petersburg Common Council Meeting Minutes

Earl Gregg Swem Library, College of William and Mary, Williamsburg, Virginia
  Charles Campbell Papers
    Anna Birdsall Campbell Diary
    Charles Campbell Diary
    Minutes of the Washington Street Church Ladies Organization

Connecticut Historical Society, Hartford
  James Deane, "Following the Flag: The Three Years' Story of a Veteran, 1862–1865"
  Michael Kelly Diary
  Edward S. Roberts Diary

William R. Perkins Library, Duke University, Durham, North Carolina

John Grammar Brodnax Papers
Brown and Williamson Tobacco Company
  "Visit Historic Petersburg" pamphlet
Charles Campbell Papers
Clopton Family Papers
Winifred A. Cowand Papers

Caleb Hampton Papers
William E. Hardy Papers
Theophilus Hunter Holmes Papers
W. Robert Leckie Papers
A. J. Leavenworth Papers
  "Journal of a Petersburg Civilian"
William Russell Diary and Papers

Snow Family Papers
Edgar Southwick Papers
John Lane Stuart Papers
Rosalia E. Taylor Papers

John R. Turner Papers
James King Wilkerson Papers
Wright Family Papers

Historic New Orleans Collection, New Orleans
  David W. Pipes Memoir

Library of Congress, Washington
  Frank R. McCoy Papers

Library of Virginia, Richmond
  Board of Public Works Papers
  Christ and Grace Episcopal Church
    Records
    Miscellaneous Microfilm, Reel 2030
  Dr. John Herbert Claiborne Letters
  S. Bassett French Biographical Sketches
    Microfilm Reels 4117–4120
  Convention Records of 1861
  Executive Papers of John Letcher

  Executive Papers of William Smith
  William Mahone Papers
    Personal Papers Collection, 1866–95
    Nathaniel Harris Letter, August 2,
    1866
  D. H. Hill Papers
  Henry Thweatt Owen Papers
  William Skinner Simpson Papers

Eleanor S. Brockenbrough Library, Museum of the Confederacy, Richmond
  Confederate Military Leaders Collection
    Letter of William J. Pegram
  Confederate States of America Collection
    Records of Military Court, Department
    of Virginia and North Carolina
  Nora Fontaine Maury Davidson
    "Cullings from the Confederacy 1862–
    1866"
  Keen Family Letters
  Thomas Rowland Papers

  Soldiers and Sailors Families
    Residents of Petersburg
  United Daughters of the Confederacy
    Collection
    Berkeley Minor, "Some Glimpses
    at the Siege of Petersburg, Partly
    from Recollections but Mainly from
    Letters and a Journal Written
    There"
  Rev. L. C. Vass Diary and Papers

National Archives and Records Administration, Washington, D.C.
  Compiled Service Record of Major James F. Milligan, CSA
  Bushrod Johnson Letter Book and Papers, 1864–65
  United States Office of the Adjutant General. Case Files of Applications from For-
    mer Confederates for Presidential Pardons, Record Group 94
  Letters Received Enlisted Branch, Record Group 94
  "Report of Buildings Occupied by U.S. Forces, Provost Marshal's Office, Petersburg,
    Virginia, May 18, 1865," by George C. Kibbe, colonel, Tenth New York Artillery,
    Record Group 292, Records of the U.S. Army, Continental, 1821–1920, Part 4,
    Entry 1712
  Southern Claims Commission Records, Record Group M1407
  "Report of Houses in Petersburg, Virginia Struck by Shells during the Siege from
    June 15, 1864 to April 3, 1865," survey conducted May 1865 by Captain Graham
    and Mr. Bowden of Petersburg, Records of the District of the Nottoway, Record
    Group 94

North Carolina Department of Archives and History, Raleigh
    William Edward Bradley Diary
    Henry Brantingham and W. H. S. Burg-
      wyn Diary
    Alexander England Family Papers
    Daniel Harvey Hill Papers
    Daniel Harvey Hill Jr. Papers
    Robert C. Mabry Papers
    Lowry Shuford Collection
    William Rufus Stephenson Papers
    Whitefield Family Papers

Petersburg National Battlefield, Petersburg
Mrs. Bessie Callender, "Personal Recollections of the Civil War"
    Historical Stories Files
      "Honor among Federals"
      "Odd Bits"
      "Protection When Necessary"

Personal Collections
    Christopher M. Calkins Collection, Petersburg, Virginia
      "Driving Tour of Civil War sites in Petersburg"
    Julie Beckwith Grossmann Collection, Petersburg, Virginia
    Eugene L. Rolfe Collection, Las Vegas, Nevada
      Diary of Private Eugene William Rolfe, *Vermont in the Civil War—One Hundred and Fiftieth Anniversary*, available online at http://www.VermontCivilWar.Org.htm
    Mrs. Anna W. Rollings Collection, Suffolk, Virginia
      Riddick Family Papers, ts. copies courtesy of Brian S. Wills, Wise, Virginia
    David Ward Collection, Lakeville, Connecticut
      GAR Record Book, C. J. Powers Post 391
      Philip R. Woodcock Diary

Union Theological Seminary, Richmond
    Dabney Papers

John Davis Williams Library, University of Mississippi, Oxford
    William C. Nelson Papers

Southern Historical Collection, Wilson Library, University of North Carolina, Chapel Hill
    James W. Albright Papers
    William D. Alexander Diary and Papers
    Anne A. Banister (Mrs. A[rchibald].
      Campbell Pryor)
      "Incidents in the Life of a Civil War
        Child"
    Jesse S. Bean Papers
    Thomas Bragg Diary and Papers
    John Grammar Brodnax Papers
    Bryan Family Papers
    Burwell Family Papers
    William J. Clarke Papers
    Confederate Hospital Records, 2nd NC
      Hospital, Petersburg
    Harrison Henry Cocke Papers
    Lucy S. Costen Papers
    De Rosset Family Papers
    Thomas Pollack Devereaux Papers
    Frank Family Papers
    Gaither Family Papers
    John Cheeves Haskell Papers
      "Reminiscences of the Confederate
        War, 1861–1865"
    Heartt-Wilson Papers
    Joyner Family Papers
    Hattie McIntosh Papers
    Anna Blue McLaurin Papers
    Phifer Family Papers
    Ruffin-Meade Family Papers
    Westwood A. Todd
      "Reminiscences"
    Samuel H. Walkup Diary and Papers

Albert M. White Papers
J. E. Whitehorne Diary
Edmund Jones Williams Letters

Fatima Massey Williams Papers
Lucy Tunstall Alston Williams Papers
William Henry Wills Papers

Alderman Library, University of Virginia, Charlottesville
George S. Bernard Diary and Papers
John H. Claiborne Papers

Vermont Historical Society, Montpelier
Lieutenant Robert Pratt Papers

Virginia Historical Society, Richmond
James W. Albright Diary
Allen Family Papers
Baylor Family Papers
Margaret Stanly Beckwith
    "Reminiscences, 1844–1865"
Bird Family Papers
Blanton Family Papers
    Jennie Friend Stephenson, "My Father
        and His Household, Before, During,
        and After the War"
Alexander Gustavus Brown Papers
J. R. Burchett Letter
Burke Family Papers
Carrington Family Papers
Clarke Family Papers
Coiner Family Papers
Thomas Conolly Diary
Giles Buckner Cooke Diary and Papers
Dearing Family Papers
Charles Henry Dimmock Papers
Thomas Claybrook Elder Papers
Eppes Family Muniments
Godwin Family Papers
Guerrant Family Papers
Abner Crump Hopkins Memoir
Conway Robinson Howard Papers
Keiley Family Papers
Keith Family Papers

Osmun Latrobe Diary
Robert Edward Lee Papers
Robert E. Lee Headquarters Papers
L. Robert Moore Papers
Mary E. Morrison Memoir
Edward Moseley Letters
Henry Chester Parry Papers
Augustus Courtney Peay Papers
James Thomas Perry Papers
Petersburg Enrolling Office Exemption
James Eldred Phillips Papers
David Washington Pipes Memoir
Eleanor Beverley (Meade) Platt Letter
Leiper M. Robinson Memoir
Roller Family Papers
Elizabeth Shenton Papers
Sixth Corps Dispatches
Stacy Family Papers
Joseph D. Stapp Letters
Elliott Lemuel Story Diary
Stuart Family Papers
William Eustace Trahern Memoir
Charles Scott Venable Papers
George Henry Venable Papers
John Bell Vincent Diary
Alvin Coe Voris Papers
David Addison Weisiger Papers
Wise Family Papers

PERSONAL COMMUNICATIONS WITH THE AUTHOR

Henderson, William D. Letter to A. Wilson Greene. December 26, 2003.
Selcer, Richard. E-mail to A. Wilson Greene. July 5, 2004.

PUBLISHED RECORDS OF THE U.S. GOVERNMENT

United States Bureau of the Census. *Agriculture of the United States in 1860, Compiled from the Eighth Census, Dinwiddie County, Virginia.* Washington, D.C., 1864.
United States Bureau of the Census. *Population Schedule of the Seventh Census of the United States: Inhabitants of Dinwiddie County, Virginia.* Washington, D.C., 1850.
United States Bureau of the Census. *Population Schedule of the Eighth Census of the United States: Inhabitants of Dinwiddie County, Virginia.* Washington, D.C., 1860.

United States Naval War Records Office. *Official Records of the Union and Confederate Navies in the War of the Rebellion.* 31 vols. Washington: U.S. Government Printing Office, 1894–1927.

United States War Department. *The War of the Rebellion: A Compilation of the Official Records of the Union and Confederate Armies.* 128 vols. Washington: U.S. Government Printing Office, 1880–1901.

NEWSPAPERS

Arkansas True Democrat
Charleston Mercury
Connecticut Western News
Grant's Petersburg Progress
Macon (Ga.) *Daily Telegraph*
New York Herald
New York Tribune
Petersburg Daily Express
Petersburg Daily Index
Petersburg Daily Register
Petersburg Semi-Weekly Register
Philadelphia Weekly Times
Richmond Daily Dispatch
Richmond Whig
Savannah (Ga.) *Republican*

PUBLISHED MEMOIRS AND PERSONAL PAPERS

Agassiz, George R., ed. *Meade's Headquarters, 1863–1865: Letters of Colonel Theodore Lyman from the Wilderness to Appomattox.* Boston: Massachusetts Historical Society, 1922.

Alexander, Edward Porter. *Military Memoirs of a Confederate: A Critical Narrative.* New York: Charles Scribner's Sons, 1907.

Archer, Fletcher H. "The Defense of Petersburg." In *War Talks of Confederate Veterans,* ed. George S. Bernard. Petersburg, Va.: Fenn and Owen, 1892.

Avary, Myrta Lockett. *Dixie after the War.* Boston: Houghton Mifflin, 1937.

Banister, Anne (Mrs. A[rchibald]. Campbell Pryor). *Incidents in the Life of a Civil War Child.* Blackstone, Va.: W.R. Turner, 1933.

Beale, G. W. *A Lieutenant of Cavalry in Lee's Army.* Boston: Gorham Press, 1918.

Benson, Susan Williams, ed. *Berry Benson's Civil War Book: Memoirs of a Confederate Scout and Sharpshooter.* Athens: University of Georgia Press, 1992.

Berlin, Ira, ed. *Freedom: A Documentary History of Emancipation, 1861–1867.* Cambridge: Cambridge University Press, 1982.

Bernard, George S., ed. *War Talks of Confederate Veterans.* Petersburg, Va.: Fenn and Owen, 1892.

Blackett, R. J. M., ed. *Thomas Morris Chester, Black Civil War Correspondent: His Dispatches from the Virginia Front.* Baton Rouge: Louisiana State University Press, 1989.

Bond, Natalie Jenkins, and Osmun Latrobe Coward, eds. *The South Carolinians: Colonel Asbury Coward's Memoirs.* New York: Vantage Press, 1968.

Carroll, Gordon, ed. *The Desolate South, 1865–1866.* Boston: Little, Brown and Company, 1956.

Chamberlayne, Churchill G., ed. *Ham Chamberlayne, Virginian: Letters and Papers of an Artillery Officer in the War for Southern Independence.* Richmond, Va.: Dietz Press, 1932.

Civil War Documents, Granville County, N.C. 2 vols. Oxford, N.C.: Granville County Historical Society, n.d.

Claiborne, John Herbert. "Last Days of Lee and His Paladins." In *War Talks of Confederate Veterans,* ed. George S. Bernard. Petersburg, Va.: Fenn and Owen, 1892.

———. *Seventy-five Years in Old Virginia.* New York: Neale Publishing, 1904.

Cockrell, Monroe F., ed. *Gunner with Stonewall: Reminiscences of William Thomas Poague.* Jackson, Tenn.: McCowat-Mercer Press, 1957.

Contributions to a History of the Richmond Howitzer Battalion. Baltimore: Butternut and Blue, 2000.

Corsan, W. C. *Two Months in the Confederate States.* London: Richard Bentley, 1863.

Corson, Blake W., ed. *My Dear Jennie.* Richmond, Va.: Dietz Press, 1982.

Couture, Richard T. *Charlie's Letters: The Civil War Correspondence of Charles E. Denoon.* n.p., 1989.

Crofts, Daniel W., ed. *Cobb's Ordeal: The Diaries of a Virginia Farmer, 1842-1872.* Athens: University of Georgia Press, 1997.

Dayton, Ruth Woods, ed. *The Diary of a Confederate Soldier: James E. Hall.* n.p., 1961.

de Pineton, Adolphe, Marquis de Chambrun. *Impressions of Lincoln and the Civil War: A Foreigner's Account.* New York: Random House, 1952.

Douglas, Henry Kyd. *I Rode with Stonewall.* Chapel Hill: University of North Carolina Press, 1940.

Dowdey, Clifford, and Louis H. Manarin, eds. *The Wartime Papers of R. E. Lee.* 2 vols. 1961. Reprint, Pennington, N.J.: 1996.

Elmore, Fletcher L., Jr., compiler. *Diary of J. E. Whitehorne 1st Sgt. Co. F Twelfth Va. Infantry A. P. Hill's Third Corps A. N. Va.* Louisville, Ky.: n.p., 1995.

French, Samuel G. *Two Wars: An Autobiography of General Samuel G. French.* Nashville: Confederate Veteran, 1901.

Gallagher, Gary W., ed. *Fighting for the Confederacy: The Personal Recollections of General Edward Porter Alexander.* Chapel Hill: University of North Carolina Press, 1989.

Girard, Charles. *A Visit to the Confederate States of America in 1863.* Tuscaloosa, Ala.: Confederate Publishing, 1962.

Gordon, Armistead Churchill. *Memories and Memorials of William Gordon McCabe.* Richmond, Va.: Old Dominion Press, 1925.

Gordon, John B., General. *Reminiscences of the Civil War.* New York: Charles Scribner's Sons, 1903.

Goree, Langston James, V., ed. *The Thomas Jewett Goree Letters.* Vol. 1, *Civil War Correspondence.* Bryan, Tex.: Family History Foundation, 1981.

Grant, Ulysses S. *Personal Memoirs of U. S. Grant.* 2 vols. New York: Charles Webster and Company, 1885.

Hagood, Johnson. *Memoirs of the War of Secession.* 1910. Reprint, Germantown, Tenn., 1994.

Harrison, Walter. *Pickett's Men: A Fragment of War History.* New York: D. Van Nostrand, Publisher, 1870.

Heartsill, William W. *Fourteen Hundred and Ninety-one Days in the Confederate Army.* Marshall, Tex.: Published by the author, 1876.

Hinton, William E. "An Eye Witness." In *War Talks of Confederate Veterans,* ed. George S. Bernard. Petersburg, Va.: Fenn and Owen, 1892.

Inman, Arthur Crew, ed. *Soldier of the South: General Pickett's War Letters to His Wife*. Boston: Houghton Mifflin, 1928.

Jones, J. William, D.D. *Christ in the Camp or Religion in the Confederate Army*. Richmond, Va.: B. F. Johnson and Co., 1887.

Jones, John B. *A Rebel War Clerk's Diary*. 2 vols. Philadelphia: J. B. Lippincott and Co., 1866.

Keckley, Elizabeth Hobbs. *Behind the Scenes*. New York: G. W. Carleton and Company, 1868.

Keiley, Anthony M. *Prisoner of War, or Five Months among the Yankees*. Richmond, Va.: West and Johnson, 1865.

Lane, Mills, ed. *Dear Mother, Don't Grieve about me. If I get killed, I'll only be dead: Letters from Georgia Soldiers in the Civil War*. Savannah: Library of Georgia, 1990.

Lankford, Nelson D., ed. *An Irishman in Dixie: Thomas Conolly's Diary of the Fall of the Confederacy*. Columbia: University of South Carolina Press, 1988.

Lawing, Mike, and Carolyn Lawing, eds. *My Dearest Friend: The Civil War Correspondence of Cornelia McGimsey and Lewis Warlick*. Durham, N.C.: Carolina Academic Press, n.d.

Ledoux, Tom, ed. *Quite Ready to Be Sent Somewhere: The Civil War Letters of Aldace Freeman Walker*. Victoria, B.C. Canada: Trafford Publishing, 2002.

Leon, Louis. *Diary of a Tar Heel Confederate Soldier*. Charlotte, N.C.: Stone Publishing Co., 1913.

McCrea, Henry Vaughan. *Red Dirt and Isinglass: A Wartime Biography of a Confederate Soldier*. Marianna, Fla.: Chipola Press, 1992.

McMurry, Richard M., ed. *Footprints of a Regiment: A Recollection of the First Georgia Regulars, 1861–1865*. Atlanta, Ga.: Longstreet Press, 1992.

Mills, Laurens Tenney. *A South Carolina Family*. n.p., 1960.

Montgomery, George F., Jr., ed. *Georgia Sharpshooter: The Civil War Diary and Letters of William Rhadamanthus Montgomery, 1839–1906*. Macon, Ga.: Mercer University Press, 1997.

Morrill, Lilly Logan, ed. *My Confederate Girlhood: The Memoirs of Kate Virginia Cox Logan*. Richmond, Va., 1932.

Moseley, Ronald H., ed. *The Stilwell Letters: A Georgian in Longstreet's Corps, Army of Northern Virginia*. Macon, Ga.: Mercer University Press, 2002.

Neese, George M. *Three Years in the Confederate Horse Artillery*. New York: Neale Publishing, 1911.

Nevins, Allen, ed. *A Diary of Battle: The Personal Journals of Colonel Charles S. Wainwright, 1861–1865*. New York: Harcourt, Brace and World, 1962.

Osborne, Frederick M., ed. *Private Osborne, Massachusetts Twenty-third Volunteers*. Jefferson, N.C.: McFarland and Company, 1999.

Owen, William Miller. *In Camp and Battle with the Washington Artillery of New Orleans*. Boston: Ticknor and Company, 1885.

Palmer, Beverly Wilson, ed. *The Selected Letters of Charles Sumner*. 2 vols. Boston: Northeastern University Press, 1990.

Pearce, T. H., ed. *Diary of Captain Henry A. Chambers*. Wendell, N.C.: Broadfoot's Bookmark, 1983.

Pickett, LaSalle Corbell. *Pickett and His Men*. Atlanta: Foote and Davies, 1899.

Porter, David Dixon. *Incidents and Anecdotes of the Civil War*. New York: D. Appleton and Company, 1885.

Porter, Horace. *Campaigning with Grant.* New York: Century Company, 1897.

Pryor, Mrs. Roger A. *My Day: Reminiscences of a Long Life.* New York: McMillan Company, 1907.

———. *Reminiscences of Peace and War.* New York: Macmillan, 1904.

Putnam, Sallie B. *Richmond during the War: Four Years of Personal Observation.* New York: G. W. Carleton and Co., 1867.

Roberts, W. H. *Drums and Guns around Petersburg.* Bowie, Md.: Heritage Books, 1995.

Robertson, James I., Jr., ed. *The Civil War Letters of General Robert McAllister.* New Brunswick, N.J.: Rutgers University Press, 1965.

Rosenblatt, Emil, and Ruth Rosenblatt, eds. *Anti-Rebel: The Civil War Letters of Wilbur Fisk.* Croton-on-Hudson, N.Y.: Published by the editors, 1983.

Sanders, George, ed. *Dear Hattie: The Civil War Letters of Mary Harriet Peek Including Those from her Brother Henry Thomas Peek of the Washington Artillery of New Orleans.* Albuquerque: Printed by the author, 1998.

Scarborough, William Kauffman, ed. *The Diary of Edmund Ruffin.* 3 Vols. Baton Rouge: Louisiana State University Press, 1972–1989.

Schiller, Herbert M., ed. *A Captain's War: The Letters and Diaries of William H. S. Burgwyn.* Shippensburg, Pa.: White Mane Publishing, 1994.

Scott, Robert Garth, ed. *Forgotten Valor: The Memoirs, Journals, and Civil War Letters of Orlando B. Willcox.* Kent, Ohio: Kent State University Press, 1999.

Sears, Stephen W., ed. *For Country, Cause and Leader: The Civil War Journal of Charles B. Haydon.* New York: Ticknor and Fields, 1993.

———, ed. *The Civil War Papers of George B. McClellan.* New York: Ticknor and Fields, 1989.

Simon, John Y., ed. *The Papers of Ulysses S. Grant.* 28 vols. to date. Carbondale: Southern Illinois University Press, 1967–.

Silver, James W., ed. *A Life for the Confederacy as Recorded in the Pocket Diaries of Pvt. Robert A. Moore.* Jackson, Tenn.: McCowat-Mercer Press, 1959.

Sloan, John A. *Reminiscences of the Guilford Grays, Co. B. Twenty-seventh N.C. Regiment.* Washington: R. O. Polkinhorn, 1883.

Smith, Gustavus W. *Confederate War Papers.* New York: Atlantic Publishing Co., 1884.

Stevens, Michael E., ed. *As if It Were Glory: Robert Beecham's Civil War from the Iron Brigade to the Black Regiments.* Madison, Wisc.: Madison House, 1998.

Stocker, Jeffrey D., ed. *From Huntsville to Appomattox. R. T. Coles's History of Fourth Regiment, Alabama Volunteer Infantry, C.S.A., Army of Northern Virginia.* Knoxville: University of Tennessee Press, 1996.

Thomas, Samuel N., Jr., and Jason H. Silverman, eds. *"A Rising Star of Promise": The Civil War Odyssey of David Jackson Logan.* Campbell, Calif.: Savas Publishing, 1998.

Tower, R. Lockwood, ed. *Lee's Adjutant: The Wartime Letters of Colonel Walter Herron Taylor, 1862-1865.* Columbia: University of South Carolina Press, 1995.

Townsend, George Alfred. *Rustics in Rebellion: A Yankee Reporter on the Road to Richmond, 1861-1865.* Chapel Hill: University of North Carolina Press, 1950.

Tribble, Byrd Barnette. *Benjamin Cason Rawlings: First Virginia Volunteer for the South.* Baltimore: Butternut and Blue, 1996.

Trowbridge, John T. *The Desolate South, 1865-1866: A Picture of the Battlefields and of the Devastated Confederacy.* New York: Duell, Sloan and Pearce, 1956.

Vandiver, Frank E., ed. *The Civil War Diary of General Josiah Gorgas.* Tuscaloosa: University of Alabama Press, 1947.

Welch, Spencer Glasgow. *A Confederate Surgeon's Letters to His Wife.* New York: Neale Publishing, 1911.

Wiatt, Alex L., ed. *Confederate Chaplain William Edward Wiatt: An Annotated Diary.* Lynchburg, Va.: H. E. Howard, 1994.

Wiggins, Sarah Woolfolk, ed. *The Journals of Josiah Gorgas, 1857–1878.* Tuscaloosa: University of Alabama Press, 1995.

Wiley, Kenneth, ed. *Norfolk Blues: The Civil War Diary of the Norfolk Light Artillery Blues.* By John Walters. Shippensburg, Pa.: Burd Street Press, 1997.

Williams, Edward B., ed. *Rebel Brothers: The Civil War Letters of the Truehearts.* College Station: Texas A and M University Press, 1995.

Wright, Stuart T., ed. *The Confederate Letters of Benjamin H. Freeman.* Hicksville, N.Y.: Exposition Press, 1974.

———, ed. *Memoirs of Alfred Horatio Belo: Reminiscences of a North Carolina Volunteer.* Gaithersburg, Md.: Olde Soldier Books, n.d.

MISCELLANEOUS PUBLICATIONS AND REFERENCE DOCUMENTS

Allardice, Bruce S. *More Generals in Gray.* Baton Rouge: Louisiana State University Press, 1995.

Bailey, James H., commentator. *Pictures of the Past: Petersburg Seen by the Simpsons.* Petersburg, Va.: Fort Henry Branch of the APVA, 1989.

Bearss, Sara, ed. *Dictionary of Virginia Biography.* 3 vols. to date. Richmond, Va.: Library of Virginia, 2000–.

Beers, Henry Putney. *The Confederacy: A Guide to the Archives of the Government of the Confederate States of America.* Washington: National Archives and Records Administration, 1986.

Cappon, Lester J. *Virginia Newspapers, 1821–1935.* New York: D. Appleton-Century Company, 1936.

The City of Petersburg,Virginia: The Book of the Chamber of Commerce. Petersburg, Va.: George W. Englehardt, 1894.

Current, Richard N., ed. *Encyclopedia of the Confederacy.* 4 vols. New York: Simon and Schuster, 1993.

DiGiuseppe, Thomas E., compiler. "Confederate 1st Company Independent Signal Corps." Reference document (ts.) provided to the author.

Dozier, Graham T., compiler. *Virginia's Civil War: A Guide to the Manuscripts at the Virginia Historical Society.* Richmond: Virginia Historical Society, 1998.

Ferslew, W. Eugene, compiler. *First Annual Directory of the City of Petersburg to Which Is Added a Business Directory.* Petersburg, Va.: George E. Ford, 1859.

Flournoy, H. W., ed. *Calendar of Virginia State Papers and Other Manuscripts.* 11 vols. Richmond, Va.: 1893.

A Guide to the Fortifications and Battlefields around Petersburg, Petersburg, Va.: Daily Index Job Print, 1866.

Ingram, E. Renee, compiler. *In View of the Great Want of Labor: A Legislative History of African American Conscription in the Confederacy.* Westminster, Md.: Willow Bend Books, 2002.

Krick, Robert E. L. *Staff Officers in Gray.* Chapel Hill: University of North Carolina Press, 2003.

Krick, Robert K. *Lee's Colonels*. Dayton, Ohio: Press of Morningside Bookshop, 1979.
Manarin, Louis H., ed. *Richmond at War: The Minutes of the City Council, 1861–1865*. Chapel Hill: University of North Carolina Press, 1966.
Pollock, Edward. *Historical and Industrial Guide to Petersburg, Virginia*. Petersburg, Va.: n.p., 1884.
Reese, George H., ed. *Proceedings of the Virginia State Convention of 1861*. 4 vols. Richmond, Va.: Virginia State Library, 1965.
Robertson, James I., Jr., ed. *Proceedings of the Advisory Council of the State of Virginia April 21–June 19, 1861*. Richmond: Virginia State Library, 1977.
Supplement to the Official Records of the Union and Confederate Armies. 70 vols. Wilmington, N.C.: Broadfoot, 1994–2000.
Wallace, Lee A., Jr. *A Guide to Virginia Military Organizations, 1861–1865*. Lynchburg, Va.: H. E. Howard, 1986.
Welcher, Frank J. *The Union Army, 1861–1865: Organization and Operations*. 2 vols. Bloomington: Indiana University Press, 1989–1993.

UNIT HISTORIES

Alderman, John Perry. *Twenty-ninth Virginia Infantry*. Lynchburg, Va.: H. E. Howard, 1989.
Andrus, Michael J. *The Brooke, Fauquier, Loudoun and Alexandria Artillery* Lynchburg, Va.: H. E. Howard, 1990.
Ashcraft, John M. *Thirty-first Virginia Infantry*. Lynchburg, Va.: H. E. Howard, 1988.
Balfour, Daniel T. *Thirteenth Virginia Cavalry*. Lynchburg, Va.: H. E. Howard, 1986.
Bell, Robert T. *Eleventh Virginia Infantry*. Lynchburg, Va.: H. E. Howard, 1985.
Best, Isaac O. *History of the 121st New York State Infantry*. Chicago: Lieut. Jas. H. Smith, 1921.
Billings, John D. *The History of the Tenth Massachusetts Battery of Light Artillery in the War of the Rebellion*. Boston: Arakelvan Press, 1909.
Bowen, James Lorenzo. *History of the Thirty-Seventh Regiment Massachusetts Volunteers, in the Civil War of 1861–1865, With a Comprehensive Sketch of the Doings of Massachusetts as a State, and of the Principal Campaigns of the War*. Holyoke, Mass.: Clark W. Bryan and Company, 1884.
Cavanaugh, Michael A. *Sixth Virginia Infantry*. Lynchburg, Va.: H. E. Howard, 1988.
Chapla, John D. *Fiftieth Virginia Infantry*. Lynchburg, Va.: H. E. Howard, 1997.
Chernault, Tracy, and Jeffrey C. Weaver. *Eighteenth and Twentieth Battalions of Heavy Artillery*. Lynchburg, Va.: H. E. Howard, 1995.
Clark, Walter, ed. *Histories of the Several Regiments and Battalions from North Carolina in the Great War, 1861–65: Written by Members of the Respective Commands*. 5 vols. Goldsboro, N.C.: Nash Brothers, 1901.
Coker, James L. *History of Company G, Ninth S.S. Regiment, S.C. Army and of Company E, Sixth S.C. Regiment, S.C. Army*. Charleston, S.C.: Press of Walker, Evans and Cogswell, 1899.
Collins, Darrel L. *Forty-sixth Virginia Infantry*. Lynchburg, Va.: H. E. Howard, 1992.
Crew, R. Thomas, Jr., and Benjamin H. Trask. *Grimes' Battery, Grandy's Battery, and Huger's Battery Virginia Artillery*. Lynchburg, Va.: H. E. Howard, 1995.
Crews, Edward R., and Timothy A. Parrish. *Fourteenth Virginia Infantry*. Lynchburg, Va.: H. E. Howard, 1995.
Dickert, D. Augustus. *History of Kershaw's Brigade*. Newberry, S.C.: E. H. Aull, 1899.

Divine, John E. *Eighth Virginia Infantry*. Lynchburg, Va.: H. E. Howard, 1983.

Driver, Robert J. *Fifth Virginia Cavalry*. Lynchburg, Va.: H. E. Howard, 1997.

Driver, Robert J., and Kevin C. Ruffner. *The First Battalion Virginia Infantry, Thirty-ninth Battalion Virginia Cavalry, Twenty-fourth Battalion Virginia Partisan Rangers*. Lynchburg, Va.: H. E. Howard, 1996.

Fields, Frank E. *Twenty-eighth Virginia Infantry*. Lynchburg, Va.: H. E. Howard, 1985.

Fortier, John. *Fifteenth Virginia Cavalry*. Lynchburg, Va.: H. E. Howard, 1993.

Gunn, Ralph White. *Twenty-fourth Virginia Infantry*. Lynchburg, Va.: H. E. Howard, 1987.

Haynes, Edwin Mortimer, Chaplain. *A History of the Tenth Regiment Vermont Volunteers, with Biographical Sketches of the Officers who fell in Battle and a Complete Roster of all the Officers and Men Concerned With it—Showing all Changes By Promotion, Death, or Resignation, During the Military Existence of the Regiment*. Lewiston, Me.: Journal Steam Press, 1870.

Henderson, William D. *The Forty-first Virginia Infantry*. Lynchburg, Va.: H. E. Howard, 1986.

———. *The Twelfth Virginia Infantry*. Lynchburg, Va.: H. E. Howard, 1984.

Gregory, G. Howard. *Fifty-third Virginia Infantry and Fifth Battalion Virginia Infantry*. Lynchburg, Va.: H. E. Howard, 1999.

———. *The Thirty-eighth Virginia Infantry*. Lynchburg, Va.: H. E. Howard, 1988.

Holland, Darryl. *Twenty-fourth Virginia Cavalry*. Lynchburg, Va.: H. E. Howard, 1997.

Jensen, Les. *Thirty-second Virginia Infantry*. Lynchburg, Va.: H. E. Howard, 1990.

Jones, Benjamin W. *Under the Stars and Bars: A History of the Surry Light Artillery*. Richmond, Va.: Everett and Waddey Company, 1909.

Jordan, Ervin L., Jr., and Herbert A. Thomas Jr. *Nineteenth Virginia Infantry*. Lynchburg, Va.: H. E. Howard, 1987.

Krick, Robert K. *The Fredericksburg Artillery*. Lynchburg, Va.: H. E. Howard, 1986.

———. *Thirtieth Virginia Infantry*. Lynchburg, Va.: H. E. Howard, 1983.

Manarin, Louis H. *Fifteenth Virginia Infantry*. Lynchburg, Va.: H. E. Howard, 1990.

Mills, George Henry. *History of the Sixteenth North Carolina Regiment in the Civil War*. Reprint. Hamilton, N.Y.: Edmonston Publishing, 1992.

Moore, Robert H. *Chew's Ashby, Shoemaker's Lynchburg and the Newtown Artillery*. Lynchburg, Va.: H. E. Howard, 1995.

———. *Graham's Petersburg, Jackson's Kanawha, and Lurty's Roanoke Horse Artillery*. Lynchburg, Va.: H. E. Howard, 1996.

———. *The Richmond Fayette, Hampden, Thomas, and Blount's Lynchburg Artillery*. Lynchburg, Va.: H. E. Howard, 1991.

Murphy, Terrence V. *Tenth Virginia Infantry*. Lynchburg, Va.: H. E. Howard, 1989.

Riggs, David F. *Seventh Virginia Infantry*. Lynchburg, Va.: H. E. Howard, 1982.

Robertson, James I., Jr. *Eighteenth Virginia Infantry*. Lynchburg, Va.: H. E. Howard, 1984.

Sherwood, George L. *The Mathews Light Artillery, Penick's Pittsylvania Artillery, Young's Halifax Artillery, and Johnson's Jackson Flying Artillery*. Lynchburg, Va.: H. E. Howard, 1999.

Sherwood, George L., and Jeffrey C. Weaver. *Fifty-ninth Virginia Infantry*. Lynchburg, Va.: H. E. Howard, 1994.

Sherwood, W. Cullen, and Richard L. Nicholas. *Amherst Artillery, Albemarle Artillery, and Sturdivant's Battery.* Lynchburg, Va.: H. E. Howard, 1996.

Sublett, Charles W. *Fifty-seventh Virginia Infantry.* Lynchburg, Va.: H. E. Howard, 1985.

Trask, Benjamin H. *Ninth Virginia Infantry.* Lynchburg, Va.: H. E. Howard, 1984.

———. *Sixty-first Virginia Infantry.* Lynchburg, Va.: H. E. Howard, 1988.

Wallace, Lee A., Jr. *First Virginia Infantry.* Lynchburg,Va.: H. E. Howard, 1984.

———. *Seventeenth Virginia Infantry.* Lynchburg, Va.: H. E. Howard, 1990.

———. *Third Virginia Infantry.* Lynchburg,Va.: H. E. Howard, 1986.

Weaver, Jeffrey C. *Branch, Harrington and Staunton Hill Artillery.* Lynchburg, Va.: H. E. Howard, 1997.

———. *Brunswick Rebel, Johnston, Southside, United, James City, Lunenburg Rebel, Pamunkey Heavy Artillery and Young's Harborguard.* Lynchburg, Va.: H. E. Howard, 1996.

———. *Fifty-fourth Virginia Infantry.* Lynchburg, Va.: H. E. Howard, 1993.

———. *Sixty-third Virginia Infantry.* Lynchburg, Va.: H. E. Howard, 1991.

———. *The Virginia Home Guards.* Lynchburg, Va.: H. E. Howard, 1996.

Wiatt, Alex L. *The Twenty-sixth Virginia Infantry.* Lynchburg, Va.: H. E. Howard, 1984.

Wyckoff, Mac. *A History of the Second South Carolina Infantry, 1861–65.* Fredericksburg, Va.: Sergeant Kirkland's Museum and Historical Society, 1994.

ARTICLES AND ESSAYS

Atwood, Joseph S. "Lincoln at Petersburg." *National Tribune*, Sept. 17, 1911.

Barnes, John S. "With Lincoln from Washington to Richmond in 1865." *Appleton's Magazine* 9, no. 5 (May 1907): 515–24.

———. "With Lincoln from Washington to Richmond in 1865." *Appleton's Magazine* 9, no. 6 (June 1907): 742–51.

Beauregard, [P.] G. T. "Four Days of Battle at Petersburg." In *Battles and Leaders of the Civil War*, vol. 4, ed. Robert U. Johnson and Clarence C. Buel, 540–44. New York: Century Co., 1887–88.

Birdsong, James G. "The Petersburg Grays." *Southern Historical Society Papers* 36 (1908): 360–61.

Bradwell, I[ssac]. G[ordon]. "Last Days of the Confederacy." *Confederate Veteran* 29 (1929): 56–58.

Butterfield, M[iles]. L. "Personal Reminiscences with the Sixth Corps, 1864–5." *War Papers Being Papers Read Before the Commandery of the State of Wisconsin Military Order of the Loyal Legion of the United States.* Vol. 4, 85–93. Milwaukee: Burdick, Armitage and Allen, 1914.

Calkins, Chris M. "A Geographic Description of the Petersburg Battlefields: June 1864–April 1865." *Virginia Geographer* 16 (Spring–Summer 1984): 16–22.

Castel, Albert. "Theophilus Holmes—Pallbearer of the Confederacy." *Civil War Times Illustrated* 16, no. 4 (July 1977): 10–17.

Collier, Charles F. "War Recollections. Story of the Evacuation of Petersburg, by an Eye-Witness." *Southern Historical Society Papers* 22 (1894): 69–73.

Colston, R[aleigh]. E. "Repelling the First Assault on Petersburg." In *Battles and Leaders of the Civil War*, vol. 4, ed. Robert U. Johnson and Clarence C. Buel, 535–37. New York: Century Co., 1887–88.

Crook, William H. "Lincoln as I Knew Him." *Harper's Monthly Magazine* 62 (June 1907): 41–48.

Davi[d]son, Miss Nora F. "Confederate Hospitals at Petersburg, Va." *Confederate Veteran* 29 (1921): 338–39.

de Pineton, Adolphe, Marquis de Chambrun. "Personal Recollections of Mr. Lincoln." *Scribner's Magazine* 13, no. 1 (Jan. 1893): 26–38.

Earp, Charles A. "Two Johns Hopkins University Confederates." *Confederate Veteran* 43, no. 5 (Sept.–Oct. 1994): 18–24.

Gordon, Leslie J. "The Generalship of George E. Pickett after the Battle of Gettysburg." In *Leadership and Command in the American Civil War*, ed. Steven E. Woodworth, 147–94. Campbell, Cal.: Savas Woodbury Publishers, 1996.

Groene, Bertram H., ed. "Civil War Letters of Colonel David Lang." *Florida Historical Quarterly* 54 (Jan. 1976): 340–66.

Hartzell, Lawrence L. "The Explanation of Freedom in Black Petersburg, Virginia, 1865–1902." In *The Edge of the South: Life in Nineteenth-Century Virginia*, ed. Edward L. Ayers and John C. Willis. Charlottesville, Va.: University Press of Virginia, 1991.

Henderson, William D. "The Evolution of Petersburg's Economy, 1860–1900." *Virginia Geographer* 16 (Spring–Summer 1984): 23–42.

Jackson, Luther P. "Free Negroes of Petersburg, Virginia." *Journal of Negro History* 12 (July 1927): 365–88.

Jordan, Ervin L., Jr. "Different Drummers: Black Virginians as Confedearte Loyalists." In *Black Southerners in Gray. Essays on Afro-Americans in Confederate Armies*, ed. Richard Rollins, 57–74. Redondo Beach, Cal.: Rank and File Publications, 1994.

Jordan, Mark H. "Gibbon's Plan for Taking Petersburg in '62." *Civil War Times Illustrated* 1, no. 3 (June 1962): 17.

Kautz, August V. "Operations South of the James River." In *Battles and Leaders of the Civil War*, Vol. 4, ed. Robert U. Johnson and Clarence C. Buel, 533–35. New York: Century Co., 1887–88.

Kilmer, George L. "Petersburg: Historic Incidents of the Closing Days before the City, Taking Possession." *Philadelphia Weekly Times*, November 28, 1885.

Kimbrough, J[oseph]. S[ydney]. "From Petersburg to Hart's Island Prison." *Confederate Veteran* 22 (1914): 498–500.

Oram, Richard W., ed. "Harper's Ferry to the Fall of Richmond: Letters of Colonel John De Hart Ross, C.S.A., 1861–1865." *West Virginia History* 45 (1984): 159–74.

Power, J. Tracy. "Robert Ransom." In *Encyclopedia of the Confederacy*, ed. Richard N. Current. 4 vols., 3:1307–8. New York: Simon and Schuster, 1993.

Pryor, Anne Banister. "A Child's Recollections of War." *Confederate Veteran* 39, no. 2 (Feb. 1931): 54–57.

Reidenbaugh, Lowell. "Micah Jenkins." In *Encyclopedia of the Confederacy*, ed. Richard N. Current. 4 vols., 2:844. New York: Simon and Schuster, 1993.

Roberts, Edward S. "War Reminiscences." *Connecticut Western News*, February 1, 1912.

Robertson, James I., Jr., ed. "English Views of the Civil War: A Unique Excursion to Virginia, April 2–8, 1865." *Virginia Magazine of History and Biography* 77 (April 1969): 201–12.

"A Sketch of 12 Months Service in the Mobile Rifle Co." *Alabama Historical Quarterly* 25, no. 1 (Spring 1963): 149–89.

Smith, James W. "The Role of Blacks in Petersburg's Carrying Trade and Service-oriented Industry, 1800–1865." *Virginia Geographer* 16 (Spring–Summer 1984): 43–54.

Wagstaff, H. M., ed. *The James A. Graham Papers, 1861–1884*. Chapel Hill: University of North Carolina Press, 1928.

Wallace, Lee A., Jr. "Musters at Poplar Lawn." *Virginia Cavalcade* 17 (Winter 1968): 4–10.

Wilcox, Cadmus M. "Defense of Batteries Gregg and Whitworth, and the Evacuation of Petersburg." *Southern Historical Society Papers* 4 (1877): 18–33.

Wixcey, William T. "First Flag in Petersburg." *National Tribune*, July 4, 1907.

Woodworth, Steven E. "General P. G. T. Beauregard and the Bermuda Hundred Campaign." In *Leadership and Command in the American Civil War*, ed. Steven E. Woodworth, 197–230. Campbell, Cal.; Savas Woodbury Publishers, 1996.

Wyatt, Edward A., IV. "The Rise of Industry in Ante-Bellum Petersburg," *William & Mary Quarterly*, 2nd Series, 17, no. 1 (Jan. 1937): 1–36.

Secondary Sources

Ayers, Edward L. *In the Presence of Mine Enemies: War in the Heart of America, 1859–1863*. New York: W.W. Norton, 2003.

Ayers, Edward L., and John C. Willis, eds. *The Edge of the South: Life in Nineteenth-century Virginia*. Charlottesville: University Press of Virginia, 1991.

Bailey, James H. *A Century of Catholicism in Historic Petersburg: A History of Saint Joseph's Parish*. n.p., 1942.

———. *Old Petersburg*. Richmond, Va.: Hale Publishing, 1976.

Baker, Jean H. *Mary Todd Lincoln: A Biography*. New York: W.W. Norton, 1987.

Barefoot, Daniel W. *General Robert F. Hoke: Lee's Modest Warrior*. Winston-Salem, N.C.: John F. Blair Publisher, 1996.

Barrett, John G. *The Civil War in North Carolina*. Chapel Hill: University of North Carolina Press, 1963.

Bearss, Ed. *River of Lost Opportunities: The Civil War on the James River, 1861–1862*. Lynchburg, Va.: H. E. Howard, 1995.

Bearss, Ed, and Chris Calkins. *The Battle of Five Forks*. Lynchburg, Va.: H. E. Howard, 1985.

Bergeron, Arthur W., Jr. *Confederate Mobile*. Jackson: University Press of Mississippi, 1991.

Bill, Alfred Hoyt. *The Beleaguered City: Richmond, 1861–65*. New York: Alfred A. Knopf, 1946.

Boney, F. N. *John Letcher of Virginia: The Story of Virginia's Civil War Governor*. Tuscaloosa: University of Alabama Press, 1966.

Bradley, Mark L. *This Astounding Close: The Road to Bennett Place*. Chapel Hill: University of North Carolina Press, 2000.

Brewer, James H. *The Confederate Negro: Virginia's Craftsmen and Military Laborers, 1861–1865*. Durham, N.C.: Duke University Press, 1969.

Bridges, Hal. *Lee's Maverick General: Daniel Harvey Hill*. New York: McGraw-Hill Book Company, 1961.

Brown, J. Willard. *The Signal Corps, U.S.A., in the War of the Rebellion*. Boston: U.S. Veteran Signal Corps Association, 1896.

Buck, Paul H. *The Road to Reunion*. Boston: Little, Brown and Company, 1937.

Burton, Brian K. *Extraordinary Circumstances: The Seven Days' Battles.* Bloomington: Indiana University Press, 2001.

Calkins, Chris. *Auto Tour of Civil War Petersburg, 1861–1865.* Petersburg, Va.: City of Petersburg, 2003.

Calos, Mary, Charlotte Easterling, and Ella Sue Rayburn, eds. *Old City Point and Hopewell: The First 370 Years.* Norfolk, Va.: Donning Co., 1983.

Carmichael, Peter S. *William R. J. Pegram: Lee's Young Artillerist.* Charlottesville: University Press of Virginia, 1995.

Cavanaugh, Michael A., and William Marvel. *The Battle of the Crater: "The Horrid Pit," June 25–August 6, 1864.* Lynchburg, Va.: H. E. Howard, 1989.

Channing, Steven A. *Crisis of Fear: Secession in South Carolina.* New York: Simon and Schuster, 1970.

Cooper, William J., Jr. *Jefferson Davis, American.* New York: Alfred A. Knopf, 2000.

Cormier, Steven A. *The Siege of Suffolk: The Forgotten Campaign, April 11–May 4, 1863.* Lynchburg, Va.: H. E. Howard, 1989.

Crofts, Daniel W. *Reluctant Confederates: Upper South Unionists in the Secession Crisis.* Chapel Hill: University of North Carolina Press, 1989.

Cummings, Charles M. *Yankee Quaker Confederate General: The Curious Career of Bushrod Rust Johnson.* 1971. Reprint, Columbus, Ohio: 1993.

Cunningham, H. H. *Doctors in Gray: The Confederate Medical Service.* Baton Rouge: Louisiana State University Press, 1958.

Dabney, Virginius. *Richmond, the Story of a City.* Garden City, N.Y.: Doubleday and Company, 1976.

Davis, Arthur Kyle. *Three Centuries of an Old Virginia Town: The Story of Petersburg, Its History and Memorials.* Richmond, Va.:, n.p., 1923.

Davis, William C. *Breckinridge: Statesman Soldier Symbol.* Baton Rouge: Louisiana State University Press, 1974.

———. *A Government of Our Own: The Making of the Confederacy.* New York: The Free Press, 1994.

———. *The Union That Shaped the Confederacy.* Lawrence: University Press of Kansas, 2001.

Detzer, David. *Allegiance: Fort Sumter, Charleston, and the Beginning of the Civil War.* New York: Harcourt, 2001.

Donald, David Herbert. *Lincoln.* New York: Simon and Schuster, 1995.

Dozier, Howard Douglas. *A History of the Atlantic Coast Line Railroad.* New York: Houghton Mifflin, 1920.

Drewry, Patrick Henry. *The Story of a Church: A History of Washington Street Church at Petersburg, Virginia, 1773–1923.* Petersburg, Va.: Plummer Printing Company, 1923.

Eanes, Greg. *"Destroy the Junction": The Wilson-Kautz Raid and the Battle for the Staunton River Bridge, June 21, 1864 to July 1, 1864.* Lynchburg, Va.: H. E. Howard, 1999.

Eaton, Clement. *A History of the Southern Confederacy.* New York: Macmillan, 1954.

Eckenrode, H. J., and Bryan Conrad. *James Longstreet: Lee's Old War Horse.* Chapel Hill: University of North Carolina Press, 1936.

Eckert, Ralph Lowell. *John Brown Gordon: Soldier Southerner American.* Baton Rouge: Louisiana State University Press, 1989.

Fishel, Edwin C. *The Secret War for the Union.* Boston: Houghton Mifflin, 1996.

Freeman, Douglas Southall. *Lee's Lieutenants: A Study in Command.* 3 vols. New York: Charles Scribner's Sons, 1942–44.

———. *R. E. Lee: A Biography.* 4 vols. New York: Charles Scribner's Sons, 1934–35.

Furgurson, Ernest B. *Ashes of Glory: Richmond at War.* New York: Alfred A. Knopf, 1996.

Ginsberg, Louis. *History of the Jews of Petersburg, 1789–1950.* Petersburg, Va.: Williams Printing Company, 1954.

Goldfield, David R. *Urban Growth in the Age of Sectionalism, Virginia, 1847–1861.* Baton Rouge: Louisiana State University Press, 1977.

Gordon, Leslie J. *General George E. Pickett in Life and Legend.* Chapel Hill: University of North Carolina Press, 1998.

Graham, Willie, and Mark R. Wenger. *Battersea: A Historical and Architectural Study. Prepared for the Friends of Battersea Committee.* Petersburg, Va.: Historic Petersburg Foundation, 1988.

Greene, A. Wilson. *Breaking the Backbone of the Rebellion: The Final Battles of the Petersburg Campaign.* Mason City, Ia.: Savas Publishing, 2000.

Harrison, Marion C. *Home to the Cockade City! The Partial Biography of a Southern Town.* Richmond, Va.: House of Dietz, 1942.

Henderson, William D. *Petersburg in the Civil War: War at the Door.* Lynchburg, Va.: H. E. Howard, 1998.

———. *The Unredeemed City: Reconstruction in Petersburg, Virginia, 1865–1874.* Lanham, Md.: University Press of America, 1977.

Hennessy, John. *The First Battle of Manassas: An End to Innocence, July 18–21, 1861.* Lynchburg, Va.: H. E. Howard, 1989.

Heslop, Page. *Pastors, Pulpits, and Petersburg: A Profile of Second Baptist Church and the Cockade City, 1854–1994.* n.p., n.d.

Hesseltine, William B. *Civil War Prisons: A Study of War Psychology.* Columbus: Ohio State University Press, 1930.

History of the Second Presbyterian Church. Petersburg, Va.: Owen Printing, 1951.

Horn, John. *The Destruction of the Weldon Railroad: Deep Bottom, Globe Tavern, and Reams Station, August 14–25, 1864.* Lynchburg, Va.: H. E. Howard, 1991.

———. *The Petersburg Campaign: June 1864–April, 1865.* Conshohocken, Pa.: Combined Books, 1993.

Howe, Thomas J. *Wasted Valor, June 15–18, 1864.* Lynchburg, Va.: H. E. Howard, 1998.

Hudson, Leonne M. *The Odyssey of a Southerner: The Life and Times of Gustavus Woodson Smith.* Macon, Ga.: Mercer University Press, 1998.

Iobst, Richard W. *Civil War Macon: The History of a Confederate City.* Macon, Ga.: Mercer University Press, 1999.

Jackson, Luther Porter. *Free Negro Labor and Property Holding in Virginia, 1830–1860.* New York: D. Appleton-Century, 1942.

———. *A Short History of the Gillfield Baptist Church of Petersburg, Virginia.* Petersburg, Va.: Virginia Printing Co., 1937.

Johnson, Robert Erwin. *Rear Admiral John Rodgers, 1812–1882.* Annapolis, Md.: United States Naval Institute, 1967.

Jones, Richard L. *Dinwiddie County: Carrefour of the Commonwealth.* Richmond, Va.: Whittet and Shepperson, 1976.

Jordan, David M. *"Happiness Is Not My Companion": The Life of General G. K. Warren.* Bloomington: Indiana University Press, 2001.

Jordan, Ervin L., Jr. *Black Confederates and Afro-Yankees in Civil War Virginia*. Charlottesville: University Press of Virginia, 1995.

Lankford, Nelson D. *Richmond Burning: The Last Days of the Confederate Capital*. New York: Viking, 2002.

Lebsock, Suzanne. *The Free Women of Petersburg: Status and Culture in a Southern Town*. New York: W.W. Norton, 1984.

Link, William A. *Roots of Secession: Slavery and Politics in Antebellum Virginia*. Chapel Hill: University of North Carolina Press, 2003.

Longacre, Edward G. *Army of Amateurs: General Benjamin F. Butler and the Army of the James, 1863–1865*. Mechanicsburg, Pa.: Stackpole Books, 1997.

Lutz, Francis Earle. *The Prince George–Hopewell Story*. Richmond, Va.: William Byrd Press, 1957.

MacRae, David. *The Americans at Home*. New York: E. P. Dutton and Co., 1952.

Marlow, Clayton Charles. *Matt W. Ransom: Confederate General from North Carolina*. Jefferson, N.C.: McFarland and Company, 1996.

Marvel, William. *Burnside*. Chapel Hill: University of North Carolina Press, 1991.

———. *Lee's Last Retreat: The Flight to Appomattox*. Chapel Hill: University of North Carolina Press, 2002.

Massey, Mary Elizabeth. *Ersatz in the Confederacy*. Columbia: University of South Carolina Press, 1952.

———. *Refugee Life in the Confederacy*. Baton Rouge: Louisiana State University Press, 1964.

McFeely, William S. *Grant: A Biography*. New York: W.W. Norton, 1981.

McPherson, James M. *Battle Cry of Freedom: The Civil War Era*. New York: Oxford University Press, 1988.

Moore, Albert Burton. *Conscription and Conflict in the Confederacy*. New York: Hillary House, 1963.

Musicant, Ivan. *Divided Waters: The Naval History of the Civil War*. New York: Harper Collins, 1995.

Newton, Steven H. *Joseph E. Johnston and the Defense of Richmond*. Lawrence: University Press of Kansas, 1998.

Nichols, Roy Franklin. *The Disruption of American Democracy*. New York: Macmillan, 1948.

Oberseider, N. L., and Suzanne Savery, eds. *Four Self-Guided Walking Tours of Petersburg, Virginia*. Petersburg, Va., 1995.

Parramore, Thomas C., with Peter C. Stewart and Tommy L. Bolger. *Norfolk: The First Four Centuries*. Charlottesville: University Press of Virginia, 1994.

Patterson, Gerard A. *From Blue to Gray: The Life of Confederate General Cadmus M. Wilcox*. Mechanicsburg, Pa.: Stackpole Books, 2001.

Porter, John W. H. *A Record of Events in Norfolk County, Virginia, From April 19, 1861 to May 10, 1862, with a History of the Soldiers and Sailors of Norfolk County, Norfolk City and Portsmouth Who Served in the Confederate States Army or Navy*. Portsmouth, Va.: W. A. Fiske, 1892.

Potter, David M. *The Impending Crisis, 1848–1861*. New York: Harper and Row, 1976.

Power, J. Tracy. *Lee's Miserables: Life in the Army of Northern Virginia from the Wilderness to Appomattox*. Chapel Hill: University of North Carolina Press, 1998.

Quarstein, John V. *CSS Virginia, Mistress of Hampton Roads*. Appomattox, Va.: H. E. Howard, 2000.

Rable, George C. *Civil Wars: Women and the Crisis of Southern Nationalism.* Urbana and Chicago: University of Illinois Press, 1989.

――――. *The Confederate Republic: A Revolution against Politics.* Chapel Hill: University of North Carolina Press, 1994.

Radley, Kenneth. *Rebel Watchdog: The Confederate States Army Provost Guard.* Baton Rouge: Louisiana State University Press, 1989.

Rives, W. C. *Historic Dinwiddie County, Virginia or the Last Long Camp Published by order of the Jamestown Exhibit Committee of Dinwiddie Co., Va.* Petersburg, Va.: Franklin Press, 1907.

Robertson, Katherine C. *Bravest Surrender: A Petersburg Patchwork.* Richmond, Va.: Press of Whittet and Shepperson, 1961.

Robertson, William Glenn. *Back Door to Richmond: The Bermuda Hundred Campaign, April–June 1864.* Newark: University of Delaware Press, 1987.

――――. *The Battle of Old Men and Young Boys, June 9, 1864.* Lynchburg, Va.: H. E. Howard, 1989.

Rogers, William Warren, Jr. *Confederate Home Front: Montgomery during the Civil War.* Tuscaloosa: University of Alabama Press, 1999.

Rosen, Robert N. *The Jewish Confederates.* Columbia: University of South Carolina Press, 2000.

Sanger, Donald Bridgman, and Thomas Robson Hay. *James Longstreet.* Gloucester, Mass.: Peter Smith, 1968.

Schiller, Herbert M., M.D. *The Bermuda Hundred Campaign.* Dayton, Ohio: Morningside House, 1988.

Schott, Thomas E. *Alexander H. Stephens of Georgia: A Biography.* Baton Rouge: Louisiana State University Press, 1988.

Schweninger, Loren. *Black Property Owners in the South, 1790–1915.* Urbana and Chicago: University of Illinois Press, 1990.

Scott, James G., and Edward A. Wyatt, IV. *Petersburg's Story: A History.* Petersburg, Va.: Titmus Optical Company, 1960.

Sears, Stephen W. *Gettysburg.* Boston: Houghton Mifflin, 2003.

――――. *To the Gates of Richmond: The Peninsula Campaign.* New York: Ticknor and Fields, 1992.

Shanks, Henry T. *The Secession Movement in Virginia, 1847–1861.* Richmond, Va.: Garrett and Massie Publishers, 1934.

Silver, James W. *Confederate Morale and Church Propaganda.* Tuscaloosa, Ala.: Confederate Publishing, 1957.

Simpson, Craig M. *A Good Southerner: The Life of Henry A. Wise of Virginia.* Chapel Hill: University of North Carolina Press, 1985.

Sommers, Richard J. *Richmond Redeemed: The Siege at Petersburg.* Garden City, N.Y.: Doubleday and Company, 1981.

Starobin, Robert S. *Industrial Slavery in the Old South.* New York: Oxford University Press, 1970.

Sutherland, Daniel E. *Seasons of War: The Ordeal of a Confederate Community, 1861–1865.* New York: The Free Press, 1995.

Taylor, Emerson Gifford. *Gouverneur Kemble Warren: The Life and Letters of an American Soldier, 1830–1882.* Boston and New York: Houghton Mifflin, 1932.

Thomas, Emory M. *The Confederate Nation: 1861–1865.* New York: Harper and Row, 1979.

Tidwell, William A. *Come Retribution: The Confederate Secret Service and the Assassi-nation of Lincoln.* Reprint. New York: Barnes and Noble Books, 1997.

Todd, Richard Cecil. *Confederate Finance.* Athens: University of Georgia Press, 1954.

Towers, Frank. *The Urban South and the Coming of the Civil War.* Charlottesville: University of Virginia Press, 2004.

Trotter, William R. *Ironclads and Columbiads: The Civil War in North Carolina, The Coast.* Winston-Salem, N.C.: John F. Blair, 1989.

Trout, W. E. *The Appomattox River Atlas.* Petersburg, Va.: Virginia Canals and Naviga-tion Society, 1990.

Trudeau, Noah Andre. *The Last Citadel: Petersburg, Virginia, June 1864–April 1865.* Boston: Little, Brown and Company, 1991.

———. *Like Men of War: Black Troops in the Civil War, 1862–1865.* Boston: Little, Brown and Company, 1998.

Waugh, John C. *Reelecting Lincoln: The Battle for the 1864 Presidency.* New York: Crown Publishers, 1997.

———. *Surviving the Confederacy.* New York: Harcourt, 2002.

Wert, Jeffry D. *General James Longstreet: The Confederacy's Most Controversial Soldier, A Biography.* New York: Simon and Schuster, 1993.

Wiley, Bell I. *The Life of Johnny Reb.* Indianapolis and New York: Bobbs-Merrill Com-pany, 1943.

Williams, T. Harry. *P. G. T. Beauregard: Napoleon in Gray.* Baton Rouge: Louisiana State University Press, 1955.

Williamson, J. Pinckney. *Ye Olden Tymes: History of Petersburg, Va., for Nearly Three Hundred Years.* Petersburg, Va.: Frank A. Owen, 1906.

Wills, Brian Steel. *The War Hits Home: The Civil War in Southeastern Virginia.* Char-lottesville: University Press of Virginia, 2001.

Wilson, Harold S. *Confederate Industry: Manufacturers and Quartermasters in the Civil War.* Jackson: University Press of Mississippi, 2002.

Wise, Stephen R. *Lifeline of the Confederacy: Blockade Running during the Civil War.* Columbia: University of South Carolina Press, 1988.

Woodworth, Steven E., ed., *Leadership and Command in the American Civil War.* Campbell, Calif.: Savas Woodbury Publishers, 1996.

Writer's Program of the Works Projects Administration in the State of Virginia: Dinwid-die County. *The Countrey of the Apamatica.* Richmond, Va.: Whittet and Shepperson, 1942.

Wyatt, Edward A. *Along Petersburg Streets.* Richmond, Va., 1943.

UNPUBLISHED PAPERS

Rice, Philip M. "Internal Improvements in Virginia, 1775–1860." Ph.D. diss., University of North Carolina, 1948.

Saval, Wallace Michael. "Montage of a City under Siege: Petersburg, 1864–65." Master's thesis, Virginia State University, 1971.

MAPS

Petersburg Public Library

Beers, F.W. C.E. Typographical Map of Petersburgh published for the Southern and Southwestern Surveying and Publishing Company, 1877.

INDEX

Dimmock, Captain Charles H. (*continued*)
and social life in Petersburg, 127, 151,
227, 233
Dimmock, Elizabeth Seldon (Mrs. Charles
H.), 140
Dimmock Line, 104, 108, 144, 168, 176–77,
184–85, 188, 246–47, 305n39
Dinwiddie County, Va., 7, 63, 198, 215;
and African Americans, 125, 218; in
election of 1860, 16; hospitals in, 210,
214; during secession crisis, 22; volun-
teers from, 46, 174
Dinwiddie Court House, Va., 25, 214, 234,
239–40, 243
District of Cape Fear (CSA), 160
District of Columbia unit: 1st Cavalry,
180–81
District of the Nottoway (US), 266, 272,
323n64
Dix, Major General John A., 137, 144–45
Dodson, Daniel, 14
Dodson, John, 36
Donnan, Alexander, 130, 231
Donnan, Mrs. John, 65
Donnan, Robert C., 42, 310n26
Douglas, Major Henry Kyd, 249
Douglas, Stephen A., 15, 16, 24, 25, 53
Drewry's Bluff, 75, 76, 90, 91, 93, 95, 106,
144, 158, 171; battle of (May 1864), 172,
173, 174
Dudley, William A., 41
Dunlop, David, 23; home of, *212, 267*
Dunlop Station, 180, 200
Dunlop Street, 199
Dunn, Andrew, 224
Dunn, Captain Archibald W., 162
Dunn, John B., 113
Dunn and Beasley Tobacco Factory, 87
Dunn's Hill, 90, 93, 95, 107, 151
Durham, N.C., 266

Early, Lieutenant General Jubal A., 203
East Hill, 59, 283n7
Eden, Major Robert C., 260–61
Edwards, Colonel Oliver, 256
Elder, Thomas Claybrook, 211, 215, 218
Elizabeth River, 43
Elliott, Private James C., 168

Elliott's Salient, 204–6
Ellis, Charles, 115
Ellis, John W., 49, 65, 284n26
Elvira (a slave), 123
Ely, Colonel Ralph, 252
Elzey, Major General Arnold, 106, 138,
144–47, 149–50, 299n34
Eppes plantation (Appomattox), 92
Erasmus (a slave), 81
Eshelman, Major Benjamin F., 153
Estelle, Katie, 128
Ettrick, Va., 7, 35, 114, 193, 210, 214, 251
Ettrick Cotton Mill 6, 113
Exchange Bank of Petersburg, 43, 44, 117

Fair Grounds (Confederate General) Hos-
pital, 85–86, 94, 111–12, 196, 202, 210,
231, 246, 256
Falconer, Alexander, 53–54
Farmville, Va., 5, 70
Ferebee, Colonel Dennis D., 180
Ferrero, Brigadier General Edward, 207,
209, 261
Fifth Street, 212
Fillmore Street, 216
First Baptist Church, 121, 233
Fisher, Captain Christopher Fry, 43, 49
Five Forks, battle of, 240–41, 242–43,
261
Flood, Daniel, 61
Ford, John A., 38
Fort: Boykin, 158; Clifton, 106, 108, 165,
168; Gregg, 246–47; Hatteras (NC), 84;
Henry, 3; Monroe, 36, 39, 61, 70, 74,
138, 144, 161, 162, 163; Moultrie (SC),
18; Powhatan, 43, 47, 98, 99, 103, 142,
280n26, 291n45; Stedman, battle of,
237–38; Sumter (SC), 18, 26, 27, 28, 31,
49, 95; Whitworth, 246–47
Foster, Major General John G., 109
Fox, Gustavus Vasa, 93
Franklin, Va., 140, 156
Franklin Street, 208
Frayser's Farm (Glendale), battle of, 95
Fredericksburg, Va., 25, 81, 109, 136, 137,
141, 142, 151
Freedmen's Bureau, 271
French, General Samuel Gibbs, 98, *99,*

Harpers Ferry, Va., 14
Harris, Brigadier General Nathaniel H., 246
Harrison Street, 48, 51
Harrison's Creek, 185
Harrison's Landing, 94, 95, 98, 102
Hart farm, 244
Hartsuff, Major General George L., 261, 262, 264–68, 271–72
Harvie, Lewis E., 22–23, 26
Hatcher's Run, 244, 245; battle of, 234–35, 236
Hatteras Island, N.C., 84
Heartsill, William W., 112, 142
Heth, Major General Henry, 247
Hicksford, Va., 147
High Street, 31, 104, 184, 216, 226, 255
Hill, Lieutenant General Ambrose Powell (A. P.), 209, 217, 219, 227, 244, 249, 319n6
Hill, General Daniel Harvey (D. H.), *97;* during Bermuda Hundred campaign, 165–66, 172; biographical information about, 96; as commander in northeastern North Carolina (1861), 84; as commander of the Department of North Carolina (1862), 96–105; as commander of the Department of North Carolina (1863), 137–38, 142–45, 155, 299n34; praises Micah Jenkins, 148; relieved of command (1864), 174; resigns, 136, 297n8; and strategic significance of Petersburg, 83, 146, 159, 183–84; as subordinate to Longstreet in North Carolina (1863), 138, 140
Hill, Jack, 257
Hill, Lossie, 180
Hincks, Brigadier General Edward W., 168, 175, 177
Hines, Dr. Peter, 94
Hinrichs, Captain Oscar, 251
Hobson, Captain Owen H., 165
Hoge, Rev. Moses Drury, 121
Hoge, Rev. William, 120–21
Hoke, General Robert F., 157–58, 159, 169, 171, 175, 184
Holmes, General Theophilus H., 89, 90, 92, 93, 95, 96, 98

Hood, Major General John Bell, 137–38, 140–41, 151
Hood, Major William, 174, 176
Hooker, Major General Joseph, 141
Hope Flour Mill, 227
Hopkins, H. L., 70
Hubbard, Colonel James, 256
Huger, Major General Benjamin, 72, 75, 84, *86,* 88, 89, 90, 91
Humphreys, Major General Andrew A., 239
Hunter, Robert M. T., 234
Hunton, Brigadier General Eppa, 153, 155
Hurt, Lieutenant Wales, 180, 182
Hymandinger, Mrs., 66

Independent Signal Corps and Scouts, 91, 141, 147
Iron Front Building, 184, 188
Island Belle, 94
Isle of Wight County, Va., 114
Ivor, Va., 115, 156, 165

Jackson, Thomas A., 87, 114, 293n9
Jackson, General Thomas J. (Stonewall), 92, 98, 109, 129, 132, 141, 143, 233
James City County, Va., 36
James River, 54, 77, 104; and the blockade, 67, 115, 263; Confederate signal stations and patrols along, 91, 95, 136, 145, 158–60; military significance of, 39, 74–75, 93, 98, 103, 138, 144, 156, 161; and Union navy, 76, 88, 90
Jamestown, 38, 279n18
Jarratt family, 8
Jarratt's Hotel, 10, 45, 49, 51, 59, 193, 225
Jarvis, William H., 14
Jefferson Street, 87, 225, 254
Jenkins, Brigadier General Micah, 140, 142, 143–44, 146–47, *148;* as ranking officer in Petersburg, 147–51, 300n43
Jerusalem Plank Road, 5, 108, 153, 176, 179, 181, 244, 258; battle of, 193
Johnson, General Bushrod R., 174, 185, 233, 240
Johnson, Sylvanius, 7
Johnson, William Ransom, 127

Merrimack (USS), 39, 74
Michie, William B., 42
Michigan units: 1st Sharpshooters, 252;
　2nd Infantry, 252; 8th Infantry, 260
Military Division of the James (US), 266,
　323n64
Milligan, James Fisher, 91, 106, 134, 138,
　141, 145, 147, 154, 158, 301n73
Mine Run, operations at, 154–55
Mobile, Ala., 119, 219
Model Farm: burns, 162; as Confederate
　bivouac, 65, 73, 85, 90, 106, 147, 156;
　as parole camp, 107, 138, 141–42; and
　surrender of Petersburg, 253; tourna-
　ment at, 227
Moncus, Mrs., 230
Monitor (USS), 74, 90, 94
Montague, Colonel Edgar B., 146
Montgomery, Ala., 21
Moore, T. V., 129
Moore's Tobacco Warehouse, 89
Morrison, Mrs. William, 257–58
Morrison, William E., 257
Mount Erin, 11
Munford, George Wythe, 131

Nansemond County, Va., 151
Nashville (CSS), 74
Nassau, Bahamas, 114–15
Nelson, Hugh, 153
Nelson, William, 223
Nelson, Major William, 99
New Bern, N.C., 105, 109, 134, 140,
　301n70; operations against, 157–58,
　160
Newmarket (race track), 10, 128, 154, 155,
　188
New Orleans, La., 60, 64, 66, 195
New Road, 181
New York, N.Y., 68, 69, 105, 263
New York Herald, 16
New York units: 6th Heavy Artillery, 261;
　10th Artillery, 261, 266; 33rd Battery,
　266; 41st Infantry, 266; 69th Infantry,
　69; 121st Infantry, 253–54
Nichols, Captain J. M., 117
Nitre and Mining Bureau (CSA), 232
Norfolk, Va., 43, 47, 61, 70, 84, 90, 94, 99,

105, 195; as economic rival to Petersburg, 5; evacuated, 75, 88; ordnance
sent to, 38; Petersburg African Americans sent to, 36, 65–66; Petersburg
troops stationed at, 33, 35, 37, 41, 44,
48, 53–54, 65, 72–74; refugees from,
70, 76, 127; during secession crisis,
17–18, 25
Norfolk and Petersburg Railroad, 5, 10,
　33, 49, 58, 73, 115, 241
North Carolina Hospital, 86, 92, 94, 112,
　113, 122
North Carolina units: Brem's Battery, 92;
　1st Cavalry, 84; 1st Infantry, 46; 2nd
　Infantry, 97; 4th Cavalry, 180; 4th In-
　fantry, 82, 83, 86; 24th Infantry, 65, 85,
　156; 27th Infantry, 97; 31st Infantry,
　157, 162, 163; 32nd Infantry, 82; 35th
　Infantry, 161; 43rd Infantry, 79; 46th
　Infantry, 97; 48th Infantry, 92, 93, 97,
　240; 49th Infantry, 92, 124; 50th In-
　fantry, 112; 51st Infantry, 165; 53rd In-
　fantry, 95; 55th Infantry, 106–7, 109,
　134; 56th Infantry, 168
Nottoway County, Va., 46, 97

Oaks Tobacco Warehouse, 223
Old Men and Young Boys, Battle of
　(June 9, 1864), 176–82; aftermath of,
　182–83, 306n54; casualties, 306n51;
　map of, 178
Old Street, 7, 11, 162, 165, 200, 211
Orange County, Va., 154
Osborne, Betty, 127
Osborne, Jean, 127
Osborne and Chieves Tobacco
　Factory, 87
Owen, Henry T., 218

Page, Betty, 127, 250
Page, Lucy, 127
Page, Dr. R. P., 112
Pamlico Sound, 84
Pamunkey River, 94, 145
Pannill, William, 44, 71, 88
Parke, Major General John G., 251, 256
Parker, Albert, 66
Parkersburg, Va., 19